MEASURING EDUCATIONAL ACHIEVEMENT

ROBERT L. EBEL

Michigan State University

PRENTICE-HALL, INC.
Englewood Cliffs, New Jersey

PRENTICE-HALL EDUCATION SERIES

PRENTICE-HALL INTERNATIONAL, INC., *London*
PRENTICE-HALL OF AUSTRALIA, PTY., LTD., *Sydney*
PRENTICE-HALL OF CANADA, LTD., *Toronto*
PRENTICE-HALL OF INDIA (PRIVATE) LTD., *New Delhi*
PRENTICE-HALL OF JAPAN, INC., *Tokyo*

©1965 by Prentice-Hall, Inc., Englewood Cliffs, New Jersey

PRINTED IN THE UNITED STATES OF AMERICA
56854-C

To Hazel June

who recalls the summer
during which the first draft
of this book was written
as especially enjoyable for all of us

Preface

We must never forget that to the degree that we are able to measure medical competence, to just that same degree will medical competence be available to our people.

NATHAN A. WOMACK, M.D.

The planning, writing, and revisions of this book have been guided by the purpose of providing prospective teachers and practicing teachers at all educational levels with the concepts, principles, and procedures that can help them to prepare better tests of educational achievement, and to use them more effectively in the advancement of learning. Hence, as compared with other introductory textbooks on educational measurement, this book devotes considerably more attention to test development and test analysis. Considerably less attention, in fact hardly any direct attention, is paid to the selection and use of standardized tests of aptitude, achievement, and personality.

Four defenses of the decision not to include a discussion of standardized tests and school testing programs in this book can be offered. First, it seemed impossible to deal adequately with both subjects— classroom testing and standardized testing—in the same course or the same textbook. Second, in terms of their frequency of use and cruciality to educational progress, classroom tests seemed to have a prior claim on the attentions of teachers. Third, the currently available textbooks seem to deal more adequately with standardized tests than with classroom tests. Finally, the instructor who is reasonably proficient in making and using his own tests is not likely to go far astray in the selection and use of standardized tests.

The students of teaching and the practicing teachers for whom this book is intended are not presumed to have had any previous special training in educational measurement. With this in mind, the author can lean in either of two directions as he attempts to make his discussions of somewhat technical matters comprehensible. He may lean in the direction of simplicity, avoiding the more complex issues and problems, or dealing with them descriptively, so as to limit the amount of close reading and critical thinking required. Or he may lean in the direction of thoroughness, not avoiding the discussion of any crucial aspect of the subject because of its presumed difficulty, but seeking to dissolve the difficulty by clarity of exposition and by the use of concrete illustrations.

An author can lose his balance by leaning too far in either direction. This book is by no means the simplest textbook on educational measurement that is available; nor is it the most thorough. But it does not avoid the discussion of difficult problems, and hence, despite the author's consistent efforts to be clear and intelligible, it may sometimes tax the student's powers of comprehension. Our hope is that the breadth of knowledge and depth of understanding a reasonably competent student can gain from a careful study of these pages will be worth the effort it may cost him.

Focused as it is on the construction and use of classroom tests of educational achievement planned, written, administered, and interpreted by school teachers and college professors, the book is oriented primarily toward the practical problems of measuring the results of learning. An effort has been made, however, not only to suggest sound principles and practices, but also to provide as much as possible in the way of philosophical, rational, and empirical bases for understanding and accepting the suggestions offered.

To acknowledge completely an author's indebtedness is clearly an impossible task. Little that is said in this book has not been said before. The author's best hope is that he has used good judgment in borrowing from the ideas of others, and has not bungled the job of integrating these into a coherent whole.

A number of staff members of the Educational Testing Service, including specifically Anna Dragositz, William Coffman, Frances

Swineford, Martin Katz, and William B. Schrader, read drafts of some of the chapters and aided immeasurably in their improvement. The original draft was read carefully, and with excellent constructive criticisms by Elizabeth Hagen. A revised draft benefitted from the perceptive comments and suggestions of Professor Tom Hastings. I gladly acknowledge the immense value of their contributions, without holding them responsible for any of the flaws I have allowed to remain. In a more general way I am indebted to my former colleagues, E. F. Lindquist, Paul Blommers, Dewey Stuit, Henry Chauncey, Henry S. Dyer, William W. Turnbull and others, for stimulation, guidance and instruction. I hope the book will do credit to their competence and bear witness to their friendly helpfulness.

Lastly may I acknowledge the indispensable contribution of my secretary, Mrs. Ethel Kinney, to the production of the several drafts of the manuscript. She typed or supervised the typing of them and directed the preparation of the figures, tables and exhibits. For her careful, persistent, competent assistance, I am deeply indebted.

ROBERT L. EBEL

Contents

I The Need
for Better Classroom Tests

*Nothing is more revealing of the purpose underlying a
course of study than the nature of the examinations given
at its close. Nothing is more effective in telling the student
what we want him to do than the method we take of finding out whether or not, and how well he has done it.*

ALEXANDER MEIKLEJOHN

Most of the tests of educational achievement used in
school and college classrooms are prepared, administered, scored,
and interpreted by classroom teachers and professors. Each student
takes many such tests during the course of his formal education.
They exert a direct and powerful influence on how he studies and
what he learns. Hence it is not unreasonable to believe that the
educational significance of locally produced classroom tests may
far outweigh that of the occasional standardized tests or program
tests the students take.

The term "classroom test" in this book means any written test
prepared by a school or college teacher for use in his own classroom. Essay tests and tests composed of mathematical problems, as
well as various types of objective tests, are included in the meaning
of the term as used here. Our concern will be with important, full-
period tests given either at the end of a unit of work or just before

1

grades are issued rather than with short quizzes and other informal "tests."

1. The importance of classroom tests

The view that classroom tests are important and that they could be, and ought to be, much better than they often are is shared by most school teachers and college professors. Occasionally one hears the suggestion that education could go on perfectly well, perhaps much better than it has in the past, if tests and testing were abolished. On other occasions one hears grudging acceptance of tests as a "necessary evil" in education. But the view of the great majority of teachers at all levels is that periodic assessment of educational progress is essential to effective education and that good tests afford very useful assistance to teachers in making those assessments.

One would have difficulty in finding among those who are inclined to discount the value of tests a teacher or professor who is not concerned about quality in education—about the achievements of his students, about the adequacy of their previous preparation, about his own success as a teacher, and about the effectiveness of the whole enterprise of education. But quality is a matter of degree. Unless some means exist for measuring it, for distinguishing between higher and lower quality, between better and poorer achievement, concern for quality will not mean very much. If tests are abandoned, it must be on the ground that better means are available for measuring educational achievement.

It is easy to understand why tests are sometimes characterized as a "necessary evil" in education. Almost all students, but especially students of average or inferior ability, approach a test with apprehension. Those who do less well than they had expected can easily find some basis for regarding the examination as unfair. Cheating on examinations is reported often enough to cast some shadows of disrepute over the whole enterprise.

Instructors, too, sometimes dislike to assume the role of examiners. Most of them prefer to be helpful rather than critical. There is something inconsiderate about probing the minds of other human beings and passing judgment on their shortcomings. There is even something presumptuous in assuming the right to set the standards by which others will be judged. And if the instructor has learned that he is not an infallible examiner, if he has experienced the critical retaliation of students who have been unfairly judged, his wishful dreams of education freed from the torments of examining and evaluation are also easy to understand. No doubt he sometimes feels like the Sergeant of Police in "The Pirates of Penzance," who sings, "Taking one consideration with another, a policeman's lot is not a happy one."

Unfortunately, there is no effective substitute for tests or examinations in most classrooms. Even in a generally critical leaflet on some aspects of contemporary testing in the public schools, the authors say,

> To teach without testing is unthinkable. Appraisal of outcomes is an essential feedback of teaching. The evaluation process enables those involved to get their bearings, to know in which direction they are going.[1]

Anxiety, unfairness, dishonesty, humiliation, and presumptuousness can be and should be minimized, but the process of examining and evaluating cannot be dispensed with if education is to proceed effectively.

Those who would abolish tests, or who regard them as an evil which must be tolerated, usually do not mean to imply that good education is possible without any assessment of student achievement whatsoever. What they sometimes do suggest is that a good teacher, working with a class of reasonable size, has no need for tests in order to make sufficiently accurate judgments of student achievement. They may also suggest that the tests they have seen, or perhaps that they have even used themselves, leave so much to be desired that a teacher is better off without the kind of "help" such tests are likely to give. In some cases they may indeed be right in this judgment. Very bad tests have been made and used. No doubt some such tests have actually been worse than no tests at all.

But again, the majority of teachers and professors are keenly aware of the limited and unsatisfactory bases they ordinarily have for judging the relative achievement of various students and of the fallibility of their subjective judgments when based on the irregular, uncontrolled observations they can make in their classroom or office.

---

[1] Joint Committee of the American Association of School Administrators, *Testing, Testing, Testing* (Washington, D.C.: American Association of School Administrators, 1962), p. 9.

They welcome the help that tests can give in providing a more extensive and objective basis for judgment. For testing is not really an alternative to teacher observation of student behavior. It is simply a specialized technique for extending, refining, efficiently recording, and summarizing those observations.

2. Can tests provide valid measures of achievement?

Precise measurement requires careful control or standardization of the conditions surrounding it. Obviously this control makes the behavior being measured artificial to some degree. Artificiality is a price that usually must be paid to achieve precision. It is a price that scientists and engineers, as well as psychologists and teachers, have usually found worth paying. For tests intended to measure typical behavior, such as personality, attitude, or interest tests, the price may sometimes be too high. That is, the behavior in the artificial test situation may be so poorly related to typical behavior in a natural situation that precise measurement of something hardly worth measuring is so much wasted effort. But for tests of educational aptitude or achievement, the gain in precision resulting from the controlled conditions that formal testing can afford usually far outweighs the slight loss in the relevance of artificial to natural behavior.

Perhaps an illustration from the field of physical ability testing may be helpful here. Judges, watching a group of children at play (the natural situation), could make rough estimates of the relative abilities of the students to run fast, jump high, or throw some object far. But the precision of the estimates obtained in such an uncontrolled, unstandardized situation would probably be quite low. The different judges would not be likely to agree with each other, or even with themselves on different occasions, in the estimates they would report. If precise estimates are desired, the judges, the children, and everyone else concerned would probably prefer to see them made under the standardized and controlled, if somewhat artificial, conditions of a regular track meet. No one would worry much about the possibility that the ones who performed best in the track and field events might seem to do similar things somewhat less well under "natural" conditions on the playground.

Because all pupils in a class usually take the same test of achievement under the same conditions, some critics have concluded that uniform written tests, particularly objective tests, disregard individual differences and even tend to suppress individuality. The fact that some classroom tests are graded by machines has served to strengthen this misconception. Mass testing and machine grading suggest a standardized uniformity in education that seems inconsistent with concern for the individual and his unique needs and potentials.

But while the tests and the processes of testing are as nearly alike for all the students in a class as we can make them, the scores of the students on the tests are not alike. Those who score high reflect superior ability and achievement. Those who score low reveal deficiencies. Tests tend to reveal differences among students, not to suppress or conceal them. In fact, uniformity in the conditions of testing is a prerequisite to unequivocal indication of individual differences. If the tests are not identical for all students, not all of the differences in their scores can be attributed to differences among them in ability or achievement.

The kind of information about individual differences that uniform tests reveal so clearly is essential to effective individualization of instruction. The unique needs of individual students can be identified and met. The unique capabilities of individual students can be identified and developed. Thus can standardized measurement serve individualized education.

The emphasis in this chapter on the value of written tests in extending a teacher's observations of student behavior and making these observations more dependable and precise is not intended to suggest that tests should be the sole means used in judging a student's educational achievement. Written tests are efficient, versatile devices for measuring many aspects of student achievement, but they cannot do the whole job. Some educational objectives may be concerned mainly with the development of physical skills or social behaviors. Direct observation is likely to provide a much better basis for assessing such skills and behaviors than would a written test. Nor should a teacher or professor ignore his own direct observations, in the classroom or elsewhere, of a student's level of understanding or ability to use knowledge, despite the fact that written tests are especially effective in measuring educational outcomes of that kind. The broader the basis of observations on which evaluation rests, the better, provided only that each observation carries no more weight in determining the final result than its appropriateness and accuracy warrant.

3. The functions of classroom tests

The major function of a classroom test is to measure student achievement and thus to contribute to the evaluation of his educational progress and attainments. This is a matter of considerable importance. To say, as some critics of testing have said, that what a student knows and can do is more important than his score on a test or his grade in a course implies, quite incorrectly in most cases, that the two are independent or unrelated. To say that testing solely to measure achievement has no educational value also implies, and again quite incorrectly in most cases, that test scores are unrelated to educational efforts, that they do not reward and reinforce effective study, penalize unproductive efforts, or tend to discourage lack of effort.

Tests can, and often do, help teachers and professors to give more valid, reliable grades. Because these grades are intended to summarize concisely a comprehensive evaluation of the student's achievement, because they are reported to the student and his parents to indicate the effectiveness of his efforts, because they are entered in the school record and may help to determine honors and opportunities for further education or future employment, it is important that teachers and professors take seriously their responsibilities for assigning accurate, meaningful grades. Students are urged, quite properly, not to study *merely* to earn high grades. But, in terms of the student's present self-perceptions and his future opportunities, there is nothing "mere" about the grades he receives.

A second major function of classroom tests is to motivate and direct student learning. The experience of almost all students and teachers supports the view that students do tend to study harder when they expect an examination than when they do not and that they emphasize in studying those things on which they expect to be tested. If the students know in advance they will be tested, if they know the kinds of knowledge and ability the test will require, and if the test does a good job of measuring the achievement of essential course objectives, then its motivating and guiding influence will be most wholesome.

Anticipated tests are sometimes regarded as extrinsic motivators of learning efforts, less desirable or effective than intrinsic motivators would be. Learning should be its own reward, providing its own intrinsic motivation for study, it is said. Fortunately, no choice need be made between extrinsic and intrinsic motivation. Both contribute to learning. Withdrawal of either would be likely to lessen the learning of most students. For a fortunate few, intrinsic motivation may be strong enough to stimulate all the efforts to learn that the student ought to put forth. For the great majority, however, the added, extrinsic motivation provided by tests and other influential factors is indispensable.

Classroom tests have other useful educational functions. The process of constructing them, if the job is approached carefully, should cause an instructor to think carefully about the goals of instruction in a course. It should lead him to define those goals operationally in terms of the kind of tasks a student must be able to handle to demonstrate achievement of the goals. On the student's part the process of taking a classroom test, and of discussing the scoring of it afterward, can be a richly rewarding learning experience. As Stroud has said,

> It is probably not extravagant to say that the contribution made to a student's store of knowledge by the taking of an examination is as great, minute for minute, as any other enterprise he engages in.[2]

Hence, testing and teaching need not be considered as mutually exclusive alternatives, as competitors for the valuable classroom hours. They are intimately related parts of the total educational process.

Awareness of the important direct contributions of test taking to student learning can lead to unwarranted disparagement of tests as measuring instruments. It is sometimes said, for example, that tests should be used to promote learning *rather than* to measure achievement, as if these two uses were somehow in conflict and

---

[2] James B. Stroud, *Psychology in Education* (New York: David McKay Co., Inc., 1946), p. 476.

mutually exclusive. Or the suggestion may be made that pupils who have taken a test will learn more if the test is not graded.

While there are situations in which test materials can be used solely as learning exercises, disregarding any evidence they could provide about levels of achievement, it would be unfortunate to leave the impression that most tests should be treated in this way. For the indirect contributions of a test to the promotion of learning can be far greater in scope and in effect than the direct contributions. What a student studies, and how he studies, in the weeks before the test can have far more to do with what he learns than his mental exercise during the hour or so while he is taking the test.

Richardson and Stalnaker, two leaders in the development of modern educational achievement testing, have insisted that,

> An achievement examination need not have direct pedagogical value in itself. . . . The purpose of achievement examining is essentially measurement for certifying academic credit. . . . An achievement examination is good or valid if it simply does a good job of measuring what it purports to measure.[3]

An educational test that does not promote learning is somehow of questionable utility. But the promotion of learning is a complex enterprise, requiring a variety of tools. Tests can be, and usually are, highly important tools for the promotion of learning. If their usefulness were judged solely in terms of what the student learns while taking the test, the greater part of their importance would be overlooked. In the case of tests, the indirect influence in promoting learning is far more potent than the direct.

It probably goes without saying that the educational value of a test depends on its quality and on the skill of the teacher in using it. Good tests, properly used, can make valuable contributions to a student's education. Poor tests, or tests misused, will contribute less and might even do educational harm.

4. Who should prepare classroom tests?

Most classroom tests must be prepared by the teacher or professor who is teaching the class. While there are many standardized tests

---

[3] M. W. Richardson and J. M. Stalnaker, "Comments on Achievement Examinations," *Journal of Educational Research,* XXVIII (1935), 425-32.

of achievement available for broad areas of subject matter, there are few that are specifically appropriate to the content and objectives of a particular unit of study, a unit that may constitute only a fraction of the whole course of study of a single subject. Some textbook publishers furnish tests to accompany their texts. These can be helpful, but too often the items included have not been carefully prepared or reviewed critically by other experts in educational measurement or in the subject field itself.

Some public education authorities, like those in New York State, prepare tests for use in state-wide programs of achievement testing. Some universities, like Michigan State, maintain evaluation services that are responsible for preparing achievement tests for their basic courses. Since these tests are usually prepared by experts in test construction, working closely with expert teachers of the subjects involved, they usually do excellent jobs of measuring educational achievement. But the substantial costs involved in the development of external tests, and the problems of matching the content of the test to the material emphasized in the classroom, make it seem unlikely that they will replace any substantial fraction of teacher-made tests in the forseeable future.

The necessity that involves most teachers in test construction brings with it some educational advantages. As has been said, the process of test construction can help the teacher clarify and define the educational objectives of a course. Classroom tests prepared by the teacher are likely to fit the content and objectives of a particular course better than would a test prepared by anyone else. Finally, when testing and teaching are in the hands of the same person, they are likely to be more effectively integrated in the total educational process than if the testing were separated from the teaching.

The necessary and desirable direct responsibility that professors and teachers have for the tests of educational achievement used in their classes does not require that every test must be a completely new and original creation of the instructor involved. There could be, and should be, much more frequent and extensive exchange of test outlines and test items among teachers of similar courses than is usually the case.

This idea of cooperation in test construction is not new. It was involved in the establishment of the Cooperative Test Service thirty years ago. It was advocated by Thurstone in an article in the *AAUP Bulletin* in 1948.[4] To help make the idea effective, a number of organizations have published collections of test items in various fields. A partial list of these collections is presented in Exhibit 1.1.

EXHIBIT 1.1

A Partial List of Published Collections of Test Items

Anderson, Howard R., E. F. Lindquist, and Harry D. Berg, *Selected Test Items in American History,* Bulletin No. 6. Washington, D.C.: National Council for the Social Studies, September 1949.

Anderson, Howard R., E. F. Lindquist, and Frederick H. Stutz, *Selected Test Items in World History,* Bulletin No. 9. Washington, D.C.: National Council for the Social Studies, September 1947.

Bureau of Examinations and Testing, *Sourcebook of Test Items for Teachers of Mathematics.* Albany, N.Y.: State Education Department, 1956.

College Entrance Examination Board, *A Description of the College Board Achievement Tests.* Princeton, N.J.: Educational Testing Service, 1962.

Dressel, Paul L. and Clarence H. Nelson, *Questions and Problems in Science,* Test Item Folio No. 1. Princeton, N.J.: Educational Testing Service, 1956.

Ebel, Robert L. and associates, *Multiple-choice Items for a Test of Teacher Competence in Educational Measurement.* National Council on Measurement in Education, 1962 (Wilbur L. Layton, Secretary-Treasurer, Iowa State University, Ames, Iowa).

Gerberich, J. Raymond, *Specimen Objective Test Items.* New York: David McKay and Co., Inc., 1956.

Morse, Horace T. and George H. McCune, *Selected Items for the Testing of Study Skills,* Bulletin No. 15. Washington, D.C.: National Council for the Social Studies, September 1949.

Individual teachers of similar courses can, and probably should, arrange for cooperative exchange of test items and test plans. Not only will such cooperation tend to reduce the labor of test construction, it will also make the tests less parochial in the educational understandings and values they reflect and, hence, more generally valid measures of educational achievement.

---

[4] Louis L. Thurstone, "The Improvement of Examinations," *American Association of University Professors Bulletin,* XXXIV (June, 1948), 394-97.

At the very least, a teacher who uses objective tests can establish and maintain a cumulative file of his own items. The best of these can be and should be reused frequently. If the items have been analyzed for discrimination and difficulty (see Chapter 11), and if the analysis data is recorded with the item, the value of such a file as an aid in future test development will be greatly increased.

When the same test item is used repeatedly it may become the subject of special study and thus lose some of its value as an un-biased indicator of the examinees' general level of achievement. Copies of tests or test items, particularly those used in basic required courses enrolling large numbers of students, do find their way into student files. This kind of dissemination of information about the questions that might be reused in a crucial examination may be limited by careful supervision of the examination, and careful collection of all test copies, but can hardly be prevented altogether.

How much the reuse of test items needs to be restricted to prevent appreciable loss of test validity depends, obviously, on the circumstances. In some extreme cases it may seem unwise to ever reuse a single item. Such cases are probably rare. In other extreme cases the identical examination has been used term after term in moderately large classes taking required courses with no appreciable loss in validity. But those were good courses and most of the students were motivated to master the content in them, not just to pass a requirement. Hence the pressure on test security and validity was low. Most courses ought to lie closer to that extreme than to the other.

The legendary "fraternity files" of old tests are seldom as complete, as diligently used, or as richly rewarding to their owners as campus folklore might suggest. And for good reasons. The student who, because of low motivation or low ability, has learned dangerously little during the term is unlikely to find much salvation in poring over copies of old tests, even when urged on and helped along by his more scholarly brothers. What do all those words mean? And even if the answers are clearly and accurately shown, how can they all be remembered until time for the examination? When the probabilities (rather than the possibilities) are assessed rationally, the danger of reusing test items tends to diminish. Probably most instructors ought to do more of it rather than less.

5. Some requirements for effective testing

If all teachers and prospective teachers were skilled in the arts
of test development and use, there would be little need for professional training in test construction. But on their own testimony, on
that of their sometimes suffering students, and on that of visiting
experts called in to advise them on their testing problems, teachers
do reveal shortcomings in their use of tests.

A good test constructor must know comprehensively and understand thoroughly the field of knowledge to be covered by the test so
that he will be able to ask significant, novel questions, express them
properly and plainly, and provide acceptable, correct answers to
them. He must be accurately aware of the level and range of understanding and ability in the group to be tested so that he can choose
problems of appropriate intrinsic difficulty and present them so that
they will have appropriate functional difficulty. He must understand
the thought processes of the students and the misconceptions which
the less capable ones are likely to have so that he can make wrong
answers attractive to those of low achievement.

He must be skilled in written expression so that he can communicate clearly and concisely the information and instructions which
make up the test and the test items. He must be a master of the
techniques of item writing, well acquainted with the most useful
forms of test items with their unique virtues and limitations, and
with the most common pitfalls to be avoided in using them. Finally,
he must be sufficiently conscious of the importance of good measures
of educational achievement and sufficiently confident of his ability
to prepare tests that will provide such measures to be willing to
spend the time and make the effort necessary to do a competent,
workmanlike job.

The traits just enumerated fall generally into one or the other
of two categories: those which contribute to good teaching as well
as good testing and those which contribute uniquely to good testing.
More of the shortcomings observed in classroom tests are probably
attributable to deficiencies in traits of the first category than in those
of the second. But the correction of deficiencies in command of subject matter, and skill in teaching, is beyond the scope of this book.
Nothing that can be said about the techniques of test construction
and use will enable an incompetent teacher to make a good test.

What a book on classroom testing may do is to help good teachers make better tests than they would otherwise.

A point worth mentioning in passing is that some instructors, outstanding in their scholarship and teaching ability, possess rather naïve notions about the requirements for effective measurement of educational achievement. Sometimes it almost seems that there must be a psychological incompatibility between expertness in subject-matter scholarship on the one hand and willingness to accept effective techniques of educational measurement on the other. The nuclear physicist, the economic theorist, the Shakespearean scholar, and many of their expert colleagues may practice and preach primitive and untrustworthy techniques of testing and grading.

The gap between what we know about how educational achievement ought to be measured and what we actually do in classroom testing is sometimes explained away as a failure in communication, which it almost certainly is. The test specialists are blamed for having developed highly abstruse concepts and a highly technical jargon that place their special knowledge beyond the reach of the typical teacher. No doubt there is some justification for this charge. But some of the responsibility may belong to the school and college teachers, too. They may have expected that their own native good sense, plus some effortless sleight-of-hand, could qualify them as experts in educational measurement. The matter is not quite that simple, as Henry Dyer has pointed out.

> I don't think the business of educational measurement is inherently simple, and I don't think it is something that can be wrapped up in a do-it-yourself kit. Any way you look at it, the measurement of human behavior is bound to be a terribly complex process, since the phenomena of human behavior are themselves as complex as anything in the universe.[5]

6. Common mistakes of teachers in testing

What are some of the mistakes that even expert teachers and eminent professors make in measuring educational achievement? What are some of their unsound practices in classroom testing?

---

[5] Henry S. Dyer, "What Point of View Should Teachers Have Concerning the Role of Measurement in Education?" *The Fifteenth Yearbook of the National Council on Measurements Used in Education* (East Lansing, Mich.: Michigan State University, 1958).

First, they tend to rely too much on their own subjective judgments, on fortuitous observations, on unverified inferences, in evaluating educational achievements. The wide difference among different judges in their evaluations of the same evidence of student achievement—that is, the unreliability of those judgments—has been demonstrated over and over again, yet many teachers have never checked on the reliability of any of their tests and may not even have planned those tests purposely to make them as reliable as possible.

Second, some teachers feel obliged to use absolute standards in judging educational achievement, which can almost always be judged more fairly and consistently in relative terms. If most of the students in a class get A's on one test and most of the same students fail another, some teachers prefer to blame the students rather than the test. They believe, contrary to much evidence, that a teacher can set a reasonable passing score on a test simply by looking at the test and without looking at any student answers to it. They believe that "grading on the curve" permits the students to set the (relative and presumably fallible) standards, instead of permitting the teacher (whose standards are presumed to be absolute and infallible) to set them.

Third, both teachers and professors tend to put off test preparation to the last minute and then to do it on a catch-as-catch-can basis. A last-minute test is likely to be a poor test. Further, such a test cannot possibly have the constructive influence in motivating and directing student learning that a good test of educational achievement ought to have and that a test planned and described to students early in the course would have.

Fourth, many teachers use tests which are too inefficient and too short to sample adequately the whole area of understanding and abilities that the course has attempted to develop. Essay tests have many virtues, but efficiency, adequacy of sampling, and reliability of scoring are not among them.

Fifth, teachers often overemphasize trivial or ephemeral details in their tests, to the neglect of the understanding of basic principles and the ability to make practical applications. To illustrate, it is probably far more important to understand the forces which brought Henry VIII into conflict with the Pope than to know the name of his second wife. Yet some teachers are more inclined to ask about the specific, incidental details than about the important general principles.

Sixth, the test questions that teachers and professors write, both essay and objective, often suffer from lowered effectiveness due to unintentional ambiguity in the wording of the question or to the inclusion of irrelevant clues to the correct response. Too few teachers avoid these hazards by having their tests reviewed by some competent colleague before the tests are used.

Seventh, the inevitable fact that test scores are affected by the particular questions or tasks included in them tends to be ignored, and the magnitude of the resulting errors (called *sampling errors*) tend to be underestimated by those who make and use classroom tests. Many of them believe that a test score will be perfectly accurate and reliable if no error has been made in scoring the individual items or in adding these to get a total score. Differences as small as one score unit are often taken to indicate significant differences in attainment.

Finally, many teachers and professors do not use the relatively simple techniques of statistical analysis to check on the effectiveness of their tests. A mean score can show whether or not the test was appropriate for the group tested in its general level of difficulty. A standard deviation can show how well or how poorly the test differentiated among students having different levels of attainment. A reliability coefficient can show how much or how little the scores on this test are likely to differ from those the same students would get on an independent, equivalent test.

An analysis of the responses of good and poor students to individual test items can show whether the items discriminate well or poorly and, if poorly, can suggest why and what needs to be done to improve the item. The calculation of these statistics is quite simple. There is no better way for a teacher or professor to continue to improve his skill in testing, and the quality of the tests he uses, than to analyze systematically the results from his tests and to compare the findings of these analyses with ideal standards of test quality, such as those discussed in Chapter 9.

7. Sources of additional information about problems in the measurement of educational achievement

Some references likely to be useful in solving classroom testing problems are given in Exhibit 1.2. The instructor who becomes a self-motivated student of the improvement of tests of educational achievement should find these sources of information helpful.

EXHIBIT 1.2

Sources of Information About Educational Achievement Tests

I. Books

Adkins, Dorothy C. and others, *Construction and Analysis of Achievement Tests*. Washington, D.C.: U.S. Government Printing Office, 1947. 292 pp.
Written by experts, largely from the point of view of civil service testing, this compact book has chapters on the planning and construction of tests, on statistics and test analysis, and on performance tests. It contains a useful glossary of technical terms used in testing.

Gray, William S. (ed.), *Tests and Measurements in Higher Education*. Chicago, Ill.: The University of Chicago Press, 1936. 237 pp.
Sixteen papers presented at the Institute for Administrative Officers of Higher Institutions by authorities like Palmer O. Johnson, Ben D. Wood, L. L. Thurstone, Ralph W. Tyler, M. W. Richardson, I. L. Kandel, and John M. Stalnaker make up the contents of this volume. In addition to describing both the examination practices then being followed in a number of colleges and the methods being used to improve those practices, the papers deal with several broad topics, such as measurement of ability to write, an appraisal of the test movement, and needed research in the field of tests and examinations. This is another volume from the early days of testing that possesses enduring value.

Green, John A., *Teacher Made Tests*. New York: Harper & Row, Publishers, 1963. 141 pp. This is a concise, elementary treatment of the planning, construction, and use of various kinds of tests—objective, performance, essay, and oral used by classroom teachers.

Hawkes, Herbert E., E. F. Linquist, and C. R. Mann, *The Construction and Use of Achievement Examinations*. Boston: Houghton Mifflin Company, 1936. 416 pp.

General considerations in test construction, including definition of objectives to be measured, theories of test construction, and practices in test construction are followed by
chapters dealing with examinations in major subject fields
and by other chapters on the functions and limitations of
examinations. While this book is not a recent publication, it
contains many sound practical suggestions for test construction.

Lindquist, E. F., *Educational Measurement*. Washington, D.C.:
American Council on Education, 1951. 819 pp.
A comprehensive book on testing containing chapters by
twenty of the leading specialists in the field. It represents
the most authoritative manual on testing currently available.
Some of the chapters will be too technical for the beginning
student. It is, however, an extremely valuable reference to
one seriously concerned with test construction and use.

Travers, Robert M. W., *How to Make Achievement Tests*. New
York: The Odyssey Press, Inc., 1950. 180 pp.
The purpose of this brief nontechnical book is ". . . to help
teachers develop the types of evaluation instruments that
are known as objective tests of achievement." The seven
chapters deal with test planning, item writing, test assembly,
administration and scoring, and score interpretation. The
scoring of free-answer examinations is discussed in an appen-
dix.

Wood, Dorothy A., *Test Construction: Development and Interpretation of Achievement Tests*. Columbus, Ohio: Charles E.
Merrill Books, Inc., 1960. 134 pp. A description of the construction, administration, scoring, and interpretation of classroom tests, addressed to experienced and prospective teachers
at all educational levels.

II. References to Periodical Literature

The Education Index, The H. W. Wilson Company, New York,
1929-present, 13 volumes.
This collection of references to current periodical articles on
education, classified by subject and author, is issued monthly
and cumulated periodically. Most of the articles related to
classroom testing will be found under the subject heading
Tests and Scales, although some others will be found under
the headings *Educational Measurements, Evaluation, Examinations,* and *Objective Tests. The Education Index* is available in many college libraries and large general libraries.

Encyclopedia of Educational Research, 3rd ed. New York: The
Macmillan Company, 1960.

Paper-and-pencil achievement tests, essay and objective, are discussed in an article entitled "Tests and Examinations," based on 133 selected references. Other types and uses of tests and other evaluation techniques are discussed in separate articles. Earlier editions (1940 and 1950) of this encyclopedia, edited by Walter S. Monroe, contain additional discussions and references on testing problems. (Chester W. Harris is the editor of the third edition.)

Psychological Abstracts. Washington, D.C.: The American Psychological Association. This bimonthly publication lists classified references on most subjects of interest to psychologists, including educational measurement. Most references are followed by brief summaries or excerpts. An annual index, by authors and subjects, is provided.

Goheen, Howard W. and Samuel Kavruck, *Selected References on Test Construction, Mental Test Theory, and Statistics, 1929-1949.* Washington, D.C.: U.S. Government Printing Office, 1950. This bibliography lists 2,544 references, classified by topic and cross-indexed by author and subject matter. It is an extremely useful compilation.

"Educational and Psychological Testing," *Review of Educational Research,* XXXII, No. 1, (February, 1962). Washington, D.C.: American Educational Research Association. (Also XI:1, 1941; XIV:1, 1944; XVII:1, 1947; XX:1, 1950; XXIII:1, 1953; XXVI:1, 1956; XXIX:1, 1959
Occasionally before February, 1941, and regularly every three years thereafter, an issue of this summary and bibliography of research studies in education has been devoted to educational and psychological testing. Useful analyses and research evidence on most testing problems can be located with the help of these periodic reviews. A recent issue listed over 800 periodical articles on testing and commented on many of them.

III. Manuals on Testing

Hubbard, John P. and William V. Clemans, *Multiple Choice Examinations in Medicine.* Philadelphia: Lea & Febiger, 1961. This is a guide to the examiner and examinee. While the focus is on examinations for medical students, the suggestions apply to examinations in other fields as well.

National Science Teachers Association, *Let's Build Quality Into Our Science Tests.* Prepared by C. H. Nelson in cooperation with the NSTA's Committee on Evaluation. Washington, D.C., 1958. This pamphlet discusses principles of testing in science, and delineates techniques for testing logical reasoning,

problem solving, application and analysis. Illustrative examples
provide the core of the discussion.

Peterson, Shailer, *Manual on the Preparation of Examinations
in the Field of Dentistry*. Chicago, Ill.: American Dental
Association, 1952. 63 pp. Chapters deal with paper-and-pencil
examinations, clinical and laboratory examinations, administration of examinations, scoring and interpreting, and statistical tools. Many illustrative test items are included. Although
oriented to examinations in dentistry, the principles of measurement discussed and illustrated have general validity.

Stodola, Quentin, *Making the Classroom Test* (Evaluation and
Advisory Service Series, No. 4). Princeton, N.J.: Educational
Testing Service, 1959. 28 pp. This guide for teachers illustrates
basic principles of test construction in relation to four typical
classroom tests. Special problems in writing and scoring tests
are also discussed.

Tinkelman, Sherman H., *Improving the Classroom Test*. Albany,
N.Y.: The State Education Department, 1956. 55 pp. This
Manual is concerned with test construction procedures for
the classroom teacher, from planning to printing. Item types
and the principles of good item writing are discussed and
illustrated.

IV. Journals and Yearbooks

Educational and Psychological Measurement, G. Frederic Kuder
(ed.), Box 6907, College Station, Durham, North Carolina.
Many excellent articles on the development and application of
educational tests appear in this quarterly journal. It is the
only periodical devoted exclusively to problems in the
measurement of individual differences.

Proceedings of the Invitational Conference on Testing Problems.
Princeton, N.J.: Educational Testing Service. Each annual
issue of these proceedings prints the papers presented at a
one-day meeting, which is one of the major events each year
for those interested in educational measurement. Over the
years most of the problems of testing in the schools have
been foci of attention and expert discussion at these meetings.

*Yearbooks of the National Council on Measurement in Edu-
cation*.
Papers presented at the NCME annual meeting are printed
in full in these yearbooks. The 18th yearbook was issued in
1961. Many of the papers deal with testing problems of
interest to classroom teachers. (Copies of the yearbooks
obtainable from Dr. Irvin J. Lehmann, Secretary of NCME,
Michigan State University, East Lansing, Michigan.)

However, the instructor should not expect simple, clear-cut, fully validated solutions to all of the questions that will occur to him. Some simple questions may touch on problems that are not simple at all, so that the best solution in any given instance will depend on a complex of interacting factors. An example of such a question is, "How can we tell how valid our tests are?" The answers authorities give to other questions may depend more on their educational value systems than on their knowledge of research findings. But for most problems, including those in both categories just mentioned, the student of educational achievement testing will find additional enlightenment in the references listed here.

Articles and books and courses on testing can help instructors to make better classroom tests and to use them more effectively without devoting much more time to the processes. But real improvement is likely to cost a real increase in time and effort on the part of the classroom teacher. How far he is willing to go along this line will be determined by the value he places on accurate evaluations of achievement and on the satisfaction he gets from doing a good job with this aspect of his responsibility as a teacher. Some competent, conscientious teachers may be willing to go a considerable distance.

8. Summary

The main conclusions to be drawn from the discussions presented in this chapter can be summarized in the following twelve propositions.

1. Good achievement in education is fostered by the use of good tests of educational achievement.
2. Most teachers recognize the essential role of measurement in education.
3. Achievement tests are given under specially devised and carefully controlled conditions to improve the precision of measurement without imparing seriously its validity.
4. Written tests provide an important basis, but not the only basis teachers should use in evaluating student achievement.
5. The primary function of a classroom test is to measure student achievement.
6. Classroom tests can help to motivate and direct student achievement, and can provide learning exercises.

7. The development of a good classroom test requires the instructor to define the course objectives in specific, operational terms.
8. Most classroom tests are and ought to be prepared by the course instructors.
9. Competence in teaching is a necessary, but not a sufficient condition, for expert test construction.
10. Construction of a good objective test requires special knowledge of testing techniques and special skill in the use of language.
11. Some common weaknesses of teacher-made tests are attributable to: (1) reliance on subjective judgments, (2) reliance on absolute standards of judgment, (3) hasty test preparation, (4) use of short, inefficient tests, (5) testing trivia, (6) careless wording of questions, (7) neglect of sampling errors, and (8) failure to analyze the quality of the test.
12. To improve their testing teachers will have to work harder, longer, more cooperatively, and with more frequent reference to manuals on test improvement.

REFERENCES

Dyer, Henry S., "What Point of View Should Teachers Have Concerning the Role of Measurement in Education?" *The Fifteenth Yearbook of the National Council on Measurements Used in Education.* East Lansing, Mich.: Michigan State University, 1958.

Joint Committee of the American Association of School Administrators, *Testing, Testing, Testing,* p. 9. Washington, D.C.: American Association of School Administrators, 1962.

Richardson, M. W. and J. M. Stalnaker, "Comments on Achievement Examinations," *Journal of Educational Research,* XXVIII (1935), 425-32.

Stroud, James B., *Psychology in Education,* p. 476. New York: David McKay Co., Inc., 1946.

Thurstone, Louis L., "The Improvement of Examinations," *American Association of University Professors Bulletin,* XXXIV (June, 1948), 394-97.

2 What Should Achievement Tests Measure?

> *If measurement is to continue to play an increasingly important role in education, measurement workers must be much more than technicians. Unless their efforts are directed by a sound educational philosophy, unless they accept and welcome a greater share of responsibility for the selection and clarification of educational objectives, unless they show much more concern with what they measure as well as with how they measure it, much of their work will prove futile or ineffective.*
>
> E. F. LINDQUIST

1. The dual problems of test construction

The test constructor faces two major problems. The first is to determine what to measure. The second is to decide how to measure it. In general, books and articles on educational testing offer more help in solving the second problem than the first. But the quality of an educational achievement test depends on how well *both* problems have been solved. How well the first problem is solved largely determines what is sometimes called the *relevance* of the test. By "relevance" we mean the apparent or obvious logical relationship between what the process of testing requires the student to do and what the process of education undertook to teach

22

him to do. How well the second problem is solved has a great deal to do with the *reliability* of the test and its practicality. By "reliability" we mean the consistency of the measurement of a particular achievement from time to time or from test to test. To the degree that a test has this kind of relevance and yields reliable scores, it can claim to be a *valid* test. A valid test of educational achievement is one composed of relevant tasks and yielding reliable scores.[1]

If the test constructor has sound and specific ideas about what constitutes educational achievement in the area of the test, he knows what to measure. But these sound and specific ideas are sometimes hard to get. For one thing, there is far more of knowledge, understanding, ability, skill, and effective behavior available for us to learn in the world than any one person could possibly learn, even if he were willing to try for maximum learning, which most of us are not. Teachers and students are constantly faced with the need to make choices between many varied things to be taught and to be learned. We keep asking ourselves and others the question Herbert Spencer asked and tried to answer a century ago. "What knowledge is of most worth?" [2] Benjamin Franklin recognized the same problem. "It would be well if they could be taught everything that is useful and everything that is ornamental: but art is long and their time is short. It is therefore proposed that they learn those things that are likely to be most useful and most ornamental." [3]

The problems of the test constructor thus have much in common with those of the curriculum maker, the textbook writer, and the classroom teacher. The test constructor, however, can borrow ideas from all of the other three. If those whose guidance he accepts are themselves well educated and if they have thought long and carefully about what achievements are of most worth, the test constructor may build a good test with their help. But the problem is not a simple one. In the foreseeable future educators will probably have to get along as best they can with somewhat imperfect, uncertain answers to the question of what to test. This, of course, is no excuse

---

[1] The concepts of test reliability and test validity are much more complex than these simple definitions may imply. They will be discussed in greater detail in subsequent chapters.

[2] Herbert Spencer, *Education: Intellectual, Moral and Physical* (New York: A. L. Burt; London: G. Manwaring, 1861).

[3] Thomas Woody, *Educational Views of Benjamin Franklin* (New York: McGraw-Hill Book Company, 1931), p. 158.

for not trying to find the best available answers, which are doubtless much better than those we often give or accept.

There is another school of thought about how to produce good tests. Instead of trying to build relevance into the tests, with rational decisions about what kinds of tasks will provide valid measures of a particular kind of achievement, the proponents of this school advocate an experimental approach. Try any kind of question or task you can think of that might work, they say, and retain in the test only those that do work, or work best. The difficulty with this approach is that it requires some basis for judging how well an item "works" as an indicator of achievement. Usually this implies some other, and presumably better, measure of the achievement in question. But this is precisely what we were setting out to create. If we already had it, we probably would not need to worry about building the new test. The use of empirical (experimental) approaches to test development do not circumvent the need for rational decisions and value judgments with respect to what should be measured. If they are not applied to the test, they have to be applied in choosing the standards by which the test is to be judged.

Publishers of standardized tests of educational achievement and directors of wide-scaled testing programs which use achievement tests face a special problem in deciding what to test. It is the problem of how to make a single test suitable for students who have been taught by different teachers using different textbooks and learning materials in courses having different orientations. The usual solution is to base the test on the elements thought to be most commonly taught. If the differences are too great to make this solution feasible, separate tests have to be provided.

The classroom teacher's problems would seem to be much simpler since only one teacher, one or the same set of textbooks, and a single approach to teaching are involved. But the advantage is less than it might seem. If a particular teacher's instruction and testing do not emphasize substantially the same achievements as those of most other teachers of the same subjects, his students may not have the achievements expected of them. Thus the test constructor must ask not only, "Do *I* consider this achievement worth having?" but also, "Do *most* good teachers of the subject regard this particular knowledge or ability worth having?"

Some differences between teachers, texts, courses, and tests are not only tolerable but probably essential if teaching is to have its maximum vitality and person-to-person effectiveness. But if the differences become too great, particularly in the more elementary courses, the students may suffer later. Thus the classroom teacher needs to be concerned about the general validity and acceptability of his value judgments and approaches to teaching. If a wholesale revision in curriculum and instruction is called for, it had best not be undertaken singlehandedly, in the relative isolation of a single classroom.

2. The measurability of educational outcomes

Education is an extensive, diverse, complex enterprise, not only in terms of the achievements it seeks to develop but also in terms of the means by which it seeks to develop them. Our understanding of the nature and process of education is far from perfect. Hence it is easy to agree that we do not now know how to measure all important educational outcomes. *But in principle, all important outcomes of education are measurable.* They may not be measurable with the tests currently available. They may not even be measurable in principle, using only paper-and-pencil tests. But if they are known to be important, they must be measurable.

To be important an outcome of education must make an observable difference. That is, at some time, under some circumstances, a person who has more of it must behave differently from a person who has less of it. If different degrees or amounts of an educational achievement never make any observable difference, what evidence can be found to show that it is, in fact, important?

But if such differences can be observed, then the achievement is measurable. For all that measurement requires is verifiable observation of a more-less relationship. Can integrity be measured? It can if verifiable differences in integrity can be observed among men. Can mother love be measured? If observers can agree that a hen shows more mother love than a female trout, or that Mrs. A shows more love for her children than Mrs. B, then mother love can be measured.

The argument, then, is this. To be important an educational outcome must make a difference. If it makes a difference, the basis for measurement exists.

To say that A shows more of trait X than B may not seem like much of a measurement. Where are the numbers? Yet out of a series of such more-less comparisons a scale for measuring the trait or property can be constructed. The Ayres scale for measuring the quality of handwriting is a familiar example of this.[4] If a sequence of numbers is assigned to the sequence of steps or intervals which make up the scale, then the scale can yield quantitative measurements. If used carefully by a skilled judge, it will yield measurements that are reasonably objective (i.e., free from the unique biases of the particular judge) and reliable (i.e., free from errors of measurement).

Are some outcomes of education essentially qualitative rather than quantitative? If so, is it reasonable to expect that these qualitative outcomes can be measured?

It is certainly true that some differences between persons are not usually thought of as more-less differences. This person is a man; that one is a woman. This person has blue eyes; that one has brown. This person speaks only French; that one speaks only German. But we can express these qualitative differences in quantitative terms. This person has more of the characteristics of a man; that one has less. This person has more eye-blueness; that one has less. This person has more ability to speak French; that one has less.

We may think of the weight of a man, his age, or the size of his bank account as quantities, while regarding his health, his friendliness, or his honesty as qualities. But it is also possible to regard all of them—weight, age, savings, health, friendliness and honesty—as qualities. And if they serve to differentiate him from other men, because he exhibits more or less of them than other men, they become quantitative qualities. It is difficult to think of any quality which interests us that cannot also be quantified. "Whatever exists at all exists in some amount," said E. L. Thorndike.[5] And William A. McCall has added, "Anything that exists in amount can be measured."[6]

---

[4] L. P. Ayres, *A Scale for Measuring the Quality of Handwriting of School Children,* Division of Education, Bulletin 113 (New York: Russell Sage Foundation, 1912).

[5] E. L. Thorndike, *The Seventeenth Yearbook of the National Society for the Study of Education,* Part II (Bloomington, Ill.: Public School Publishing Company, 1918), p. 16.

[6] William A. McCall, *Measurement* (New York: The Macmillan Company, 1939), p. 15.

Are some outcomes of education too intangible to be measured? No doubt there are some that we speak of often, like critical thinking or good citizenship, that are so difficult to define satisfactorily that we have given up trying to define them specifically. To this extent they are intangible. To this extent they are hard to measure. To this extent they are also hard to teach purposefully. We may feel intuitively that critical thinking and good citizenship are immensely important. But if we don't know very clearly what we mean by those terms, it is hard to show that the concepts they might stand for are in fact important.

The processes of education which a particular student experiences probably have subtle and wholly unforeseen effects on him, and possibly on no one else. Some of these effects may not become apparent until long after the student has left school. These, too, could be regarded as intangible outcomes. It is unlikely that any current tests, or any that could conceivably be built, would measure these intangibles satisfactorily. In individual instances they might be crucially important. But since they may be largely accidental, subtle, and quite possibly long delayed in their influence, the practical need to measure them may be no greater than the practical possibility of measuring them.

Some of the belief that certain important outcomes of education are difficult to measure may stem from a confusion between measurement and prediction. For example, most people agree that it is quite difficult at present to measure motivation or creativity. But those who want to measure motivation or creativity are interested mainly in future prospects, not in present status or past achievements. They are less interested in the motivation or the creative achievements a person has shown in the past than in how hard he will work and how successfully he will create in the future.

Difficult as the problems of measuring some complex human traits are, they are much simpler than the problems of predicting unusual future success, especially if that success requires a fortunate coincidence of many influences. To help keep our thinking straight we probably should not charge those difficulties to the limitations of educational measurement. We might charge them in part to the somewhat indefinite generality of the concepts (motivation, creativity, etc.) involved, in part to the complexity of human behavior, and in part to our own cherished, if partly imaginary, freedom of choice and action.

Finally, it should be recognized that paper-and-pencil tests do have some limitations. They are well adapted to testing verbal knowledge and understanding and ability to solve verbal and numerical problems. These are important educational outcomes, but they are not all. One would not expect to get far using a paper-and-pencil test to measure children's physical development. Perhaps such a test could be made to yield somewhat better measures of the social effectiveness of adults, but even here the paper-and-pencil test is likely to be seriously limited. Both performance tests of physical development and controlled observations of behavior in social situations would be expected to offer more promise than a paper-and-pencil test.

However, it is important to remember that the use of alternative measures of achievement does not in any way lessen the need for objectivity, relevance, reliability, and validity. To achieve these qualities of excellence in measurement may well be even more difficult in performance testing and observational rating than it is in paper-and-pencil testing. But the usefulness of the measurements depends on them.

3. The problem of quantification

To say that anything that exists is potentially measurable is not to say that we already know how to measure it, that we can quickly discover how best to measure it, or that it can be measured successfully by means of a paper-and-pencil test. One of the major tasks of research workers in any new field is to discover effective means of *quantifying* the characteristics they choose to study. By "quantifying" we mean discovering ways of getting numbers attached to examples of the quality so that differences in the numbers correspond at least roughly to the perceived differences in the quality. To quantify temperature, for example, we put some mercury in a glass tube and attach it to a specially devised ruler. The length of the mercury column yields numbers which correspond generally with our perceptions of temperature, but which are considerably more refined and dependable.

A description of the process of quantifying a characteristic constitutes what some scientists call an "operational definition" of it. Often such characteristics start out as rather vague concepts, based on hunches or hypotheses. The process of devising a method of measurement for the characteristic, that is, of quantifying it, forces the scientist to become more specific. If this operational definition does not satisfy him or if the numbers it yields turn out to be harder to get or less useful than he had hoped, he may try another. If two different methods of quantification of the same variable are suggested and if the measures obtained by the two methods are not identical or directly proportional, one of the methods will have to be discarded, or two different variables will have to be recognized. The interesting point is that the process of measurement requires, and results in, a very specific definition of the thing to be measured.

An illustration may help to make this clear. Suppose you are asked to say which of three gasoline stations at an intersection is the biggest. Assume that no generally accepted method of measuring the size of a gasoline station is known. Your problem is to *quantify* the somewhat indefinite concept "bigness of a gasoline station." That is, you have to find some aspect of the station you can count or measure that will give you numbers which correspond to your notions of bigness.

You might choose, for example, to count the number of pumps, or the number of employees, or the number of cars that stop in a typical day. Or you might choose to measure the number of gallons of gasoline sold in a typical day or the cubic feet in the service building. You might choose some combination of some of these measures. When you had made the choice, and not before, "bigness" as applied to gasoline stations would become measurable. What is more, that concept of "bigness" would then come to have a definite meaning. The methods of measuring such a concept, and thus the meaning of the concept, are not to be discovered. They have to be invented.

A similar problem is faced, and a similar solution must be worked out, in quantifying any aspect of educational achievement, from reading readiness to understanding of quantum mechanics. In some areas the nature of educational achievement has been well defined, and these definitions are generally accepted. In others the situation is less stable and orderly. But we are likely to waste time if we set out to discover the *true* measure of intelligence or spelling ability or architectural aptitude. We will have to invent the process of quantification and test it in terms of the usefulness of the measures it yields.

Thorndike defended the measurability of human traits by arguing that whatever exists at all exists in some amount. But such attributes as the bigness of a gasoline station, the curvature of a line, the hardness of a stone, or the intelligence of a child do not exist in quite the same sense that a gasoline station, a line segment, a gem stone, or a school child may be said to exist. The attributes are abstractions which we invent. We know they are measurable simply because grossly different amounts of them can be perceived by the unaided senses. The problems of measuring these attributes is essentially that of developing devices to aid the senses, to refine the gross perceptions, to make our quantitative reports more precise, more reproducible, more objective, in short more reliable. This is part of the test constructor's problem as he tries to decide what to measure.

4. The uses and limitations
of educational objectives in test development

An educational achievement test should seek to measure what the process of education has sought to achieve. Hence the test constructor needs to be concerned with educational objectives, both those which relate to the total process of education and those which relate specifically to the course or subject for which the test is being constructed. The tests he builds ought to be as consistent as possible with the educational objectives of the society, the school, and the test constructor himself.

One of the uses of any statement of educational objectives is to remind all concerned that education should be a purposeful activity, not simply a routine ritual. The steady influx of pupils to be educated and the organization of these pupils into a succession of annual class groups, each of which follows much the same program of studies as it advances through the institution, give the process of education a repetitive characteristic that could easily become a fixed routine. Often the educational needs of a society seem to change faster than the programs of the society's educational institutions. Indeed, some educators seem to make a virtue of the traditional in education, regardless of the educational needs of the contemporary society. It is occasionally useful to ask of any subject of study or method of instruction the simple question, "Why?" and to insist on an answer that makes sense. The formulation of educational objectives can be the occasion for asking such questions. Another use of educational objectives, related to the first, is in the redirecting of educational emphases. Often the motivation for this redirection is the observation that instruction in the schools is not adequately meeting the needs of the day. Herbert Spencer's essay on the purposes of education begins by deploring the overemphasis on the *ornamental* in education, to the neglect of the useful.[7] Spencer evaluated knowledge from the standpoint of its contribution to five categories of activities which constitute human life:

1. Self-preservation
2. Securing the necessities of life
3. Rearing and discipline of offspring
4. Maintenance of proper social and political relations
5. Gratification of the tastes and feelings

When the secondary school continued in the traditions of college preparation while rising enrollments were generating needs for terminal, general, and vocational education, the Commission on the Reorganization of Secondary Education sought to redirect its emphases by formulating the now famous seven cardinal principles as the main objectives of education:[8]

1. Health
2. Command of fundamental processes
3. Worthy home membership
4. Vocation
5. Citizenship
6. Worthy use of leisure
7. Ethical character

Statements of educational objectives often accompany efforts to reorient instruction in a particular field of study. A group of social

---

[7] Spencer, *op. cit.*

[8] National Education Association Commission on Reorganizing Secondary Education, *Cardinal Principles of Secondary Education,* U.S. Office of Education, Bulletin No. 35 (Washington, D.C., 1918).

studies teachers in the Wisconsin Improvement Program listed these
specific goals for teaching in the social studies:[9]

1. Transmit our cultural heritage.
2. Provide intellectual exercise for the discipline of the mind.
3. Promote moral and spiritual values.
4. Develop democratic citizenship.
5. Promote good mental health.
6. Teach important historical facts and generalizations.
7. Promote the attitude that history is interesting and useful.
8. Teach time and space relationships.
9. Promote aesthetic sensitivities.
10. Acquaint students with basic historical references.
11. Provide instruction and practice in the skills of writing notes
    from lectures, writing essay examinations, locating informa-
    tion, judging the validity of evidence, drawing conclusions
    from data, skill in working in a group, and facility in oral ex-
    pression.

Even more narrowly specific statements of objectives can be formulated for particular courses, units of study, or even individual les-
sons.

General statements of educational objectives are useful to the test
constructor as guides to the areas to be covered and to the direction
of emphasis in his test. Highly specific statements may be useful in
suggesting particular questions or types of questions to ask. But
statements of objectives have limitations too.

Sometimes instead of aiming to be directive they aim to be inclusive. Instead of suggesting that the schools or the teacher of a particular course do this *instead* of that, they seem to suggest that the
schools do both this *and* that, as well as everything that anyone has
suggested it might also be good to do. Frequently they include
highly attractive terms like "critical thinking," "creative produc-
tivity," or "good citizenship," which everyone can endorse but few
can define. Such all-inclusive statements of objectives may be of
some use as systems of grouping or classification, but they have little
directive value.

---

[9] Robert L. Ebel, "The Problem of Evaluation in the Social Studies," *Social
Education*, XXIV (January, 1960), 6-10.

Another limitation of statements of educational objectives grows out of the very large number of things to be learned and abilities to be acquired. To attempt to list them all would be an enormous task. The task of getting agreement on some order of priorities would be even greater. And if the job were ever completed, the list would be so long, and so subject to criticism, that few would ever bother to read it. The alternative of a comprehensive listing in detail of all objectives is to list names or descriptions of only the major categories of objectives. This is the alternative ordinarily chosen. It gives some indication of coverage and emphasis but is usually too general and indefinite to be of much direct help to the test constructor.

It is important to realize, as was pointed out in a recent yearbook of the National Society for the Study of Education, that specific educational goals are not derived by logical deduction from a single basic statement of the meaning and purpose of life.[10] Rather, they seem to arise out of recognitions of specific needs in the complex business of living. As Grieder has said,

> Are not the goals of a society largely unformulated, like the unwritten British Constitution? They develop slowly and through a continuous process of interaction among various segments and levels of a society, and among societies.[11]

Flanagan has proposed an empirical approach to the formulation of educational goals.[12] By collecting and classifying descriptions of actual observations of effective and ineffective behavior in particular fields of activity (the so-called critical incidents), investigators would be able to develop a more general summary listing of the critical requirements for success in that activity. Thus far this suggestion has not made serious inroads into the more conventional armchair procedures for formulating educational objectives.

A serious effort to take some of the vagueness out of statements of educational objectives at the college level has been made by Bloom

---

[10] Warren Findley and Others, "The Relation of Testing Programs to Educational Goals," *The Impact and Improvement of School Testing Programs,* Part I, Chap. 2. Sixty-Second Yearbook of the National Society for the Study of Education (Chicago: The University of Chicago Press, 1963).

[11] Calvin Grieder, "Is It Possible to Word Educational Goals?" *Nation's Schools,* LXVIII (October, 1961), 10ff.

[12] John C. Flanagan, "The Critical Requirements Approach to Educational Objectives," *School and Society,* LXXI (May 27, 1950), 321-24.

and his co-workers.[13] They have produced a system for the classification of educational objectives which they call a "taxonomy." The term "taxonomy" is derived from two Greek words, *taxis,* meaning "arrangement," and *nomos,* meaning "law." Hence a "taxonomy" is a lawful or an orderly arrangement. That part of the study of plants and animals which is concerned with classifying them into a succession of ever narrower and more specific groups—phyla, classes, orders, families, etc.—is biological taxonomy. Bloom's taxonomy is a taxonomy of educational objectives.

The original publication, the book cited, dealt only with cognitive objectives, grouped in six major classes:

1. Knowledge   4. Analysis
2. Comprehension   5. Synthesis
3. Application   6. Evaluation

More recently, the taxonomy has been extended to affective objectives, having to do with attitudes, values, interests, and appreciation. The five major classes of affective objectives in this taxonomy are:

1. Receiving   4. Organization
2. Responding   5. Characterization
3. Valuing

A taxonomy for a third area of educational objectives dealing with the development of psychomotor (muscular) skills is yet to be completed. Since value judgments were specifically outlawed during its development, the taxonomy provides no directive guidance as to objectives of higher or lower priority.

But the taxonomy does attack one of the major limitations of some other formulations of objectives, i.e., indefiniteness. For accompanying each description of a subclass of objectives are illustrative items taken from actual tests. Even where the subclasses are not clearly distinct, and the appropriateness of a stated objective or a test item to one rather than another subclass is not clearly apparent, the items do help to reduce the uncertainty regarding what a particular objective or set of objectives means. The taxonomy also

---

[13] Benjamin S. Bloom and Others, *Taxonomy of Educational Objectives* (New York: David McKay Co., Inc., 1956).

provides a collection of illustrative test items that can be most useful to the test constructor.

In summary, the test constructor needs to be informed about and interested in the educational objectives in the field of his test. A good statement of objectives can help him extend and balance the coverage of his test and check on the appropriateness of its emphasis. But even the best such statement is likely to leave him with many item ideas to discover and many value judgments to make. Ordinarily he will need considerable help from course outlines, textbooks, and even other tests in deciding what should go into the test and what should be left out.

5. Behavioral goals of education

The history of education indicates that most subjects of study were introduced into the educational program in response to real and immediate needs. With changing times these needs sometimes disappeared, but successive generations of scholars who in their turn became teachers tended to continue teaching the same things they had been taught. Partly in response to the persistence of irrelevant knowledge in the curriculum and partly in reaction to the vagueness of many statements of objectives, some educators like Ralph Tyler began to urge that objectives should be defined in terms of desired behavior.[14] The purpose of education, they suggested, is not to accumulate knowledge but to change behavior. Their suggestions have borne fruit in two volumes setting forth the goals of education in behavioral terms.[15] The efforts of a great many carefully selected educators went into the production of these reports whose development was supervised by Educational Testing Service, with financial support from the Russell Sage Foundation.

The defects in education which led to this development are real defects and need to be corrected. All knowledge is not of equal worth, as Herbert Spencer argued a century ago. The knowledge

---

[14] Ralph W. Tyler, "A Generalized Technique for Constructing Achievement Tests," *Educational Research Bulletin*, Ohio State University, Columbus, Ohio, X (1931), 199-208.

[15] Nolan C. Kearney, *Elementary School Objectives* (New York: Russell Sage Foundation, 1953); and Will French and Associates, *Behavioral Goals of General Education in High School* (New York: Russell Sage Foundation, 1957).

that we ask teachers to teach and students to gain command of needs to be reviewed frequently to reassess its power and its relevance to contemporary needs. Educational objectives which are stated so vaguely that it is difficult to learn by observing what the scholar can do, whether he has attained them or not, are not likely to provide useful guides to either teaching or testing.

But the remedy proposed, that of defining educational objectives in terms of desired behavior, also has shortcomings. It appears to assume that despite the highly complex and rapidly changing world in which we live, a teacher can know years ahead of time how the scholar ought to behave in a given set of circumstances. It also seems to assume that the teacher is entitled to prescribe his behavior for him. Both of these assumptions may be open to serious question. An alternative to the definition of educational objectives as descriptions of specific acts or general patterns of desired behavior is their definition in terms of relevant and powerful knowledge, the command of which seems well calculated to give the scholar the capacity to adapt his behavior effectively in the face of a complexity of varied, changing situations.

The power of knowledge as a tool for the attainment of human aspirations can hardly be doubted. But it is not all-powerful. It cannot guarantee the results we seek. This leads to the question of what other means might be used to attain our goals. What alternative to reason based on knowledge is there which the schools might cultivate in order to help human beings to live better?

One alternative to knowledge and reason as a basis for behavior is simple conditioning. Much of the behavior we exhibit is conditioned behavior. Human beings are almost as adept as other animals in learning to do the things that their environment rewards and to avoid the things that it punishes. In the case of very young children, conditioning may be the only effective means of education. As our experiences accumulate, as our awareness develops, reflective thought becomes available as a means of problem solving and of education. But the adult remains susceptible to conditioning, however rationally he may seek to behave. Fortunate success or unfortunate failure can encourage or discourage future efforts along the same line. The attitudes and values a person holds, even his beliefs, are attributable to conditioning as well as to reflective thought.

No doubt a case could be made in favor of conditioning as the exclusive means of education in a static society dedicated to the strength and stability of the group. But that is not the kind of a society in which we live nor the ideal to which we are dedicated. We respect the worth and dignity of the individual and seek to facilitate his maximum development as a free man. This means that we must be concerned with the cultivation of his rational powers. Quoting the Educational Policies Commission:

> To be free, a man must be capable of basing his choices and actions on understandings which he himself achieves and on values which he examines for himself. . . . The free man, in short, has a rational grasp of himself, his surroundings, and the relation between them.[16]

Emphasis on desired behavior as an educational outcome has encouraged test builders to write items which describe specific situations and call for the examinee to choose the most appropriate or effective behavior in that situation. Here is an example.

> Jim has a movie date for Saturday night but is short on cash. His brother Bob has $5.00 that he is willing to loan for a week at 5 per cent interest, provided Jim will give him some security. Jim offers any one of the following items. Which should Bob accept if he is a prudent businessman?
>
> 1. Jim's class ring
> 2. Jim's new sweater
> *3. Jim's car keys
> 4. Jim's football

Items such as this can have the virtue of testing the examinee's ability to behave effectively in a given situation.

But items of this type are subject to two weaknesses. They tend to require lengthy descriptions of the problem setting and thus to become time consuming and inefficient sources of information on achievement. They also tend, because of the difficulty of communicating fully and clearly all the factors which might be relevant to the choice of an answer, to become somewhat ambiguous as problems and somewhat indeterminate as to the correct response. Taken

---

[16] National Education Association Educational Policies Commission, *The Central Purpose of American Education* (Washington, D.C.: National Education Association, 1961), p. 4.

together these weaknesses may account for the rather lower reliability for tests of this type than is ordinarily obtained when using
more direct measures of knowledge. There is little evidence that the
situational tests are more valid measures of command of substantive
knowledge than are the simpler, more direct tests. The test constructor may wish to experiment with items of this type, but in the
absence of empirical evidence of their superiority there are no compelling reasons for insisting on their use.

Those who have urged that educational goals be expressed in
terms of desired behavior have wisely sought emphasis on meaningful statements of useful educational outcomes. They have not advocated conditioning as the primary means of human education. They
have not tried to promote a static society. The aim they have been
pursuing may not be significantly different from that expressed by
the phrase "command of substantive knowledge." If so, the concerns
expressed in the foregoing paragraphs may seem to be more concerned about the use of particular words than about the purposes
and means of education.

But it seems important to suggest strongly that the proper starting
point of educational planning in a democracy is not the kind of behaviors present adults desire future adults to exhibit, but rather the
kind of equipment that will enable them to choose their own behaviors intelligently. A major problem of education is to identify
the elements of knowledge whose command will be most useful to
the student in contributing to a good life for himself, in the best
society he can help to develop. From this point of view educational
achievement should be judged more in terms of what the student
can do than in terms of what he typically *does* do. If there is any
sizable discrepancy in the long run between the two, something must
be wrong either with what education has taught him how to do or
with what society rewards him for doing.

6. The cognitive outcomes of education

If we look at what actually goes on in our school and college
classrooms and laboratories, libraries and lecture halls, it seems
reasonable to conclude that the major goal of education is to
develop in the scholars a *command of substantive knowledge.*

Achievement of this kind of cognitive mastery is clearly not the only concern of teachers and scholars engaged in the process of education. But the command of substantive knowledge is, and ought to be, the central concern of education.

Pursuit of knowledge is clearly the business of scholarship. The power of knowledge has been so generally acknowledged, from ancient to modern times, that it may seem surprising that anyone would challenge cognitive mastery as the central purpose of education. Yet it has been, and is being, challenged. Knowledge alone is not enough, says the businessman. It does not guarantee financial success. Knowledge alone is not enough, says the college president. It does not guarantee scholarly achievement. Knowledge alone is not enough, says the religious leader. It does not guarantee virtue. Knowledge alone is not enough, says the philosopher. It does not guarantee happiness.

They are all right, of course. Knowledge alone is *not* enough. But in this complex world of chance and change no one thing, nor any combination of things, ever will be enough to *guarantee* financial success or scholarly achievement or virtue or happiness. Few would deny that the command of substantive knowledge does contribute mightily to the attainment of these other, more ultimate goals. Further, it is difficult to name any other human ability which can be developed that is likely to contribute more than, or as much as, knowledge to the attainment of these goals. It is even more difficult to describe what sorts of things the schools ought to be doing to develop the alleged noncognitive ingredients of success, achievement, virtue, or happiness.

But what is *substantive knowledge?* And what is meant by *command* of knowledge? Consider the first question. A whole branch of philosophy, epistemology, is devoted to a study of what it is and how it is acquired. Perhaps a simpler approach will suffice here.

A person's knowledge includes everything that he has experienced as a result of his perceptions of his external environment or as a result of his internal reflections or thought processes. All this history of his living becomes a part of his knowledge. Psychologists suggest that nothing a person has experienced is ever completely and permanently forgotten. It all remains somewhere, however deeply buried and overlaid with other experiences. The problem of learning, in the modern view, is not so much how to get things into the mind as it is how to get them out again when they are needed. The problem is less one of storage than it is of ready access.

As defined in *Webster's New Collegiate Dictionary*, "knowledge" is:

1. Familiarity gained by actual experience
2. Acquaintance with fact; hence, scope of information
3. The act or state of understanding; cognition
4. That which is gained and preserved by knowing; enlightment; learning; also, broadly, the sum of information conserved by civilization

These definitions suggest the scope of the concept of knowledge, and its relationship to or identity with experience, fact, information, understanding, enlightment, and learning.

The kind of knowledge that schools and colleges are most concerned with is verbal knowledge. To the degree that a person's experiences of external affairs and internal thoughts can be expressed in words, they become a part of his verbal knowledge. Because verbal knowledge can be recorded, thought about, and communicated so conveniently, it is a very powerful form of knowledge. Possession of skill in using verbal knowledge may be the source of, and certainly provides the clearest evidence of, man's superiority over the lower animals.

Schools are sometimes criticized for excessive concern with verbal knowledge, at the expense of nonverbal knowledge growing out of direct, firsthand experiences in the laboratory, the shop, or outside the school room altogether. Such directly obtained knowledge, it is pointed out, provides the foundation on which the truth and usefulness of all verbal knowledge must rest. For some students, and indeed for some scholars as well, that foundation appears to be none too broad and none too firm. To strengthen and extend it is to add important new dimensions to a person's understanding of the words and sentences with which he deals.

All this can be granted without abandoning the proposition that development of a student's command of useful verbal knowledge is the principal function of formal education. Direct experience is essential as a foundation, but it provides little more than the foundation. It is the verbal knowledge, through which those experiences are integrated, interpreted, and communicated that makes possible the intelligent behavior of a human being and the culture of a human society.

There is already a great store of recorded human verbal knowledge in the world. Day by day it increases. Indeed it seems to some observers to be increasing so rapidly that they speak frighteningly of the "explosion of knowledge." In some fields, fortunately few, new knowledge almost appears to make an old scholar's learning obsolete in his own lifetime.

Not all of the items in this store of knowledge—the names, dates, events, concepts, ideas, and propositions—are of equal value. Some are of limited, temporary interest. Some are indefinite and inaccurate. One of the most important and most difficult tasks of the educator is to sort out the more valuable from the less valuable. It is easy to say that those items of knowledge which are most widely useful, or most central to the structure of a body of knowledge, should be regarded as most valuable. But to apply these abstract criteria to specific items in specific areas of knowledge, the educator must make a multitude of difficult decisions usually in the absence of really adequate evidence. The task is not easy, but it is essential. Whether in curriculum construction, test development, or any other activity concerned with the content of education, the educator's first problem is to pass sound judgments on the potential usefulness of various kinds and items of knowledge.

The second major problem of the educator is to manage the learning process so as to develop the student's *command* of knowledge. To have command of knowledge is to have ready access to it and full comprehension of its scope, its limitations, and its implications. Hence to develop command of knowledge requires development of relationships a person knows, the better his command of the items generalizations, between concepts and principles. The more of these relationships a person knows, the better his command of the items they relate and the more likely he is to recall them when they might be useful to him.

Relating is understanding. Thunder is understood better when it is related to lightning. Fermentation is understood better when it is related to bacteria. Fluid pressure is understood better when it is related to depth and density. In general, the understanding of any separate thing involves seeing its relations to other things. The knowledge a person understands he has command of, and the knowledge he commands he also understands.

Command of knowledge obviously involves thinking, which both requires and produces it. Thus while knowledge and thinking are not identical, they are closely related. To say that the purpose of education is not to acquire knowledge but to develop the ability to think is to establish a false antithesis. Knowledge and thinking are not mutually exclusive or even alternative goals of education. Each demands the other. One cannot be in favor of thinking but opposed to knowledge. Nor can the power to think be increased appreciably except by increasing the store of knowledge at the command of the thinker. Faulty thinking usually reflects limited or erroneous knowledge, or failure to make careful and unbiased use of it.

Objective tests, composed as they are of many separate, independent items, are sometimes supposed to be useful only for measuring isolated bits of factual information. This supposition involves several questionable assumptions:

1. Whatever characterizes a test must also characterize the thing it tests.
2. Information can be, and often is, stored in the form of isolated bits.
3. The questions on objective tests are familiar questions, to which pat answers can be recalled if they ever were learned.

But if the test is a good test consisting largely of novel problems, to which answers must be thought through with the help of information previously acquired, and if it is true that the availability of relevant information depends on how well it has been integrated into a consistent, meaningful network of relations, then objective tests are not so severely limited. Discrete items can test, and usually do test, command of knowledge, that is, ability to use it to solve new problems.

Cohen and Nagle have made two comments about knowledge that seem particularly useful in this context.[17] They say (1) that knowledge is of propositions and (2) that a proposition is anything which

---

[17] Morris R. Cohen and Ernest Nagel, *An Introduction to Logic and Scientific Method* (New York: Harcourt, Brace & World, Inc., 1934), p. 27.

can be said to be true or false. Propositions are expressed in sentences, but not all sentences are propositions. Those expressing questions or commands cannot be said to be true or false, nor can those which report purely subjective wishes or feelings. Propositions are always declarative sentences about objects or events in the external world. For example:

> The earth is a planet in the solar system.
>
> A body immersed in a fluid is buoyed up by a force equal to the weight of fluid displaced.
>
> As we consume or acquire additional units of any commodity, the satisfaction derived from each additional installment tends to diminish.
>
> William J. Bryan failed in his bid for election to the presidency of the United States in the campaign of 1896.

The relation of propositions such as these to objective test items of the true-false type is direct and simple. Less obvious, but no less true, is the fact that a proposition like those above are implicit in most other types of objective test items—multiple choice, matching, short answer, or completion. What we test, beyond the student's ability to understand the language used in the test item, is his knowledge of the proposition that makes one answer correct and others incorrect. All of the propositions cited above appear to deserve a a place in the "information conserved by civilization." But there are some other sentences expressing propositions which probably do not deserve such preservation. For example:

> Rain fell in New York City on December 6, 1962.
>
> The cost of living in Canada advanced two-fifths of a point during October 1962.
>
> Work-limit tests are mentioned on page 366 of *Educational Measurement,* edited by E. F. Lindquist.

Objective test items ought not to be based on propositions such as these but sometimes, unfortunately, they may be.

The closeness of this relation between the propositions which constitute our knowledge and the items needed for our objective tests may suggest a convenient source of good test items. Simply pick out of a good textbook or reference work a number of sentences expressing important propositions and use these as the basis for test items in the desired form. Basically this is an excellent idea, but it does involve some problems.

Relatively few of the sentences encountered in even a good text or reference work are intended to express propositions about the external world. Many are quite indefinite. Many are offered modestly as tentative hypotheses. Many depend heavily on the context for their meaningfulness or accuracy. Many are in the nature of explanatory comments to the reader to help him follow the author's line of thought. Sometimes the basic proposition implicit in a paragraph or section of a text is never stated succinctly and explicitly by the author. Finally, many of the declarative sentences which seem important and necessary in an extended discourse on a topic do not seem important enough in isolation to be selected in the limited sampling of propositions that must constitute a test.

Thus, despite the fact that the major goal of education is to develop in the scholars a command of substantive knowledge and despite the fact that all knowledge is knowledge of propositions, it is not easy to discover ready-made propositions which are suitable as bases for objective test items. For to be suitable, such propositions need to meet at least four requirements:

1. They must be worded as accurately and unambiguously as the precision of knowledge and language allow in a reasonably concise statement.
2. They must be acceptable as established truth by a preponderance of experts in the field.
3. They must be regarded as the propositions most worthy of knowing and remembering by a preponderance of experts in the field.
4. They must express principles and ideas not generally known by those who have not studied in the field.

The difficulty of finding or creating propositions which meet these standards in some areas of study may raise questions about the value of study in that field. If good examinations are difficult to build in a field, it may be because the supporting structure of substantive knowledge is weak.

Another problem involved in the use of proposition sentences from text and reference books as the source of test items is that of testing command of knowledge, not just superficial acquaintance with certain verbal stereotypes. This problem is likely to be most acute in building true-false tests but can be very troublesome in other item types as well. But since the concepts and relationships involved in one proposition can usually be involved in a variety of other propositions, or in alternative wordings of the same proposition, this difficulty can usually be overcome satisfactorily.

Substantive knowledge, as the term is used here, encompasses more than knowledge of facts and principles. It includes, for example, both knowledge of words and other symbols and the objects or concepts they stand for. A person who can read general or technical literature in his native language or in a foreign language, or who can read music or a blueprint, demonstrates command of substantive knowledge.

Substantive knowledge encompasses understanding and ability to explain, for understanding consists mainly of knowing the relations between things. To understand the seasons, for example, one must know the relation between the orbital motion of the earth and the declination of the sun and between that declination and the degree of concentration of solar energy on the surface of the earth. The more one *knows* about the relations among these and other relevant factors, the better he *understands* the seasons.

Substantive knowledge also includes mental skills, such as the ability to add fractions, to diagram a sentence, to play chess, or to design a bridge. While it is probably safe to say that the person who exhibits more skill in any of these areas than another person knows more than the other, it is even safer to say that he has better command of the relevant knowledge. Proficiency in mental skills requires ready availability of the relevant knowledge.

7. The problem of rote learning

Concern is sometimes expressed over the emphasis some tests are supposed to place on mere knowledge to the neglect of higher mental processes. Some tests are thought to require nothing more than recognition, or simple recall of isolated factual details. Test builders are often urged to shun tests of this type in favor of tests that emphasize comprehension, interpretation, application, analysis, synthesis, or evaluation. They are warned to guard against items which can be answered on the basis of sheer rote memory.

Any test which can be prepared for most effectively by concentration on rote learning and which therefore encourages students to neglect meaning and understanding in their pursuit of knowledge is a bad test. Such tests can be built and have been built. Undoubtedly, too, some students, in some situations, concentrate on memorization of words with little concern for meanings. But the extent of rote learning, and the educational harm it may do, have probably been somewhat exaggerated.

One source of overconcern with rote learning may be failure to distinguish clearly between incomplete understanding, on the one hand, and rote learning on the other. Students, and adults too, sometimes reveal woeful ignorance of important matters. But it may not be quite correct to charge these deficiencies to an excess of rote learning in the schools. Perhaps the trouble is not rote learning, but no learning. Instead of too much learning of the wrong kind, the deficiencies we exhibit may imply too little learning of any kind.

There is another factor which limits somewhat the danger of rote learning. From the point of view of the learner, rote learning is seldom a very attractive occupation. It is dull, hard work, with no promise of any long-term value. A student may engage in it, out of desperation, in the hope of getting by a quiz or examination, but it seldom rewards him with any sense of permanent achievement.

Finally, rote learning is relatively inefficient and ineffective. Even if a student's sole aim is temporary recall of the answers to a set of questions given to him in advance, he will ordinarily find *understanding*, even limited understanding, a better ally than rote learning. For understanding involves perception of simplifying structural unities, in the variety of aspects and details, which aid memory and recall. A student who chooses to rely on rote learning is seldom likely to do as well on a test as one who seeks the aid of understanding, even when the questions in the test call for nothing more than the recall of isolated factual details.

In summary, because rote learning may be far less common than our fears of it imply, because it is generally unattractive and ineffective, the danger that tests which emphasize factual knowledge will reward and encourage rote learning may not be serious.

8. The problem of meaningless verbalization

There is, however, a related danger which may deserve to be taken more seriously. It is the danger of confusing verbal facility and fluency, on the one hand, with command of substantive knowledge on the other. To the degree that test questions demand only acquaintance with verbal stereotypes, with oft-repeated word sequences or associations, to the degree that they may be answered successfully on the basis of word-word associations alone, without clear perceptions of word-thing relationships, to that degree the tests may be measuring superficial verbal facility instead of command of substantive knowledge.

Written tests depend heavily upon words. Words are versatile and essential instruments for thinking and communicating. But they represent the means, not the ends, of learning. Their usefulness to us depends upon our nonverbal knowledge of what they symbolize.

It is possible, indeed it is not uncommon, for speakers or writers to use words with more concern for fluency and grace in expression than for the accuracy of the ideas being expressed. Most students, and most adults as well, recognize and use more words, phrases, even stereotyped sentences, than they understand clearly. One of the main responsibilities of the test maker as he works with words in his test questions, or with the verbal responses scholars give to some of them, is to make sure that mere verbal facility does not pass for substantive knowledge.

9. The problem of forgetting

The acquisition of knowledge as an educational goal is sometimes discounted on the grounds that 1) most of what is learned is quickly forgotten and (2) it is wasteful of time and effort to "stuff the mind" with facts which are readily available in a set of good reference works. There is some truth in both of these contentions, but they do not argue so strongly as they may seem to against the pursuit of knowledge as the primary goal of education.

Forgetting does occur, of course, but what is forgotten, and how much, depends largely on how much command of the knowledge the student actually achieved, and how well selected (i.e., how useful) was the knowledge he sought or was required to pursue. The more command the student achieves, the more he understands or grasps a unifying structure in the knowledge he is studying, the less he is likely to forget, particularly of the central, unifying principles. The more useful the knowledge, the more likely he is to practice and thus maintain his command over it.

Reference works are valuable accessories to the effective utilization of knowledge, but they are poor substitutes for command of knowledge. How effectively they can be used depends to a considerable degree on how much the user already knows. One whose mind is deliberately kept empty of facts which are available in reference works is unlikely to have much interest in those facts or to know how to find them if he should be interested. Further, his progress is likely to be very slow. The "ready availability" of facts in good reference works is something of an illusion. Finding the particular fact one needs can be a frustrating, time-consuming enterprise. It is hard to beat a well-stocked mind as a ready-reference source of information.

10. Noncognitive outcomes of education

Test constructors are sometimes asked to measure noncognitive human traits, such as motivation, persistence, flexibility, creativity, etc. One advisory committee for a selection testing program suggested the need for measures of the following characteristics:

1. *Flexibility in Thinking:* the ability to change or reevaluate an accepted hypothesis in the light of new evidence
2. *Balanced Judgment:* the ability to evaluate and weigh the importance of quantitative and semiquantitative factors in a complex in which the absolute or "true" value of these factors is unknown and to arrive at a *reasonable* hypothesis among the many *possible* hypotheses which the complex of factors provides
3. *Critical Perception:* the ability to evaluate the printed page or the spoken word in an impartial, nongullible manner
4. *Educability:* the capacity for continuous intellectual growth
5. *Selectivity:* the ability to select from a mass of learned material those elements which are relevant to the problem at hand

6. *Synthesizing Ability:* the ability to perceive unity and relatedness among apparently discrete areas of knowledge
7. *Cultural Awareness:* a broad interest in, and sensitivity to, the world of which the individual is a part

Another mentioned these as needing measurement:

1. Ability to make the intuitive leap from inconclusive evidence to a reasonable hypothesis
2. Ability to break set—to back away from a stone wall and look for another way around it
3. Ability to maintain poise and effectiveness in a changing situation—to adapt to sudden changes in the rules of the game

But test constructors have had very little success in measuring traits of this kind. Three considerations may help to explain the difficulty.

In the first place, these traits are seldom very clearly defined. A definition of adequate clarity for purposes of measurement is necessarily an operational definition. That is, it must describe how one can tell which of a pair of individuals characteristically exhibits the trait in question more frequently or more strongly. If the trait is a general one, manifesting itself in different ways in different situations, the definition must encompass all its manifestations. These requirements of an adequate definition are difficult to meet, so difficult, apparently, that few definitions seem to exist for even the most popular noncognitive traits mentioned above. Not knowing very definitely what he is being asked to measure, the test constructor's difficulty in measuring it is quite understandable.

In the second place, at least some of these traits may be little more than convenient verbal fictions, invented for the purpose of explaining the causes of behavior. That is, they may seem to provide plausible explanations of behavior whose real causes are unknown or too complex to be dealt with conveniently. In this they may serve something of the same function as the evil spirits of the ancients, to which disease and death used to be attributed, or to the demons presumed to be the cause of irrational behavior. Terms like "persistence" or "flexibility," originally and quite legitimately used simply to *describe* behavior, have been subtly transformed by the alchemy of trait psychology into *causes* of behavior. Again, it is not surprising that test constructors have trouble measuring an entity that is more a matter of rationalization than of solid evidence.

In the third place, any paper-and-pencil test, however it may be labeled, is likely to be perceived and dealt with by an examinee essentially as a cognitive task. The examinee simply cannot behave noncognitively in responding to it. He *will* recall and select and evaluate and decide. He will inevitably *think* how he ought to answer. The evidence is clear that almost all personality tests can be faked and will be faked if it is in the examinee's best interests (as he sees them) to do so. Those which are sufficiently disguised to forestall faking are likely to be too ambiguous to provide meaningful data. A paper-and-pencil test is thus inherently limited as a measure of personality traits. A cognitive task is poorly adapted to the measurement of noncognitive characteristics.

In view of these difficulties, the prospects are not bright for *measuring* noncognitive outcomes of education, at least for purposes of recognizing and rewarding achievement. As Vernon has said:

> The testing or assessment of personality is fraught with so many difficulties . . . that even the application of the highest psychological skill and technical accomplishment cannot be expected to bring about rapid success.[18]

If a personality *inventory* (rather than a *test*) is used as a convenient means of collecting summary data on the ways the respondent has behaved in the past, it can have considerable value. Focusing on crucial aspects of behavior, and getting honest reports from an observer who is most directly and intimately acquainted with that behavior, it can provide information that may be extremely useful to an expert counselor. For assessing educational achievement in the classroom, however, the typical instructor is unlikely to be able, and may not really need, to *measure* noncognitive educational outcomes.

11. Development of mental abilities as an educational goal

The development of mental abilities is sometimes proposed as the primary purpose and goal of education. Stroud, for example, has said, "All education is in large measure a cultivation of the higher

---

[18] Philip E. Vernon, *Personality Tests and Assessments* (London: Methuen & Co., Ltd., 1953), p. 206.

mental processes, even instruction in the basic skills or so-called tool subjects." [19] Later, in the same passage he explains, "By the cultivation of the higher mental processes is usually meant instruction in reflective, relational, and inferential thinking." C. H. Judd has compiled a book on the subject.[20] But some other writers on educational psychology do not mention the subject at all.

It is not always clear what the term "mental ability" is intended to mean. It could mean no more nor less than "development of ability to think," to use the words of the Educational Policies Commission. Perhaps it is simply intended to emphasize the use of knowledge, as opposed to its possession. If so, development of mental abilities is not so much an alternative to acquisition of knowledge as an extension to include assimilation of knowledge, which is essentially the same extension as that implied by the phrase "command of substantive knowledge." It is hard to see how mental abilities can be developed or can exist apart from knowledge.

The use of the plural term "mental abilities" suggests that several separate abilities are involved. Presumably these are not intended to refer to the so-called mental faculties of attention, memory, imagination, reason, will, temperament, and character that were thought to be independent, general powers of the mind in the nineteenth century. Studies of transfer of training do not support the belief that such abstract mental faculties or abilities exist or that development and strengthening them by study in one area of knowledge will make them available for use in any other area. Presumably a mental ability is something more general than, for example, ability to spell the word *Constantinople,* ability to add 7 and 9, or ability to complete and balance the chemical equation for the preparation of oxygen from potassium chlorate.

Thus it would seem that the concept of mental abilities or processes is quite indefinite. No generally recognized catalog of mental processes with titles and definitions for distinctly different mental processes seems to exist. There is no reliable classification of such processes into higher and lower levels. Even if we agree that the term "mental process" means no more nor less than the term

---

[19] James B. Stroud, *Psychology in Education* (New York: David McKay Co., Inc., 1946), p. 198.

[20] C. H. Judd, *Education as Cultivation of the Higher Mental Processes* (New York: The Macmillan Company, 1936).

"thinking," we have no very clear notions of what processes may be involved or of how the "higher" processes may differ from the "lower." Daydreaming seems different from problem solving, but at present we can only guess in what way and to what extent different mental processes may be involved.

There is, however, one point on which most educational psychologists now seem to agree. The mind does not consist of separate faculties which can be cultivated independently. It functions as a unit, and all aspects of its functioning—attention, perception, memory, volition, emotion, etc.—are likely to be involved whenever the mind is active. The objects of thought may be more or less complex and the procession of thoughts may be more or less purposefully directed and controlled, but so far as we now know, the mind probably functions in essentially the same way regardless of its task. It must certainly need different kinds of knowledge to cope effectively with different kinds of problems, knowledge of processes as well as knowledge of content, but there seems to be no good basis for suggesting that different, whether higher or lower, types of mental functions need to be involved.

Examiners frequently classify their test questions in terms of content (knowledge) and process (ability). But even this distinction sometimes gets blurred. Does a problem in simple addition involve knowledge or ability or both? If both, how can the two be distinguished? Why do they need to be distinguished? It is conceivable that one student could have mastered the "content" of mathematics, or grammar or literature, better than another and yet be less adept than he is in using the "processes" involved, but the difficulty of clearly distinguishing between content and process makes evidence on this hypothesis hard to get.

Attempts to write test items which will require the highest levels of mental processes involve several hazards. One is that they may be quite difficult and thus call for more than ordinary examinees are capable of delivering. Such items are not likely to contribute much effective measurement. Another is that they may involve fairly complex situations, which require many words to describe and may present the examinee with problems of comprehension and interpretation which may be irrelevant to the main purpose of the examination. Characteristics of this kind are likely to lower the precision and the efficiency of the test question.

In order to describe the items in a test adequately it seems necessary to specify more than the areas or topics of subject matter with which they deal. Categories of mental abilities or processes have sometimes been used to provide a second dimension to the test outline. But in view of the difficulty of distinguishing clearly between different mental abilities and processes, it may be advisable to avoid this mentalistic approach as much as possible. One alternative is to describe different test items in terms of the kind of task they present rather than in terms of the somewhat hypothetical processes that may be involved in their solution. For example, different kinds of questions used in typical classroom tests may:

1. Ask what a particular term means
2. Ask for a particular fact or principle
3. Ask the explanation of something
4. Ask the solution to a problem

By including a variety of tasks like these the test can probably cover adequately most of the outcomes of instruction in most courses without becoming involved with the intangibilities of mental processes or abilities.

One of the propositions advanced by Richardson and Stalnaker in their "Comments on Achievement Examinations" was this: "Proposition III. The form of a test gives no certain indication of the ability tested." In discussing this proposition they said:

> We wish to digress enough to point out that psychologists do not know what abilities are involved in procedures such as writing examinations. The nature of these mental operations had best be left alone when discussing test form.[21]

This advice was given in 1935, but it would still appear to be sound.

12. Summary

Some of the main ideas developed in this chapter may be summarized in the following eleven statements.

1. Determination of what to measure is a critical, difficult problem in achievement test construction.

---

[21] M. W. Richardson and J. M. Stalnaker, "Comments on Achievement Examinations," *Journal of Educational Research*, XXVIII (1935), 425-32.

2. The need for rational decisions and value judgments with respect to what should be measured cannot be circumvented by using experimental procedures for test validation.

3. Any important outcome is necessarily measurable, but not necessarily by means of a paper-and-pencil test.

4. Educational outcomes which are said to be intangible because of the lack of good definitions of them are as difficult to attain through purposeful teaching as they are to measure through achievement tests.

5. Any measurement of an educational achievement should be relevant, reliable, and objective, regardless of whether it is derived from a paper-and-pencil test or from some other technique of measurement, such as a performance test or a rating of observed behavior.

6. The development of a measurement process requires the invention and selection of appropriate operations for quantifying the thing to be measured.

7. Some human characteristics we would like to measure do not really exist as things to be measured until they have been operationally defined in a particular process of measurement.

8. Statements of educational objectives are useful in redirecting educational emphases from past to present needs.

9. Guidance in determining what to measure may be obtained from a statement of educational objectives.

10. Some statements of educational objectives are vaguely general instead of being clearly specific, and uncritically inclusive rather than purposefully selective.

11. Objectives defined in terms of desired behavior are concretely meaningful but may emphasize specific end products at the expense of more general means toward those ends.

12. The use of conditioning as a means for improving the effectiveness of human behavior is more appropriate in the early years of life than it is after formal schooling has begun.

13. A major goal of education is to develop in the student a command of substantive knowledge.

14. A person's knowledge consists of everything that he has experienced as a result of his perceptions of external stimuli or internal thought processes.

15. The problem of learning is less one of getting things into the mind than it is of finding ways to get them out again when they are needed.

16. The first problem of the educator is to decide what kinds and items of knowledge will be most useful to the student. His second problem is to manage the learning process so that the student develops a command of this body of knowledge.

17. Command of knowledge is demonstrated by its use in problem solving, decision making, explanation, argumentation, and prediction.

18. Rote learning cannot lead to command of knowledge and is unlikely to be used extensively by students.

19. Uncritical acceptance of words of vague or uncertain meaning interferes with development of command of knowledge.

20. The greater a student's command of a body of knowledge, the less he is likely to be troubled by forgetting it.

21. No really satisfactory solutions have been found to the difficult problem of measuring noncognitive educational achievements.

22. Little is known at present about the nature and measurement of so-called higher mental processes.

REFERENCES

Ayres, L. P., *A Scale for Measuring the Quality of Handwriting of School Children,* Division of Education, Bulletin 113. New York: Russell Sage Foundation, 1912.

Bloom, Benjamin S. and Others, *Taxonomy of Educational Objectives.* New York: David McKay Co., Inc., 1956.

Cohen, Morris R. and Ernest Nagel, *An Introduction to Logic and Scientific Method,* p. 27. New York: Harcourt, Brace & World, Inc., 1934.

Ebel, Robert L., "The Problem of Evaluation in the Social Studies," *Social Education,* XXIV (January, 1960), 6-10.

Findley, Warren and Others, "The Relation of Testing Programs to Educational Goals," *The Impact and Improvement of School Testing Programs,* Part I, Chap. 2. Sixty-Second Yearbook of the National Society for the Study of Education. Chicago: The University of Chicago Press, 1963.

Flanagan, John C., "The Critical Requirements Approach to Educational Objectives," *School and Society,* LXXI (May 27, 1950), 321-24.

French, Will and Associates, *Behavioral Goals of General Education in High School.* New York: Russell Sage Foundation, 1957.

Grieder, Calvin, "Is It Possible to Word Educational Goals?" *Nations Schools,* LXVIII (October, 1961), 10ff.

Judd, C. H., *Education as Cultivation of the Higher Mental Processes.* New York: The Macmillan Company, 1936.

Kearney, Nolan C., *Elementary School Objectives*. New York: Russell Sage Foundation, 1953.

McCall, William A., *Measurement*, p. 15. New York: The Macmillan Company, 1939.

National Education Association Commission on Reorganizing Secondary Education, *Cardinal Principles of Secondary Education*, U.S. Office of Education, Bulletin No. 35. Washington, D.C.: NEA, 1918.

National Education Association Educational Policies Commission, *The Central Purpose of American Education*, p. 4. Washington, D.C.: NEA, 1961.

Richardson, M. W. and J. M. Stalnaker, "Comments on Achievement Examinations," *Journal of Educational Research*, XXVIII (1935), 425-32.

Spencer, Herbert, *Education: Intellectual, Moral and Physical*. New York: A. L. Burt; London: G. Manwaring, 1861.

Stroud, James B., *Psychology in Education*, p. 198. New York: David McKay Co., Inc., 1946.

Thorndike, E. L., *The Seventeenth Yearbook of the National Society for the Study of Education*, Part II, p. 16. Bloomington, Ill.: Public School Publishing Company, 1918.

Tyler, Ralph W., "A Generalized Technique for Constructing Achievement Tests," *Educational Research Bulletin*, X (1931), 199-208.

Vernon, Philip E., *Personality Tests and Assessments*, p. 206. London: Methuen & Co., Ltd., 1953.

Woody, Thomas, *Educational Views of Benjamin Franklin*, p. 206. New York: McGraw-Hill Book Company, 1931.

3 How to Plan a Classroom Test

We have faith that whatever people now measure crudely by mere descriptive words, helped out by comparative and superlative forms, can be measured more precisely and conveniently if ingenuity and labor are set at the task. We have faith also that the objective products produced, rather than the inner condition of the person whence they spring, are the proper point of attack for the measurer, at least in our day and generation.

EDWARD L. THORNDIKE

The preparation of any classroom test involves a number of decisions. Some of these should receive explicit attention but are often left to chance or contingency. The planning of an examination need not be an elaborate, laborious process. However, it is almost axiomatic that a little advance attention to some of these decisions is likely to improve a test substantially. Here, then, are some of the points on which decisions may need to be made and some of the considerations which could influence those decisions.

1. Decide when to test

To some extent the frequency and times of classroom testing are determined by institutional regulations on marking and reporting. Most instructors find it necessary or advisable to test at least twice during a semester. Some give hour tests every three or four weeks.

Tests given at shorter intervals can sample smaller units of instruction more intensively, but there is no limit to the amount of instruction that can be sampled by a single test and no inherent reason why a test which samples a small unit intensively is better than a test which samples a large unit more diffusely.

Frequent testing has the advantage of providing a more reliable basis for evaluation and of keeping both instructor and students more currently informed of student progress. But preparing and scoring frequent tests could consume a large share of the instructor's time, unless he has a stockpile of good test questions and unless he is equipped to handle test administration and scoring efficiently. It might in extreme cases even encroach undesirably on time for class instruction. Too frequent testing could conceivably lead to overemphasis on test-passing as a goal for study. However, it is probably safe to say that few classes are overexposed to good tests. Educational psychologists have long recognized the educational value to students of the process of taking a good test. Taking a classroom test is somewhat like going through a learning program. The educational values of such programs, and of the teaching machines used to present them, have been objects of considerable interest and study in recent years.

If instructors had complete freedom of choice in scheduling their tests, most would probably choose a midmorning hour. Some would prefer a midweek day. This degree of freedom is seldom available and there is little if any evidence or strong logic to support preference for a particular hour or day.

2. Decide what kind of questions to use

The most commonly used types of test questions are the essay (or discussion) type, the objective (or short-answer) type, and the mathematical-problem type. The subject matter of courses in mathematics, some sciences, engineering, and a few other subjects lends itself so well to problem type examinations that these are widely, almost universally, used in such courses. For many other courses either the essay or the objective type may be more appropriate than the problem type. A brief comparison of the characteristics of these types of test questions seems to be in order at this point.

To begin, let us dispose of some common misconceptions. It is not true that one type tests real understanding whereas another tests only superficial knowledge. As Richardson and Stalnaker have said, "The form of a test gives no certain indication of the ability tested." [1] It is not true that luck is a large element in scores on one type and nearly or totally absent in another. On the contrary, all three types can require much the same kind and level of ability, and if carefully handled can yield results of almost equal reliability. A good essay test or a good objective test could be constructed so that it would rank a group of students in nearly the same order as that resulting from a good problem test. But this is not to say that all three types can be used interchangeably with equal ease and effectiveness.

Vernon has called attention to evidence that

> while . . . tests of the same objectives employing different forms tend to give discrepant results (e.g., essay and new-type), tests in the same form which are aimed at different school subjects or different intellectual functions inter-correlate very highly.—For many purposes the simpler tests show superior validity, and it is doubtful how far the more complex ones do bring in the 'higher' intellectual functions at which they are aimed.[2]

Relative to the objective test, both essay and problem tests are easier to prepare. But the objective test can be scored more rapidly and more reliably (unless very special and unusual pains are taken) than either of the other types, particularly the essay type. Where very large groups of students must be tested, the use of objective tests generally permits a gain in efficiency with little if any loss in validity. But where classes are small, the efficiency advantage is in the opposite direction, and essay or problem tests should be preferred.

The problem type has the advantage of greater intrinsic relevance —of greater identity with on-the-job requirements—than either of the other types. Many superficial or purely academic questions have been included in essay and objective tests. But this fault could and should be avoided.

Neither essay nor problem-type tests, because of the length and complexity of the answers they require and because these answers

---

[1] M. W. Richardson and J. M. Stalnaker, "Comments on Achievement Examinations," *Journal of Educational Research*, XXVIII (1935), 425-32.

[2] Philip E. Vernon, *Educational Testing and Test Form Factors*, Research Bulletin 58-3, Educational Testing Service, Princeton, N.J., February, 1958.

must be written by hand, can sample as widely as is possible in an objective test. Writing is a much slower process than the reading on which objective tests depend. It is sometimes claimed that ability to choose an answer is different from, and less significant than, ability to produce an answer. But most of the evidence indicates that these abilities are highly related.

In considering the relative merits of essay, problem, and objective tests, it is important to remember that the only useful component of any test score is the objectively verifiable component of it, regardless of the type of test from which is was derived. To the degree that a test score reflects the private, subjective, unverifiable impressions and values of one particular scorer, it is deficient in meaning and hence in usefulness to the student who received it or to any one else who is interested in this ability or achievement.

In objective tests and problem tests there is often a good deal more objectivity than in essay tests. The student usually has a more definite task, and the reasons for giving or withholding credit are more obvious to all concerned. But it is well to remember that even the objective test is based on many subjective decisions as to what to test and how to test it. For the problem test there is an additional element of subjectivity in scoring which is not present in the objective test. How much credit to give for an imperfect answer and which elements to consider in judging degree of perfection are often matters of spur-of-the-moment, subjective decision when scoring problem tests.

The most commonly used types of completely objective test items are multiple-choice, true-false, matching, and classification. Many other types have been described in more comprehensive catalogs of objective test items.[3]

The multiple-choice type is widely adaptable and relatively high in ability to discriminate between better and poorer students. It is somewhat more difficult to write than some other item types, but its advantages seem so apparent that it has become the type most widely used in tests constructed by specialists. Theoretically, and this has been verified in practice, a multiple-choice test with a given number of items can be expected to show as much reliability in its scores as

---

[3] Robert L. Ebel, "Writing the Test Item," in *Educational Measurement,* ed. E. F. Lindquist (Washington, D.C.: American Council on Education, 1951); and J. Raymond Gerberich, *Specimen Objective Test Items* (New York: David McKay Co., Inc., 1956).

a typical true-false test with almost twice that number of items. Here is an example of the multiple-choice type.

> *Directions:* Write the number of the best answer to the question on the line at the right of the question.
>
> *Example:* Which is the most appropriate designation for a government in which control is in the hands of a few men?
> 1. Autonomy   4
> 2. Bureaucracy   —
> 3. Feudalism
> 4. Oligarchy

The true-false item is the simplest to prepare and is also quite widely adaptable. It tends to be less discriminating, item for item, than the multiple-choice type, and somewhat more subject to ambiguity and misinterpretation. The high proportion of items that can be answered correctly by chance, and the random error that chance responses introduce in the scores, is a major limiting factor. This limitation cannot be overcome by introducing the conventional guessing correction. However it can be largely overcome by a special scoring procedure, based on the examinee's indication of how much he was guessing on each answer given. This procedure will be described in Chapter 5. Here is an example of the true-false type.

> *Directions:* If the sentence is essentially true, encircle the letter "T" at the right of the sentence. If it is essentially false, encircle the letter "F."
>
> *Example:* A substance that serves as a catalyst in a chemical reaction may be recovered unaltered at the end of the reaction.
>
> (T) F

The matching type is efficient in that the same set of responses can be used with a cluster of several similar stimulus words. But this is also a limitation since it is sometimes difficult to get clusters of questions or stimulus words which are sufficiently similar to make use of the same set of responses. Further, questions whose answers can be no more than a word or a phrase tend to be somewhat superficial and to place a premium on purely verbalistic learning. An example of the matching type is given here.

Directions: On the blank before the title of each literary
work place the letter that precedes the name
of the person who wrote it.

Literary Works	*Authors*
b 1. *Paradise Lost*	*a.* Matthew Arnold
	b. John Milton
e 2. *The Innocents Abroad*	*c.* William Shakespeare
	d. Robert Louis Stevenson
d 3. *Treasure Island*	*e.* Mark Twain

The classification type is less familiar than the matching type, but
possibly more useful in specific situations. Like the matching type,
it uses a single set of responses but applies these to a large number
of stimulus situations. An example of the classification type is the
following.

Directions: In the following items you are to express the
effects of exercise on various body processes and sub-
stances. Assume that the organism undergoes no change
except those due to exercise. For each item blacken answer space.

1. If the effect of exercise is to definitely *increase* the
   quality described in the item
2. If the effect of exercise is to definitely *decrease* the
   quantity described in the item
3. If exercise should have no *appreciable effect,* or *an
   unpredictable effect* on quantity described in the
   item

27. Rate of heart beat   ■ ② ③
28. Blood pressure   ■ ② ③
29. Amount of glucose in the blood   ① ■ ③
30. Amount of residual air in the lungs ① ■ ③
31. Etc.

The short-answer item, in which the student must supply a word,
phrase, number or other symbol is semiobjective. It has the apparent advantage of requiring the examinee to think of the answer,
but this advantage may be more apparent than real. Some studies
have shown a very high correlation between scores on tests composed
of parallel short-answer and multiple-choice items, when both mem-

bers of each pair of parallel items are intended to test the same knowledge or ability.[4]

This means that students who are best at producing correct answers tend also to be best at *identifying* them among several alternatives. Accurate measures of how well a student can identify correct answers tend to be somewhat easier to get than accurate measures of his ability to produce them. There may be special situations, of course, where the correlation would be much lower.

The disadvantages of the short-answer form are that it is limited to questions which can be answered by a word, phrase, symbol, or number and that its scoring tends to be subjective and tedious. Item writers often find it difficult to phrase good questions on principles, explanations, applications, or predictions that can be answered in a word or phrase and that can be answered satisfactorily by *only* one specific word or phrase. Here are some examples of short answer items.

> *Directions:* On the blank following each of the following questions, partial statements, or words, write the word or number that seems most appropriate.
>
> *Examples:*
> What is the valence of oxygen? <u>-2</u>
> The middle section of the body of an insect is called the **thorax.**
> What major river flows through or near each of these cities?
>
> | Cairo | **Nile** |
> | Calcutta | **Ganges** |
> | New Orleans | **Mississippi** |
> | Paris | **Seine** |
> | Quebec | **St. Lawrence** |

Some authorities suggest that a variety of item types be used in each examination in order to diversify the tasks presented to the

---

[4] Alvin C. Eurich, "Four Types of Examinations Compared and Evaluated," *Journal of Educational Psychology*, XXVI (April, 1931), 268-78; and Desmond L. Cook, "An Investigation of Three Aspects of Free-response and Choice-type Tests at the College Level," *Dissertation Abstracts*, XV (1955), 1351.

examinee. They imply that this will improve the validity of the test or make it more interesting. Others suggest that the test constructor should choose the particular item type which is best suited to the particular question or problem he wishes to present. There is more merit in the second of these suggestions than in the first, but even the second should not be accepted as an absolute imperative in test construction. Several item forms are quite widely adaptable. A test constructor can safely decide to use primarily a single item type, such as multiple-choice, and to turn to one of the other forms only when it becomes clearly more efficient to do so. The quality of a classroom test depends much more on giving proper weight to various aspects of achievement, and on writing good items of whatever type, than on choice of this or that type of item.

In the interest of useful measurement the examiner should seek, whatever test form he uses, to make his measurements as objective as possible. A measurement is objective to the extent that it can be independently verified by other competent measurers. It is entirely conceivable that measurements obtained from a good essay test could be more objective in this sense than measurements obtained from a poor multiple-choice test. On the other hand it is fair to say that those who use essay tests tend to worry less about the objectivity of their measurements and evaluations than those who use multiple-choice tests.

Each of us is a different person, living largely in a unique world created by his own special history of experiences. It is not surprising that we sometimes find it difficult to agree on perceptions, meanings, and values. But since the harmony of our relationships and the effectiveness of our common enterprises depends on agreement, it is important for us to establish as much identity as possible among ourselves in these perceptions, meanings, and values. This is only another way of saying we need to be as objective as possible in all things, including the measurement of achievement.

In most cases teachers have chosen to use the type of question which seems most useful to them, or which they feel most competent to use effectively. However, it is possible that the force of habit and some unwarranted assumptions may have prevented some teachers from using other types that would actually be more advantageous to them. The classroom testing practices of many school and college faculties probably could be improved by periodic review of the types of tests that are being used, in comparison with those that might be used.

3. Decide how many questions to include in the test

The number of questions to include in a test is determined largely by the amount of time available for it. Many tests are limited to fifty minutes, more or less, because that is the scheduled length of the class period. Special examination schedules may provide periods of two hours or longer. In general, the longer the period and the examination, the more reliable the scores obtained from it. However, it is seldom practical or desirable to prepare a classroom test which will require more than three hours.

It is useful to consider the collection of questions, or items, which make up a test as a sample from a hypothetical population of all possible questions that might be used in such a test. A fifth-grade teacher, for example, might obtain one hundred words for a final spelling test by taking every fifth word from the total list of five-hundred words studied during the term. The five hundred words constitute the population from which the one hundred word sample is drawn. In the case of this example the population of possible questions is real and definite. But for most tests it is not. That is, there is almost no limit to the number of different problems that could be invented for use in an algebra test, nor is there any limit to the number of different questions that could be stated for use in a history test. Constructors of tests in these subjects, as in most other subjects, have no predetermined, limited list from which to draw the sample of questions to be used in the test. But their tests are samples, nevertheless, because they include only a fraction of the questions that could be asked in each case. A major problem of the test constructor is to make the sample he uses fairly represent the total population of questions that would be appropriate for the test he is building.

The more extensive the area of subject matter or abilities that the test is intended to cover, the larger the population of potential questions. The size of this population places an upper limit on the size of the sample that can be drawn from it. That is, the sample cannot be larger than the population. But population size does not place a *lower* limit on the size of the sample. A population of 1,000 potential items can be sampled by a test of ten, fifty, or a hundred items. So can a population of 100,000 potential items. The larger the population, the more likely it is to be heterogeneous, that is, to include diverse and semi-independent areas of knowledge or ability. To achieve equally accurate results, a somewhat larger sample is required in a heterogeneous than in a homogeneous field. Apart from this, the size of the population bears only a slight relation to the most advantageous size of sample.

If length of testing time does not determine the length of a test, the accuracy desired in the scores, and the diversity of types of questions in the hypothetical population of questions should determine it. The larger the number of items in the sample, and the more homogeneous the population to be sampled, the more accurate the scores from the test will be as measures of achievement in the field.

For various reasons there is a growing trend to make tests include few enough questions so that most students have time to attempt all of them when working at their own normal rates. One reason for this is that speed of response is not a primary objective of instruction in most high school and college courses and hence does not contribute valid indications of achievement. In many areas of proficiency, speed and accuracy are not highly correlated. A second reason is that examination anxiety, severe enough even in untimed tests, is accentuated when pressure to work rapidly as well as accurately is applied. A third is that efficient use of an instructor's painstakingly produced test requires that most students respond to all of it.[5] In some situations speed tests may be appropriate and valuable, but these situations seem to be the exception, not the rule.

The number of questions that an examinee can answer per minute depends on the kind of questions used, the complexity of the thought processes required to answer it, and the examinee's work habits. The fastest student in a class may finish a test in half the time required by the slowest. For these reasons it is difficult to specify precisely how many items to include in a given test. Experience with similar tests in similar classes is the best guide. Lacking that, the test constructor might assume that typical multiple-choice

---

[5] Robert L. Ebel, "Maximizing Test Validity in Fixed Time Limits," *Educational and Psychological Measurement*, XIII (1953), 347-57.

items can be answered by even the slower students at the rate of one per minute, and that true-false items can be answered similarly at the rate of two per minute. If the proposed items are longer or more complex than usual, these estimates may need to be revised. The time required by an essay question or a problem depends on the nature of the question or problem. Sometimes it is helpful for the test constructor to specify how much time he wishes the examinee to spend on each question or problem.

4. Decide what emphasis to give to various aspects of achievement

Educational achievement in most courses consists in acquisition of command of a fund of usable knowledge and in the development of ability to perform certain tasks. Knowledge can be conveniently divided into knowledge of vocabulary and knowledge about matters of fact. Abilities usually include ability to explain and ability to apply knowledge to the taking of appropriate action in practical situations. Some courses aim to develop other abilities, such as ability to calculate, ability to predict, etc.

A rather detailed analysis of educational objectives for student achievement has been published by Bloom and his associates.[6] Their taxonomy includes test items appropriate for each objective or category of achievement. Dressel and his colleagues have published outlines of test content in terms of subject matter and pupil achievements, and also have presented illustrative items.[7] These are instructive guides in planning classroom tests. They serve to broaden the test constructor's perspectives on what to test and how to test it.

But some of the words used to identify achievements are more impressionistic than objectively meaningful. Some categories of educational achievements are based on hypothetical mental functions, such as comprehension, analysis, synthesis, scientific thinking, recognition, etc., whose functional independence is open to question. Those who currently attempt to describe mental processes and func-

---

[6] Benjamin S. Bloom and Others, *Taxonomy of Educational Objectives* (New York: David McKay Co., Inc., 1956).

[7] Paul L. Dressel, *Comprehensive Examinations in a Program of General Education* (East Lansing, Mich.: Michigan State College Press, 1949).

tions may be a little, but not much, better off than sixteenth-century map makers.

> So geographers in Afric maps
> With savage pictures fill their gaps
> And o'er unhabitable downs
> Place elephants for want of towns.[8]

Unless mental processes are directly related to obvious characteristics of different kinds of test questions, it is somewhat difficult to use them confidently in planning a test or analyzing its contents. As Thorndike put it, "We have faith also that the objective products produced, rather than the inner condition of the person whence they spring, are the proper point of attack for the measurer, at least in our day and generation." [9] Occasionally, too, the specified areas of achievement are so closely related to specific units of instruction that it is difficult to regard them as pervasive educational goals.

Most of the questions used in many good classroom tests can be classified with reasonable ease and certainty into one or another of the following seven categories:

1. Understanding of terminology (or vocabulary)
2. Understanding of fact and principle (or generalization)
3. Ability to explain or illustrate (understanding of relationships)
4. Ability to calculate (numerical problems)
5. Ability to predict (what is likely to happen under specified conditions)
6. Ability to recommend appropriate action (in some specific practical problem situation)
7. Ability to make an evaluative judgment

Multiple-choice test items illustrating each of these categories are presented in Exhibit 3.1.

---

[8] Jonathan Swift, "On Poetry, A Rhapsody," *The Portable Swift* (New York: The Viking Press, Inc., 1948), p. 571.

[9] Edward L. Thorndike, "The Nature, Purposes, and General Methods of Measurement of Educational Products," *The Measurement of Educational Products*, Part II, Seventeenth Yearbook, of the National Society for the Study of Education, 1918, p. 160.

EXHIBIT 3.1

Multiple-Choice Items Intended to Test Various Aspects of Achievement

I. *Understanding of terminology*
   A. The term "fringe benefits" has been used frequently in recent years in connection with labor contracts. What does the term mean?
      1. Incentive payments for above-average output
      2. Rights of employees to draw overtime pay at higher rates
      3. Rights of employers to share in the profits from inventions of their employees
      *4. Such considerations as paid vacations, retirement plans, and health insurance
   B. What is the technical definition of the term "production"?
      1. Any natural process producing food or other raw materials
      *2. The creation of economic values
      3. The manufacture of finished products
      4. The operation of a profit-making enterprise

II. *Knowledge of fact and principle*
   A. What principle is utilized in radar?
      1. Faint electronic radiations of far off objects can be detected by supersensitive receivers.
      *2. High-frequency radio waves are reflected by distant objects.
      3. All objects emit infrared rays, even in darkness.
      4. High-frequency radio waves are not transmitted alike by all substances.
   B. The most frequent source of conflict between the western and eastern parts of the United States during the course of the nineteenth century was:
      *1. The issue of currency inflation
      2. The regulation of monopolies
      3. Internal improvements
      4. Isolationism vs. internationalism
      5. Immigration

III. *Ability to explain or illustrate*
   A. If a piece of lead suspended from one arm of a beam balance is balanced with a piece of wood suspended from the

other arm, why is the balance lost if the system is placed in a vacuum?

   1. The mass of the wood exceeds the mass of the lead.

   2. The air exerts a greater buoyant force on the lead than on the wood.

   3. The attraction of gravity is greater for the lead than for the wood when both are in a vacuum.

 *4. The wood displaces more air than the lead.

B. Should merchants and middlemen be classified as producers or nonproducers? Why?

   1. As nonproducers, because they make their living off producers and consumers

   2. As producers, because they are regulators and determiners of price

 *3. As producers, because they aid in the distribution of goods and bring producer and consumer together

   4. As producers, because they assist in the circulation of money

IV. Ability to calculate

A. If the radius of the earth were increased by three feet, its circumference at the equator would be increased by about how much?

   1. 9 feet   *3. 19 feet

   2. 12 feet   4. 28 feet

B. What is the standard deviation of this set of five measures— 1, 2, 3, 4, 5?

   1.   1   4. $\sqrt{10}$

 *2. $\sqrt{2}$ 5.   None of these

   3.   9

V. Ability to predict

A. If an electric refrigerator is operated with the door open in a perfectly insulated sealed room, what will happen to the temperature of the room?

 *1. It will rise slowly.

   2. It will remain constant.

   3. It will drop slowly.

   4. It will drop rapidly.

B. What would happen if the terminals of an ordinary household light bulb were connected to the terminals of an automobile storage battery?

   1. The bulb would light to its natural brilliance.

*2. The bulb would not glow, though some current would flow through it.

3. The bulb would explode.

4. The battery would go dead in a few minutes.

VI. *Ability to recommend appropriate action*

A. Which of these practices would probably contribute *least* to reliable grades from essay examinations?

   *1. Weighting the items so that the student receives more credit for answering correctly more difficult items

   2. Advance preparation by the rater of a correct answer to each question

   3. Correction of one question at a time through all papers

   4. Concealment of student names from the rater

B. "None of these" is an appropriate response for a multiple-choice test item in cases where:

   1. The number of possible responses is limited to two or three.

   *2. The responses provide absolutely correct or incorrect answers.

   3. A large variety of possible responses might be given.

   4. Guessing is apt to be a serious problem.

VII. *Ability to make an evaluative judgment*

A. Which one of the following sentences is most appropriately worded for inclusion in an impartial report resulting from an investigation of a wage policy in a certain locality?

   1. The wages of the working people are fixed by the one businessman who is the only large employer in the locality.

   2. Since one employer provides a livelihood for the entire population in the locality, he properly determines the wage policy for the locality.

   3. Since one employer controls the labor market in the locality, his policy may not be challenged.

   *4. In this locality, where there is only one large employer of labor, the wage policy of this employer is really the wage policy of the locality.

B. Which of the following quotations has most of the characteristics of conventional poetry?

   1. "I never saw a purple cow;
      I never hope to see one."

   *2. Announced by all the trumpets of the sky
      Arrives the snow and blasts his ramparts high."

3. "Thou art blind and confined,
   While I am free for I can see."
4. "In purple prose his passion he betrayed
   For verse was difficult.
   Here he never strayed."

Items belonging to the first category always designate a term to be defined or otherwise identified. Items dealing with facts and principles are based on descriptive statements of the way things are. Items testing explanations usually involve the words "why" or "because." Items belonging to the fourth category require the student to use mathematical processes to get from the given to the required quantities. Items which belong in both categories five and six are based on descriptions of specific situations. The *prediction* items specify all of the conditions and ask for the future result, whereas the *action* items specify some of the conditions and ask what other conditions (or actions) will lead to a specified result. In judgment items the response options are statements whose appropriateness or quality is to be judged on the basis of criteria specified in the item stem.

The usefulness of these categories in the classification of items testing various aspects of achievement depends on the fact that they are defined mainly in terms of overt item characteristics rather than in terms of presumed mental processes required for successful response. The appropriate proportions of questions in each category will vary from course to course, but the better tests tend to be those with heavier emphasis on applications of knowledge rather than on mere ability to reproduce its verbal representations. But it is more difficult to write good application questions than reproduction questions, and unless the test constructor decides explicitly in advance what proportion of the questions in his test should relate to each specified aspect of achievement, and carries out his decision, his test may suffer.

5. List topics for test items which provide a representative sample of the items of knowledge or of the abilities considered appropriate for inclusion in the test

An area of information or an ability is appropriate to use as the basis for an objective test item in a classroom test if it has been given specific attention in instruction. Emphasis in an achievement test on things that were not taught or assigned for learning is hard to justify.

One approach to defining the appropriate universe for sampling is to list as topics, in as much detail as seems reasonable, the areas of knowledge and abilities toward which instruction was directed. In the simplest case, where instruction is based on a single text, section headings in the textbook may provide a satisfactory list of such topics. If sections are regarded as about equal in importance, and if there are n times as many of them as of items needed for the test, the instructor might systematically sample every nth topic as the basis for a test item.

EXHIBIT 3.2

Illustrative Portions of Topic Lists
for a Test on Classroom Testing

List A—Vocabulary
1. Aptitude test
2. Bimodal distribution
3. Composite score
4. Expectancy table
5. Factor analysis
6. Etc.

List B—Knowledge
1. Achievement quotients
2. Types of test items
3. Essay tests
4. Kuder-Richardson formulas
5. Educational uses of tests
6. Etc.

List C—Explanation
1. Correction for attenuation
2. Use of standard scores
3. Cross validation
4. Separate answer sheet
5. Guessing correction formula
6. Etc.

List D—Application
1. Reporting scores
2. Test selection
3. Sources of information
4. Judging test quality
5. Item writing
6. Etc.

List E—Calculation
1. Mean
2. Index of item difficulty
3. Index of item discrimination
4. Percentile rank
5. Reliability coefficient
6. Etc.

If the various sections of the text are not reasonably equal in importance or if no single text provided the basis for teaching, the instructor may wish to create his own list of topics. Perhaps separate lists of vocabulary items, items of information, and topics involving explanation, application, calculation, or prediction may be required. This last approach may make it easier to maintain the desired balance among the several aspects of achievement. Illustrative portions of lists of topics for various aspects of achievement are shown in Exhibit 3.2.

6. Decide what level and distribution of difficulties are appropriate for the questions included in the test

There are two ways in which this problem can be approached. One is to include in the test only those problems or questions which any student who has studied successfully should be able to answer. If this is done, most of the students should be expected to answer most of the questions correctly. To put it somewhat differently, so many correct answers are likely to be given that many of the questions will not be very effective in discriminating among various levels of achievement—best, good, average, weak, and poor.

The other approach is to choose the questions likely to contribute most information as to relative levels of achievement among the students tested. This requires preference for somewhat harder questions, so that approximately half the students would be expected to do well on them and the other half poorly. This second approach will generally yield more reliable scores for the same amount of testing time. But it may be more worrisome to the students who take it and will not seem to reflect any minimum standards of competence for a passing score.

Some instructors believe that a good test includes some difficult questions to "test" the better students and some easy questions for the poorer students. This belief might be easier to justify if each new unit of study in a course or each new idea required the mastery of all preceding units and ideas presented in the course. In such a course students would differ in how far they had successfully progressed through it rather than in how many separate ideas they had grasped.

Few courses illustrate such perfect sequences of units and ideas.

A student who has missed some of the early ideas or done poorly in some of the early units of study will usually be handicapped in later study, but the sequence of development is seldom so rigidly fixed that his early lapses or deficiencies preclude later progress. Foreign language courses and courses in some branches of mathematics and engineering show more sequential dependence than those in other areas, but even in them the dependence is far from absolute.

For most courses of study the difference between good and poor students is less in how far they have gone than in how many things they have learned to know and to do. In such courses, and unless the students are extremely variable and the test extremely reliable, there is no need to vary the difficulty of the questions on purpose. Theoretical analyses and experimental studies demonstrate quite convincingly that in most situations tests whose questions are neither very difficult nor very easy are best. Richardson, for example, found that

> . . . a test composed of items of 50 per cent difficulty has a general validity which is higher than tests composed of items of any other degree of difficulty.[10]

And Gulliksen concluded on the basis of a theoretical analysis that

> In order to maximize the reliability and variance of a test the items should have high intercorrelations, all items should be of the same difficulty level, and the level should be as near 50 percent as possible.[11]

7. Decide whether or not to apply a "correction for guessing"

Objective test scores are sometimes "corrected for guessing" by subtracting a fraction of the number of wrong answers from the number of right answers. The purpose of such corrections is to encourage examinees to omit answers instead of guessing blindly when they encounter questions beyond the scope of their knowledge. Although the guessing correction is applied during the scoring process and does not influence the preparation of the test appreciably, the

---

[10] Marion W. Richardson, "The Relation Between the Difficulty and the Differential Validity of a Test," *Psychometrika*, I, No. 2 (June, 1936), 33-49.

[11] Harold Gulliksen, "The Relation of Item Difficulty and Inter-item Correlation to Test Variance and Reliability," *Psychometrika*, X (June, 1945), 79-91.

decision concerning it should be made before the test is given. For one thing, the question is likely to be asked when the test is given and the instructor should be prepared to give a definite, honest answer. For another, the beneficial effect of a guessing correction, if any, is more psychological than mathematical. If the announcement of a correction for guessing induces examinees to avoid responses based on blind or near blind guesses, it can perhaps improve the reliability and validity of the scores.

Any sweeping recommendation for or against guessing corrections is likely to be confounded by specific situations in which a contrary recommendation seems called for. But there are certain considerations which ought to influence the decision. These are discussed in detail in Chapter 7. It may be helpful to list the main points in that discussion here.

1. Scores corrected for guessing will usually rank students in about the same relative positions as do the uncorrected scores.
2. The probability of getting a respectable score on a good objective test by blind guessing alone is extremely small.
3. Well-motivated examinees who have time to attempt all items guess blindly on few, if any, items.
4. Ordinarily no moral or educational evil is involved in the encouragement of students to make the best rational guesses they can.
5. A student's rational guesses can provide useful information on his general level of achievement.
6. If a test is speeded, a guessing correction removes the incentive for slower students to guess blindly.
7. Scores corrected for guessing may include irrelevant measures of the examinee's test wiseness or willingness to gamble.
8. Correction for guessing complicates the scoring somewhat and tends to lower the accuracy of the scores.

In terms of the number and complexity of the arguments for and against correction for guessing and in terms of the strength of convictions held by partisans of either alternative, the decision to correct or not to correct for guessing appears momentous. In terms of practical consequences, it probably is not momentous. Since the application of guessing tends to complicate the scoring process, the burden of proof would seem to fall on the advocates of correction.

Most objective classroom tests probably can be scored quite satisfactorily by counting correct responses only. Exceptional circumstances, however, may warrant or even require a guessing correction.

8. Decide what means and what format to use in presenting the test to the students

Objective tests are almost always presented to students in printed booklets. Some careful attention to legibility and attractiveness in the arrangement and typing of the copy is usually well worthwhile. The use of separate answer sheets greatly simplifies scoring without adding seriously to the student's problem of response.

As illustrated in Exhibit 3.3, listing responses to multiple-choice items rather than arranging them in tandem makes the student's task easier. Considerable space can be saved if multiple-choice items are printed in double columns rather than across the page. Designation of alternatives by number is simple and convenient, unless many items include small-digit responses which might be confused with response numbers. In this case letters probably should be used.

EXHIBIT 3.3

A Comparison of Listed and Tandem Responses

Listed	*Tandem*
What does religious tolerance mean?	What does religious tolerance mean? (1) Making all people belong to one church. (2) Believing everything in the Bible. (3) Believing in science instead of the church. (4) Allowing people to believe what they wish.
1. Making all people belong to one church	
2. Believing everything in the Bible	
3. Believing in science instead of the church	
*4. Allowing people to believe what they wish	

Oral presentation of true-false items can be reasonably satisfactory, but other item forms may be too complex for this means. Some instructors have been well satisfied with the projection of objective test items on a screen in a partly darkened room. The cost of slides or film strips may be less than that of paper and printing, and they may be more convenient to prepare. Further, problems associated with differences among students in rate of work will be largely eliminated. Experiments have shown that most students can be paced to respond to objective test items more quickly than they do when working at their own rates, with no decrease in accuracy of response and no appreciable increase in tension (see Chapter 7).

On the other hand, there are some obvious drawbacks to test administration by visual projection. The student's attention is not fixed so firmly on his own answer sheet. The job of the test administrator is more tedious and limiting. There must be enough light to facilitate marking the answer sheets, but not so much as to make reading the projected test item difficult. Finally, make-up examinations present a serious problem with projected tests. Hence it seems likely that most objective tests will continue to be presented in printed form.

Open-book examinations, in which the examinees are permitted to bring and use textbooks, references, and class notes, have attracted some interest and attention, both on the part of instructors and of educational research workers. Instructors have seen in them a strong incentive for students to study for ability to use knowledge rather than for ability simply to remember it. Such examinations also encourage instructors to eschew recall-type test questions in favor of interpretation and application types. In this light there is much to be said in favor of the open-book examination. On the other hand, students soon learn that the books and notes they bring with them to classes are likely to provide more moral than informational support. Looking up the facts or formulas needed may take considerable time. The student who tries to make much use of his references is likely to run out of time before completing the test.

Tussing reported favorably on experiences with an open-book final examination program at El Camino College.[12] He reached the following conclusions:

1. Open-book tests can be constructed and used in all the traditional test forms—essay, multiple-choice, true-false, etc.
2. Fear and emotional blocking are reduced.

---

[12] Lyle Tussing, "A Consideration of the Open-book Examination," *Educational and Psychological Measurement,* XI (1951), 597-602.

3. There is less emphasis on memory of facts than on practical problems and reasoning.
4. Cheating is eliminated.
5. The approach is adaptable to the measurement of student attitudes.

An experimental comparison of scores on the same multiple-choice examination, administered as an open-book examination in one section and as a closed-book examination in another section of the same course in child psychology was reported by Kalish.[13] He concluded that although "the group average scores are not affected by the examination approach, the two types of examinations measure significantly different abilities." Kalish also suggested some possible disadvantages of the open-book examination:

1. Study efforts may be reduced.
2. Efforts to overlearn sufficiently to achieve full understanding may be discouraged.
3. Note-passing and copying from other students are less obvious.
4. More superficial knowledge is encouraged.

The take-home test has some of the same characteristics as the open-book test, with an additional advantage and an additional disadvantage. The advantage is removal of the pressure of time which often limits the effectiveness of a classroom open-book test as a true open-book test. The disadvantage is the loss of assurance that the answers a student submits represent exclusively his own achievements. For this reason the take-home test often functions better as a learning exercise than as an achievement test. Students may be permitted, even encouraged, to collaborate in seeking answers in which they have confidence. The efforts they sometimes put forth and the learning they sometimes achieve under these conditions can be a pleasant surprise to the instructor. But the take-home test must be scored and the scores must count in order to achieve this result. Also, it probably goes without saying, the correct answers should be reported to the students, with opportunity for them to question and discuss. In this, as in most other situations involving the use of tests, it is hazardous to use a test of low or unknown quality. Student cross-examination can be devastating.

---

[13] Richard A. Kalish, "An Experimental Evaluation of the Open-book Examination," *Journal of Educational Psychology*, XLIX (1958), 200-204.

9. Decide whether, and if so how, to determine the passing score on the test

The traditional student attitude toward tests is that the most important outcome is whether one passed or failed the test. Many instructors, retaining the student's point of view, share this attitude. But it is usually not a particularly useful attitude. Unless a particular test is the sole basis for the pass or fail decision, which it seldom should be, precisely defining a passing score on it may be more bother and cause more trouble than it is worth.

The operational significance of academic failure is that the student receives no credit for the course and sometimes must repeat it. This is a serious, complex decision which should be made deliberately and after full consideration of all relevant factors. Usually several persons other than the teacher—the administrator, the student's advisor, even the student himself—should be consulted before the decision is finally made. It should seldom be a purely clerical, automatic, impersonal decision.

Students have a right to know in advance the basis on which the instructor will decide whether to pass or fail a student and the proportion of a group that is likely to fail. Students also have a right to know how their scores on a test will affect their chances of passing. If approximately 10 per cent are expected to fail, and if a student's score places him in the lowest 20 per cent, he should know that he is in trouble. But it is seldom helpful to differentiate sharply those who have "passed" a particular test from those who have "failed" it, if the test is only one of many factors that will ultimately determine passing or failure.

Educational achievement is a continuous variable. No great gulf is fixed between those who pass and those who fail until the final decision is made. Any cutting score is at least partly arbitrary, and some failures, as well as some passes, can properly be attributed to chance, to bad or good luck, as the case may be. There is no way of avoiding the arbitrariness or the influence of chance in the ultimate decision, but there is no point in multiplying the problem by making pass or fail decisions on each test.

Some instructors believe that what one must know to pass a course is fixed by the course content and by subsequent demands on the student. They hold that decisions to pass or fail can and should be made in terms of impersonal, absolute standards set by the subject matter. These beliefs seldom can withstand critical analysis. Course content is usually selected on the basis of subjective decisions, often by individual instructors. As such, it hardly possesses the characteristics of an absolute standard of achievement. Nor is it ordinarily possible for the constructor of an objective test to gauge the difficulty of his items precisely enough to define a fixed standard of achievement with respect to that content. Those who use essay tests apply a flexible subjective scale of evaluation which permits them to say, "A score of 75 per cent on this test is passing," without failing too many. But with an objective test the die is cast when the test is made and the test constructor's lack of precisely applicable absolute standards of achievement is all too apparent when the test is scored. The essay-test grader finds it easier to circumvent this limitation.

All this suggests that when a passing score on a test must be determined, a number of factors should be considered. Probably the relative standing of the student in the group should be the most influential of these. The proportion of failures in a class ordinarily should be fairly constant from class to class. It is absurd to decree that, in any class, exactly 7 per cent of the students should fail. But it is even more absurd to tolerate measurement practices which allow the proportion of failures, in comparable groups, to fluctuate from 0 to 50 per cent. Theoretically, absolute standards have generally proved quite unreliable. Relative standards are not ideal, but they do make an important contribution to stability and fairness in setting the passing score, in the rare instances where failure must be determined from a single test.

10. Determine to test important outcomes of instruction

It may be important to conclude by re-emphasizing the importance, as well as the difficulty, of one crucial area of decisions, the decisions on what to test. Some of the most serious weaknesses of classroom tests are due to uncritical acceptance of conventional answers to this question.

Many teachers admit that their tests do not adequately reflect the really important outcomes of their courses. Some are convinced that no test, and certainly no objective test, could adequately measure student achievement of these objectives. Others are skeptical of this view. They are persuaded that all defensible outcomes of education are inherently objective, and hence testable. The problems of educational measurement, they think, can be solved. So, obviously, do we.

11. Summary

The principal ideas developed in this chapter may be summarized in twelve statements.

1. More frequent testing tends to provide a more reliable basis for evaluation.
2. The form of a test gives no certain indication of the ability tested.
3. Although they are extensively interchangeable, each type of objective test item possesses a few unique advantages and disadvantages.
4. Whatever form of test or type of item an examiner uses, he should seek to make his measurements as objective as possible.
5. Most classroom tests of achievement should be short enough, in relation to the time available, so that almost all students have time to attempt all of the items.
6. Items intended to test various aspects of achievement can ordinarily be classified more reliably on the basis of overt item characteristics than on the basis of the mental processes they presumably require.
7. An outline of topics dealt with in instruction provides a useful basis for developing test items that will sample the desired achievement representatively.
8. In most tests of achievement, items of moderate difficulty, which are answered correctly by from 40 per cent to 70 per cent of the examinees, contribute the greatest amount of useful information.
9. Application of a correction for guessing will not improve nor impair the validity of scores from most achievement tests very much.
10. Objective classroom tests usually are, and should be, presented in printed test booklets.
11. Determination of a passing score on classroom tests of educational achievement is ordinarily unnecessary and undesirable.

12. The most crucial decision the test constructor must make is what to test.

REFERENCES

Bloom, Benjamin S. and Others, *Taxonomy of Educational Objectives*. New York: David McKay Co., Inc., 1956.

Cook, Desmond L., "An Investigation of Three Aspects of Free-response and Choice-type Tests at the College Level," *Dissertation Abstracts*, XV (1955), 1351.

Dressel, Paul L., *Comprehensive Examinations in a Program of General Education*. East Lansing, Mich.: Michigan State College Press, 1949.

Ebel, Robert L., "Maximizing Test Validity in Fixed Time Limits," *Educational and Psychological Measurement*, XIII (1953), 347-57.

————, "Writing the Test Item," in *Educational Measurement*, ed. E. F. Lindquist. Washington, D.C.: American Council on Education, 1951.

Eurich, Alvin C., "Four Types of Examinations Compared and Evaluated," *Journal of Educational Psychology*, XXVI (April, 1931), 268-78.

Gerberich, J. Raymond, *Specimen Objective Test Items*. New York: David McKay Co., Inc., 1956.

Gulliksen, Harold, "The Relation of Item Difficulty and Inter-item Correlation to Test Variance and Reliability," *Psychometrika*, X (June, 1945), 79-91.

Kalish, Richard A., "An Experimental Evaluation of the Open-book Examination," *Journal of Educational Psychology*, XLIX (1958), 200-204.

Richardson, M. W. and J. M. Stalnaker, "Comments on Achievement Examinations," *Journal of Educational Research*, XXVIII (1935), 425-32.

Richardson, Marion W., "The Relation Between the Difficulty and the Differential Validity of a Test," *Psychometrika*, I, No. 2 (June, 1936), 33-49.

Swift, Jonathan, "On Poetry, A Rhapsody," *The Portable Swift*, p. 571. New York: The Viking Press, Inc., 1948.

Thorndike, Edward L., "The Nature, Purposes, and General Methods of Measurement of Educational Products," *The Measurement of Educational Products*, Part II, p. 160. Seventeenth Yearbook, of the National Society for the Study of Education, 1918.

Tussing, Lyle, "A Consideration of the Open-book Examination," *Educational and Psychological Measurement*, XI (1951), 597-602.

Vernon, Philip E., *Educational Testing and Test Form Factors*, Research Bulletin 58-3, February, 1958. Educational Testing Service, Princeton, N.J.

4 The Characteristics
and Uses of Essay Tests

The teacher who, without experience or technical train-
ing, has endeavored to use objective tests for his own class
has often been dissatisfied with the results and rightly so.
. . . Nearly every teacher, however, considers himself fully
capable of setting a satisfactory essay test in his own course
or subject, and of reading the answers at least to his
own satisfaction. . . . Norms, correlations, reader or test
reliability, and validity do not worry the teacher. If he
knows what they are, he ignores them in dealing with his
own classroom situation. The popularity of the essay
question should not, therefore, be misinterpreted to indi-
cate that it is the most suitable form for many purposes,
that it is in a "healthy" condition, or that improvements
are not needed.

JOHN M. STALNAKER

1. Some differences between essay and objective tests

Two major forms of written tests are available for general use in classroom tests of educational achievement. These are essay tests (including, for convenience, tests based on numerical problems) and objective tests. One of the first problems of the constructor of a classroom test is to decide which type to use. There are some significant differences between the two which need to be considered in reaching this decision.

1. *An essay test question requires the student to plan his own answer and to express it in his own words. An objective test item requires him to choose among several designated alternatives.*

The task of composing an adequate, original answer to a novel question can be a revealing indication of the level of educational achievement. To recall relevant principles and factual details, the student must have command of an ample store of knowledge. He must be able to relate these facts and principles, to organize them into a coherent and logical progression, and then must do justice to these ideas in his written expression. Recall is involved in the composition of an answer to an essay test question, but it would be a gross oversimplification to characterize an essay test as *simply* a measure of recall.

It is also a gross oversimplification to characterize an objective test as simply a measure of recognition. For the task of making a wise choice among superficially plausible alternative answers to a novel question can also be a revealing indication of the level of educational achievement. In this case, also, the student must have command of a wealth of relevant principles and factual details. He must be able to relate these facts and principles and to organize them into a sound basis for decision.

It is sometimes suggested that objective tests are inevitably more superficial and less realistic tests of a student's knowledge than are essay tests, since in suggesting possible answers to him the examiner has done the more important part of his task for him. But most good objective test items require the examinee to develop, by creative, original thought, the *basis* for choice among the alternatives. Good objective test items do not permit correct response on the basis of simple recognition, sheer rote memory, or meaningless verbal association. Consider the nature of the thought processes involved in selecting an answer to this question.

> A child buys jelly beans which the grocer picks up, without regard for color, from a tray containing a mixture of jelly beans of three different colors. What is the smallest number of jelly beans the child can buy and still be certain of getting at least four jelly beans of the same color?

The answers provided are 4, 7, 10, and 12.

Assume that the examinee is seeing this particular problem for the first time, so that he cannot answer it successfully by simple recall of an answer that someone else has told him. Assume, too, that problems of this kind are not of sufficient practical importance to have been made the subjects of special study and direct teaching of techniques for solution. These assumptions call attention to an important general principle of educational measurement. What a test item measures, that is, what a successful response to it indicates, cannot be determined on the basis of the item alone. Consideration must also be given to the examinee's previous experiences. These may differ significantly for different examinees. But in the case of the foregoing problem, the assumptions mentioned above may be quite reasonable.

How much different would the thought processes be, and how much more difficult would the problem be, if no answers were suggested and the task required production of the answer rather than selection? Producing an answer is not necessarily a more complex or difficult task, or one more indicative of achievement, than choosing the best of the available alternatives.

In Cook's study, where the same questions were presented to college students in two forms of a test, one in which the student had to think of and write out an answer, the other in which he simply chose the best of several answers, the correlation between scores for the same students on the two forms was as high as would be expected if both of them were measuring the same achievement.[1] Table IX of Cook's unpublished dissertation shows a correlation of .97 between the scores for 152 college freshmen on two 60 item tests of knowledge of contemporary affairs, one composed of completion (free-response) items and the other of multiple-choice items. When this correlation was corrected for unreliability of the two tests (.87 for the completion test and .86 for the multiple-choice test) it rose to .99. This means that, within the limits of their accuracy of measurement, the two tests appeared to be measuring identical aspects of achievement.

The game of chess, which few would regard as a simple or superficial exercise in thinking, is essentially a multiple-choice test. At each move the player's problem is to choose the best of a limited number of alternatives. What the alternatives are is always fairly obvious. Even a novice can easily list all the moves permitted by the rules of the game in a particular situation. Ordinarily there are only a few of these that a competent player would regard as good possibilities. The test of his skill is in the quality of the choices he makes, in his perception of the implications and consequences of

---

[1] Desmond L. Cook, "An Investigation of Three Aspects of Free-response and Choice-type Tests at the College Level," *Dissertation Abstracts*, XV (1955), 1351.

the choices he makes. The complex of considerations that makes one move better than another in the game of chess is similar in nature, though probably considerably more involved, than the complex of considerations that makes one alternative better than another in a good multiple-choice test question.

The making of choices among limited and clearly defined alternatives is a realistic part of the affairs of government, of business, and of ordinary living. Shall we use the atomic bomb or not? Shall we grant employee demands or risk a prolonged strike? Shall we vacation at the shore or in the mountains? Leaders in government spend much time dealing with the questions that confront them by issuing statements (as if they were essay test questions) and by making choices (as if they were objective test questions). Skill in doing both is valuable to the leader, and leaders are seldom equally good at doing both. But if the populace had a clear choice between a man good at making statements but weak on decisions and another weak on making statements but good at making decisions, is there any doubt which they should choose? The first might find it easier to get elected, the second would make a better leader.

The contribution of skill in written expression to success in answering essay test questions is both an advantage and a disadvantage. Written expression is an important skill. Essay tests encourage its cultivation and give practice in it (though the practice may sometimes be practice in *bad* writing—hasty, ill-considered, and unpolished). This is the advantage. The disadvantage is that skill in writing, or lack of it, may influence the scorer's judgment regarding the content of the answer. Uniform, legible handwriting and fluent, graceful sentences can compensate for some deficiencies in content. On the other hand, flaws in spelling, grammar, or usage can detract from the scorer's evaluation of the content.

2. *An essay test consists of relatively few, more general questions which call for rather extended answers. An objective test ordinarily consists of many rather specific questions requiring only brief answers.*

Relatively broad essay questions have the advantage of requiring more integration and organization of knowledge than do the more specific objective test questions. But it would not be correct to say that objective test questions deal only with isolated factual details, that they encourage the fragmentation of knowledge. The student who has organized and integrated his knowledge, who understands what he knows, will fare better than one who has not on either an objective or an essay test. He will remember better what he has learned, and have it more readily available when a test question calls for its use.

The larger number of questions found typically in objective tests gives them a considerable advantage as reliable samples of a field of achievement. In general, the larger the number of independent elements in the sample of tasks used in an achievement test, the more accurately performance on those tasks will reflect achievement in the whole field. The answer to a complex essay test question often does involve many separate elements of achievement, but these are dealt with as a more or less integrated whole by both the student and the grader, not as independent elements.

Few, if any, experimental studies of the sampling reliability of essay tests relative to that of objective tests have been made. The difficulty of obtaining sufficiently reliable grading of essay test answers may be part of the reason. But there have been some theoretical analyses of the problem. Ruch has illustrated the direct relation between the extensiveness of the sample of tasks in a test and the precision with which different levels of achievement can be differentiated.[2] Posey has shown that an examinee's luck, or lack of it, in being asked what he happens to know is a much greater factor in the grade he receives in a ten-question test than in one of one hundred questions.[3] His charts, reproduced in Figure 4.1, show the distributions of expected scores for three students on three tests. One student is assumed to be able to answer 90 per cent of all the questions that might be asked him on the subject of the test. Another is assumed to be able to answer 70 per cent of such questions, and the third is assumed capable of answering only 50 per cent of them. That is, if the test was a complete test, including all possible questions, one student's score would be 90 per cent exactly,

---

[2] G. M. Ruch, *The Objective or New-type Examination* (Chicago: Scott, Foresman & Company, 1929), p. 56.

[3] Chesley Posey, "Luck and Examination Grades," *Journal of Engineering Education*, December, 1932, pp. 292-96. Reproduced by permission of Chesley Posey and the *Journal of Engineering Education*.

another's 70 per cent exactly, and the third's 50 per cent exactly. Few tests, however, can be complete tests. Almost always they are samples, and the particular sample of questions chosen has much to do with the score a student receives on the test. Posey's chart for

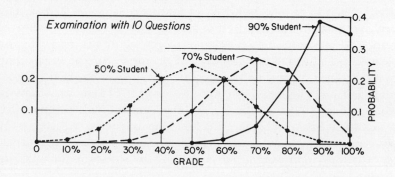

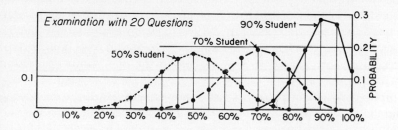

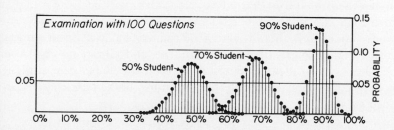

Figure 4.1. Relation of the Number of Questions in an Examination to the Sharpness of Discrimination of Different Levels of Ability*

---

* Chesley Posey, "Luck and Examination Grades," *Journal of Engineering Education*, December, 1932, pp. 292-96. Reproduced by permission of Chesley Posey and the *Journal of Engineering Education*.

the ten-question examination shows, for example, that the 50-per cent student (one capable of answering half of all possible questions correctly) has a probability of .24 (twenty-four chances in one hundred) of getting a score of 50 per cent on a sample of ten questions from the total population of possible questions. He has twenty chances in one hundred of getting a score of 60 per cent, twelve chances in one hundred of getting 70 per cent, five chances of getting 80 per cent, and one chance of getting 90 per cent. He also has twenty chances in one hundred of getting a score of 40 per cent, twelve chances of getting 30 per cent, five chances of getting 20 per cent, and one chance of getting 10 per cent. These variations in scores (from 10 to 90 per cent) that an individual might receive when his true score (the score he ought to receive) is 50 per cent are known as "sampling errors" since they are attributable to variations from sample to sample in the questions included in the test.

Now the main point of Posey's chart is that as the number of questions in the examination increases, the spread of scores (due to sampling errors) decreases. In the ten-question examination, the 90-per cent student has more than one chance in one hundred of getting a score as low as 60 per cent. In the one hundred-question examination the 90-per cent student has less than one chance in one hundred of getting a score as low as 80 per cent. With the decreasing spread of sampling error score distributions goes a decreasing overlap in the distributions for students of different levels of ability. This means that the larger the number of questions in the test, the smaller the probability that a less able student will be given a higher score than the more able student. In the examination with one hundred questions, there is very little chance of a 50-per cent student scoring higher than a 70-per cent student, and almost no chance of the 70-per cent student scoring higher than the 90-per cent student. In the examination with only ten questions, both these chances are much greater.

3. Students spend most of their time in thinking and writing when taking an essay test. They spend most of their time reading and thinking when taking an objective test.

Just as skill in writing may be a somewhat irrelevant factor determining a student's grade on an essay test, so skill in reading may also be a somewhat irrelevant factor determining a student's grade on an objective test. In neither case, ordinarily, can we claim that the test is a pure measure of command of knowledge, uncontaminated by skills of expression or interpretation.

Perhaps a distinction should be made between the kind of routine thinking students do while they are reading an objective test question or writing an essay test answer and the kind of reflective thinking which precedes the writing or follows the reading. Measured in word units, reading is a much faster process than writing. The typical student can probably read at least ten times as many words per minute as he can write. If the objective test questions involve about the same number of words as the essay test answers, a student should be able to spend a greater proportion of his time in reflective thought when taking an objective test than when taking an essay test. Observation of student behavior in taking both kinds of tests indicates that this inference is probably warranted. It would be hard to prove that this fact makes objective tests better than essay tests, but it may help to answer the argument that they are seriously worse.

4. The quality of an objective test is determined largely by the skill of the test constructor. The quality of an essay test is determined largely by the skill of the reader of student answers.

One clear and intentional implication of this statement is that both essay and objective tests vary in quality. If the quality, as measures of educational achievement, were to be determined for all tests, both essay and objective, given at a particular educational institution in a specified year, it is almost a certainty that the difference in quality between the best and poorest of either type would be greater than the difference in quality between the best examples of the two types, or the poorest examples.

It is probably true, on the other hand, that the typical essay test falls farther short of its potential as a measure of educational achievement than does the typical objective test. Fewer systematic efforts are made to improve the quality of essay than of objective types. This may be due in part to the greater difficulty of obtaining data for analysis of essay test quality. It may also be due to the belief of some essay test users that quality is inherent in the form of the test and needs no confirmation or criticism from the statistician.

Writing good objective test items requires a high degree of skill in precise and meaningful verbal expression. Teachers of composition, who specialize in cultivating effective expression and who are themselves highly skilled in this art, should be encouraged to employ that skill more frequently in the writing of objective test items. Perhaps item writing may seem unattractive to some of them because it demands more conventional precision than creative imagination in expression. In item writing, perhaps unlike creative writing, the more nearly a sentence means exactly the same thing to every person who reads it (the less it leaves to the individual's imagination), the more claim it has to respect as an example of literary craftsmanship.

> 5. *An essay examination is relatively easy to prepare but relatively tedious and difficult to score accurately. A good objective examination is relatively tedious and difficult to prepare but relatively easy to score accurately.*

This distinction may actually be most relevant, and properly most influential, in determining the situations in which essay tests are most appropriate. If a test is to be widely used, with large numbers of students, the instructor is likely to save time in the long run by taking time at the start to prepare a good objective examination. But if the test is destined for limited use, with relatively few students, the instructor is likely to save time by devoting little of it to the preparation of the test (i.e., by using an essay test) and by devoting most of his time for the examination in reading the student responses.

Where the line is drawn between a wide-use test and a limited-use test will depend on the preferences of the instructor and on his relative facility as a writer of objective test items or a reader of essay test answers. Some instructors may find objective testing more efficient than essay testing with groups as small as twenty-five. Others may prefer to use essay testing until the groups become larger than fifty.

6. *An essay examination affords much freedom for the student to express his individuality in the answer he gives, and much freedom for the scorer to be guided by his individual preferences in scoring the answer. An objective examination affords much freedom for the test constructor to express his knowledge and values but gives the student only the freedom to show, by the proportion of correct answers he gives, how much or how little he knows or can do.*

Beyond any reasonable doubt, an objective test affords less freedom than an essay test. The behavior of both the student and the scorer is more fully controlled. Indeed, the essay test has sometimes to be characterized as a projective test, in which the student's interests and values do more than the examiner's questions to determine what the response will be.[4]

However attractive the word "freedom" and the concept it represents may be, we should remember that its values are specific, not universal. In some situations it is useful, in others harmful. A break in the steering mechanism can increase the freedom of motion of an automobile, perhaps disastrously. A cashier who exercises too much freedom in his use of company funds may get into trouble. Even the freedom that astronauts experience from the pull of gravity can create all kinds of problems.

To a considerable degree, freedom is the enemy of precision in measurement. The more precisely any magnitude is to be measured, the more fully the process of measurement must be described and standardized; the more carefully all the variables which might affect the result must be controlled. Because the objective test item does provide a more uniformly standardized, carefully controlled process of measurement than does the essay test, it is, and should be, regarded as a technical advance in the measurement of educational achievement.

The freedom of the student and the scorer in essay testing, and of the test constructor in objective testing, all contribute to the lack of accuracy, that is, to the unreliability of the scores obtained. To the extent that an essay test question allows a student to choose what he will write about, it permits different students to run dif-

---

[4] Verner M. Sims, "The Essay Examination Is a Projective Technique," *Educational and Psychological Measurement*, VIII (1948), 15-31.

ferent races, and thus increases the difficulty of comparing their performances. The scorer's freedom to express himself in his evaluations also contributes to the unreliability. This freedom also allows him to respond, in his evaluations, to what he already knows or believes about the student. A good answer from a poor student tends to be discounted. A poor answer from a good student tends to be evaluated more highly than its merits deserve.

Objective test items, particularly multiple-choice items, are sometimes charged with giving students the false idea that there is one and only one right answer to every question. Life really isn't that simple, it is pointed out. An essay test, which permits or encourages diverse answers, and on which the actual conclusion reached is less important than the cogency of the reasons for giving it, is claimed to be truer to life, and hence a better test.

Several aspects of this view warrant comment. It is not at all obvious, in the first place, that students ever do get a generally oversimplified conception of the nature of things by their exposure to the *form* of multiple-choice test items, which is what the critics object to. No evidence to support this contention seems to have been gathered. Nor is its truth obvious on logical grounds. On the contrary, a student who struggles to choose the best of several plausible possibilities, and who sometimes discovers later that his choice was not the best, is likely to be impressed by the complexity of the problem, and by the good case that can sometimes be made, as Banesh Hoffman has shown, for a second- or third-rate answer.[5]

If a test includes questions like these:

1. What is the best form of national government?
2. What is the optimum class size?
3. What is the function of religion?

and if the examinee, to get credit for proper knowledge must answer:

1. The parliamentary system
2. Twenty-five pupils
3. Preparation for eternal life

complaints are certainly in order. These answers *do* imply a simplic-

---

[5] Banesh Hoffman, *The Tyranny of Testing* (New York: Crowell-Collier Publishing Co., 1962).

ity that is seldom found in life to questions of this level of complexity.

The problem here is not in the form, but in the content of the questions. No doubt questions like the last three above have been asked, and answers like these have been expected, in some multiple-choice tests. But objective test items do not need to venture so far into the quicksands of opinion, bias, and dogma as the foregoing questions do. Nor do they need to be limited to such narrowly factual Who? What? When? Where? questions as:

> Who was the presidential candidate of the Republican party in 1948?
>
> What is the square root of 1936?
>
> In what year was the first artificial Earth satellite launched?
>
> In what state was Abraham Lincoln born?

Between the first extreme of generalization and the second extreme of detail there is ample room for the test constructor to ask significant questions that permit defensible answers. Here are a few examples:

> How did the Marshall Plan contribute to European recovery?
>
> What determines the period of revolution of an Earth satellite?
>
> Why does milk sour more quickly in a warm room than in a refrigerator?

When questions like these are used as the basis for multiple-choice test items, the "correct" answers offered are likely to be terse and incomplete. But if the item writer is skilled, such partial correct answers, combined with equally partial incorrect answers, can do all of the job that the test item is intended to do, i.e., to discriminate sharply between those who are more capable and those who are less capable of producing an adequate answer to the question.

No brief answer to a complex question is likely to be as adequate as a more extended answer. But this does not mean that a student's command of knowledge related to the question can only be judged on the basis of an extended answer. Nor does it mean that a student of normal intelligence will ever mistake the terse expression of the essence of a correct response for a complete statement of all there is to say on the subject.

Some questions which we encounter in life are indeterminate in the present state of our knowledge. There is no consensus, even among experts, as to the correct answer. Different individuals or groups may believe strongly in quite different answers. It may sometimes be appropriate to refer to such a question in a test so as to determine the student's awareness that it is controversial, or his acquaintance with various points of view respecting it. But a test author should seldom ask such a question and accept only his view as the correct answer, even though he is fairly convinced that in time all other experts will come to agree with him. The scope of verified human knowledge is so wide that neither courses of instruction nor examinations need to hold students responsible for accepting particular beliefs that are being strongly challenged by others.

But for most questions there is sufficient consensus among experts to permit them to differentiate consistently a better answer from a poorer answer. This is all that is required to make the question determinate. If such a question also differentiates clearly between students of high and low achievement, it is likely to be useful in an objective test.

Essay test answers sometimes give the instructor clues to the student's thought processes. But the diverse and random nature of these clues, as well as the uncertainty that the reader will notice them or interpret them correctly, means that they seldom provide reliable indices of the general quality of the student's thought processes.

The writers of essay test questions sometimes deliberately choose indeterminate issues as the basis for their questions. What the student concludes, they say, is unimportant. The evidence on which he bases his conclusion and the cogency of his arguments in support of it are said to be all-important. These are probably the best justifications that can be afforded for the use of controversial, indeterminate questions in an examination. That they provide an adequate justification is open to question, for more direct, specific, and reliable tests of a student's command of relevant knowledge are available. More direct, specific, and reliable tests of his ability to differentiate sound from unsound arguments are also available. It is difficult to discern any good reason for testing these aspects of achievement by the indirect means and in the poorly controlled setting provided by an indeterminate test question.

The suggestion that the examiner should be more concerned with the student's processes of thinking than with the conclusions he reaches also deserves a close look. There ought to be a reasonably close relation between quality of thought processes and quality of conclusions reached. Rarely, by accident, a student might reach the proper conclusion for the wrong reasons. Usually, reaching correct conclusions will require the use of the correct evidence and thought processes. It is impossible in principle for wholly adequate evidence and reasoning to lead to faulty conclusions. In general, a process of thinking can be no better than the conclusion it leads to. Whether the thing produced is an idea or an automobile, the quality of the process of production will always be judged, in the long run, by the quality of the thing it produces.

> 7. *In objective test items the student's task and the basis on which the examiner will judge the degree to which it has been accomplished are stated more clearly than is usually true of essay tests.*

Essay test questions can be highly definite, accompanied by detailed, explicit directions to the student. Often they are not. The scoring of answers to essay test questions can also be guided by detailed, explicit directions. Often it is not. The more detailed and explicit the directions to both student and scorer, the more objective and reliable the measurements obtainable from an essay test question.

The fact that objective test items are more definite and explicit than typical essay test questions helps to account for the much more frequent criticisms of the objective test items. Many of these criticisms allege that the best answer is inadequate or that one of the wrong answers is, in fact, as good as, or better than, the answer designated as correct. The source of the trouble is the provision of answers along with the questions, and with the indication that one of these is better than the others.

Essay test questions escape these hazards by leaving the student to create an explicit answer and allowing the scorer to rate its adequacy without producing his own version of an ideal answer or describing the basis of quantifying the difference he perceives between the student's answer and his ideal. The deficiencies that an essay question may have are seldom so readily available for observation as those of an objective test item.

> 8. *An objective test permits, and occasionally encourages, guessing. An essay test permits, and occasionally encourages, bluffing.*

A student could guess blindly at the answers to an objective test. If the test were very short and simple, say ten true-false test items, he might even expect to get a perfect score by blind guessing, once in about every thousand attempts. If he is very poorly prepared, or if the test is inordinately difficult, he might accidentally get a higher score by blind guessing than he would get by considering carefully his response to each question. But seldom if ever would he *expect* to do better by blind guessing. Hence, while blind guessing is possible on an objective test, it is seldom likely to be profitable.

Nor is it likely to be prevalent. Students guess blindly on an examination only when they have no knowledge relevant to the question whatsoever, only when they are running out of time, or when they have run out of the motivation necessary to make the effort to select an answer on rational grounds. The alternative to blind guessing is not certainty of response, but rational consideration of the response. If the student has any knowledge whatever relevant to the questions and if he uses that knowledge to the best of his ability, he is not guessing blindly and his answer to the test question contributes usefully to the measurement of his achievement.

The greater the contribution that blind guessing makes to the determination of students' scores on an examination, the lower the reliability of those scores. If all students were to guess blindly on the answers to all the items in an objective test, the expected value for the reliability of their scores would be zero. Hence, if scores on an objective test show high reliability, it is safe to conclude that the role played by guessing in determining those scores was small. (However, low reliability does not necessarily indicate a large amount of guessing.) Thus, though the possibility and occurrence of guessing on objective tests cannot be denied, the seriousness of its influence on objective test scores is often overestimated.

A corresponding weakness of essay tests is bluffing. A student who is hard put to answer adequately the particular question asked can transform it subtly into a related question that is easier for him to answer. If he does the task he has substituted for the examiner's task well, the reader may not even notice the substitution. Or the student may concentrate on form rather than on content, on elegant presentation of a few rather simple ideas, in the hope that this may divert the reader's attention to the lack of substantial content. Stephen Leacock offered the following suggestions along these lines.[6]

*   *   *   *   *

To the Editor of the *Princetonian:*

Sir: You are kind enough to refer to certain of my writings in regard to the difficulties and fallacies of written examinations. You ask me if there is any way—if I have your phrase right—to "get by." I think there is.

Every student should train himself to be like the conjurer Houdini. Tie him as you would, lock him in as you might, he got loose. A student should acquire this looseness.

For the *rudiments* of education, there is no way round. The multiplication table has got to be learned. They say Abraham Lincoln knew it all. So, too, the parts of speech must be committed to memory, and left there. The names of the Wessex Kings from Alfred (better Aelfoydd) to his Danish successor Half-Knut should be learned and carefully distinguished from the branches of the Amazon.

But these rudiments once passed, education gets easier and easier as it goes on. When one reaches the stage of being what is called a ripe scholar, it is so easy to verge on imbecility.

Now for college examinations, once the student is let into college, there are a great number of methods of evasion. Much can always be done by sheer illegibility of handwriting and by smearing ink all over the exam paper and then crumpling it up into a ball.

But apart from this, each academic subject can be fought on its own ground. Let me give one or two examples.

Here, first, is the case of Latin translation—the list of extracts from Caesar, Cicero, etc., the origin of each always indicated by

---

[6] Stephen Leacock, *The Daily Princetonian,* Princeton, N.J., January 26, 1938.

having the word Caesar, etc., under it. On this we seize as our opportunity. The student doesn't need to know one word of Latin. He learns by heart a piece of translated Caesar, selecting a *typical* extract, and he writes that down. The examiner merely sees a faultless piece of translation and notices nothing—or at least he thinks that the candidate was given the wrong extract. He lets him pass.

Here is the piece of Caesar as required:

These things being thus this way, Caesar although not yet did he not know neither the copiousness of the enemy nor whether they had frumentum, having sent on Labienus with an impediment he himself on the first day before the third day, ambassadors having been sent to Vercingetorix, lest who might which, all having done, set out.

Caesar

Cicero also is easily distinguished by the cold, biting logic of his invective. Try this:

How now which, what, oh Catiline, infected, infracted, disducted, shall you still perfrage us? To what expunction shall we not subject you? To what bonds, to what vinculation, to how great a hyphen? I speak. Does he? No.

Cicero. In (and through) Catiline

The summation of what is called the liberal arts course is reached with such subjects as political theory, philosophy, etc. Here the air is rarer and clearer and vision easy. There is no trouble at all in circling around the examiner at will. The best device is found in the use of quotations from learned authors of whom he has perhaps —indeed, very likely—never heard, and the use of languages which he either doesn't know or can't read in blurred writing. We take for granted that the examiner is a conceited, pedantic man, as they all are—and is in a hurry to finish his work and get back to a saloon.

Now let me illustrate.

Here is a question from the last Princeton examination in Modern Philosophy. I think I have it correct or nearly so.

"Discuss Descartes' proposition, 'Cogito ergo sum,' as a valid basis of epistemology."

Answer:

"Something of the apparent originality of Descartes' dictum, 'cogito ergo sum,' disappears when we recall that long before him Globulus had written, 'Testudo ergo crepito,' and the great Arab scholar Alhelallover, writing about 200 Fahrenheit, had said, 'Indigo ergo gum.' But we have only to turn to Descartes' own brilliant contemporary, the Abbe Pate de Foie Gras, to find him writing, 'Dimanche, lundi, mardi, mercredi, jeudi, vendredi, samedi,' which means as much, or more, than Descartes' assertion. It is quite likely that the Abbe himself was acquainted with the words of Pretzel, Weiner Schnitzel, and Schmierkase; even more likely still he knew the treatise of the low German, Fisch von Gestern, who had already set together a definite system or scheme. He writes: 'Wo ist mein Bruder? Er ist in dem Hause. Habe ich den Vogel gesehen? Dies ist ein gutes Messer. Holen Sie Karl und Fritz und wir werden alle ins Theater gehen. Danke Bestens.' "

There, one can see how easy it is. I know it from my own experience. I remember in my fourth year in Toronto (1891) going into the exam room and picking up a paper which I carelessly took for English Philology; I wrote on it, passed on it and was pleasantly surprised two weeks later when they gave me a degree in Ethnology. I had answered the wrong paper. This story, oddly enough, is true.

Stephen Leacock

*   *   *   *   *

Not all readers of essay examinations are easy to bluff. Students likely to be most in need of the kind of assistance that bluffing might give them are unlikely to be talented in the art of bluffing. Like guessing on objective tests, the seriousness of the problem of bluffing on essay tests can easily be overestimated.

> *9. The distribution of numerical scores obtained from an essay test can be controlled to a considerable degree by the grader; that from an objective test is determined almost entirely by the test.*

For most objective tests the maximum possible raw score is determined by the number of questions on the test. Each correct response usually contributes one score unit. Each incorrect response contributes nothing and may, in some cases, result in subtraction of a fraction of a score unit. On a good test the lowest score obtained by any examinee is likely to be not far above the score which might be obtained by blind guessing.

For most essay tests the maximum possible raw score, as well as the minimum passing score, can be determined by the grader. Often the maximum number of points allowed for each of the questions is set so that the maximum possible score on the whole test is 100. Whether the grader allows no points, five points, or even seven points for a seriously inadequate answer is a matter for his own decision. Thus, no matter how inappropriate an essay test may be in difficulty, the grader can adjust his standards so some, but not too many, will receive scores below some preset minimum passing score.

For these reasons the problem of test item difficulty is of much greater concern to those who construct objective tests than it is to those who construct essay tests. Also, the hazards of a predetermined passing score are much greater on an objective than on an essay test.

Some graders of essay test questions will insist that they are not influenced by concern over how many will fail in their grading of essay test answers. They will claim to use *absolute* standards, based on their judgments of how well a student ought to do on a question of the kind being graded. But research studies like those of Starch and Elliott suggest that these so-called absolute standards are, in fact, highly personal and subjective.[7] Reliance on such *absolute* standards, in preference to relative standards (i.e., those determined by the performances of other students in the group) almost inevitably lowers the precision of the measurements obtained from essay tests.

2. Some similarities of essay and objective tests

The foregoing nine statements call attention to some of the differences between essay and objective tests. There are also some respects in which they are alike.

> 1. *Either an essay or an objective test can be used to measure almost any important educational achievement that any written test can measure.*

The "almost" in the foregoing statement is required by the fact that no good objective tests of certain achievements, like the

---

[7] Daniel Starch and E. C. Elliott, "Reliability of Grading High School Work in English," *School Review*, XX (1912), 442-57.

quality of a student's handwriting, exist or are likely to be produced. IIis spelling ability can be tested objectively. His vocabulary can be tested objectively. His ability to punctuate, capitalize, and apply the principles of grammar and rhetoric can be tested objectively. Substantial studies have shown that objective tests of ability in written composition correlate more highly with teacher estimates of that ability, based on extensive observation, than do scores on typical essay tests of ability in written composition.

Many of the traits that essay tests have been said to measure, such as critical thinking, originality, and ability to organize and integrate, are not at all clearly defined. The characteristics of answers to essay test questions that serve to indicate which students have more and which have less of these traits are seldom decribed or illustrated. When the scores awarded to essay test answers are explained or defended, when the reasons why a student did not get the maximum possible on a question are specified, they usually turn out to be some combination of these deficiencies:

1. Incorrect statements were included in the answer.
2. Important ideas necessary to an adequate answer were omitted.
3. Correct statements having little or no relation to the question were included.
4. Unsound conclusions were reached, either because of mistakes in reasoning or because of misapplication of principles.
5. Bad writing obscured the development and exposition of the student's ideas.
6. There were egregious errors in spelling and the mechanics of correct writing.

Mistakes in the first four categories can be attributed either to weaknesses in the student's command of knowledge or to lack of clarity and specificity in the examiner's question. Mistakes in the last two categories indicate weakness in the student's ability in written expression or reflect the difficulties of the hand in keeping up with a mind racing ahead under the pressure of a time-limit test. As essay tests are typically used, the unique functions they have that are beyond the scope of objective tests seem somewhat limited and indefinite. Odell's scales for rating essay test answers suggest strongly that the length of a student's answer may be closely related to the score it receives.[8] Longer answers tend to receive the higher ratings.

> 2. *Either an essay or an objective test can be used to encourage students to study for understanding of principles, organization and integration of ideas, and application of knowledge to the solution of problems.*

That the nature of the examination expected affects the preparation students make for it is attested by experience, reason and research.[9] Surveys of student opinion about thirty years ago suggested that students then studied more thoroughly in preparation for essay examinations than for objective examinations. More recent evidence is scanty and inconclusive.

With respect to the influence of examinations on study, the really important question is not how students *say* they study for examinations of different kinds, or even how they *actually* do study, but how these differences affect their achievement. In the absence of adequate evidence on this point, which may be difficult to get, we may turn to some inferences which seem to be reasonable.

1. The kind of study and achievement that a test stimulates is probably more a function of the kind of questions asked on it than of the mode of student response.
2. To the degree that tests in different form measure the same kinds or aspects of achievement, they should stimulate the same kind of study and have the same effect on achievement.

An illustration of the use of essay and objective questions to test essentially the same educational achievement is given in Exhibits 4.1 and 4.2. These tests were devised for use in a dental prosthetics test. The instructor had always used essay questions but was interested in the more reliable scores and greater convenience in scoring which objective tests might afford. He was dubious, however, about the possibility of writing a number of independent objective test

---

[8] Charles W. Odell, *Scales for Rating Pupils' Answers to Nine Types of Thought Questions in English Literature* (Bureau of Educational Research; University of Illinois, Urbana, Ill., 1927).

[9] George Meyer, "An Experimental Study of the Old and New Types of Examination: II Methods of Study," *Journal of Educational Psychology*, XXVI (1935), 30-40; and Paul W. Terry, "How Students Review for Objective and Essay Tests," *Elementary School Journal*, XXXIII (1933), 592-603.

items relating to the same complex process without having one question give away the answer to another.

To explore this possibility, the professor of dentistry supplied an essay test question and an ideal answer to it. This is displayed in Exhibit 4.1. Then a series of multiple-choice items were written on the basis of this essay-type answer. Eight of these are shown in Exhibit 4.2. Items 2 and 3 are interlocking items. That is, the question asked in item 3 gives some clues as to the best answer to item 2. Hence only one of the two items should be used in any one test.

EXHIBIT 4.1

Essay Test Question and Answer

Q. Sometimes a bridge will not go in place properly when being tried in the mouth after being soldered. If the operator should consider it advisable or necessary to unsolder, reassemble, and resolder the bridge, describe how this should be done.

A. The operator should first determine which joint or joints are to be unsoldered. The parts of the bridge should never be separated with a saw or disc, as this leaves a wide space to be filled in with solder. Instead, the bridge should be held in a blow-torch flame in such a way that the flame is directed on the joint to be unsoldered. Only enough heat must be used to melt the solder, and care must be used not to melt or distort an abutment piece.

When the parts of the bridge have been separated, they should be pickled in acid to clean them of oxide. It will be necessary to use a disc or stone to smooth and reduce the amount of solder at the joints before the bridge will go into place in the mouth. This must be done till all parts of the bridge can be reassembled in the mouth.

Place some Parr's flux wax on all contact points of the abutment pieces and pontics (this is done with the pieces outside the mouth), then place all pieces back in the mouth. The Parr's flux wax will hold the parts in place, and the wax is soft enough so the pontics can be moved around to a certain extent to get them in the right position. When positioned properly, the joints should be reinforced with sticky wax, which is hard and brittle and will hold the parts firmly together. Then to further reinforce and strengthen the bridge so the parts will not be disarranged while taking the impression, a short piece of wire about 16 gauge should be bent and placed along the buccal or labial surface of the bridge and the approximating teeth and held firmly in place with sticky wax. All this waxing must be done with the field perfectly dry because any moisture will positively prevent the wax from holding.

Then a small, shallow impression tray is selected, filled with a fast-setting impression plaster and a shallow occlusal impression (if for a posterior bridge) or lingual and incisal impression (if for an anterior bridge) is secured. The impression is removed from the mouth, the bridge also removed and reassembled in the impression, the joints filled with Parr's flux wax, the plaster impression given a coat of separating medium, and the exposed parts of the bridge covered with soldering investment. When the investment is set, the plaster impression is cut away and more soldering investment applied in the proper manner to provide for correct soldering. The case is now ready to be heated and soldered in the regular way.

EXHIBIT 4.2

Corresponding Multiple-choice Items

The following eight items deal with the problem of separating, reassembling, and resoldering a bridge which will not go into place properly after being soldered.

1. Which joint or joints should be separated?
   a. The joint between pontics and smallest abutment piece
   b. Any single joint (the faulty joint must be located by trial and error)
   c. All that were originally soldered
   *d. Only the one or ones which appear responsible for the failure to fit

Note: Only one of the following two items should be used.

2. Should the joints be separated using a saw or disc rather than heat?
   a. No, because the saw might damage the original castings

*b. No, because the saw will leave too large a gap to be filled with solder
c. Yes, because the use of heat might damage the original castings
d. Yes, because the saw leaves a clean joint ready for resoldering

3. Should the flame be concentrated on the joint to be unsoldered? Why
   a. No, because the bridge may crack if heated unevenly
   b. No, because the abutments must be thoroughly heated before the solder will melt
   *c. Yes, to avoid damage to the other pieces
   d. Yes, to avoid delay in separation

4. After the bridge has been separated what, if anything,

needs to be done before reassembling it in the patient's mouth?

*a. The pieces should be cleaned in acid, and the joints smoothed with a stone

b. The pieces should be cleaned in acid, but the joints should not be smoothed

c. The joints should be smoothed, but the pieces need not be cleaned in acid

d. Reassembling should begin as soon as the bridge has been separated

5. What is used initially to hold the pieces together on reassembly in the patient's mouth?

a. Sticky wax

*b. Parr's flux wax

c. Impression plaster

d. Soldering investment

6. Which of the following materials—flux wax, sticky wax, metal wire, and soldering investment—are used to hold the pieces of the reassembled bridge in place prior to taking the impression?

a. All of them

b. All but metal wire

*c. All but soldering investment

d. Only flux wax and sticky wax

7. What precaution is necessary in using sticky wax?

a. It must not be allowed to touch gum tissues.

b. It must be applied in separate thin layers to avoid cracking.

c. The surface to which it is applied must be moist.

*d. The surface to which it is applied must be dry.

8. What function does the plaster impression have in the process of resoldering the bridge?

*a. It holds the parts in place while soldering investment is applied.

b. It holds the parts in place while they are being soldered.

c. It permits the resoldered bridge to be checked before insertion in the patient's mouth.

d. It has no function in resoldering the bridge.

In view of the many potent factors other than examinations which affect how, and with what success, students study, in view also of the fact that these factors may interact in complex ways to facilitate or to inhibit learning, the chances are small that research will ever demonstrate clearly that either essay or objective tests have the more beneficial influence on study and learning.

3. The use of both types involves the exercise of subjective judgments.

In objective testing the subjectivity is concentrated in the process of test construction. In essay testing it affects both the selection and statement of the test questions and the evaluation of student answers. Good objective test construction aims to make the selection of things to test, and the preparation and selection of items to test them, as objective as possible. Good essay testing aims to make the standards for judging the quality of student answers as objective as possible.

The subjectivity of judgments can be reduced by pooling the opinions of experts. This is done in the construction of objective tests for use in wide-scale testing programs by the appointment of committees of examiners to develop the test specifications and to review the individual test items. It is done in the reading of essay answers in a wide-scale testing program by the appointment of committees of readers who develop standards for judging the answers and who compare their scoring of selected answers to achieve as much uniformity as possible. Instructors can seldom manage the extra assistance and effort that these procedures require, but they do represent a standard of excellence to be approached as closely as possible, as often as possible.

4. The value of scores from either type of test is dependent on their objectivity and reliability.

The score on any test is a means of communicating and recording a measurement or an evaluation. It is useful only insofar as it is meaningful. It must mean something to the person who determined it, not only at the moment of determination, but days or weeks later. It must mean as nearly as possible the same thing to the student who receives it as it did to the teacher who assigned it. To the degree that other qualified observers would assign different scores, the measurement lacks objectivity and hence utility. Measurements of school achievement, like other reports, must be trustworthy in order to be useful. To be trustworthy means that they are capable of independent verification. If the same teacher were to assign totally different scores to the same essay test answer on different occasions, or if different teachers were to disagree in the same way, our confidence in the scores would be shaken and their usefulness diminished.

From this point of view, objectivity is an essential characteristic of any measurement, including any test score, whether the score is derived from an objective test or an essay test. Just as some degree of subjectivity is involved in measuring achievement by means of either essay or objective tests, so some degree of objectivity is essential in the scores which those tests yield.

Some aspects of educational achievement can be measured with high objectivity more easily than other aspects. Some aspects of educational achievement are more important than others. Unfortunately, the most important things are not necessarily the easiest to measure objectively. (We should beware, however, of the fallacy of assuming that if an aspect of education is hard to measure objectively, it is, ipso facto, important—or that if it is easy to measure objectively, it is, ipso facto, trivial.) We cannot afford to shun the measurement of important aspects of educational achievement simply because it is hard to measure them objectively. But it would be equally bad to settle for alleged measures of these aspects of achievement which are seriously lacking objectivity.

3. When to use essay or objective tests

On the basis of these considerations of the differences and similarities between essay and objective tests, some general recommendations can be summarized.

Use essay tests in the measurement of educational achievement when:

1. The group to be tested is small, and the test should not be reused.
2. The instructor wishes to do all possible to encourage and reward the development of student skill in written expression.
3. The instructor is more interested in exploring the student's attitudes than in measuring his achievements. (Whether an instructor *should* be more interested in attitudes than achievement and whether he should expect an honest expression of attitudes in a test he will evaluate, seem open to question.)

4. The instructor is more confident of his proficiency as a critical reader than as an imaginative writer of good objective test items.

5. Time available for test preparation is shorter than the time available for test grading.

Use objective tests in the measurement of educational achievement when:

1. The group to be tested is large, or the test may be reused.
2. Highly reliable test scores must be obtained as efficiently as possible.
3. Impartiality of evaluation, absolute fairness, and freedom from halo effects are essential.
4. The instructor is more confident of his ability to express objective test items clearly than of his ability to judge essay test answers correctly.
5. There is more pressure for speedy reporting of scores than for speedy test preparation.

Use either essay or objective tests to:

1. Measure almost any important educational achievement which a written test can measure.
2. Test understanding and ability to apply principles.
3. Test ability to think critically.
4. Test ability to solve novel problems.
5. Test ability to select relevant facts and principles, to integrate them toward the solution of complex problems.
6. Encourage students to study for command of knowledge.

4. Suggestions for preparing essay tests

Both essay and objective tests can make important contributions to the measurement of educational achievement. Although they differ in significant ways and although there are particular situations in which one or the other is especially appropriate, they are to a considerable extent interchangeable. More important than which form is used is how well it is used. Test specialists have paid less attention to the improvement of essay tests than they have to the improvement of objective tests, but this does not mean that essay tests are beyond the need or the possibility of improvement.

The most basic and general suggestion for the improvement of essay tests is that the performance of essay tests should be evaluated systematically against objective standards of test quality set in advance by the test constructor himself. A number of possible standards of quality are suggested in the chapter on judging test quality.

One of the most important standards of quality, and one which has been emphasized in this chapter, is test reliability. In the case of essay tests, score reliability is affected significantly by the reliability with which the answers are read and graded, that is, by the agreement between the grades of different readers. Provision for this kind of check as part of the evaluation of test performance would be most desirable.

The quality of the individual questions in an essay test, as reflected in their difficulty and discriminating power, can also be determined by adapting the techniques described in Chapter 11. Revision or replacement of items which are too easy or too difficult, which fail to discriminate well for other reasons, or which result in student answers on whose scoring readers tend to disagree will help considerably to improve test reliability. If the items in the test are not to be reused, such an analysis may suggest the kinds of items, or the characteristics of items, most likely to contribute to test reliability. Hence the analysis will contribute indirectly to the improvement of essay tests.

Implicit in what has been said in this chapter about the values and limitations of essay tests are a number of suggestions for improving the questions of which these tests are composed.

1. Ask questions, or set tasks, which will require the student to demonstrate his command of essential knowledge.

Such questions will not simply call for reproduction of materials presented in the textbook or in other instructional materials. Instead of looking exclusively backward to the past course of instruction, they will also look forward to future applications of the things learned. The questions will be based on novel situations or problems, not on the same ones as were used for instructional purposes.

Many different types of questions may be used as the basis for essay (or objective) test questions. An outline of types of thought questions found in science textbooks has been prepared by Curtis and may be suggestive.[10] It is shown in Exhibit 4.3. Clearly, some of the illustrative questions are more suitable for use as short answer than as essay questions. Clearly, too, additional background information on the question, or guidance as to the type of answer desired,

EXHIBIT 4.3

Types of Thought Questions in Textbooks of Science
(Outlined by Francis D. Curtis in *Science Education*, September, 1943)

1. Comparison and contrast
   a. What are the differences between weather and climate?
   b. In parallel columns compare the eye and the camera, noting all similarities and differences.
2. Decision for or against
   a. Will air serve as well as oil in a hydraulic press? Explain.
   b. Which system of measurement is more logical to use if you have learned both equally well? Justify your answer.
3. Application of facts or principles already learned in new situations
   a. Suggest ways of correcting annoying reverberations in a hall or church.
   b. A glass stopper is stuck in a bottle and cannot be removed by twisting or tapping it. Suggest a way of loosening it.
4. Classification
   a. To what class of lever does the wheelbarrow belong?
   b. From your observation of the number of legs this specimen has, to what group of animals do you think it belongs?
5. Relationships involving cause and effect
   a. What is the relation between efficiency and friction of a machine?
   b. What would be the result of washing a piece of cake down your throat without chewing it?
6. Example or illustration
   a. Name a parasite.
   b. Describe a case that you have actually witnessed where friction proved to be a disadvantage.
7. Statement of author's aim or purpose in the selection or arrangement of materials
   a. Why are hydrogen and oxygen studied before water?
   b. Why do you think the main divisions of plant and animal life are presented early in the book?

---

[10] Francis D. Curtis, "Types of Thought Questions in Textbooks of Science," *Science Education*, XXVII (1943), 60-67.

8. Criticism of the adequacy, correctness, or relevancy of a situation, statement, or diagram
   a. What was your main source of error?
   b. From your observation, what criticism should you offer of the posture diagram?

9. Inference from data
   a. From the facts presented what do you think will be likely to happen in Niagara Falls during the next million years or so?
   b. What do you conclude concerning the relative rate of heat radiation from a dull and from a shiny object?

10. Discussion
    a. Present arguments for and against the introduction of the metric system in place of the English system in this country.
    b. Discuss photosynthesis.

11. Outline
    a. Outline a method for removing tarnish from copper.
    b. List in order the various blood vessels through which the blood would flow in circulating from your toe to your heart and back.

12. Explanation or definition
    a. What is meant by persistence of vision?
    b. Tell in your own words what erosion is.

13. Simple recall
    a. What is the chemical formula for water?
    b. How many legs has an insect?

14. Summary
    a. What characteristics do all satellites of the sun have in common?
    b. What facts can you state about lines of force?

15. Observation
    a. Where does the diagram show most of the planetoids to be?
    b. What are the characteristics of the oxygen which has just been made by heating potassium chlorate and manganese dioxide?

16. Formulation of new questions
    a. What questions occurred to you while performing this experiment?
    b. Write three additional questions based on this experiment that you would like to have answered.

would need to be supplied to make some of the questions usable. Similar lists have been published by Wesley and by Monroe and Carter.[11]

---

[11] Edgar B. Wesley and Stanley P. Wronski, *Teaching Social Studies in High Schools* (4th ed.; Boston: D. C. Heath & Company, 1958), pp. 356-57; and

>   2. *Ask questions which are determinate in the sense that experts could agree that one answer is better than another.*

Indeterminate questions are likely to function in some measure as exercises in exposition, whose relation to effective behavior may be quite remote. Such questions may not be highly relevant to the measurement of a student's useful command of essential knowledge. Further, and most importantly, the absence of a good best answer may make it much more difficult for a reader to judge the student's competence from the answer he gives. On controversial questions, which many indeterminate questions are, the reader's opinions and biases may have considerable influence on his evaluation of the student's answer.

>   3. *Define the examinee's task as completely and specifically as possible withont interfering with measurement of the achievement intended.*

The question should be carefully phrased so that the examinee fully understands what he is expected to do. If it is not clearly evident in the question itself, add an explanation of the basis on which his answer will be evaluated. Do not allow him more freedom than is necessary to measure the desired achievement. If the question permits variation in the extent and detail of the answer given and if you are not testing his judgment on this point, specify about how long his answer is expected to be.

>   4. *In general, give preference to more specific questions, that can be answered more briefly.*

The larger the number of independently scorable questions, the higher the sampling reliability of the test is likely to be. Narrower questions are likely to be less ambiguous to the examinee and easier for scorers to grade reliably. Occasionally the instructor may be required, in order to test some essential aspects of student achievement, to base an essay test on only a few very broad questions. These

Walter S. Monroe and Ralph E. Carter, *The Use of Different Types of Thought Questions in Secondary Schools and Their Relative Difficulty for Students,* University of Illinois Bulletin, Vol. 20, No. 34 (April 13, 1923).

occasions are not frequent, however, and the instructor should be sure that the need for extended answers is sufficient to warrant the probable loss in score reliability.

> 5. *Avoid giving the examinee a choice among optional questions unless special circumstances make such options necessary.*

If different examinees answer different questions, the basis for the comparability of their scores is weakened. The scores are likely to be somewhat less variable when students choose the questions they can answer best than when students must answer all the same questions. Hence the reliability of the scores would be expected to be somewhat less. Experimental studies indicate that this expectation is justified.

Meyer found that when college students in psychology were given the choice of omitting one of five essay questions, only 58 per cent of them omitted the question on which they would do least well.[12] He "suggested that unless the various questions are weighted in some suitable fashion the choice form of essay examination be discontinued." Stalnaker concluded a survey of the problems involved in the use of optional questions with these words:

> No experimental evidence has been published to show that skills and abilities can be adequately sampled by the use of optional questions; on the other hand, several studies have shown that optional questions complicate measurement and introduce factors of judgment which are extraneous to the ability being measured. For sound sampling, it is recommended that optional questions be avoided and that all examinees be asked to run the same race.[13]

Optional questions are sometimes justified on the ground that giving the student a choice of the questions he is to answer makes the test "fairer" to him. But if all the questions involve, as they ordinarily can, essential aspects of achievement in a course, it is not unfair to any student to ask him to answer all of them. Further, an

---

[12] George Meyer, "The Choice of Questions on Essay Examinations," *Journal of Educational Psychology*, XXX (1939), 161-71.

[13] John M. Stalnaker, "The Essay Type of Examination," in *Educational Measurement*, ed. E. F. Lindquist (Washington, D.C.: American Council on Education, 1951), p. 506.

opportunity to choose among optional questions may not help the well-prepared student at all. It may help the poorly prepared student considerably. This does not make the test fairer to all concerned.

Optional questions may be justifiable when a test of educational achievement must cover a broad area, and when the students who take it have been trained in only part of the whole area. Even in such a situation, however, the advantages of using optional questions may not outweigh the disadvantages. Optional tests, separately scored, might be preferable to a common test, yielding a single score, based on different sets of questions.

6. Test the question by writing an ideal answer to it.

Writing the ideal answer at the time the question is drafted serves an immediate purpose. It gives the test constructor a check on the reasonableness of the question and the adequacy of his statement of it. He may see how some change in the question could make the question easier, if that seems desirable, or more difficult, if that seems desirable, or more discriminating, which is always desirable. Also useful, if it can be arranged, is to have someone else who should be able to answer the question try to answer it. Comparison of his answer with that of the test constructor's might shed additional light on its suitability and might suggest additional ways of improving it.

The deferred purpose served by drafting an ideal answer to each essay test question is to provide guidance, and a point of reference, for the instructor when he begins to grade the students' answers. If someone other than the instructor is to grade the questions or to help with the grading, the ideal answer is almost indispensable to uniformity in grading.

5. Suggestions for grading essay tests

As has been mentioned, the quality of the measurement of educational achievement which results from the use of essay tests is heavily dependent on the quality of the grading process. The competence of the grader is the key to the quality of this process, and no suggestions given here can compensate for deficiencies in that competence. But even competent graders may inadvertently do things that make the results less reliable than they ought to be. Here are some suggestions for the grader of essay test answers to consider if he is anxious to make his work as precise as possible.

> *1. Write out an ideal answer to the question and decide whether to use analytic scoring or global-quality scaling.*

No matter which type of scoring is used, it is helpful to have a "perfect" answer to serve as a guide and standard. In the case of analytic scoring, crucial elements of the ideal answer are identified and scored more or less separately. The higher the proportion of these crucial elements appearing in the student's answer and the less they are contaminated by inaccuracies or irrelevancies, the higher the student's score. Analytic scoring can pay attention not only to the elements of an ideal answer, but also to relations between these elements, that is, to the organization and integration of the answer. But if these relationships are complex and subtle, analytic scoring may prove to be too cumbersome and tedious to be effective.

An illustration of competent and painstaking analytic scoring of essay test answers is provided by the procedures of the Examination Service of the American Institute of Certified Public Accountants.[14]

> During the first eight to ten days after the examination, the section chairmen and the reviewers develop the grade sheets, the grading guides, and the notes for the reviewers. The grade sheets for each subject indicate the acceptable items in the answers and their assigned weights. One grade sheet is attached to each candidate's papers; it becomes a permanent record of the points earned. The grading guide describes the concepts, ideas, reasons, entries, amounts, and other items which constitute an acceptable answer; it also provides instructions on how to interpret certain items that may appear on the candidates' papers as well as instructions covering the techniques of grading and scoring. A copy of the grading guide is given to each grader and reviewer.

An alternative is global-quality scaling. In using this method, the grader simply reads the answer for a general impression of its adequacy. He may transform that impression into a numerical grade, record the grade, and go on to the next answer. A better procedure,

---

[14] Association of Certified Public Accountant Examiners, *Report of the CPA Examination Appraisal Commission* (New York: ACPAE, 1961), p. 24.

providing the grader with an opportunity to check the consistency of his grading standards as applied to different papers, involves the sorting of answers into several piles corresponding to different levels of quality. Sorting before marking permits, even encourages, the grader to reconsider his decisions in the light of experience with all of the students' answers. It lessens the probability that he would give a higher score to one of two answers which, on rereading, seem to be of equal quality.

Scorers who use the sorting process in connection with global-quality scaling of answers usually try to make the size of each pile approximate some predetermined ideal. That is, they may try to put about the same number in each pile. Or they may try to approximate a normal distribution. With three piles the approximate goals might be:

Low	Middle	High
25%	50%	25%

or with five piles:

Lowest	Lower	Middle	Higher	Highest
5%	25%	40%	25%	5%

Scorers sometimes find it advantageous to use a three-stage process of sorting, dividing the answers after initial reading into three approximately equal piles in the first stage and then subdividing each of these after rereading into three more piles, yielding nine levels of quality in all. The third step in the process is to compare the papers in level 6 (upper third of the original middle group), with those in level 7 (lower third of the original upper group), to make sure that the level-7 papers are actually better than those in level 6. Papers from the upper third of the original lower group (level 3) would also be compared for the same purpose with those from the lower third of the original middle group (level 4).

How many piles to use in the sorting and whether to make the intended distribution equal across piles or roughly normal are matters of preference and convenience. The more piles used, the greater the precision of scoring, provided the answers differ enough, and the scorer is perceptive enough, to make confident, reliable decisions as to the classifications of the individual papers.

As part of one dental aptitude test, examinees are required to carve a lump of plaster into some regular shape, such as the block letter "I" shown in Figure 4.2.[15] The lump of plaster supplied to the student has only one smooth flat side to start with. The examinee's task, using a carving knife, is to produce an object which

Figure 4.2. Block Carving Shape for a Dental Aptitude Test

resembles the specified shape as closely as possible and on which all angles are right angles, all edges are straight lines, and all surfaces flat.

Initially, these objects were scored analytically, measuring and scoring each angle, each edge and each surface. The process seemed more tedious than necessary. The alternative of holistic scoring was tried. The judge would look at each block and then place it on one of several piles graded from "excellent" to "awful." Holistic scoring seemed to yield slightly more consistent ratings for the same student from block to block or from judge to judge than analytic scoring.

As a general rule, global-quality scaling is simpler and faster than analytic scoring. In some situations it may be more reliable. But it does not provide any clear justification of the grade assigned, nor does it give any indication to the student of how his answer fell short of the mark. Analytic scoring can provide such indications. It is well suited to questions which are likely to elicit detailed, uniformly structured answers.

2. *Grade the answers question by question rather than student by student.*

This means that the grader will read the answers to one question on all students' papers before going on to the next question. Such

[15] R. V. Smith and H. V. Freeman, "Report on Aptitude Testing in Dentistry at University of Iowa," *Proceedings, 12th Annual Meeting,* American Association of Dental Schools, 1936, pp. 214-28.

a procedure is obviously required in the global-quality scaling just described. It is advantageous in analytic scoring as well, since concentration of attention on one question at a time helps to develop specialized skill in scoring it.

3. If possible, conceal from the grader the identity of the student whose answer he is grading.

The purpose of this procedure is to reduce the possibility that biases or halo effects will influence the scores assigned. Ideally, the answers to different questions would be written on separate sheets of paper, identified only by a code number. These sheets would be arranged into groups by question for the grading process and then recombined by the student for totaling and recording. By this process one can reduce not only the halo effect associated with the student's name and reputation, but also that which might result from high or low scores on preceding answers. The purpose is, of course, to make the essay test scores measure actual achievement, as reflected by performance on the test, as accurately as possible.

4. If possible, arrange for independent grading of the answers, or at least a sample of them.

Independent grading is the only real check on the objectivity, and hence on the reliability, of the grading. It is troublesome to arrange and time consuming to carry out, however. Hence it is seldom likely to be undertaken on the initiative of the classroom teacher. But if a school or college were to undertake a serious program for the improvement of essay examinations, such a study of the reliability of essay-test grading would be an excellent way to begin.

To get independent grades, at least two competent readers would have to grade each question, without consulting each other and without knowing what grades the other had assigned. At least one hundred, preferably three hundred, answers should be given this double, independent reading. (The answers need not all be to the same question. Reading the answers of thirty students to each ten questions would be quite satisfactory.) The correlation between the pairs of grades would indicate the reliability of grading the questions. Then the Spearman-Brown formula (discussed on pp. 327-328,

Chapter 10) could be applied to estimate the reliability of grading for the test as a whole.

6. Summary

The main conclusions to be drawn from the discussions presented in this chapter can be summarized in the following twenty propositions.

1. An essay demands that a student write well. An objective test demands that he read well.

2. Essay tests ordinarily consist of a few questions that call for extended answers. Objective tests ordinarily consist of many questions that call for brief answers.

3. The bulk of a student's time is spent in reading and thinking when he takes an objective test. His time is spent mainly in thinking and writing when he takes an essay test.

4. In objective testing the skill of the test constructor is crucial. In essay testing the competence of the scorer is crucial.

5. Essay tests are easier to prepare and harder to score than objective tests.

6. In an essay test the examinee has more freedom to show his individuality, and the scorer more opportunity to depend on his personal opinions, than in an objective test.

7. The examinee's task and the basis for evaluating his performance tend to be specified more clearly on objective than on essay tests.

8. Objective tests sometimes permit guessing. Essay tests sometimes permit bluffing.

9. It is easier for the examiner to control the distribution of essay than of objective test scores.

10. The important aspects of educational achievement that can be measured by objective tests are largely identical with those that can be measured by essay tests.

11. Good objective tests and good essay tests can both test understanding, applications, problem solving, and the organization of ideas.

12. Subjective judgment is involved in both essay and objective testing.

13. Scores from either essay or objective tests must possess objective meaning to be useful.

14. Essay tests save time when the group to be tested is small. Objective tests save time when the group to be tested is large.

15. Good essay test questions require the student to demonstrate command of essential knowledge.

16. The reliability of essay test scores can be improved by making the questions specific enough so that all good answers must be nearly identical.

17. The reliability of essay test scores can ordinarily be improved by asking more questions that call for short answers than by asking fewer questions that call for long answers.

18. Optional questions should be avoided in essay testing.

19. The quality of an essay question can be tested and reliable scoring facilitated by attempting to write an ideal answer to it.

20. The reliability of reading essay answers can be improved by grading them question by question, by concealing the name of the examinee, and by arranging for several independent gradings.

REFERENCES

Association of Certified Public Accountant Examiners, *Report of the CPA Examination Appraisal Commission,* p. 24. New York: ACPAE, 1961.

Cook, Desmond L., "An Investigation of Three Aspects of Free-response and Choice-type Tests at the College Level," *Dissertation Abstracts,* XV (1955), 1351.

Curtis, Francis D., "Types of Thought Questions in Textbooks of Science," *Science Education,* XXVII (1943), 60-67.

Hoffman, Banesh, *The Tyranny of Testing.* New York: Crowell-Collier Publishing Co., 1962.

Meyer, George, "An Experimental Study of the Old and New Types of Examination: Two Methods of Study," *Journal of Educational Psychology,* XXVI (1935), 30-40.

———, "The Choice of Questions on Essay Examinations," *Journal of Educational Psychology,* XXX (1939), 161-71.

Monroe, Walter S. and Ralph E. Carter, *The Use of Different Types of Thought Questions in Secondary Schools and Their Relative Difficulty for Students,* University of Illinois Bulletin X, No. 34. University of Illinois, Urbana, Ill., April 13, 1923.

Odell, Charles W., *Scales for Rating Pupils' Answers to Nine Types of Thought Questions in English Literature.* Bureau of Educational Research, University of Illinois, Urbana, Ill., 1927.

Peterson, S., "Forecasting the Success of Freshmen Dental Students Through the Aptitude Testing Program," *Journal of the American Dental Association,* XXXVII (1948), 259-65.

Posey, Chesley, "Luck and Examination Grades," *Journal of Engineering Education* (December, 1932), pp. 292-96.

Ruch, G. M., *The Objective or New-type Examination,* p. 56. Chicago: Scott, Foresman & Company, 1929.

Sims, Verner M., "The Essay Examination Is a Projective Technique," *Educational and Psychological Measurement,* VIII (1948), 15-31.

Stalnaker, John M., "The Essay-type of Examination," in *Educational Measurement,* p. 506, ed. E. F. Lindquist. Washington, D.C.: American Council on Education, 1951.

Starch, Daniel and E. C. Elliott, "Reliability of Grading High School Work in English," *School Review,* XX (1912), 442-57.

Terry, Paul W., "How Students Review for Objective and Essay Tests," *Elementary School Journal,* XXXIII (1933), 592-603.

Wesley, Edgar B. and Stanley P. Wronski, *Teaching Social Studies in High Schools* (4th ed.). Boston: D. C. Heath & Company, 1958.

5 How to Use True-False Tests

He who would distinguish the true from the false must have an adequate idea of what is true and false.
SPINOZA

True-false test items enjoyed considerable popularity in the early days of objective testing. Although they still appear in achievement tests constructed by teachers for their own use, they have almost disappeared from the tests constructed by specialists for use in wide-scale testing programs. Even among nonspecialists, including the teachers who make them and the students who must take them, true-false items tend to be regarded as one of the least satisfactory forms for use in objective test construction.

· 1. Criticisms of true-false test items

There are several reasons for this disfavor. In the first place, true-false items are suspected, with good reason, of being particularly susceptible to chance error resulting from guessing. A student guessing blindly on a one-hundred item true-false test would expect to get a score of 50. In a group of forty-five students, all of whom guess blindly on all of the items in a one-hundred item true-false test, one student would be expected to get, purely by chance, a score as high as 60. Another would be expected to get a score as low as 40. The remaining scores would be expected to fall between these limits. Differences between students in these chance scores would have no necessary relation to differences between students in levels of achievement.

Of course, the assumptions of this example are quite unrealistic. Not all of a group of forty-five students would be likely to guess blindly at all of the items on a test. But the problem of guessing on true-false tests cannot be completely disposed of by this argument. Ordinary true-false tests are typically less reliable than multiple-choice tests of equal length (i.e., equal numbers of items). Chance errors due to the guessing of some students on some items are probably part of the reason.

In the second place, true-false items are frequently judged to be trivial. Any sentence from a textbook looks to the uncritical eye as if it might be used as a true-false test item. If such sentences are not culled carefully, a test based on them may indeed be filled with trivia.

In the third place, if true-false items are based directly on sentences from textbooks, there is a danger that they might encourage and reward sheer verbal memory. A student, perceiving a familiar pattern of words, such as "ontogeny repeats phylogeny" or "the properties of the elements are periodic functions of their atomic weights," may be able to identify it correctly as true or false without any very clear notion of what it means.

In the fourth place, many sentences that look like they might be useful as true or false statements prove not to be worded carefully enough or not to include enough background information or qualifications to enable even an expert to judge with assurance whether they are true or false. A frequent report of students who have taken a true-false test is that many of the items seemed highly ambiguous. Teachers who are pressed to defend the truth or falsity of such items are sometimes inclined to agree.

In the fifth place, unlike a multiple-choice item, the true-false item does not provide any explicit alternative in relation to which the relative truth or falsity of the item can be judged. Each statement must be judged in isolation to be true enough to be called true (i.e., true enough so that the test constructor probably intended it to be true), or false enough to be called false. This lack of a comparative basis for decision contributes to the ambiguity of some true-false test items.

Finally, true-false items have been criticized as educationally harmful on the ground that they expose the student to error. The presentation of false statements as if they might be true may, it has been feared, have a negative suggestion effect, causing the student to believe and remember statements which were never intended to be true. Experimental studies of this effect have found it to be slight, if indeed it exists at all. Ruch tentatively concluded that the negative suggestion effect in true-false tests is probably much smaller than is sometimes assumed and is fully offset by the net positive teaching effects.[1] And as Ross point out,

> Modern psychology recognizes the importance of the total situation or configuration in learning. Whether or not a false statement is dangerous depends largely upon the setting in which it appears. A false statement in the textbook, toward which the characteristic pupil attitude is likely to be one of passive, uncritical acceptance, might easily be serious. But the situation is different with the items in a true-false test. Here the habitual attitude of the modern pupil is one of active, critical challenge.[2]

Thus the list of objections to the use of true-false test items, some more justified than others, is long. But there are also several things to be said in favor of true-false test items.

2. Advantages of true-false test items

In the first place, they provide a simple, direct, and fundamental test of the student's knowledge. Acquisition of command of knowledge is, we have suggested previously, the central purpose of education. All knowledge is knowledge of propositions. One essential purpose of experimental science is to test the truth or falsity of hypothetical propositions. The essential purpose of logical reasoning is to test the truth or falsity of deductive propositions. Propositions are expressed in sentences. These sentences may be true or false. This is the stuff of which human knowledge (and true-false tests) are made. The basic relation between propositions and true-false test items is one reason for including a separate chapter on true-false

---

[1] G. M. Ruch, *The Objective on New-type Examination* (Chicago: Scott, Foresman & Company, 1929), p. 368.

[2] C. C. Ross, *Measurement in Today's Schools* (2d ed.; Englewood Cliffs, N.J.: Prentice-Hall, Inc., 1947), p. 349.

tests in this book, and for placing it before the chapter on multiple-choice tests, which are currently the most popular form.

In the second place, true-false items are quite efficient. The number of independently scorable responses per thousand words of test or per hour of testing time tends to be considerably higher than that for multiple-choice test items. Sometimes this advantage in efficiency of true-false items is lost as a result of ambiguity in the test items or as a result of examinee guessing. If these disadvantages are controlled, as they can be by proper item writing and test administration procedures, the higher efficiency of the true-false items can be expected to result in test scores of higher reliability.

In the third place, most instructors are likely to find the task of writing reasonably good true-false items to be simpler and less time consuming than the task of writing equally good multiple-choice items. This is not to say that writing good true-false items is as simple or that it can be done as rapidly as most teachers might wish. Care must be taken to select important propositions as a basis for the test items, to use originality in phrasing them so as to make it difficult for a student to respond correctly on a basis of superficial verbal memory, and to word them precisely so as to avoid intrinsic ambiguity. But because true-false items are simpler in structure than multiple-choice items, they tend to be simpler to write and somewhat less subject to technical weaknesses.

3. Equivalence of true-false and multiple-choice item forms

Implicit in most multiple-choice test items are one true statement and several false statements. For multiple-choice items also test knowledge. They, too, are based on propositions. Though no experiments of this kind seem to have been reported, it is a reasonable hypothesis that most multiple-choice test items could be converted into equivalent true-false test items with no serious change in what is measured or in the precision of measurement. If the conversion were done properly, there might even be an improvement in the reliability of the scores obtained.

Exhibit 5.1 illustrates corresponding items in multiple-choice and true-false forms designed to test essentially the same aspects of achievement. None of the items in either version test recall of iso-

EXHIBIT 5.1

Corresponding Multiple-choice and True-False Test Items

Multiple-choice Version	True-false Version

Multiple-choice Version

1. James wants to put a fence around a garden which is 60 feet long and 45 feet wide. How many feet of fencing will he need?

   a. 90 feet   c. 120 feet
   b. 105 feet   *d. 210 feet

2. The equation $X^2 + Y^2 = 4$ is represented graphically by

   *a. a circle
   b. an ellipse
   c. a parabola with its base on the X-axis

3. How can one generate enough electric current to light a flashlight bulb?

   a. By rubbing two good conductors of electricity together
   b. By dipping two strips of zinc in dilute sulphuric acid
   c. By connecting the north pole of a magnet to the south pole, using a coil of wire
   *d. By rotating a coil of wire rapidly near a strong magnet

4. What does religious tolerance mean?

   a. Admitting everyone to the same church
   b. Accepting religious teachings on faith
   c. Altering religious belief so that it does not conflict with science
   *d. Allowing people to believe what they wish

True-false Version

1a. It will take 105 feet of fencing to put a fence around a garden which is 60 feet long and 45 feet wide. (F)

1b. It will take 210 feet of fencing to put a fence around a garden which is 60 feet long and 45 feet wide. (T)

2a. The graph of $X^2 + Y^2 = 4$ is a circle. (T)

2b. The graph of $X^2 + Y^2 = 9$ is an ellipse. (F)

2c. The graph of $X^2 + Y^2 = 1$ is a parabola with its base on the Y-axis. (F)

3a. One can generate enough electric current to light a flashlight bulb by dipping two strips of zinc in dilute sulphuric acid. (F)

3b. One can generate enough electric current to light a flashlight bulb by rotating a coil of wire rapidly near a strong magnet. (T)

4a. Religious tolerance means admitting everyone to the same church. (F)

4b. Religious tolerance means allowing people to believe what they wish. (T)

4c. Religious tolerance means altering religious beliefs so that they do not conflict with science. (F) lated, factual details that are likely to have been taught directly. All of the items require explanation, interpretation, or application. Each of the multiple choice questions has been used as a basis for several true-false questions, only one of which could be used in any one test. However, the relative brevity of the true-false items means that more such items, yielding more independent item scores, can be answered in a test of the same duration.

The prevailing preference for the multiple-choice form of test item has led some item writers to use this form when the content of the item is really better suited to the true-false form. Two illustrations are presented in Exhibit 5.2. These two multiple-choice items are essentially collections of true-false statements. When the multiple-choice items are separated into true-false items, all of which could be used in the same test in this case, considerably more infor-

EXHIBIT 5.2

Items Better Suited to True-False Than to Multiple-choice Form

Multiple-choice Version	*True-false Version*	
1. Which of these is not characteristic of a virus?	1*a*. A virus can live only in plant and animal cells.	(T)
a. It can live only in plant and animal cells.	1*b*. A virus can reproduce itself.	(T)
b. It can reproduce itself.		
* c. It is composed of very large living cells.	1*c*. A virus is composed of very large living cells.	(F)
d. It can cause diseases.	1*d*. A virus can cause diseases.	(T)
2. Given △ *PQR* with median *RS*. Which of the following must be true?	2*a*. The median of a triangle is perpendicular to the side it intersects.	(F)
a. RS is perpendicular to PQ.	2*b*. The median of a triangle bisects the angle from which it is drawn.	(F)
b. *RS* bisects < *QRP*.		
c. △ PQR is a right triangle.	2*c*. A triangle with a median is a right triangle.	(F)
*d. None of the above.	2*d*. The median of a triangle divides it into two triangles of equal area.	(T)

mation (i.e., a large number of independent item scores) about the
student's achievement can be obtained from the same test content.

On the other hand, there are occasional multiple-choice items,
such as those involving qualitative comparisons between specific
examples, which would probably be more awkard to handle in true-
false form. Two illustrations of multiple-choice items of this type
are provided in Exhibit 5.3. However, despite occasional exceptions
such as these, it seems safe to say that most aspects of educational
achievement which can be tested using one of the two forms can also
be tested satisfactorily using the other.

EXHIBIT 5.3

Items Better Suited to Multiple-choice Than to True-False Form

1. Which of the following sentences is stated most emphatically?

   a. If my understanding of the question is correct, this
   principle is one we cannot afford to accept.

   b. One principle we cannot afford to accept is this one,
   if my understandng of the question is correct.

   * c. This principle, if my understanding of the question
   is correct, is one we cannot afford to accept.

   d. This principle is one we cannot afford to accept, if
   my understanding of the question is correct.

2. Which of the following couplets has the characteristics of Robert
   Frost's poetry most apparently?

   * a. "I opened the door so my last look
   Should be taken outside a house and book."

   b. " 'Tis the human touch in this world that counts,
   The touch of your hand and mine."

   c. "Dear Girl! the grasses on her grave
   Have forty years been growing."

   d. "Think still of lovely things that are not true.
   Let wish and magic work at will in you."

4. Confidence weighting of responses to true-false test items

If the potential virtues of true-false test items are to be realized,
some of the most serious defects associated with them must be cor-

rected. Prominent among these defects is the possibility of correct response by chance or very inadequate understanding.

When true-false items are administered in the usual way, the difference in average ability or achievement between those who answer an item correctly and those who answer it incorrectly may not be as great as it ought to be. Among those who answer correctly there are some who understand the point so thoroughly that there is no doubt about their entitlement to credit for a correct response. There are others whose grasp of the points is less firm and who are more or less lucky to have chosen the correct answer. Among those who answer incorrectly there are some simply misinformed on the point involved and whose incorrect response was firmly preordained. There are others who have some relevant information and whose failure to answer correctly was at least to some degree a matter of bad luck.

These considerations suggest a means for sharpening the discrimination of true-false items. Instead of being given only two alternative responses, an examinee might be given five, like those displayed in Table 5.1. He would thus be given the opportunity of double credit for a correct answer, at the risk of an equal penalty for an error, on the items which he felt he could answer confidently. He is encouraged to answer, for single unit credit and no penalty for error, all other items for which he has some basis for response. Finally, he is given the opportunity of omitting an item, in preference to guessing blindly on it, without losing the score he might expect to get by the blind guessing. This extension of the options available to an examinee in responding to a true-false test item, so that the credit or penalty he receives depends on his confidence in

TABLE 5.1

Confidence-weighted Responses to True-False Test Item

Response Number	Significance of the Response	Right	Wrong	Omit
		\multicolumn{3}{c}{Score Value}	
1	The statement is probably true.	2	−2	
2	The statement is possibly true.	1	0	
3	I have no idea.			0.5
4	The statement is possibly false.	1	0	
5	The statement is probably false.	2	−2	

the correctness of the answer, is referred to here as "confidence weighting."

The system of scores in Table 5.1 defines an optimum strategy for the student. He should not ask for double credit on an item, at the risk of a penalty, unless he thinks that the odds are two to one or better that his answer will be correct. This is illustrated in Table 5.2. So long as the proportion correct is above two-thirds, the student's score will be higher if he indicates higher confidence in his response. But when the proportion correct falls below two-thirds, his score will be higher if he responds only at the lower level of confidence.

TABLE 5.2

**Relation of Scores to Proportions of Items
Correct on a One Hundred-item True-False Test**

	Confidence of Response	
Proportion Correct	Low (Possible)	High (Probable)
80%	80	120
70%	70	80
67%	67	68
66%	66	64
60%	60	40
50%	50	0

Other systems of confidence weighting than that described in Table 5.1 are possible. One which avoids fractional scores, and which requires odds of more than three to one on correctness of response before a confident response becomes advantageous, uses these weights in scoring:

For an omitted response	0
For a tentative response (true or false)	
if correct	1
if incorrect	−1
For a positive response (true or false)	
if correct	2
if incorrect	−4

With these scoring weights, if a student gives tentative (low-weight) answers to twelve questions and is right on nine of them, his score on those items would be $9 - 3 = 6$. If he had chosen to give positive (high-weight) answers of the same kinds to the same twelve questions, his score would have been $18 - 12 = 6$. Thus whenever the odds are better than three to one of correct response, the examinee is likely to gain by choosing the higher weight. If the odds are less than three to one, it is to his advantage to choose the lower weights.

5. Confidence weighting and personality

Are scores weighted for confidence in this way measures of a personality trait as well as of knowledge? Does the bolder student have a consistent advantage over his more cautious classmate? Or does the advantage run in the other direction? A simplified sample problem may help to see the answer to this question.

Consider an eighty-item true-false test which is being taken by a particular student. To simplify the example let us assume that he knows enough about the answers to forty of these items so that his probability of giving a correct answer is $p = .75$ (three correct out of every four attempts) but that he is less well equipped to answer the other forty, so that his probability of giving a correct answer is $p = .60$ (three correct out of every five attempts). If he understood the limits of his own knowledge perfectly with respect to each item, he would answer all forty of the $p = .75$ items with high confidence and all forty of the $p = .60$ items with lower confidence. The result would be a score for him of 64.

But suppose, being brashly confident, he answered all eighty of the questions with high confidence. His score would then be 56. Or suppose being timidly cautious, he answered all eighty of the questions with low confidence. His score would then be 54. In either case, being too confident or too cautious he loses.

Finally, suppose he is neither overconfident nor overcautious but simply unaware of what he knows well and what he knows poorly. This leads him to mark twenty of the forty $p = .75$ items with high confidence and the other twenty with low confidence. It leads him also to mark twenty of the forty $p = .60$ items with high confidence, and the other twenty with low confidence. In this case his score would be 56. Again he loses relative to the score of 64 he might have obtained by having and using knowledge about the quality of his own knowledge.

The inferences to be drawn from this illustration are that in a true-false test in which the student rates his own answers, in terms of his confidence in them, the things that count most toward the size of his score are (1) his knowledge of the subject and (2) his knowledge about the quality of his own knowledge. When either or both of these are deficient, his score suffers. The distribution of his responses will suggest whether he has been too confident, too cautious, or unable to differentiate between what he knows well and knows poorly. But the total test score he receives is not a measure of his willingness or reluctance to gamble to any appreciable extent. It reflects mainly what he knows about the subject and to a lesser degree what he knows about the state of his own knowledge with respect to the subject.

Of course it is possible to use data from a student's responses to a confidence weighted test to obtain a score which *does* reflect willingness to gamble. Swineford derived such a score by dividing the number of errors on items for which the examinee requested maximum credit, at the risk of maximum penalty, by the total number of errors.[3] Intercorrelations of these gambling scores on four tests ranged from about .2 to about .8 and were sufficient to reveal a common factor of tendency to gamble. A score of this kind has interesting possibilities for research and perhaps might have some uses in guidance as well.

6. Empirical studies of confidence weighting

A study of specially weighted responses to true-false test items has been reported by Soderquist, who found that graduated credit for the examinee's degree of confidence in his answer, accompanied by graduated penalties for misplaced confidence, improved the reliability of true-false test scores significantly.[4]

The results of some other experimental trials of this system of confidence weighting of responses to true-false test items are shown in

---

[3] Frances Swineford, "Analysis of a Personality Trait," *Journal of Educational Psychology,* XXXII (1941), 438-44.

[4] Harold O. Soderquist, "A New Method of Weighting Scores in a True-False Test," *Journal of Educational Research,* XXX (1936), 290-92.

Table 5.3. All three tests were administered in periods of approximately one hour. The improvement factors indicate by how much the original test would have had to be lengthened, under conventional scoring, to achieve the same reliability as was obtained by weighted scoring. The gains attributable to the weighted scoring are equivalent to those that would have been expected had seventy to eighty-five items been added to the tests.

TABLE 5.3

Reliability of Conventional and Weighted True-False Test Scores

Test	Number of		Reliability		Improvement Factor
	Items	Students[d]	Conventional	Weighted	
Cronbach[a]	100	30	.574	.713	1.84
Vocabulary[b]	150	30	.765	.828	1.48
Thorndike[c]	101	30	.728	.821	1.72

[a] Based on the material in Cronbach's *Essentials of Psychological Testing*. This test was administered experimentally and taken by the students anonymously.

[b] A test of terms used in educational measurement. The terms in the test had not been studied individually and specifically.

[c] Based on the material in Thorndike and Hagen's *Measurement and Evaluation in Psychology and Education*. This was the final examination in the course.

[d] A group of thirty graduate students enrolled in a course on educational measurement at the University of Southern California in August, 1960.

Reliability coefficients of .80 or higher for classroom tests of educational achievement are quite respectable. This is especially true since these tests were composed of items that had not been selected or revised on the basis of previous tryout. The weighted scoring added a little to the work of scoring, but the gain in reliability may be worth the extra effort. In sum, this system of weighted scoring might supply a considerable part of the answer to the problem of unreliability due to guessing on true-false tests.

7. The problem of ambiguity

A second major problem that needs solution if true-false test items are to be used effectively in the measurement of educational achievement is the problem of ambiguity. It may be useful to begin by drawing a distinction between intrinsic ambiguity and apparent ambiguity. Students who say, "If I interpret the statement this way, I'd say it is true. But if I interpret it that way, I'd have to say it is false," are complaining about apparent ambiguity. But if experts in the field have the same difficulty in interpreting the same statement, the trouble may be intrinsic ambiguity.

Apparent ambiguity is a result, in part, of inadequacies in the student's knowledge. He has trouble interpreting the statement because the words mean something a little different to him than they do to the expert or because they do not bring to his mind as readily as they do to the expert's the associations necessary to make the intended interpretation clear. Hence apparent ambiguity is not only unavoidable, it may even be useful. By making the task of responding correctly harder for the poorly prepared than for the well-prepared student, it can help to discriminate between the two.

Thus a student's report that he does not understand a test question is not necessarily an indictment of the question. It may be, rather, an unintentional confession of his own shortcomings.

Intrinsic ambiguity, on the other hand, the kind of ambiguity that troubles the expert as much as or more than it troubles the novice, is not helpful at all. It probably can never be eliminated, since language is inherently somewhat abstract, general, and imprecise. But in the statements used in true-false test items it should be minimized.

The first line of defense against intrinsic ambiguity is the knowledge of the test constructor and his skill in using words to communicate his ideas as plainly as possible. The second line of defense is critical review of the items by other equally competent experts in the field covered by the test. Many instructors will have to rely mainly on their own knowledge and skill. Comments from students after the test has been returned may call attention to some intrinsic ambiguities that need correction. But the possibility that a statement *could be* misinterpreted, or indeed even the fact that it *was* misinterpreted, does not convict the statement of serious intrinsic ambiguity.

Statements that suffer from intrinsic ambiguity contribute little to, and may even detract from, the reliability of the test scores. The instructor who is seeking to make his tests as reliable as possible will guard as carefully as he can against intrinsically ambiguous true-false items. If his test produces scores of high reliability, he can feel confident that the items in it have not been seriously weakened by ambiguity. But if the scores are less reliable than he desires, intrinsic ambiguity in some of his test items may be to blame.

8. The problem of significance

A third problem involved in the use of true-false tests is that of choosing significant statements as a basis for the items. Most declarative sentences are intended to be true statements and hence might conceivably be used in a true-false test. However, as one reads an expository passage in a textbook, it comes as something of a surprise to find how few of the sentences would actually make good true-false test items. Some of them serve only to keep the reader informed of what the author is trying to do or to remind him of the structure and organization of the discussion. Some are so dependent for their meaning on sentences which precede or follow them that they are almost meaningless out of context. Some are intended only to suggest an idea, not to state it positively and precisely. Some include a whole logical argument, involving two or three propositions, in a single sentence. Some are intended not to describe what is true, but to prescribe what ought to be true. Some are expressed so loosely and so tentatively that there is hardly any possible basis for doubting them. In all the writing we do to preserve the knowledge we have gained and to communicate it to others there seem to be very few naturally occurring nuggets of established knowledge.

For this reason it is seldom possible to find in a text or reference work a sentence which can be copied directly for use as a true statement or transformed by a simple reversal for use as a false statement. The task of writing good true-false test items is more a task of creative writing than of copying. And it may be fortunate that it is so. For it helps the test constructor to avoid the hazard of writing items which would encourage and reward the learning of meaningless verbal sequences.

9. Suggestions for writing true-false test items

It may now be useful to restate the suggestions for writing true-false test items that were expressed or implied in the preceding discussions of ambiguity and significance and to add some others.

1. Base true or false items on propositions that are likely to be significant and useful in dealing with a wide variety of situations and problems.

2. Express the proposition as simply and as clearly as possible. Use words whose meanings are definite and precise.

3. Include enough background and information and qualifications so that the truth or falsity of the statement does not depend on some special, uncommon assumption.

4. Make the true statements true enough and the false statements false enough so that experts would unanimously agree on the answer.

5. Choose and state propositions so that their truth or falsity is not immediately obvious to every reasonable person.

6. Let each test item express a single idea. Avoid complex statements which unnecessarily combine several ideas. If it is necessary to include explanatory or qualifying elements in the statement, indicate clearly which part is to be judged true or false.

7. Do not create false statements from true ones simply by inserting the word "not." The task of judging the truth or falsity of a statement which says that something is *not* so can become highly and needlessly complex.

8. Word the statements so that sheer memory of words, empty phrases, or meaningless sentences will not permit a correct answer.

9. Guard against irrelevant clues, such as specific determiners, which would permit a test-wise but unprepared examinee to respond correctly.[5] Specific determiners refer to sweeping terms like "all," "always," "none," "never," "impossible," "inevitable," etc. Statements including such terms are likely to be false. On the other hand, statements including such qualifications as "usually," "sometimes," "often," etc. are likely to be true.

10. Illustrations of good and poor true-false items

Some good true-false items are shown in Exhibit 5.4. They include items testing factual knowledge, interpretations, computations, and applications. None of the items reproduces a conventional verbalization and hence none is likely to be answered successfully on that basis alone. Item 9, based on a comparison of two things, in this

---

[5] Ina H. Brinkmeier and G. M. Ruch, "Specific Determiners in True-False Statements," *Journal of Educational Research,* XXII (1930), 110-18.

case two quantities, and Item 10, based on a conditional if-then proposition, illustrate types that deserve wider use in true-false tests. Items 8 and 10 illustrate attractive false statements. The student who associates carbon dioxide with limewater on a very superficial

EXHIBIT 5.4

Illustrative True-False Test Items

(T) 1. Hodgkin's disease is characterized by an increase in the size of the lymph nodes.

Subject: Pathology
Level: College
Type: Fact

(F) 2. A receiver in bankruptcy acquires title to the bankrupt's property.

Subject: Business Law
Level: College
Type: Fact

(T) 3. Protective tariffs were consistent with the principles of the mercantilist system.

Subject: Economics
Level: College
Type: Interpretation

(T) 4. An eclipse of the sun can only occur when the moon is new.

Subject: Astronomy
Level: High School
Type: Interpretation

(F) 5. The radius of a circle whose area is 75 would be greater than 5.

Subject: Arithmetic
Level: Upper Grades
Type: Computation

(T) 6. The quantity 11,800 can also be written 11.8×10^3.

Subject: Mathematics
Level: High School
Type: Interpretation

(F) 7. The complete combustion of one molecule of $C_{24}H_{50}$ requires seventy-four molecules of oxygen.

Subject: Chemistry
Level: High School
Type: Computation

(F) 8. Limewater is a convenient source of carbon dioxide.

Subject: Chemistry
Level: High School
Type: Fact

(T) 9. More heat energy is required to warm a gallon of cool water from 50°F. to 80°F. than to heat a pint of the same cool water to boiling point.

Subject: Physics
Level: High School
Type: Computation

(F) 10. If heat is supplied at a constant rate to melt and vaporize a substance, the temperature of the substance will increase at a constant rate also.

Subject: Physics
Level: High School
Type: Application

basis is likely to mark Item 8 true. One who responds to Item 10 on the basis of common sense, ignoring the heat absorption and constancy of temperature during melting and vaporization, is likely to mark it as true also.

But none of the items provides a complete pattern, on the basis of which good items can be written by imitation alone. The instructor's thorough mastery of the subject, his skill in verbal communication, and his ingenuity in creating new settings for familiar principles and in devising plausible-looking false statements are the really important qualifications for the writing of effective true-false items.

The items in Exhibit 5.5 illustrate faults the writer of true-false items should be aware of and should shun. Items 1, 2, and 3 violate the first principle in Section 9 of this chapter, which suggests that true-false items should be based on significant and useful propositions.

Items 1 and 2 also illustrate the use of poorly chosen sentences rather than essential ideas as the basis for true-false items. The truth or falsity of Item 1 is of concern only to the writer and the reader of a particular passage. Item 2 is clearly intended to express the author's own enthusiasm for camping. It is not intended to express precisely a proposition that the author has discovered and that could be tested for truth or falsity.

Item 3 is trivial. What it says is hardly worth knowing. What it omits—the nature of the relation and of its significance—is far more important.

Item 4 violates the second principle, which suggests that true-false items should be expressed as simply and clearly as possible. The wording of this item is careless and redundant. The essential idea could be expressed much more clearly and simply in these words:

> 4. Costs for the construction and maintenance of United States highways in a state are shared by both state and Federal governments. (T)

Item 5 does not include sufficient information or qualification (Principle 3, p. 138) to make it unequivocally false. A single rain cloud may weigh more than 100,000 tons, but one cubic foot of it may weigh approximately the same as a cubic foot of air. Whether it is called light or heavy depends on whether one considers density or total weight. Even a very well-informed person would have trouble deciding which interpretation was intended.

EXHIBIT 5.5

Faulty True-False Items

1. Two pitfalls should be avoided in writing true-false test items. (F)
2. Camping has a good past, a better present, and an almost unlimited future. (T)
3. The relation between a parasite and its host is significant. (T)
4. When you see a highway with a marker which says "Iowa U.S. 218" you know that the construction and upkeep of that road is built and maintained by the state and Federal governments. (T)
5. Rain clouds are light in weight. (F)
6. Merit is an important factor affecting a teacher's salary. (F)
7. Frozen foods of the highest quality may be ruined in the kitchen. (T)
8. Insurance agencies may be either specialized or general. (T)
9. As a result of mistakes in our foreign policy, the Communists won control of China after World War II. (T)
10. Life is a continuous process of choice-making, sacrificing one human value for another, which goes through the following steps: spontaneous mental selections regarding everything we want, conflicting preferences hold each other in check, hesitation becomes deliberation as we weigh and compare values, finally a choice or preference emerges. (T)
11. Columbus did not make four voyages of exploration to the Western hemisphere. (F)
12. For every action there is an equal and opposite reaction. (T)
13. Objective tests are useful in measuring all aspects of educational achievement. (F)
14. Stars send out light that twinkles. (T)

Item 6 violates the fourth principle. It is not sufficiently true or false so that experts could be expected to agree on the answer. Across the country it is no doubt true that the salaries of good teachers are higher than the salaries of poor teachers. However it is also true that the salary schedules of many school systems, and the minimum salaries specified in many state codes, do not include merit as a factor related to salary at all.

Items 7 and 8 are too obviously true on a common-sense basis to function well at test items (Principle 5). Who could doubt the possibility of cooking any kind of food badly, or the possibility of general as well as specialized insurance agencies. The trouble with Items 7 and 8 is that they were based on accessory sentences in a discussion, not on an important uncommon idea.

Principle 6 is violated by items 9 and 10. Item 9 involves two elements, whose truth or falsity is not necessarily identical. It is true that the Communists won control of China following World War II. Whether this was a result of mistakes in our foreign policy is less clear, even to experts. If it were true and if the item writer wished to make clear that this was what the item was testing, he might reword it to read:

> 9. The Communists won control of China following World
>   War II because of mistakes in our foreign policy. (T)

Item 10 is an even more obvious example of failure to narrow a statement to a single issue and to focus on it as a basis for testing. Nor does it reflect very clear expression of logical thinking. To defend such a statement as true simply because it is quoted verbatim from some authoritative source is to place a premium on sheer verbal memory and a penalty on independent thought and understanding.

Item 11 violates Principle 7. A false statement has been created simply by inserting a "not" in an otherwise true statement. An examinee might easily disagree with the statement and then mark it true because he knows that what it says essentially *is* true. Columbus *did* make four voyages of exploration to the Western hemisphere.

Item 12 could unduly reward an examinee who learns words instead of understandings (Principle 8). It is an instructional cliché. A student might identify it as something he has seen or heard from a usually reliable source, and correctly identify it as a true statement on that basis, without any real conception of its meaning or any ability to use it.

Item 13 illustrates how the discriminating power of a true-false item may be spoiled by a specific determiner, in this case the word "all" (Principle 9). Even an enthusiastic teacher of a course in classroom testing would have reservations about so sweeping a statement. Most of his students would reject it on a common-sense basis.

Item 14 violates Principle 4, either because of the carelessness in expression or the limited knowledge of the person who wrote it. There is no more "twinkling" in the light sent out by Arcturus or Polaris than there is in the light sent out by the sun. But the light from distant stars, viewed through air currents typical of our atmosphere, *appears* to twinkle when viewed from the Earth. A better statement of Item 14 might be:

> 14. The light from stars appears to twinkle more than the light from planets. (T)

11. Techniques for developing true-false test items

True-false items are based on propositions that the test constructor regards as important and relevant to the purposes of the test. A large part of the art of writing good true-false test items is the art of selecting the right propositions on which to base them. The test constructor's knowledge of the subject matter of his test, and perhaps his educational values as well, will determine the quality of his selections of propositions to test.

Beyond the selection of propositions to test, however, there are two other skills essential to the writing of good true-false items. There is skill in finding novel restatements of the essence of the proposition, or significant implications of it, so as to write true statements that will be seen as true only by those who understand the proposition. There is also skill in clothing some antithesis of the proposition in words and phrases that sound familiarly and sincerely true, to confound the student whose knowledge is superficially verbalistic.

Ideally, true-false items are written as pairs of one true and one false expression of the same essential point. If the item writer cannot think of a plausible false alternative to a true statement, or a nonobvious true alternative to a false statement, then the proposition under consideration is probably not suitable as a basis for a true-false test item. It goes without saying that one would seldom want to use both members of a true-false pair in the same test. Further, in the illustrations that follow where diverse approaches to testing the same basic idea are illustrated, only one approach would ordinarily be used in testing a particular idea in a single test. Different approaches, of course, might be used in testing different ideas in the same test.

Five suggestions are offered for developing true items. The suggestions are illustrated with items that might be derived from these two more or less conventionally stated propositions.

1. The economic philosophy of mercantilism involved government regulation of business to serve national interests.
2. An eclipse is caused by the shadow of one body in the solar system falling on another.

No special suggestions for writing false items are offered beyond the general suggestion of wording some contradiction of the true statement so that it sounds plausible. But, following the general recommendation that true-false items be written in pairs, a false version of each true statement is illustrated.

Suggestion 1. Restate the essential idea in different words.

True versions	False versions
Under the mercantile system, laws controlling production and trade are enacted for the purpose of strengthening the entire country.	Under the mercantile system, industries regulate their own production and prices.
When some of the light from a star like the sun to a planet like the earth is blocked by some other body like the moon, an eclipse is said to occur.	When light from a star like the sun is reflected from a planet like the earth onto some other body like the moon, an eclipse is said to occur.

Suggestion 2. Restate a part of the original idea.

True versions	False versions
The mercantile system requires legislative support.	The mercantile system requires corporate income taxes.
All eclipses involve shadows.	If light rays could not be bent, eclipses could not occur.

Suggestion 3. Relate the basic idea to some other idea.

True versions	False versions
Mercantilism and free trade are incompatible.	Mercantilism requires free trade.

True versions	False versions
An eclipse of the moon can only occur when the moon is full.	An eclipse of the moon can only occur when the moon is new.

Suggestion 4. Develop implications of the basic idea.

True versions	False versions
Mercantilism requires a strong central government.	Mercantilism requires strong local autonomy in government.
Prediction of eclipses requires information on the orbital motions of the bodies involved.	Prediction of eclipses requires information on the inclination of the earth's axis.

Suggestion 5. Infer the effect of different (even impossible) circumstances.

True versions	False versions
If there were no trade between nations, mercantilism would be pointless.	If there were no trade between nations, mercantilism would be far more effective.
If there were no luminous astronomical bodies like the sun, eclipses would not be observed.	Eclipses cannot occur in the presence of luminous stars.

The foregoing are not all the possible true-false items that could be developed on the essential ideas underlying mercantilism and eclipses. Probably some much better than those displayed here could be composed. But these illustrations may serve to show the diverse variations that can be developed as means for testing a student's command of an idea. They may suggest that true-false items are not limited to testing simple recall but can present novel problems for the examinee to think through and attempt to solve.

Each true statement that is included in a test should permit the test constructor to say of it: "The truth of this statement is not obvious to everyone, but I can provide evidence to show that it is essentially true." Each false statement that is included in a test should permit the test constructor to say of it: "This statement reads like a plausibly true statement, but I can provide evidence to show that it is essentially false." If the items pass these tests, they are likely to be good true-false test items.

12. Desirable balance between true and false statements

Several investigators have found that false statements tend to discriminate somewhat more sharply between students of high and low achievement than do the true statements.[6] This may be due to what is called an "acquiescent response set." In the absence of firm knowledge a student seems more likely to accept than to question a declarative statement whose truth or falsity he must judge.

Instructions for preparing true-false tests sometimes suggest that about the same number of false statements as true should be included in the test. But if the false statements tend to be higher in discrimination, it would be advantageous to include a higher proportion of them, perhaps as many as 60 per cent. One cannot afford to go too far in this direction, however. If a test constructor were to make a practice of including as many as three false statements to each true statement, the students would be likely to recognize the imbalance and might use it to gain an unwarranted advantage in answering doubtful questions. "When in doubt, mark it false" would be a good rule to follow when false statements outnumber true statements appreciably.

13. Summary

Some of the main ideas developed in this chapter are summarized in the following fifteen statements.

1. True-false items have lost favor, perhaps unjustifiably, since the early days of objective testing.
2. True-false items have been criticized for triviality, for ambiguity, for encouragement of rote learning, for susceptibility to guessing, and for exposing students to error instead of to truth.

---

[6] Lee J. Cronbach, "Studies of Acquiescence as a Factor in True-False Test," *Journal of Educational Psychology*, XXX (1942), 401-15; Robert L. Ebel, "Some Tests of Competence in Educational Measurement," *The 17th Yearbook of the National Council on Measurements Used in Education* (East Lansing, Mich.: Michigan State University, 1960), pp. 93-104; Alexander G. Wesman, "The Usefulness of Correctly Spelled Words in a Spelling Test," *Journal of Educational Psychology*, XXXVII (April, 1946), 242-46.

3. True-false items are efficient and convenient and can provide direct tests of a student's command of essential knowledge.

4. Many important aspects of achievement can be tested equally well by using either true-false or multiple-choice test items.

5. The influence of guessing on true-false test scores can be limited by a system of scoring that awards extra credit for right answers, as the risk of extra penalties for wrong answers, to those answers that the examinee gives confidently.

6. Confidence-weighted scores on true-false tests reward examinees whose confidence matches their knowledge and penalize examinees whose confidence is too great or too small.

7. Empirical studies show that confidence weighting improves test reliability.

8. Good true-false items may appear ambiguous to novices but should not appear ambiguous to experts.

9. Few textbook sentences are significant enough, and meaningful enough out of context, to be used as the true statements in a true-false test.

10. The difference between true statements and false statements in a true-false test should be so wide that the true statements are not spoiled nor false statements created by minor imperfections.

11. Good true-false statements express single, not multiple, ideas.

12. In general, good false statements are not created by inserting the word "not" in a true statement.

13. Avoid give-away adjectives like "sometimes," "usually," or "often" in true statements, or "always," "never," or "impossible" in false statements.

14. Make false items plausible by using familiar words and phrases in seemingly straightforward factual statements.

15. False statements tend to make more discriminating test items than true statements.

REFERENCES

Brinkmeier, Ina H. and G. M. Ruch, "Specific Determiners in True-False Statements," *Journal of Educational Research*, XXII (1930), 110-18.

Cronbach, Lee J., "Studies of Acquiescence as a Factor in True-False Tests," *Journal of Educational Psychology*, XXX (1942), 401-15.

Ebel, Robert L., "Some Tests of Competence in Educational Measurement," *The Seventeenth Yearbook of the National Council on Measurements Used in Education,* pp. 93-104. East Lansing, Mich.: Michigan State University, 1960.

Ross, C. C., *Measurement in Today's Schools* (2d ed.), p. 349. Englewood Cliffs, N.J.: Prentice-Hall, Inc., 1947.

Ruch, G. M., *The Objective or New-Type Examination,* p. 368. Chicago: Scott, Foresman & Company, 1929.

Soderquist, Harold O., "A New Method of Weighting Scores in a True-False Test," *Journal of Educational Research,* XXX (1936), 290-92.

Swineford, Frances, "Analysis of a Personality Trait," *Journal of Educational Psychology,* XXXII (1941), 438-44.

Wesman, Alexander G., "The Usefulness of Correctly Spelled Words in a Spelling Test," *Journal of Educational Psychology,* XXXVII (April, 1946), 242-46.

6 How to Write Multiple-Choice Test Items

Having written three words, the poet must choose a fourth. It doesn't just happen: it must be chosen. And having written four he must choose a fifth. And so on for all the elements of the poem—every image, every metric emphasis, every last comma must be selected for admission. The good poet is defined by the quality of the choices he makes—by the exactness of his demands, and by the rigidity of his refusal to make cheap choices.

JOHN CIARDI

1. The use of multiple-choice items in classroom testing

Multiple-choice test items are currently the most highly regarded and widely used form of objective test item. They are adaptable to the measurement of most important educational outcomes—knowledge, understanding, and judgment; ability to solve problems, to recommend appropriate action, to make predictions. Almost any understanding or ability that can be tested by means of any other item form—short answer, completion, true-false, matching or essay—can also be tested by means of multiple-choice test items.

The form of the multiple-choice item, with the stem asking or implying a direct question, provides a realistic, naturally appropriate setting for testing student achievement. There tends to be less indirectness and artifice in multiple-choice than some other item forms. Students often find multiple-choice questions less ambiguous than completion or true-false items. Instructors find it easier to defend the correct answers to them.

Finally, multiple-choice items seem to both instructors and students to be less susceptible to chance errors resulting from guessing than true-false items. It is easy to exaggerate the harm done by guessing, and, as pointed out in Chapter 5, true-false items can be used with special instructions for administration and scoring that will practically eliminate guessing. But as these two forms are ordinarily used, correct response by guessing is unquestionably a more serious handicap of true-false than of multiple-choice test items.

In spite of their virtues, multiple-choice test items have not escaped the attention of critics. Some of the criticisms reflect a general mistrust of all objective testing techniques. These critics allege that objective test questions are inevitably superficial, ambiguous, and conducive to guessing. They say or imply that the only good way to test is the old way they prefer to use—namely, essay testing. Other critics find fault with specific test items, alleging that the questions are ambiguous, the correct answers incorrect, or the distractors as good as or better than the intended correct answer.

Few objective tests or test items are so perfect as to be above reproach from a persistent, perceptive critic. But there are at least two weaknesses in the general indictments that have been issued against all multiple-choice tests and test items. First, the criticisms are seldom supported by unbiased experimental data, despite the fact that relevant data would be fairly easy to obtain. Most of the flaws pointed out should lower the discriminating power of the items and the reliability of the test scores. Some of the critics, instead of obtaining or even welcoming experimental evidence, tend to discredit statistical methods of testing the quality of items or tests, without suggesting any procedure to replace it other than their own intuitions (and occasionally those of a few friends) and what seems to them to be plain common sense.

In the second place, the critics seldom attempt seriously to make a good case for a better way of measuring educational achievement. Even the most ardent advocate of objective testing does not claim perfection. He acknowledges that multiple-choice test questions can be subject to serious flaws and that, in general, they are not as clearly meaningful and sharply discriminating as they should be. He agrees wholly with the observation that objective test scores are not as reliable as they might be and ought to be for maximum value. But he is likely to reject the suggestion that multiple-choice testing should be abandoned. He is fairly certain that whatever might replace it would have most of the same shortcomings, probably to an even greater degree. In addition, he has reason to believe that the implied alternative, essay testing, would be much less convenient to use in many situations. He would accept and respect dependable evidence that there are much better ways for measuring educational achievement. But he is not likely to consider seriously any recommendations accompanied by expressions of disdain for experimental evidence.

Multiple-choice test items can serve a useful purpose in the measurement of educational achievement. This chapter will present nine suggestions for making effective use of this item form. Then some illustrations of desirable characteristics of multiple-choice test items will be presented.

2. Suggestions for preparing good multiple-choice test items

1. Develop multiple-choice test items on the basis of independently meaningful and demonstrably valid statements of relevant, important ideas.

Most items of information about word meanings or matters of fact and the basis of most explanations, decisions, calculations, and predictions can be expressed as statements or propositions. In practice, few item writers take the trouble to express the ideas they are testing in written statements, but ideas of this kind are implicit in most of the questions they ask. Novices at item writing and even some experienced professionals find that explicit statements of item ideas are useful in selecting the most promising ideas and in developing sound multiple-choice test items from them. Samples of topics for items in a test on classroom testing, adequate statements of item ideas related to these topics, and the translation of the ideas into multiple-choice test items are illustrated in Exhibit 6.1.

EXHIBIT 6.1

Examples of Item Topics, Item Ideas, and Test Items for a Test on the Construction of Classroom Tests

Topic: Table of specifications

Idea: The test constructor should draw up an outline or table of specifications, indicating the relative emphasis that will be given to each of the various areas of content or objectives of instruction.

Item: What is the principal function of the table of specifications for a test?

1. To enable the scorer to know which response to each item is correct

2. To help students prepare properly for the test

*3. To guide the test constructor toward writing the appropriate numbers of various kinds of items

4. To provide data for calculating reliability of test scores

Topic: Test difficulty

Idea: An objective classroom test is of appropriate difficulty if the mean score is about midway between the maximum possible score and the expected chance score.

Item: A sixty-item objective test composed of four-response multiple-choice items is given at the end of a course. What data would provide the best evidence as to whether or not the test is of appropriate difficulty?

*1. The class mean of the numbers of items answered correctly is 27.5.

2. The distribution of scores is approximately normal.

3. A few items are answered correctly by all students.

4. The reliability coefficient for the test is .50.

Topic: Spearman-Brown formula

Idea: The Spearman-Brown formula is used to estimate the reliability of a test similar to a given test, but of different length.

Item: When is the Spearman-Brown formula useful in estimating test reliability?

1. When the same test has been given twice to the same group

2. When the only available data are the number of items in the test and the mean and standard deviation of the scores

3. When one knows the number of items in the test and the difficulty of each item

*4. When a coefficient of correlation between scores on the odd-numbered items and on the even-numbered items in test has been calculated

A good practical reason for basing multiple-choice test items on well selected statements of appropriate ideas is that statements of this kind provide the foundation for good instruction in many courses. Good materials of instruction—texts, references, lecture notes, etc.—should provide a convenient source from which to select key statements for conversion into test items.

But many of the statements teachers utter or text authors write are not entirely meaningful apart from the context in which they appear. Many are only suggestive, not definitive. Many are not wholly true or objectively verifiable. Many are not entirely relevant to the purposes of instruction in the course. These statements differ widely in importance. Many are quite trivial. Some teachers invent their own terminology and emphasize their own opinions. Items based on such unique visions of truth are not likely to have the general validity essential to good test items. Some ideas are so commonplace and others so abstruse that questions based on them would almost inevitably be too easy or too difficult to differentiate effectively among levels of achievement in the groups to be tested.

Laws, principles, and generalizations tend to be more important than specific incidents or details. However, the statements of such laws, principles, and generalizations may be memorized as relatively meaningless word sequences. This calls attention to one danger in basing multiple-choice test items on statements identical with those that have been used in instruction. The wording of the item may duplicate the statement so closely that verbal memory could provide as good a basis for correct response as would clear understanding. Good item writing avoids this danger by rephrasing the idea or seeking novel illustrations or applications of it. The aim of good item writing is to yield evidence of understanding, of command of the idea as a tool in thinking, rather than evidence of recall of the conventional verbal expression of the idea.

To a considerable degree the quality of any educational achievement test depends on the meaningfulness, truthfulness, relevance, and importance of the ideas on which the test items are based. If the test constructor can supplement his own subjective judgments of these qualities with those from competent colleagues, their consensus is likely to yield an even better test.

2. Choose item topics and ideas and write multiple-choice test items with a view to maximizing the discriminating power of the items.

The uses made of multiple-choice tests of classroom achievement usually require single scores for each student tested. The main purpose of such scores is to summarize and express numerically the student's general level of competence in the area covered by the test. The complex nature of mental abilities, and the limitations of available techniques for assessing them, limit most test scores to relative meaning and limit the precision of even that relative meaning. For a test item to contribute substantially to the precision of relative measures of general competence in a complex, often heterogeneous area of achievement, it must discriminate. That is, students having more of the general competence the test is intended to measure should have greater success than students of less competence in answering each test question correctly.

Methods of measuring the discriminating power of a test item and of improving item discrimination are presented and discussed in Chapter 11. But it is important for the test constructor to keep this requirement in mind during the initial writing of multiple choice or any other type of item for use in an educational test. The job of the item is to discriminate different levels of achievement in the area covered by the course. Most students of high achievement should answer it correctly. Most students of low achievement should miss it. The item writer should choose topics and ideas for testing which are likely to discriminate in this way. He should word the question and the intended correct answer to it and should choose and word the distracters so as to enhance the probable difference between good and poor students in their success on the item.

The basis on which the item discriminates is extremely important. For classroom tests of educational achievement that basis should not be general intelligence, or reading ability, or test-wiseness. Each item should require understanding or ability whose development is a special objective of the particular course of study. Even a bright, sophisticated student should have trouble with the item unless he has learned, in that course or elsewhere, the particular understanding or ability the item is testing.

It is sometimes suggested that the final examination for a course should be given as a pretest early in the course so that final course marks can be based on the student's growth during the course, not on what he knew before starting the course as well. Some objections that have been raised to basing marks on apparent growth are discussed in Chapter 13. But there is another, perhaps better, reason for giving the course final as a pretest. Such a procedure will help to identify items that are unlikely to discriminate on the basis of specific course achievement. If most of the students can answer an achievement test question before that achievement has been taught, then either the question is a poor question or that particular achievement need not be taught in the course in question.

The following assignment has been used in courses on test construction to emphasize the importance of writing test items for the purpose of discrimination.

Discrimination Item Assignment

Write one copy of a short paragraph (three to seven sentences) expressing an idea which is sure to be new to practically all members of this class, and which you feel is important for them to know. Then write one copy of a four-response multiple-choice item designed to discriminate between those who have this idea and those who do not. Turn in the item on one sheet of $8\frac{1}{2}$ x 11 paper with your name on the face of it and the correct response on the back. Keep the paragraph.

At the next class meeting after the items have been turned in, the class will be divided into two approximately equal groups in separate rooms. The members of each group will read their paragraphs to each other. When all paragraphs have been read the students will take a test composed of items written by members of both groups. Each student will also be asked to pick out the five items (other than his own) that deal with the most important ideas, and the five he considers least important.

Your score on this assignment will be (1) the difference in proportions of correct response between the group that heard your paragraph and the other group, plus (2) the proportion of the total group rating your item as one of the five most important.

The effect of this practice exercise is to artificially create two groups of students which do not differ appreciably in general level of ability but which can, and should, differ greatly in their competence to answer specific questions. To score highly on the assignment the student must succeed in (1) choosing an important new idea, (2) writing a concise, clear exposition of the idea, and (3) translating the idea into a multiple-choice test question that all the student's classmates are likely to consider important but that only those who have heard the exposition will be able to answer correctly. The student's individual items are either read twice to the class slowly or presented by means of an opaque projector. This assignment serves to call attention to the importance of item discrimination and also to make the students keenly aware of shortcomings in item writing, or in the choice of ideas to test, which may spoil the discriminating power of a test item.

> *3. Arrange to write the initial item drafts so that subsequent revision and assembly into the finished test will be as convenient as possible.*

Revision is facilitated if the initial draft is written in pencil and if each item is written, well spaced, on a separate sheet of paper. The sheet should be identified by words or a code indicating what type of question (vocabulary, factual, etc.) is being asked and what topic it deals with. If based on an explicitly stated item idea, the idea may be written on the page and a specific reference to its source may be indicated. It is best not to number the items until they have been arranged in the order in which they will appear in the test.

Quite naturally the first part of the item to be written is the question or introductory statement. This is usually referred to as the "stem" or "lead" of the item. Not so obviously, the next part to be written in the first draft is the intended answer. The intended answer is the most important alternative and deserves priority in attention while the question it is supposed to answer is fresh in mind. If an adequate answer cannot be written, there is no point in worrying about distracters.

But while the intended answer should be written next after the item stem, it should not always be written in the space directly below the item stem on the page. Its placement among the responses should be varied randomly even in the first drafts of the items. Unless this is done, an unbiased review of the item is difficult to manage. The best approach to a critical review of the substance of a test item is for the reviewer to act like an examinee—to seek the correct answer to the item. Such an approach obviously requires that the correct answer should not always appear at the same place among the alternatives. One way to manage this operation is to prepare a reasonably random sequence of the digits one to four and use it as a guide to placement of correct responses among the four alternatives. A random sequence can be obtained from a well-shuffled deck of cards if each club is recorded as a one, each diamond as a two, each heart as a three, and each spade as a four.

An otherwise formidable task of item writing can be made more manageable if the total number of items required is divided into a daily quota. An item writer familiar with his material and working from an adequate test plan may be able to turn out the first drafts of ten promising multiple-choice items in an hour or two. By working this long each day for ten days, he may produce an entire test.

The order in which test items are arranged in the final form of the test is not critical. If different types of items—multiple choice, matching, etc.—are included in the same test, there is some advantage in grouping each type together. It is sometimes desirable, for psychological reasons, to begin the test with several rather easy items to help relieve the initial tension examinees sometimes feel. But for most classroom tests the items do not, and should not, vary widely in obvious difficulty. Hence it is not feasible, even if it were considered desirable, to arrange them very precisely in order of difficulty. There is some logic, but not overwhelming, in arranging the items in topical groups. There is little reason to arrange them by type of question, vocabulary, factual, etc., unless a separate score on each kind of question is to be obtained.

> 4. *Begin the item with a stem question or incomplete statement to which a reasonably adequate answer or completion can be given concisely and for which plausible wrong answers can be found.*

The function of the item stem is to acquaint the examinee with the problem that is being posed for him. Ideally, it should state or imply a specific question. While words can sometimes be saved without loss of clarity by using an incomplete statement as the item stem, a direct question is often better. Not only does a direct question tend to present the student with a more specific problem, it also may focus the item writer's purposes more clearly and help him to avoid irrelevance or unrelatedness in the distracters. Incidentally, one easy way to start a bad multiple-choice test item is to use the subject of a sentence as the item stem and its predicate as the correct response.

When an incomplete sentence is used as the item stem, the problem it presents to the examinee will usually be clearest if the omitted part comes at the end of the sentence, not the beginning or a middle portion. However, if the part omitted is only a word, short phrase, or number, the location of the missing portion is less crucial.

Novel questions and novel problem situations reward the critical-minded student who has sought to understand what he was taught. They penalize the superficial learner. It is usually desirable to avoid using the same questions or problems in a test that were used in instruction. In general, bona fide questions such as would be asked by a person honestly seeking information are likely to be more important than quiz-type questions, which would only be asked by someone who already knew the answer. Here is an example of a bona fide question:

> Who were the Huks in the Philippines?
> 1. A tribe of primitive head-hunters
> *2. A Communist-supported rebel group
> 3. Wealthy Philippine landowners and industrialists
> 4. Members of the minority party in the Philippine legislature

This is a question which might occur naturally to a person seeking information. It is not one which has been invented to test a student's recall of particular instructional materials. It is consistent with the idea that the main objectives of instruction are to impart information useful outside the classroom. In contrast, a quiz-type question like the following is less desirable:

> J. B. Matthews, one-time employee of Senator McCarthy's subcommittee, charged that a large number of supporters of Communism in the United States would be found in which of these groups?
> 1. Wall Street bankers
> 2. Newspaper editors
> 3. Professional gamblers
> *4. Protestant clergymen

This item is typical of one asked by someone who already knows the answer and simply wishes to see if the examinee knows it also. It is not a natural, honest question. While it may discriminate between those having more and those having less information, often it is related only indirectly to fundamental objectives of education.

It sometimes seems desirable to phrase the stem question to ask not for the correct answer, but for the incorrect answer. For example, "Which of these is *not* a means of heat transmission?" Such questions should be used sparingly and carefully. They tend to trap the examinee, who easily forgets while pondering his answer that he is looking for a wrong answer, not a correct one. Negatively stated items seem most attractive when used in relation to formal categories or unique lists of causes, factors, etc. Frequently such categories and lists are matters of organizational convenience and lack the general validity or importance which make them good bases for test items.

Another common device for adapting multiple-choice items to questions which seem to require several correct answers is to add to the correct answers listed separately the alternative "all of the above" as the correct response. But use of this response is strictly appropriate only if all the preceding alternatives are thoroughly correct answers to the stem question, and even then there is the inherent ambiguity in this device. A correct answer should not be wrong simply because there are other correct answers. "All of the above" should be used sparingly as an alternative to multiple-choice test items.

The response "none of the above" is also sometimes used as the intended answer when no other good answer is provided or as a distracter when a good answer is provided. It is particularly useful in multiple-choice arithmetic or spelling items where the distinction between correctness and error is unequivocal. But this response, like "all of the above," should *not* be used unless the best answer is a thoroughly correct answer.

It is usually desirable to express the stem of the item so that it asks as directly, accurately, and simply as possible for the essential knowledge or ability which the item is intended to test. The following item stem seems needlessly complex:

> Considered from an economic viewpoint, which of these
> proposals to maintain world peace derives the least sup-

port from the military potentialities of atomic energy?
1. An international police force should be established.
2. Permanent programs of universal military training
should be adopted.
*3. Sizes of standing military forces should be in-
creased.
4. The remaining democratic nations of the world
should enter into a military alliance.

Even after repeated careful readings, the meaning of this item stem
is not clear. It involves a negative approach and seems to combine
two dissimilar bases for judgment, economics and atomic energy.
The wording of this item might seem to reflect lack of clarity in the
thinking of the person who wrote it.

Informational preambles which serve only as window dressing and
do not help the examinee understand the question he is being asked
should ordinarily be avoided. But it is well to specify all conditions
and qualifications necessary to make the intended response definitely
the best of the available alternatives. If many descriptive or qualifying ideas are required, the clearest expression may be achieved by
placing them in separate introductory sentences. In general, the item
writer should avoid addressing the examinee personally, as if asking
for his opinion rather than for a general truth. Try to avoid implying something in the item stem which is not strictly true, even
though this does not interfere logically with the choice of a correct
response to the item. For example:

Why is blood plasma often preferred to whole blood for
transfusions?
1. Whole blood may carry disease germs.
*2. Whole blood must be "typed" to match the blood
of the patient.
3. Plasma can be prepared synthetically.
4. Plasma contains more disease-fighting white corpus-
cles than whole blood.

It is incorrect to state that blood plasma is preferred to whole blood.
If whole blood of the proper type is available, it is usually preferred.
The stem should ask what advantage blood plasma has over whole
blood, for it is true that the plasma need not be typed.

5. *Phrase the intended correct response so that it is thoroughly correct or clearly adequate, expressed as clearly and concisely as possible, without providing clues which give it away to the clever but poorly prepared student.*

Ideally, the intended answer to a multiple-choice question should be a thoroughly correct answer, admitting no difference of opinion among adequately informed experts. This kind of absolute correctness, however, is difficult to achieve except in formal logical systems or in statements which simply reproduce other statements. Few, if any, inductive truths or experimentally based generalizations can be regarded as absolutely true. The test constructor must base many of his items on propositions which are not known certainly to be absolutely true but which are strongly probable. But he should guard against basing items on statements whose validity would be challenged by competent scholars.

In this connection there are two damaging extremes to avoid. One is failure to qualify the question or problem sufficiently to exclude alternative interpretations which lead to different but equally defensible correct answers. The other is qualifying the question in such a way that its truth becomes unequivocal but the question itself becomes inconsequential. For example, it is important to know why the armed forces of the United States were ordered into combat in Korea in 1950, but it is difficult to give a thoroughly correct answer to such a question. On the other hand, it is quite easy to give an unequivocally truthful answer to the question, "What explanation for U.S. military action in Korea was given in an editorial in the *Chicago Tribune* on Friday, June 30, 1950?" But the answer to such a reiterative type of question may not be highly important. The item writer must often steer between the Scylla of indefiniteness and the Charybdis of triviality. He should never settle for a best answer when a correct answer to the same question is available. He should be sure that, in the eyes of competent experts, his best answer is clearly better than any other alternative offered. But he should not avoid important questions, simply because no absolutely and completely correct answer is available for them.

The correct response to a multiple-choice test item sets the pattern for the other responses, the distracters. All responses should be parallel in grammatical structure, semantically similar, and roughly equivalent in length and complexity, since all are intended to be alternative responses to the same question. Obviously the alternatives should be described completely enough to be clearly meaningful, but no words should be wasted in the process and needless structural complexity should be avoided. Parallel structure sometimes requires that all responses should begin with the same word. But if the same group of words is repeated in each response, the possibility of including that phrase only once in the stem should be considered.

Brevity in the responses simplifies the task for the examinee by removing an irrelevant source of difficulty. Brief responses also tend to focus attention on the essential differences among the alternatives offered. Other things being equal, the multiple-choice test item having the shorter responses will be the better. But a test composed largely of items using one-word responses or very short phrases is likely to place more emphasis on vocabulary than on command of knowledge. The item writer should not sacrifice importance and significance in the questions to gain brevity in the responses.

Some irrelevant clues to the correct answer in multiple-choice test items may be due to lack of parallelism in the alternatives offered. There is a tendency for item writers to express the correct answer more carefully and at greater length than the other alternatives. Sometimes revealing key words from the item stem, or their synonyms, are repeated in the correct answer. Sometimes the correct response is more consistent grammatically or semantically with the item stem than are the other responses. Sometimes the correct response is more general and inclusive than any distracter. Sometimes a familiar verbal stereotype is used as the correct answer, so that a student can respond successfully simply by recalling vaguely that he had encountered those same words before. Finally, it sometimes happens that the stem of one item will inadvertently suggest the answer to another item. Here are some examples of items which provide irrelevant clues:

> When used in conjunction with the T-square, the left vertical edge of a triangle is used to draw:
> *1. Vertical lines
> 2. Slant lines
> 3. Horizontal lines
> 4. Inclined lines

The use of the word "vertical" in both the stem and the correct response of this item provides an obvious clue.

> The minor differences among organisms of the same kind
> are known as:
>   1. Heredity
>   *2. Variations
>   3. Adaptation
>   4. Natural selection

The plural term "differences" in the stem calls for a plural response. This points directly to response 2 as the correct response.

> The major weakness of our government under the Articles of Confederation was that
>   1. There were no high officials.
>   *2. It lacked power.
>   3. It was very difficult to amend.
>   4. There was only one house in Congress.

There is an obvious relation between lack of power and weakness of government. If one knew nothing about the Articles of Confederation, he would nevertheless tend to choose the correct answer on this common-sense basis alone.

> How did styles in women's clothing in 1950 differ most
> from those in 1900?
>   1. They showed more beauty.
>   2. They showed more variety.
>   3. They were easier to clean.
>   *4. They were easier to live in, to work in, to move in,
>   and were generally less restrictive.

The greater detail used in stating the correct response makes it undesirably obvious.

> History tells us that all nations have enjoyed participation in:
>   1. Gymnastics
>   2. Football
>   *3. Physical training of some sort
>   4. Baseball

Response 3 obviously provides a more reasonable completion to the stem statement than any of the other responses. It represents a consistent style of expression. This is one of the dangers inherent in the use of incomplete statement item stems.

All of these irrelevant clues to the correct answer are undesirable, of course, and should be avoided. It is entirely appropriate to plant such clues deliberately in the distracters to mislead the test-wise but poorly prepared student. To give all of the relevant clues—those useful to well prepared examinees—while avoiding the irrelevant clues is an important part of the art of writing multiple-choice test items.

> 6. *Choose and phrase the incorrect alternatives (distracters) so that they are thoroughly wrong or clearly inadequate, yet plausible enough to appeal to substantial numbers of poorly prepared examinees.*

Many multiple-choice test items prove to be too difficult or low in discrimination because the item requires examinees to make very fine distinctions between correct and incorrect responses. Perhaps the item writer's efforts to write plausible distracters led him to incorporate too much truth in them. Or perhaps he used his own keen perceptions of subtle differences in meaning as a standard for estimating the capabilities of his less capable students. To avoid these pitfalls the item writer should seek to maximize the ratio of plausibility to correctness in his distracters. He should ask not only, "Does this distracter look good enough for some students to choose it?" but also, "Could it, by any stretch of the imagination, be defended as a correct answer to the question?" Unless the answer to the first question is "yes" and the second "no," he should try again. The following item illustrates plausible but totally incorrect distracters:

> To what did the title of the Broadway musical *Top Banana* refer?
> 1. The dictator of a Central American country
> 2. The warden of a penitentiary
> *3. The leading comedian in a burlesque theater
> 4. The president of a large fruit company

Bananas are fruits from Central America. The phrase "top banana" sounds like slang which penitentiary inmates might use. Hence these distracters have been well chosen to plant common-sense clues that will attract those who lack the knowledge the item is designed to test.

Common practice in writing multiple-choice test items calls for three or four distracters, so that four or five alternatives are provided in each item. If good distracters are available, the larger the number of alternatives, the more highly discriminating the item is likely to be. However, as one seeks to write more distracters each additional one is likely to be somewhat weaker. There is some merit in setting one's goal at three good distracters to each multiple-choice item and in struggling temporarily to reach this goal. Not all good distracters are immediately apparent. Some will emerge only after considerable brain-racking.

On the other hand, there is no magic in four alternatives and no real reason why all items in a test should have the same number of alternatives. It is quite possible to write a good multiple-choice test item with only two distracters (three responses), and occasionally with only one distracter, as Smith, and Ebel and Williams have shown.[1] After tryout, some items can actually be improved by dropping distracters which don't distract poor students, or which do distract good ones.

A student may sometimes arrive at the correct answer to a multiple-choice test item through a process of elimination. Rejecting responses that seem unsatisfactory, he is finally left with one that he selects as the right answer, not because he has any basis for choosing it directly, but simply because none of the others will do.

The availability of this process of elimination is sometimes regarded as a weakness of the multiple-choice item form. A student gets credit for knowing something that he really doesn't know, it is charged. Most specialists in test construction, however, do not disapprove of the process of answering by elimination and do not regard the process as a sign of weakness in multiple-choice items in general, or in an item where the process is particularly useful. (It might be noted in passing that an item which uses the response "none of the above" as a correct answer *requires* the student to an-

---

[1] Kendon Smith, "An Investigation of the Use of 'Double Choice' Items in Testing Achievement," *Journal of Educational Research,* LI (1958), 387-89; and Robert L. Ebel and Bob G. Williams, "The Effect of Varying the Number of Alternatives per Item on Multiple-choice Vocabulary Test Items," *The 14th Yearbook of the National Council on Measurements Used in Education* (East Lansing, Mich.: Michigan State University, 1957), pp. 63-65.

swer by a process of elimination.) There are two reasons why this process is not generally deplored by the test specialists.

In the first place, the function of achievement test items is primarily to contribute to a measure of general achievement in an area of study. They are not intended primarily to provide an inventory of which particular bits of knowledge or which particular skills a student has. The achievement of a student who answers items 1, 3, and 5 correctly but misses 2 and 4 is regarded as equal to the achievement of another student who answers items 2, 3, and 4 correctly but misses 1 and 5. Identifying exactly which things a student has achieved or failed to achieve is a matter of secondary importance in an achievement test.

In the second place, the knowledge and ability required to properly eliminate incorrect alternatives can be, and usually is, closely related to the knowledge or ability that would be required to select the correct alternative. If education does not consist in the accumulation of unrelated bits of information, if the development of a meaningful network of related facts and concepts is essential, then the fact that a student responds in a reflective, problem-solving manner, choosing the best answer by rational processes (including the process of elimination), should be applauded rather than deplored.

In practice, few multiple-choice test items are likely to be answered correctly solely by eliminating incorrect choices. Far more often the process of choice will involve comparative judgments of this alternative against that. It is unlikely that an examinee who is totally ignorant of the correct answer would have knowledge enough to eliminate with certainty the incorrect alternatives. This is especially likely to be true if the item is well enough constructed so that all the available alternatives, correct and incorrect, have some obvious basic similarity. For this and the other reasons just given it seems safe to conclude that the problem of answer choice by a process of distracter elimination need not be regarded as a serious one.

7. Word the item as clearly, simply, and correctly as possible.

The purpose of the words and syntax chosen in writing a multiple-choice test item is to communicate explicit meaning as efficiently as possible. Habits of colorful, picturesque, imaginative, creative writing may serve the item writer badly by impairing the precision and definiteness of his communication of thought. Few written words are read with such careful attention to meaning, expressed and implied, as those in objective test items. Item writing makes rigorous demands on the vocabulary and writing skill of the test constructor as well as on his mastery of the subject matter of the test and his familiarity with the characteristics of the students to be tested. Simple carelessness in grammar, usage, punctuation, or spelling may interfere with the effectiveness of an item and will certainly reflect no credit on the item writer. Skill in expository writing and careful exercise of that skill are essential to the production of good objective test items.

> 8. *Modify the item, if necessary, so that it is reasonable to expect about half the examinees to answer the item correctly.*

Common sense would suggest that a good test should include some easy and some difficult items along with those of intermediate ease or difficulty. In most classroom tests, however, especially at the high school and college levels, reasonable theoretical models predict and experimental studies confirm that the most reliable and valid scores will be obtained by giving preference to items of medium difficulty.

For free-response items an item of medium difficulty is one which about 50 per cent of the examinees answer correctly. For choice-type items, where the possibility of blind guessing exists, an item of medium difficulty can be defined as one on which the proportion of correct responses is midway between the expected chance proportion and 100 per cent. Thus a true-false item of medium difficulty would be answered correctly by about 75 per cent of the examinees. A multiple-choice item offering five alternative responses would be medium in difficulty when answered correctly by about 60 per cent of the examinees (since 60 per cent is midway between 20 per cent, the chance success proportion for items of this type, and 100 per cent).

Items of the same average difficulty for a group have widely different apparent difficulties for specific students. An item that the best student answers incorrectly will be answered correctly by many students of lower ability. In most courses, the best student is distinguished most clearly from the rest not by his superior ability to answer the very hardest questions, but by his ability to answer more questions of all levels of difficulty.

An item so easy that all examinees answer it correctly, or so difficult that none answers it correctly, yields no information about relative levels of achievement. An item of 50 per cent difficulty can yield the maximum amount of this kind of information. Fortunately, items in a midrange of difficulty, say from 30 per cent to 70 per cent success, are almost as productive of differential information as are items of 50 per cent difficulty. No item writer can predict precisely how difficult his items are likely to be. If he aims at fifty per cent, he is likely to produce items that actually range quite widely in difficulty. The point is that he usually should not deliberately try to write some very easy and other very difficult items.

Some instructors and students disapprove of tests on which the typical student succeeds in answering correctly only about half of the questions. It seems to reflect ineffectiveness of teaching and a low level of mastery of course objectives. It is contrary to the tradition of percentage marking, in which 100 represented perfection and 70 or 75 substantial achievement, but barely enough to justify advancement to the next grade or course.

Objective tests could be built on which the typical student would score 70 per cent correct, 75 per cent correct, or even higher. But such a test would be relatively inefficient, including many items which nearly all students answer correctly. Items of this kind yield relatively little information useful in differentiating levels of achievement. Further, the notion that traditional percentage standards for marking and passing provide absolute standards of achievement rests on assumptions easily shown to be unreasonable or contrary to fact. In most cases an instructor is well advised to discard this notion and to concentrate on building the most efficient and reliable tests he can. This calls for items of intermediate difficulty, and the closer they cluster about 50 per cent, the better the test will ordinarily be.

To some extent the difficulty of a multiple-choice test item is inherent in the idea on which it rests. There are, however, techniques which give the writer of a multiple-choice test item some control over the difficulty of the items he produces on a given topic. He can generally make the stem question easier by making it more general or harder by making it more specific, as the following items illustrate:

A tariff is a tax on:
1. Gifts of money
*2. Goods brought into a country
3. Income of immigrants
4. Real estate

Only the most general notions about a tariff are required to successfully respond to this item. It is suitable for use at the lowest level of achievement in this area. A much higher degree of knowledge of tariffs is required to respond successfully to the following item.

A high protective tariff on Swiss watches in the United States is intended to most directly benefit:
1. Swiss watchmakers
2. United States citizens who buy Swiss watches
3. United States government officials
*4. United States watchmakers

This pair of items illustrates how the generality or specificity of a question can be used to help control its difficulty.

The item writer can make the correct response easier to select by making the alternatives more heterogeneous and harder by making them more homogeneous. In some cases, several items of information or demonstrations of ability can be called for in the same item and the correct response arranged so that a student who knows or can do any one of the several will be able to choose the intended response.

By using techniques such as these, the test constructor can often salvage an appropriate item idea which seems initially to be much too easy or too difficult. If the techniques seem ineffective, the appropriateness of the idea as a basis for testing achievement may be open to question.

9. *Arrange for competent, independent review and revision of the initial item draft.*

A person reacting to test items written by another can often detect errors, ambiguities, or idiosyncrasies of conception which might interfere with the ability of a test item to discriminate validly among various levels of achievement. If the reviewer also has specific competence in the field covered by the test, his suggestions are likely to be more numerous, more relevant, and more generally helpful. A school-wide requirement that every objective classroom test be independently reviewed by a staff member other than the author and that the names of both be printed on the final form might do more than any other step to improve the quality of objective classroom tests and the grades based on them. An analogous step, which might also yield great improvement, would be the requirement that each essay test answer be read and graded independently by the instructor and a competent colleague, with the names of each and the grades they each assigned reported to the student.

If the item writer cannot arrange for independent review of his items, he should put the first drafts aside for a few days and then review them himself. This is not nearly so effective as review by another person, but it is far better than no review at all. In each case the reviewer should ask these questions: Is the item based on an appropriate idea? Does the stem present a clear problem? Is the correct response adequate and better than any other response? Are the distracters likely to attract mainly students of low achievement? Is the wording clear? Is the difficulty appropriate?

If possible, the reviewer should react to each item as an examinee would, seeking the best answer and then checking his choice against the key. This approach increases his likelihood of detecting serious flaws in the item.

One difficulty is likely to arise when objective test items are reviewed independently, a difficulty which can be minimized if both the item writer and the reviewer are aware of it. It is the tendency for their individual preferences in matters of style to become sources of disagreement on matters irrelevant to the basic quality of the item. Both item writer and reviewer should cultivate the ability to discriminate between essential elements of item quality and incidental item characteristics. They should focus their attention and discussion on the essentials, on the issues closely related to the basic quality of the item.

3. **Illustrations of desirable and undesirable characteristics of multiple-choice test items**

The items which follow have been collected from a variety of sources. Some of them were prepared for tests of understanding of contemporary affairs in the early 1950's. While these may no longer be suitable for use, the principles of item writing they illustrate are still valid. The illustrations have been grouped in nine sets to illustrate characteristics of the item:

A. Topics	*D*. Responses	*G*. Clues
B. Approach	*E*. Distracters	*H*. Difficulty
C. Stem	*F*. Wording	*I*. Arrangement

Brief comments accompany each item to explain its virtues or short-comings. These items may also serve to suggest the variety of approaches or styles which may be used in formulating multiple-choice test items.

A. Topics

1. *Item permitting a correct answer (Desirable, if possible)*

   What happened in 1953 to the proposed act of Congress granting statehood to Hawaii?
   a. It was passed by both the House and the Senate.
   b. It was defeated in both the House and the Senate.
   *c. It was passed by the House but not by the Senate.
   d. No act regarding statehood for Hawaii was introduced in either the House or the Senate.

There are some matters of fact which provide a suitable basis for correct answer items. Some judgment is involved in determining whether or not a governor is "successful" (Item 3 below), but no judgment is involved in describing what each house of Congress did with a particular measure.

2. *Item using citation of authority (Undesirable)*

   What does Ross say about the Kuder-Richardson method for calculating test reliability?

   *a. It involves assumptions which are likely to be diffi-
       cult to meet in the ordinary test situation.
    b. It produces coefficients which are higher than
       those obtained by the split-halves procedure.
    c. It is the simplest and generally most satisfactory
       method.
    d. It takes account of both pupil errors in response
       and sampling errors among the items.

What a particular writer has to say on this point is probably less
important than what experts generally agree to be true. If there is
no consensus among experts on the matter, probably no student
should be held responsible for knowing what one writer believes.
Incidentally, the current opinion of experts tends to favor the use
of the Kuder-Richardson formula.

   3. *Item requiring best answer (Desirable)*
      Which statement best characterizes the man ap-
      pointed by President Eisenhower to be Chief Justice
      of the United States Supreme Court?
       a. An associate justice of the Supreme Court who
          had once been a professor of law at Harvard.
    *b. A successful governor who had been an unsuccess-
          ful candidate for the Republican presidential
          nomination.
       c. A well-known New York attorney who successfully
          prosecuted the leaders of the Communist party in
          the United States.
       d. A Democratic senator from a Southern state who
          had supported Eisenhower's campaign for the
          presidency.

For many of the most important questions which need to be asked,
it is impossible to state an absolutely correct answer within the
reasonable limits of a multiple-choice test item. Even if space limitation were not a factor, two experts would probably not agree on
the precise wording of the best possible answer. The use of the type
of item which has one best answer permits the item writer to ask
much more significant questions and frees him from the responsibility of stating a correct answer so precisely that all authorities
would agree that the particular wording used was the best possible
wording.

4. *Item based on matter of opinion (Permissible)*
Which of these statements is most consistent with
Jefferson's concept of democracy?
a. Democracy is part of the divine plan for mankind.
b. Democracy requires a strong national government.
*c. The purpose of government is to promote the welfare of the people.
d. The purpose of government is to protect the people from radical or subversive minorities.

The responses to this question represent generalizations on the basis of Jefferson's speeches and writings. No authoritative sanction for one particular generalization is likely to be available. Yet scholars familiar with Jefferson's work would probably agree on a best answer to this item. In such cases the use of an item based on expert opinion is entirely justifiable.

5. *Item admitting no best answer (Undesirable)*
Which event in the following list has been of the
greatest importance in American history?
*a. Braddock's defeat
b. Burr's conspiracy
c. The Hayes-Tilden contest
d. The Webster-Hayne debate

It is unlikely that scholars can agree on which of the events listed is of the greatest importance in American history. The importance of an event depends on the point of view of the judge and the context in which he is thinking of it. Unless experts can agree on a best answer, it should not be used as a test item.

6. *Item dealing with an incidental detail (Undesirable)*
This question is based on the advertising campaign
of Naumkeag Mills to retain the market leadership of
Pequot bed linen. What was the competitive position
of Pequot products in 1927?
a. Ahead of all competitors among all customers
*b. Strong with institutional buyers but weak with
household consumers
c. Second only to Wamsutta among all customers
d. Weak with all groups of consumers

This advertising campaign may provide excellent illustrations of the problems involved and the practices to follow in advertising campaigns. But it seems not entirely appropriate to measure a student's ability to handle an advertising campaign by asking him to recall the details of one illustration used in instruction.

7. *Item based on unique organization of subject matter (Undesirable)*
   The second principle of education is that the individual:
   a. Gathers knowledge   c. Responds to situations
   b. Makes mistakes   *d. Resents domination

The only person capable of answering this question is one who has studied a particular book or article. Whether a given principle of education is first or second is usually a matter of little importance. Educators have not agreed on any particular list of principles of education or any priority of principles. This item shows an undesirably close tie-up to the particular organization of subject matter used by a particular instructor or writer.

8. *Item based on novel question (Desirable)*
   If the radius of the earth were increased by 3 feet, its circumference at the equator would be increased by about how much?
   a. 9 feet   *c. 19 feet
   b. 12 feet   d. 28 feet

Requiring a student to predict what would happen under certain unusual, even impossible, circumstances is a good way of measuring his understanding of the principle involved. Mechanical computation of the answer to a problem like the one above is apt to be much more tedious than estimation on the basis of thorough understanding of the relationship.

9. *Item requiring selective recall (Desirable)*
   Which of the following was an important development in Canada during 1953?
   *a. Rapid business and industrial growth
   b. A severe and widespread economic depression
   c. A marked trend toward Communism in provincial governments

d. Appearance of a strong movement favoring unification of the United States and Canada

Unless this item had been made the specific object of instruction, it will function as a test of a student's ability to recall a variety of information about Canada, to select that which is relevant, and to base a generalization upon it.

B. *Approach*

10. *Item using descriptive responses (Desirable)*
    What is monogamy?
    a. Refusal to marry
    b. Marriage of one woman to more than one husband
    c. Marriage of one man to more than one wife
    *d. Marriage of one man to only one wife

Inexperienced item writers tend to seek items having very short responses. This seriously limits the significance and scope of the achievements which can be measured. In an item measuring vocabulary knowledge, it is usually better to place the term to be defined in the item stem and to use definitions or identifications as the responses. The same principle should apply to nonvocabulary items. One-word responses need not be avoided altogether, but they should seldom be prominent in any test.

11. *Item using label responses (Undesirable)*
    A marriage in which one woman marries one man is called

    a. unicameral   *c*. monotheism
    b. dualism   *d. monogamy

This item illustrates how Item 10 might be inverted to give one-word responses. But when changed in this way it may be somewhat less realistic. It is true that people frequently search their minds for a word to express a particular concept. But seldom does that concept have the characteristics of a formal definition, such as the stem of Item 11. Further, and perhaps more importantly, it is usually somewhat more difficult to get good distracters for a one-word correct response than for a phrase or sentence. When this is true, item discrimination may suffer.

12. *Item showing artificial inversion (Undesirable)*

A man hits a ball into the air to a height of 15 feet
or more and it comes down within 2 feet of the net.
He is attempting to perfect the

a. High pass   c. High lob
b. High volley   *d. High set-up

Item 12 shows artificial inversion of a test item to gain short
responses. It is not likely that a coach or a player would often need
to be able to answer a question like the one above. It would seem
much more useful for them to know how best to practice a particular
maneuver, such as the high set-up. A question asking this directly
would look more practical and might even provide better discrimination.

13. *Item using indirect approach (Undesirable)*

Which leaf layer makes it possible for the plants to
get the raw materials needed for photosynthesis?

a. Upper epidermis   c. Spongy layer
b. Palisade layer   *d. Lower epidermis

While it is true that the pores through which the leaf cells of most
plants obtain gases needed for photosynthesis occur mainly in the
lower epidermis, it is unnecessarily and undesirably indirect to
speak of the lower layer as "making it possible" for the plants to
get the raw materials. Further, not all plants have their stomata in
the lower epidermis. A notable exception, for example, is the water
lily. A direct question on the function of the stomata might be
preferable.

14. *Item asking examinee his opinion (Undesirable)*

What do you consider the most important objective
of the staff meetings?

*a. To establish good working relations with your
    staff
b. To handle routine matters
c. To help teachers improve instruction
d. To practice and exemplify democracy in admini-
    stration

There is one sense in which any answer to this item must be considered a correct answer. On the other hand, what the item writer obviously wished to determine was the examinee's judgment concerning the most important objective of staff meetings, for the purpose of checking that judgment against authoritative consensus in the matter. It would be better to ask him directly to choose the most important objective of staff meetings. His answer will obviously be what he considers the most important objective, but it will be open to criticism and possible correction if it differs from the judgment of recognized experts.

15. *Item combining two elements to give four responses (Desirable)*

What was the general policy of the Eisenhower administration during 1953 with respect to government expenditures and taxes?
   a. Reductions of both expenditures and taxes
  *b. Reduction of expenditures, no change in taxes
   c. Reduction in taxes, no change in expenditures
   d. No change in either expenditures or taxes

One common difficulty with four-response multiple-choice items is that of securing four good alternatives. An obvious solution to this problem in some cases is to combine two questions with two alternatives each to give the necessary four alternatives.

16. *Item combining a question with an explanation (Desirable)*

Has the average size of farms in the United States tended to increase in recent years? Why?
   a. Yes, because as the soil loses its natural fertility more land must be cultivated to maintain the same output
  *b. Yes, because the use of farm machinery has made large farms more efficient than small farms
   c. No, because the difficulty in securing farm labor has forced many farmers to limit their operations
   d. No, because large family farms tend to be subdivided to provide smaller farms for the children

This is a variation of the preceding type of item in which essentially two questions, having two or more alternatives each, are combined to give four alternatives.

C. *Stem*

17. *Item using incomplete stem (Undesirable)*
Physiology teaches us that
*a. The development of vital organs is dependent upon muscular activity.
b. Strength is independent of muscle size.
c. The mind and body are not influenced by each other.
d. Work is not exercise.

Like Item 19, Item 17 poses no specific question. Physiology could teach a variety of things. While there may be somewhat greater danger of this lack of specificity when incomplete sentences are used as item stems, this item would be just as bad if the stem read, "What does physiology teach us?"

18. *Item using negative stem (Undesirable)*
In the definition of a mineral which of the following is incorrect?
a. It was produced by geologic processes.
b. It has distinctive physical properties.
c. It contains one or more elements.
*d. Its chemical composition is variable.

Items that are negatively stated, i.e., that require an examinee to pick an answer which is not true or characteristic, tend to be somewhat confusing. They appear unusually attractive to examination writers because so much of the instructional material is organized in terms of parallel subheadings under a main topic. This suggests the easy approach of asking for something which is *not* one of those subheadings. However, such questions are rarely encountered outside the classroom and thus lack the practical relevance that is usually desirable.

19. *Item asking no specific question (Undesirable)*
In comparing the period of heterosexual adjustment of our culture with those of other cultures, it must be concluded that
*a. There are tremendous differences that can only be explained on a cultural basis.

b. There are large differences which must be explained by the interaction of biology and the more influential culture.

c. Although there are some differences, the biological foundation of puberty is fundamental.

d. In most cultures puberty is the period of heterosexual adjustment.

There is a wide variety of conclusions possible on the basis of a study of a particular period of human development. Until the examinee reads the responses, he has no clear idea of what the question is asking. The item as a whole is not focused on any single specific problem. This opens the way for confusing multiple interpretations.

20. *Item using an introductory sentence (Permissible)*

The term "creeping socialism" appeared frequently in political discussions in 1953. Which of these is most often used to illustrate "creeping socialism"?

*a. Generation and distribution of electric power by the Federal government

b. Communist infiltration of labor unions

c. Gradual increase in sales and excise taxes

d. Participation of the United States in international organizations such as the United Nations

The use of a separate sentence frequently adds to the clarity of the item stem if it is necessary to present background information as well as to ask the question itself. Combining these two elements into a single-question sentence probably would make it considerably more complex.

21. *Item including a necessary qualification (Desirable)*

What change occurs in the composition of the air in a lighted airtight room in which the only living things are growing green plants?

a. Carbon dioxide increases and oxygen decreases.

*b. Carbon dioxide decreases and oxygen increases.

c. Both carbon dioxide and oxygen increase.

d. Both carbon dioxide and oxygen decrease.

As originally worded this item simply asked, "What change occurs in the composition of the air in a room in which green plants are growing?" Only if one specifies that the room is lighted, so that

photosynthesis can take place, that it is air-tight, so that changes in
the composition will not be neutralized by ventilation, and that
there are no other living things which might consume the oxygen
faster than it is produced, is it possible to give a firm answer to this
question.

    22. *Item involving "window dressing" (Undesirable)*
        While ironing her formal, Jane burned her hand
        accidentally on the hot iron. This was due to a
        transfer of heat by
      *a. Conduction
       b. Radiation
       c. Convection
       d. Absorption

The introductory sentence suggests that the item involves a practical
problem. Actually the question asked calls only for knowledge of
technical terminology.

    23. *Item involving an "instructional aside" (Undesirable)*
        In purifying water for a city water supply, one
        process is to have the impure water seep through
        layers of sand and fine and coarse gravel. Here many
        impurities are left behind. Below are four terms, one
        of which will describe this process better than the
        others. Select the correct one.
       a. Sedimentation
      *b. Filtration
       c. Chlorination
       d. Aeration

The primary purpose of a test item is to measure achievement.
While much learning may occur during the process of taking a test,
deliberate inclusion of instructional materials may reduce its effectiveness as a test more than its instructional value is increased. It
might be better to ask the purpose of filtration in purifying city
water supplies or the type of filter used.

    D. Responses

    24. *Item showing inappropriate responses (Undesirable)*
        The chief difference between the surface features of
        Europe and North America is that

a. The area of Europe is larger.
b. Europe extends more to the South.
c. The Volga River is longer than the Missouri-Mississippi.
*d. The greater highlands and plains of Europe extend in an east-west direction.

Only the correct answer really describes a surface feature of Europe. Either the question should not be limited to "surface features" or the responses given should all conform to that category.

25. *Item showing nonparallel responses (Undesirable)*
    Slavery was first started
    *a. At Jamestown settlement
    b. At Plymouth settlement
    c. At the settlement of Rhode Island
    d. A decade before the Civil War

The first three responses are places; the fourth is a time. Use of a direct question stem might help to prevent this type of ambiguity, which could make it possible for more than one answer to be correct.

26. *Item using indistinct responses (Undesirable)*
    Meat can be preserved in brine due to the fact that
    a. Salt is a bacterial poison.
    *b. Bacteria cannot withstand the osmotic action of the brine.
    c. Salt alters the chemical composition of the food.
    d. Brine protects the meat from contact with air.

Both responses a and b could be judged correct. Response b simply explains why response a is correct. It is undesirable to have only one of two almost equally correct responses be considered the correct response.

27. *Item including complicating elements in the responses (Undesirable)*
    Systematic geography differs from regional geography mainly in that
    a. Systematic geography deals, in the main, with physical geography, while regional geography concerns itself essentially with the field of human geography.

   b. Systematic geography studies a region system-
      atically, while regional geography is concerned
      only with a descriptive account of a region.
 * c. Systematic geography studies a single phenomenon
      in its distribution over the earth in order to supply
      generalizations for regional geography, which
      studies the arrangement of phenomena in one
      given area.
   d. Systematic geography is the modern scientific way
      of studying differentiation of the earth's surface,
      while regional geography is the traditional and
      descriptive way of studying distribution of phe-
      nomena in space.

It is a principle of good item writing that the responses should be
as simple and clearly distinct as possible. In an item of this type it
is very difficult to perceive and keep in mind the essential distinction between the alternative responses. A better question might ask,
"What is the characteristic of systematic geography which distinguishes it essentially from regional geography?"

   28. *Item using "none of these" appropriately (Desirable)*
       Which word is misspelled?
       a. Contrary   c. Extreme   e. None of these
      *b. Tendancy   d. Variable

Whenever each of the responses can be judged unequivocally as
correct or incorrect in response to the question posed in the item
stem, it is appropriate to use "none of these" as a response. It would
also be appropriate to use "all of these" in a similar situation where
more than one perfectly correct answer is possible.

   29. *Item using "all of these" and "none of these" inappro-
       priately (Undesirable)*
       What does the term "growth" mean?
      *a. Maturation   d. All of these
       b. Learning   e. None of these
       c. Development

Since no word means exactly the same as "growth," this item
appears more suited to best-answer than to correct-answer form.
"All of these" or "none of these" are usually considered inappropriate responses to best-answer items.

30. *Item using quantitative scale of responses (Desirable)*
How did (*A*) the estimated amount of petroleum discovered in new fields in 1953 compare with (*B*) the amount extracted from producing fields in the same year?
   a. *A* was practically zero.
   b. *A* was about half of *B*.
   c. *A* just about equaled *B*.
   *d. *A* was greater than *B*.

In many situations the precise value of a quantitative answer is less important than knowledge of the general level of that value. It is frequently possible to categorize the responses to represent intervals on a scale of quantities. This presents a systematic approach to testing in quantitative situations. The use of code letters for the two quantities to be compared shortens the response options and probably adds to their clarity.

31. *Item using qualitative scale of responses (Desirable)*
Some cases of lung cancer have been attributed to smoking. What was the status of this idea in 1953?
   a. The theory had been clearly established by medical evidence.
   *b. It was a controversial matter and some experts considered the evidence to be inconclusive.
   c. The theory had been clearly disproved by surveys of smokers.
   d. The theory was such a recent development that no tests of it had been completed.

The responses to this item represent a scale of values from complete establishment to complete indefiniteness. The use of a qualitative scale of responses helps to systematize the process of test construction and to suggest desirable responses.

E. *Distracters*

32. *Item using true statements as distracters (Desirable)*
What is the principal advantage of a battery of lead storage cells over a battery of dry cells for automobile starting and lighting?

a. The storage cell furnishes direct current.
b. The voltage of the storage cell is higher.
*c. The current from the storage cell is stronger.
d. The initial cost of the storage cell is less.

It is not necessary that the incorrect responses to a test item be themselves incorrect statements. They simply need to be incorrect answers to the stem question. Lead storage cells do furnish direct current, at a higher voltage than dry cells, but this is not the reason why the storage cell is preferred. Judgments concerning the relevance of knowledge may be as important as judgments concerning its truth. Multiple-choice items should make frequent use of this device for testing an achievement which is sometimes thought to be testable only by using essay examinations.

33. *Item using stereotypes in distracters (Desirable)*
Which of these has effected the greatest change in domestic plants and animals?
a. Influence of environment on heredity
b. Organic evolution
*c. Selective breeding
d. Survival of the fittest

Phrases like "organic evolution" or "survival of the fittest," which a student may have heard without understanding, provide excellent distracters at the elementary level of discrimination for which this item is intended.

34. *Item using obscure distracters (Undesirable)*
A chaotic condition
a. Asymptotic   c. Gauche
*b. Confused   d. Permutable

If the words "chaotic" and "confused" represent an appropriate level of difficulty for this vocabulary test, then the remaining terms used as distracters are obviously too difficult. It is unreasonable to expect the examinee to know for sure that one of them might not be a better synonym for "chaotic" than the intended correct answer. The use of distracters which are at a lower level of difficulty than the correct answer is sometimes criticized because it permits a student to respond successfully by eliminating incorrect responses. However, students who can respond successfully on this basis usually possess more knowledge than those who cannot. Hence the discriminating power of an item is not impaired by this characteristic.

35. *Item using a highly implausible distracter (Undesirable)*

    Which of the following has helped most to increase the average length of human life?
    a. Fast driving
    b. Avoidance of overeating
    c. Wider use of vitamins
    *d. Wider use of inoculations

Some teachers may feel that the abilities of some of their students cannot possibly be underestimated, but they should not let this feeling of frustration lead them to employ such an unreasonable distracter as the first response to this item.

36. *Item involving verbal trick (Undesirable)*

    Horace Greeley is known for his
    a. Advice to young men not to go west
    b. Discovery of anesthetics
    *c. Editorship of the *New York Tribune*
    d. Humorous anecdotes

Insertion of the "not" in the first response spoils what would otherwise be the best answer to the question. This makes the item test the examinee's alertness more than it tests his knowledge of Horace Greeley.

F. *Wording*

37. *Item using imprecise wording (Undesirable)*

    Why do we have warmest weather in summer?
    a. The sun is nearest the earth in summer.
    *b. The sun's rays strike the earth most directly in summer.
    c. The air is freer of clouds in summer.
    d. The prevailing winds blow from the south in summer.

It is not accurate to say the sun's rays strike the earth any more directly in summer than they do at any other time of the year. What

is true is that the sun's rays are more nearly vertical to the surface
and hence are concentrated on a smaller area than is true when they
strike the earth's surface on a slant.

38. *Item showing needless repetition in responses*
    (Undesirable)
    Which is the best definition for a vein?
    *a. A blood vessel carrying blood going to the heart
    b. A blood vessel carrying blue blood
    c. A blood vessel carrying impure blood
    d. A blood vessel carrying blood away from the heart

This item could probably be improved by using an incomplete
statement stem such as, "A vein is a blood vessel carrying———."
Occasionally some repetition provides the most convenient way of
making the item clear, but in this case the repetition seems excessive.

39. *Item showing ineffective expression (Undesirable)*
    Among the factors listed which have contributed to
    rapid expansion of cut-over land, the most impor-
    tant during recent years has been
    a. Confiscatory taxation of standing timber
    *b. High prices for lumber
    c. Rapid growth of population
    d. Rising standards of living

Item stems should be not only grammatically correct, but should
represent the most effective expression of the question idea. Reword-
ing the item to read, "What has been the most important cause for
the rapid increase in cut-over lands in recent years?" would seem
to improve it.

G. *Clues*

40. *Item using stereotyped phrases in the correct answer*
    (Undesirable)
    Which best describes what happens when work is
    done?
    *a. A force operates through a distance.
    b. A force is exerted.
    c. Energy is destroyed.
    d. Potential energy is changed to kinetic.

The statement that work is done whenever a force operates through a distance is a somewhat abstract statement. It could be remembered by one who concentrates on verbal recall almost as well as by one who has grasped the underlying concept of work in concrete situations.

41. *Item using stereotyped answer (Undesirable)*
    How did Columbus discover America?
    a. He was blown off his course by a violent storm.
    *b. He was seeking a water route to the Orient.
    c. Queen Isabella sent him to make discoveries.
    d. He was fleeing persecution in Spain.

Stereotyped answers like the one used as the correct response to this item and Item 40 could encourage superficial learning. Hence they seldom ought to appear in good test items.

42. *Item whose distracters are too similar (Undesirable)*
    The large number of insect species alive today is evidence of
    a. Their relative freedom from attacks of predators
    *b. Perfection of their adaptation to their environment
    c. Their very complex structure
    d. Their great ability to produce many young

In this item the distracters are all much less general than the correct response. This similarity makes the correct response more obvious than it probably ought to be.

43. *Items which interlock (Undesirable)*
    What, if anything, developed in 1955 with respect to relations between Egypt and Soviet Russia?
    a. A Russian military force invaded Egypt.
    b. Egypt accused members of the Russian embassy of spying and broke off diplomatic relations.
    c. Soviet Russia supported Egypt's demand for independence from Britain.
    *d. The Egyptian government arranged to buy arms from Soviet Russia.
    How did the Western powers react to Egypt's agreement to buy arms from Soviet Russia ?
    a. They approved it as a gesture of good will.

     b. They pointed out that it was a private affair
between Egypt and Russia.
  c. They pointed out that it was a threat to peace in
the eastern Mediterranean.
     d. They protested that Egypt was aiding a potential
enemy.

The second of the two items above provides the answer to the first.
Attempts to cover the same small unit of subject matter too intensively, or on diverse levels of comprehension, may lead to interlocking test items. The best preventative is careful review of the items
after they have been written.

H. *Difficulty*

    44. *Easier item using heterogeneous responses*
        (Permissible)

        An embargo is
   a. A law or regulation
     b. A kind of boat
     c. An embankment
     d. A foolish adventure

The responses to this item vary widely. Because of their wide differences, only an elementary knowledge of embargoes is required for
successful response.

    45. *Harder item using homogeneous responses (Permis-
        sible)*

        An embargo is
     a. A tariff
     b. A customs duty
   c. The stoppage of goods from entry and departure
     d. An admission of goods free of duty

Although the same question is implied in both Items 44 and 45, the
homogeneity of the responses in Item 45 requires a considerably
higher level of knowledge about embargoes and hence makes the
item more difficult.

    46. *Easier item involving multiple clues (Permissible)*

        Which of the following are outstanding contempo-
rary pianists?

*a. Robert Casadesus and Rudolph Serkin
 b. Patrice Munsel and Marian Anderson
 c. Claude Debussy and Ignace Paderewski
 d. Alan Paton and Alec Guinness

The use of the names of two individuals fitting the specification in the item stem makes it somewhat easier. The examinee need only know one of the contemporary pianists, or know one in each of the three distracters is not a contemporary pianist, to respond successfully.

I. Arrangement

47. *Item with response placed in tandem (Undesirable)*
    The balance sheet report for the Ajax Canning Company would reveal   (a.) The company's profit for the previous fiscal year   (*b.) The amount of money owed to its creditors   (c.) The amount of income tax paid (d.) The amount of sales for the previous fiscal period.

Responses in tandem save some space but are much more difficult to compare in the process of selection than those placed in list form.

48. *Item with unnatural sequence of responses (Undesirable)*
    The population of Denmark is about
    a. 2 million
    b. 15 million
   *c. 4 million
    d. 7 million

Whenever the responses for an item form a quantitative or qualitative scale, they normally should be arranged in order of magnitude from smallest to largest or largest to smallest. This may avoid some confusion on the part of the examinee and eliminate an irrelevant source of error.

4. Illustrative reading interpretation test items

Reading interpretation tests, involving a passage of background reading material and a set of multiple-choice questions relating to the passage, are used more often in tests of academic aptitude, of general educational development, or of reading ability in the lower grades than in classroom achievement tests. One example of a section from such a test seems appropriate in this chapter because it provides an illustration of some of the contrasts between expertly and inexpertly written multiple-choice test items.

Both sets of items were written on the basis of the same passage of background material. The inexpertly written items were produced by some beginning students in a class in test construction. The following pages show (*A*) the instructions given the students of item writing, (B) the background reading material, (*C*) the students' items, and (*D*) the items written by expert examiners.

A. READING TEST ASSIGNMENT

Construct a test of fifteen multiple-choice items over the reading passage on "hail." Assume that the student will have the reading selection before him as he takes the test.

The purpose of the test is to determine how thoroughly the student understands the material he has read. Understanding cannot be measured by items which in the stem or the correct response repeat the exact phraseology of the reading passage. Questions which deal with specific information in the passage must always involve paraphrases.

Understanding of a reading passage is revealed in part by the student's recognition of implications not specifically stated in the passage. It is also revealed by the student's ability to generalize the main idea or subject matter of the paragraph or of the entire selection.

Finally, understanding is revealed by the student's recognition of the organization of paragraphs or of the selection as a whole. He should know which ideas are main ideas and which contribute to the support of these main ideas.

Include items dealing with all these aspects of understanding and interpretation in the test which you prepare.

B. READING PASSAGE ON HAIL

One of the three kinds of icy particles that fall from the sky is called "hail." It consists of icy lumps, called "hailstones," ranging from the size of a small pea up to that of a big orange. While hailstones do occur in a variety of shapes, most of them are spherical, like sleet. A hailstone differs from other icy particles in that it is built up of alternate layers of clear and snowy ice. Usually it has a snowy center surrounded by from one to a dozen or more icy coats arranged like the skins of an onion.

Hailstorms are commonest in the warmer half of the year and in temperate regions, but they may occur at any season and in almost any part of the world. Hail is fairly common in the tropics and is occasionally observed in polar regions. While hail has been known to fall continuously in one place for more than an hour, it ordinarily falls for a short time only.

A hint to how hail is formed is furnished by the appearance of the typical hailstone. The layers of clear and snowy ice are evidently acquired during several journeys of the stone up and down between cold and warm levels of air. At the high, cold levels the hailstone is coated with snow. At lower, warmer levels it is covered with rain, which turns to ice as the stone is again carried upward. This action continues until the stone is too heavy for the air current to support; then is falls to the earth. It is probable that this process can take place only at the front of a thunderstorm, where there are strong upward currents.

The heavy hailstones hitting down upon the earth often cause great damage. The loss caused by hail throughout the world is estimated to average more than $200 million a year. The greatest part of this loss results from destruction of growing crops. Grapes, olives, tobacco, and hops are among the cultivated crops most readily injured. Of course, other types of damage occur, too. Skylights, roofs of greenhouses, and other exposed glass are often broken during a hailstorm. Human beings are very rarely injured by hail, but livestock in open fields are sometimes killed.

Probably nowhere else in the world are crop losses so great as in the vine-growing districts of Southern Europe. Two curious practices, based on the false belief that men can prevent hailstorms, have long been common in these regions. One of these is "hail-shooting," which consists of shooting cannon balls, bombs, or rockets at the clouds. Millions of dollars have been wasted in this way. The other practice is the use of the hail-rod, which is really a form of lightning rod. This was introduced when it was mistakenly believed that hail was caused by electrical action. There is no proof that either of these preventive schemes has any effect on hailstorms.

In contrast to such useless efforts, the practice of insuring crops against hail has proved a great benefit to farmers in the Old World for more than a hundred years. Hail insurance has recently become popular in America also. In some European countries, and in certain parts of the United States and Canada, the hail insurance business is handled by the government. The Department of Agriculture recently reported that the amount of hail insurance in force in this country was more than $500 million.

C. INEXPERTLY WRITTEN ITEMS ON HAIL PASSAGE

1. The origin of hail is caused by
    a. Atmospheric pressure
    b. Strong ascending currents of air
    c. Horizontal stratification
  *d. Vapor condensing in whirling air currents
2. Large pellets of ice called hail are made of
    a. Concentric layers of ice
    b. Frozen raindrops
  *c. A spongy mass of ice and snow
3. Hail usually occurs during the summer because
  *a. It is formed in violent storms.
    b. The extreme heat causes the stones to be released.
    c. The summer is the only time of year hail can form.
4. The great damage due to hailstorms leads us to believe
    a. Their paths are many miles in width.
  *b. Their paths are a few miles in length and width.
    c. Their paths are many miles in length.
5. Hail is not seasonal, in fact, winter hail is formed by
    a. Very large hailstones
    b. Very small hailstones
    c. Melting snowdrops
  *d. Frozen raindrops and thus called "sleet"
6. As hail falls almost any place in the world we may realize that
    a. It is caused by the winds of the temperate zone.
    b. Its fall is only in regions of extreme heat.
    c. Its fall is only in regions of great rainfall.
  *d. It may fall wherever the proper air pressure is.

7. The shape of hailstones is
   a. Always round
   *b. Of many varied shapes
   c. Spherical
8. The reason for the shell of ice in hail is
   *a. Hail is built of condensing vapor being whirled up and down in violent currents.
   b. It freezes as it comes through each layer of atmosphere.
   c. It is suspended by rising currents of air.
9. In the vineyards of Southern Europe schemes for the prevention of hailstorms are based on the theory of
   a. Hail caused by atmospheric pressure
   *b. Electricity caused hailstorms
   c. Whirling air currents
10. Hail insurance is beneficial to farmers all over the world because it
    a. Is handled by the governments
    *b. Protects farmers against acts of nature
    c. Saves farmers money spent on other methods of prevention
11. The rolling white squall cloud at the beginning of a thunderstorm is
    *a. A hail factory
    b. A cirrus cloud
    c. A cumulus cloud
12. The size of a hailstone depends on
    a. The temperature of the atmosphere
    *b. The violence of the whirl it receives
    c. The amount of moisture in the air
13. Hail is
    a. Diminutive specks of compact snow
    b. Particles of ice
    *c. Alternate layers of clear and snowy ice
14. The size of hailstones is
    a. Of one definite size
    *b. From pea size to large as lemons
    c. Infinitesimal in size

15. Hailstorms last
   a. Just a few minutes
 *b. From a few minutes to a half-hour
   c. Very long periods of time

D. EXPERTLY WRITTEN ITEMS ON HAIL PASSAGE

1. What is the *purpose* of the first paragraph?
   a. To tell how large hailstones sometimes become
   b. To explain that there are three kinds of hail
   c. To prove that hail and sleet are not the same thing
 *d. To describe hail
   e. To compare hailstones with onions

2. If you made a trip from the equator to the north pole, during what part of your journey would you be most likely to run into hailstorms?
   a. The first part
 *b. The middle part
   c. The last part
   d. As likely on any one part as on another

3. Which of the following is true of hailstorms?
 *a. They sometimes produce hailstones as large as apples.
   b. They most often occur in the tropics.
   c. They produce particles, constructed in sections like oranges.
   d. They most often occur in winter.
   e. They are caused by atmospheric electricity.

4. In an outline of this article, there are three subtopics under the heading "Objects damaged by hail." Two of these subtopics are "Growing crops" and "Livestock." What is the other subtopic?
   a. Tobacco   d. Poultry
 *b. Exposed glass   e. Cattle
   c. Olives

5. What is the main idea of the fifth paragraph?
   a. The vine-growing districts of Southern Europe suffer the greatest crop losses from hail.
   b. There are two ways to prevent hail from falling.
   c. Millions of dollars have been spent to prevent hailstorms.
   *d. Attempts to prevent hailstorms have been unsuccessful.
   e. Hail is not caused by electrical action.

6. Why is a hailstone made up of layers of clear and cloudy ice?
   a. It has fallen through several clouds, some of which are much colder than others.
   b. It has been charged several times by the electricity in the thunderstorm.
   *c. It has been repeatedly blown up into cold air after falling into warmer air.
   d. It has fallen through alternate layers of cold and warm air.
   e. It becomes so heavy that the cloud cannot support it.

7. The greatest losses from hail are caused by damage to which of the following?
   a. Automobile tops   d. Skylights
   *b. Plants   e. Livestock
   c. Greenhouses

8. Suppose we wish to divide this article into two parts and make up a heading for each part. Which of the following would make the best heading for the first part of the article?
   a. Kinds of storms
   b. Crops injured by hail
   c. Value of hail insurance
   d. Appearance of hail
   *e. Description of hail and hailstorms

9. What is the main idea of the sixth paragraph?
    a. Hail insurance was used widely in the Old World before it spread to America.
    b. Great amounts of money are spent each year to pay for damage done by hail.
    *c. Hail insurance is a successful and increasingly popular protection against loss from hailstorms.
    d. Everybody should carry hail insurance.
    e. Governments have begun to take an interest in hail insurance.

10. How does hail differ from sleet?
    a. Hail is composed of particles of frozen water.
    *b. Hail is made up of alternate layers of clear and snowy ice.
    c. Hail is often spherical in shape.
    d. Hail sometimes falls steadily for an hour.
    e. Hail often accompanies severe storms.

11. In the appearance of hailstones what gives us an idea of how they are formed.
    a. Their spherical shape   *d. Their layer structure
    b. Their unusual size   e. Their weight
    c. Their smooth surface

12. Why does it hardly ever hail except when there are thunderstorms?
    *a. Other storms do not have such strong upward movements of air.
    b. Only thunderclouds are heavy enough to keep the hail from falling before it melts.
    c. There is not enough moisture in other types of storms.
    d. The electricity in thunderstorms is necessary for the formation of hail.

13. Which one of the following purposes probably was uppermost in the mind of the author when he wrote this article?
    a. To indicate how foolish are the European ideas of preventing hailstorms
    *b. To give general information concerning hail
    c. To entertain the people who would read the article
    d. To prevent people from being afraid of hail
    e. To urge people to buy hail insurance

14. Which one of the following would make the *best* title
for this article?
  a. How to tell hail from other icy particles
 *b. Hail and the damage it does
  c. Prevention of damage from hail
  d. Value of hail insurance
  e. Why we have hailstorms

Note that the inexpertly written items tend to be stated imprecisely and to involve logical flaws. If hail consists of large pellets
of *ice,* should those pellets be said to consist of a spongy mass of ice
and *snow?* (Item 2). The first paragraph of the reading passage
implies quite clearly that sleet is not a form of hail (Item 5), but
rather, a different form of icy particle. Violent storms occur in
winter, too (Item 3). Our notions of the area affected by a hailstorm
are based on direct observation, not on inferences from the damage
they do (Item 4). And if we were to relate area affected to amount
of damage, logic would suggest that response *b* was the poorest of
the three.

To say that the shape of hailstones is "of many varied shapes" is
linguistically a bit awkward (Item 7). The indicated correct response
to Item 8 describes the formation of hail more impressionistically
than exactly. The correct response to Item 9 would be stated more
precisely if it indicated a theory *that* "hailstorms are caused by
atmospheric electricity." "Updraft," or "upward current of air,"
might be preferable to "whirl" as part of the correct answer to
Item 12. "Formation" would seem better than "origin" in the stem
of Item 1.

The responses to Items 3, 8, and 9 are not as parallel as would be
desirable. The responses to Item 14 do not complete the stem phrase
as sensibly and smoothly as they might. Only response *d* in Item 6
is logically consistent with the statement in the stem that hail falls
almost any place in the world. But the suggested correct response
does not express a very good reason for its wide range of occurrence.
The clouds which bring hailstorms are more characteristically black
than white (Item 11). It may be useful in teaching to characterize
such clouds as hail factories, but emphasis on such instrumental
figures of speech in an examination is open to question.

While these inexpertly written items reveal many technical flaws in item writing, the basic weakness seems to be lack of thorough understanding of hailstorms and lack of ability to express ideas exactly in writing. The items written by the experts tend to be longer, but they appear also to call for more thorough understanding of the background material. If both sets of items had been tried out, some of the students' items might have proved to be quite difficult, but the difficulty would usually arise from irrelevant ambiguity, not from the presentation of a penetrating but fair task of interpretation.

5. Summary

Some of the main ideas developed in this chapter are expressed in the following twenty-five statements.

1. The most highly regarded and widely used form of objective test item at present is the multiple choice.
2. Multiple-choice test items should be based on sound, significant ideas that could be expressed as independently meaningful propositions.
3. The wording of a multiple-choice item should not follow familiar textbook phraseology so closely that verbal memory without comprehension will provide an adequate basis for response.
4. The main job of most multiple-choice test items is to differentiate between students of higher and lower achievement.
5. Giving the final examination as a pretest will help to identify items that can provide valid measures of specific achievements in the course.
6. Drafting each multiple-choice item in pencil and double spaced on a separate sheet of paper will facilitate revision of the item and its assembly into the test.
7. The stem of a multiple-choice item should state or clearly imply a specific direct question.
8. Item stems including the word "not" and asking in effect for an incorrect answer tend to be superficial in content and confusing to the examinee.
9. The responses "none of the above" and "all of the above" are appropriate only when the answers given to a question are

absolutely correct or incorrect (as in spelling, arithmetic problems, etc.).

10. The intended answer should be clear, concise, correct, and free of clues.

11. All of the responses to a multiple-choice test item should be parallel in point of view, grammatical structure, and general appearance.

12. The distracters in a multiple-choice item should be definitely incorrect but plausibly attractive to the uninformed.

13. While most multiple-choice items provide at least four alternative answers, good ones can be written with only two or three alternatives.

14. A student who selects the correct response to a multiple-choice item by eliminating the incorrect responses demonstrates useful achievement.

15. To function properly a multiple-choice item must be expressed in carefully chosen words and critically edited phrases.

16. In general the best multiple-choice test items are those that about one half of the examinees answer correctly.

17. Some multiple-choice items can be made easier by making the question more general and the responses more diverse, or harder by making the question more specific and the responses more similar.

18. Subsequent, and preferably independent, review of the drafts of multiple-choice test items is likely to improve their quality.

19. Some of the most effective multiple-choice test questions call for a best answer rather than an absolutely perfect correct answer.

20. Items testing recall of incidental details of instruction or special organizations of subject matter are ordinarily undesirable.

21. The stem of a multiple-choice item should be expressed as concisely as possible without sacrificing clarity or omitting essential qualifications.

22. The responses to a multiple-choice item should be expressed simply enough to make clear the essential differences among them.

23. True statements that do not provide good answers to the stem question often make good distracters.

24. The responses to a multiple-choice item should be listed rather than written one after another in a compact paragraph.

25. The reading interpretation items written by novices on a passage tend to be stated imprecisely and to reveal imperfect understanding of the passage.

REFERENCES

Ebel, Robert L., "Writing the Test Item," in *Educational Measurement,* ed. E. F. Lindquist. Washington, D.C.: American Council on Education, 1951.

————, and Bob G. Williams, "The Effect of Varying the Number of Alternatives per Item on Multiple-choice Vocabulary Test Items," *The Fourteenth Yearbook of the National Council on Measurements Used in Education,* pp. 63-65. East Lansing, Mich.: Michigan State University, 1957.

Engelhart, Max D., "Suggestions for Writing Achievement Exercises to be Used in Tests Scored on the Electric Scoring Machine," *Educational and Psychological Measurement,* VII (1947), 357-74.

————, "Unique Types of Achievement Test Exercises," *Psychometrika,* VII (1942), 103-16.

Hoffman, Banesh, "Best Answers or Better Minds," *American Scholar,* XXVIII (Spring, 1959), 195-202.

————, "Testing," *Physics Today,* XIV (October, 1961), 38-42.

————, "The Tyranny of Multiple-choice Tests," *Harper's Magazine,* CCII (March, 1961), 37-44.

Mosier, Charles I., M. Claire Myers and Helen G. Price, "Suggestions for the Construction of Multiple-choice Test Items," *Educational and Psychological Measurement,* V (1945), 261-71.

Multiple-choice Questions: A Close Look. Princeton, N.J.: Educational Testing Service, 1963.

Multiple-choice Items for a Test of Teacher Competence in Educational Measurement, National Council on Measurement in Education. Ames, Iowa: Iowa State University, 1962.

Smith, Kendon, "An Investigation of the Use of 'Double-choice' Items in Testing Achievement," *Journal of Educational Research,* LI (1958), 387-89.

Weitzman, Ellis and W. J. McNamara, "Apt Use of the Inept Choice in Multiple-choice Testings," *Journal of Educational Research,* XXXIX (1946), 517-22.

Wesman, Alexander G. and George K. Bennett, "The Use of 'None of These' as an Option in Test Construction," *Journal of Educational Psychology,* XXVII, 541-49.

7 How to Administer and Score
an Achievement Test

In view of their crucial importance in the whole chain of events from the conception of the test to the use of scores in conferences with individuals, it seems highly unfortunate that the giving and scoring of tests are frequently treated very casually by both the authors and the users of tests.

ARTHUR E. TRAXLER

Unless the class is very large, unless the classroom is poorly suited for test administration, or unless other special problems are encountered, test administration usually is the simplest phase of the whole testing process. In the administration of external, standardized tests, the golden rule for the test administrator is: *Follow the directions in the manual precisely.* In classroom testing there usually is no manual and the need for rigidly standardized conditions of test administration is much less. Nevertheless, in test administration, as in most other matters, advanced planning usually pays dividends. Also there are some persistent problems associated with test administration, such as the questions of test time limits, of guessing on objective tests, and of cheating. These topics, together with the problems of efficient scoring of objective tests, will provide the subject matter of this chapter.

1. Test presentation

The questions for essay or problem tests are sometimes written on the chalkboard as the test period begins. This saves duplication costs and helps to maintain the secrecy of the questions, but it gives the teacher the double responsibility of copying the questions and of getting the students started to work on them, at a time when minutes are precious and when everyone is likely to be somewhat tense. And when the blackboard has been erased, no one has a valid record of exactly what the questions asked.

Oral dictation of test questions, especially short-answer or true-false questions has been tried with some success, but most students prefer to be able to look at the question while they are trying to decide on an answer to it. Putting the questions on slides and projecting them in a semidarkened room has also been tried.[1] It enables the examiner to pace the students and insures that each examinee will give at least brief consideration to each question. Studies indicate that examinees answer about as many questions correctly when they are forced to hurry as when they choose their own pace. If the rate of question presentation is rapid, more questions can be asked and more reliable scores obtained in a given testing period. But the students are generally unhappy with this kind of time pressure.

Probably the best method of test presentation is to duplicate enough copies so that each student can have one. In printed test copy, legibility of print and of format are prime considerations. Some classroom tests are duplicated unskillfully, on inadequate equipment. Questions may be crowded too closely together. Instead of being listed in a column, the response options to multiple-choice questions may be written in tandem to form a continuous, hard-to-read paragraph. Faults like these can be avoided by taking pains with the layout and duplication of test copy. Most modern standard-

---

[1] H. A. Curtis and Russell P. Kropp, "A Comparison of Scores Obtained by Administering a Test Normally and Visually," *Journal of Experimental Education*, XXIX (1961), 249-60; and Curtis and Kropp, *Experimental Analyses of the Effects of Various Modes of Item Presentation on the Scores and Factorial Content of Tests Administered by Visual and Audio-visual Means*, Department of Educational Research and Testing, Florida State University, Tallahassee, Florida, 1962, p. 83.

ized tests provide reasonably good models for the classroom teacher
to copy.

2. Preparing the students

In addition to preparing the test for the students, it is important
to prepare the students for the test. To begin with, they usually
should know that a test is coming. Any important test should be
announced well in advance. If a test is to have a desirable effect in
motivating and directing efforts to learn, the students not only
need to know that a test is coming but they need also to know the
kinds of achievements that the test will require them to demonstrate.
This means that the instructor should plan his tests *before* the course
begins, as part of the over-all planning for the course.

Some instructors favor surprise tests in the belief that such tests
keep the students studying regularly and discourage cramming. In
some situations these tactics may be necessary and effective. Most
instructors, however, see some elements of unfairness in surprise
tests. Further, cramming is unlikely to be effective with, or to be
encouraged by, a test of a student's command of knowledge. Such
command cannot be achieved in a few short sessions of intensive
cramming. Cramming is most essential and effective if the test requires no more than superficial memory for prominent details.
Advance announcement and description of a good test is likely to
do more to encourage effective study than the surprise administration of a test, especially if its nature has been kept secret from
the students.

3. Developing skill in test taking

In addition to knowing that a test is coming, and to knowing
what, in general, to expect in it, the student needs to know how to
give a good account of himself on the test. The measurement of a
student's achievement requires his active cooperation. If he lacks
skill in test taking, his score may fall short of indicating all of his
achievement. Test taking is not a highly specialized skill. It is not
difficult to master. But almost anyone who has taken more than a
few tests can testify from his own experience how easy it is to go
astray on an examination, how failure to heed all directions, or care-

lessness, or unwarranted assumption, or ignorance of some crucial rule of the game has marred an otherwise creditable test performance.

What are some of the legitimate and essential test-taking skills that an examinee ought to possess?

1. He ought to be aware of the danger of failing to read or listen attentively when directions for taking the test are presented and of the danger of failing to follow those directions exactly.

2. He should find out the basis on which his responses will be scored. Will points be subtracted for wrong responses or for errors in spelling, grammar, or punctuation? Will any questions carry more weight than others?

3. He should be aware of the premium which most human scorers, and most scoring machines, place on legibility and neatness. Accordingly, he should take pains in writing his answers or marking the answer sheet.

4. He should put himself in the best possible physical and mental shape for taking the test. Fatigue induced by an all night cram session, even when partially offset by coffee, is a heavy handicap to the test taker. He should realize that last-minute cramming is a poor substitute for consistent effort throughout the course, particularly if the test he is facing is likely to be a well-constructed measure of his command of knowledge. Some anxiety is useful in keeping the examinee up to doing his best, but jitters are even less helpful than fatigue.

5. He should pace himself so as to have time to consider and respond to all the test questions. This means that he must not puzzle too long over a difficult question or problem, nor extend too long his answer to an essay test question, even when a long answer seems easy to write.

6. He should know that ordinary guessing corrections really do not penalize even blind guessing, but simply seek not to reward it. Hence, he should conclude that his best interests usually will be served by attempting an answer to all questions, even those which he has only a slight basis for answering.

7. In answering an essay question, he should take time to reflect, to plan, and to organize his answer before starting to write. He should decide how much he can afford to write in the time available. And in all cases he should write something, however flimsy it may seem to be, as an answer.

8. If he is making responses on a separate answer sheet, he should check frequently to be sure his mark actually indicates the response he intended and that it is marked in the spaces provided for that question.

9. If possible, he should save time to reread his answers, to detect and correct any careless mistakes.

Since examinations do count, students and their teachers are well advised to spend some time considering how to cope with them most skillfully. Some good books on the subject, giving more detailed helps than we have suggested here, are available.[2]

4. The problem of test-wiseness

Concern is more often expressed over an excess of test-taking skill than over a deficiency. The suggestion is made that some examinees have developed this skill to such a degree that it enables the examinee to score well on a test for which he is otherwise almost totally unprepared.

There is some real basis for this concern. Certain tests, especially certain kinds of intelligence tests, include novel, unique, highly specialized tasks, such as figure analogies, number series, etc. For test problems of this character the main problem of the examinee is to "get the hang of" solving them. They do not reflect previous learning, nor is the skill developed in solving these test problems likely to be practically useful in other settings. Their use in intelligence testing is justified on the grounds that brighter students will get the hang of solving novel problems sooner, and more fully, than duller students.

Items of this type are seldom used in classroom tests. But there are common faults in item writing which may allow an examinee to substitute test-wiseness for knowledge. Specific determiners in true-false items provide one illustration. Statements including the words "always" or "never" tend to be false statements; those including words like "usually" or "seldom" tend to be true. Another illustration is provided by the tendency of writers of multiple-choice items to express the correct response more carefully than the dis-

---

[2] Joseph C. Heston, *How to Take a Test* (Chicago: Science Research Associates, 1953); and Herschel Manuel, *Taking a Test* (New York: Harcourt, Brace & World, Inc., 1956).

tracters and hence to make it longer and more fully qualified than the distracters. The test constructor must guard against these and other faults if his test is to measure specific subject competence rather than general test-taking sophistication. But if the test is a good measure of achievement, one which tests command of knowledge, and if it is free of technical flaws, more error in measurement is likely to originate from students who have too little, rather than too much, skill in taking tests.

5. The problem of test anxiety

The problem of test anxiety was mentioned in the preceding section. Anxiety is a frequent side-effect of testing, whether that testing occurs in the classroom, on the athletic field, in the art exhibit hall, in the court room, in the conference room where a crucial business decision is being discussed, or in the legislative chamber where a bill is being debated. Test anxiety in the classroom is not something unique. It is a part, though hopefully not too large a part, of life itself.

Because human beings are complex and the situations in which they are tested are diverse, it is unlikely that any simple, universal answers will be found to questions concerning the cause and cure of test anxiety. Some research has been done on test anxiety, particularly among young children. However, the measurement of anxiety is no simple problem. It is not surprising that few generalizations of wide applicability can be defended solidly on the basis of research findings. However, combining what controlled experimentation has reported with common observations of human behavior, it is possible to offer a few generalizations that seem reasonably safe.

1. There is a negative correlation between level of ability and level of test anxiety.[3] Those who are most capable tend to be least anxious when facing a test.
2. There is a positive correlation between level of anxiety and level of aspiration. Those who are most anxious when facing a test tend to be those who have the greatest need or desire to do well on it.

---

[3] Irwin G. Sarason, "Empirical Findings and Theoretical Problems in the Use of Anxiety Scales," *Psychological Bulletin* (1960), pp. 403-15.

3. Mild degrees of anxiety facilitate and enhance test performance. More extreme degrees are likely to interfere with and depress test performance.

4. The more frequent a student's contact with tests of a particular type given for a particular purpose, the less likely he is to be the victim of extreme anxiety.

5. Test anxiety can be educationally useful if it is distributed, at a relatively low level, throughout the course of instruction, instead of being concentrated, at a relatively high level, just prior to and during an examination. Skillful teaching involves the controlled release of the energy stimulated by test anxiety.

Evidence to support the belief that some students of good or superior achievement characteristically go to pieces and do poorly on every examination is hard to find. Since individuals differ in many respects, it is reasonable to suppose that they may differ also in their tolerance of the kind of stress which tests generate. On the other hand, it is conceivable that apparent instances of underachievement on tests may actually be instances of overindication of ability in other situations. That is, a student whose achievement is really quite modest may have cultivated the poise, the ready response, the verbal facility, and the pleasing manners which enable him to pass for an accomplished and promising scholar in all save impersonal test situations. All things considered, a teacher is well advised to take with several grains of salt a student's claim that his test performances never do justice to his real achievements.

6. Administering the test

Normally, as suggested earlier, the actual administration of the test involves relatively few and simple problems. Since the time available for the test is usually limited, and seldom as long as some of the students wish, every available minute should be used to good advantage. By giving preliminary instructions before the day of the test, by organizing the test materials for efficient distribution, by keeping last-minute oral directions and answers to questions as brief as possible, the test can be started promptly to give each student the maximum amount of time to work on it. Corresponding provisions for efficient collection of materials and advance notice to the students that all work must stop when time is called, help to conclude the test on time and in an orderly fashion.

To aid the students in pacing themselves, it is helpful for the teacher to write a statement like this on the chalkboard near the beginning of the test.

> No more than ———— minutes remain for you to work on this test.
>
> If you have not reached item ———— you are working too slowly.

By changing the numbers entered in these statements every ten or fifteen minutes, the teacher can help the students find time to consider all questions.

During almost any test administration, some students are likely to feel the need of asking some questions. Questions such as those growing out of errors in the test copy or ambiguities in the directions or the test questions require answers if the students are to respond properly. A teacher should help a student to understand the tasks but should stop short of helping him to solve them. Sometimes the dividing line is hard to determine.

Such questions as those stimulated by obvious but noncritical typographical errors should not even be asked. Since the process of asking and answering a question during the course of an examination is always disturbing to others, even if it is done as quietly and discreetly as possible, and since the answer to one student's question might possibly give him an unfair advantage over the others, students should be urged to avoid all but the most necessary questions. Advice to them on this point can well be given prior to the day of the examination.

7. The problem of cheating

In addition to giving directions, answering questions, and helping the students keep track of time, the instructor has at least one other major responsibility during the course of administering a test. That is to prevent cheating. This problem, which students, teachers, and educational administrators tend to agree is serious, seems to receive more attention in the popular press than in technical books and articles on testing. Cheating on examinations is commonly viewed as a sign of declining ethical standards or as an inevitable consequence of increased emphasis on test scores and grades.

Any activity of a student or group of students whose purpose is to give any of them higher grades than they would be likely to receive on the basis of their own achievements is cheating. Thus the term covers a wide variety of activities, such as:

1. The side-long glance at a fellow student's answers
2. The preparation and use of a crib sheet
3. Collusion between two or more students to exchange information on answers during the test
4. Unauthorized copying of questions or stealing of test booklets in anticipation that they may be used again later on
5. Arranging for a substitute to take an examination
6. Stealing or buying copies of an examination before the test is given, or sharing such illicit advanced copies with others

While these various forms of cheating differ in seriousness, none can be viewed with indifference. The typical student has many opportunities to cheat. Some circumstances may even encourage him to cheat. But there is none which justifies him in doing so. A student may conclude, not without some justification, that the ethical standards of many of his fellow students are not very high, at least where cheating on examinations is concerned. He may go on to infer that this fact requires him to lower his own standards or justifies him in doing so. Whatever other conditions may contribute to it, cheating would not occur if all students were to recognize that it is always dishonest and usually unfair.

Some acts of cheating are no doubt motivated by desperation. The more extreme the desperation, the more ambitious and serious the attempt to cheat is likely to be. A cause contributing to cheating is carelessness on the instructor's part in safeguarding the examination copy before it is administered and in supervising the students during the examination.

As already mentioned, emphasis on grades is sometimes blamed as a primary cause of cheating. But since grades are, or should be, symbols of educational achievement, the blame, if any is warranted, should be directed toward emphasis on individual efforts to achieve. No doubt most students would find it easier to resist the temptation to cheat if no advantage of any consequence was likely to result from the cheating. But refusal to recognize and reward achievement may be as effective in reducing achievement as in reducing cheating. Such a price seems too heavy to pay.

Increased use of objective tests has also been blamed as a cause of cheating. The mode of response to objective tests makes some kinds of cheating easier, but the multiplicity of questions makes other kinds of cheating more difficult. No form of test is immune to all forms of cheating. The quality of a test, however, may have a direct bearing on the temptation it offers to students to cheat. Demand for detailed, superficial knowledge encourages the preparation of crib sheets. If the examination seems to the students unlikely to yield valid measures of their real achievements, if it seems unfair to them in terms of the instruction they have received, if their scores seem likely to be determined by irrelevant factors anyway, the crime of cheating may seem less serious.

What cures are there for cheating? The basic cure is related to the basic cause. Students and their teachers must recognize that cheating is dishonest and unfair and that it deserves consistent application of appropriate penalties—failure in the course, loss of credit, suspension, or dismissal. Reports on the prevalence of cheating, sometimes exaggerated no doubt, should not be allowed to establish cheating as an acceptable norm for student behavior or to persuade instructors that cheating is inevitable and must be accommodated as gracefully as possible.

It is the responsibility of the instructor to avoid any conditions which make cheating easy—before, during, or after an examination. The security of the examination must be safeguarded while it is being written and duplicated and when it is stored. If the class is large and if the students cannot be seated in alternate seats, alternate forms of the examination should be distributed to students sitting in adjacent seats. Alternate forms satisfactory for this purpose can be provided by arranging the same questions in different order. Finally, the instructor should take seriously the task of proctoring his examinations as part of his responsibility to the majority of students who will not cheat and who should not be penalized for their honesty.

A teacher has considerable authority in his own classroom. It should not be abused through overuse under stress or through underuse when the situation requires it. If the teacher is satisfied beyond any reasonable doubt that a student is cheating, the teacher needs no other justification for:

1. Collecting the examination materials and quietly dismissing the student from the room
2. Voiding the results of the examination, requiring an alternative make-up examination, or giving the student a failing grade on the examination
3. Bringing the incident to the attention of the school authorities if further action seems necessary

8. Honor systems

One frequently mentioned proposal for dealing with problems like cheating involves establishment of an honor system. Honor systems vary, but they have in common a cultivation of the student's sense of responsibility for personal honor and for the honor of the group. They vary in the responsibilities they place on the students for maintaining the system and in the means used for dealing with infractions.

Those honor systems which obligate students to inform designated authorities of the dishonorable acts of other students require a drastic change in one aspect of the code of human behavior—that which forbids talebearing. The honor sought by the honor system thus must be purchased at the price of another kind of honor, that of loyalty to one's close associates. It is not surprising that systems of this kind sometimes break down.

Honor systems seem to work best in educational institutions whose moderate size and rich traditions encourage strong group identification and loyalties. The spirit of honor on which the system depends seldom arises or maintains itself spontaneously. It must be cultivated carefully and continuously. The things which must be done, or avoided, to maintain personal honor and the honor of the group are usually clearly defined in a code or by well-rehearsed tradition. The degree to which student experience with an honor system in such an environment cultivates a general and lasting spirit of personal honor in a world where no such system is in effect may be open to question. That such systems have worked to limit, or even eliminate, cheating in certain institutions seems beyond doubt. That such systems sometimes break down, disastrously, is also beyond doubt. What is not beyond doubt is the widespread belief that adoption of the honor system is a feasible answer to the problem of cheating on examinations in almost any school or college.

9. Loss of test security

Instructors and administrators, especially at the college level, are occasionally beset by rumors that copies of this or that examination are "out" in advance of the scheduled administration of the examination. Sometimes the rumors are founded on fact. More often they are founded on a misunderstanding and spread in the colloquies of anxious students. Finally the rumor (not so identified, of course) reaches the ears of the instructor, often via one or a number of anonymous telephone calls. What is the instructor to do then?

The first thing to do is to try to determine whether or not the rumor is founded on fact. This is the instructor's responsibility and he should spare no effort in the pursuit of evidence. If he is ready to enlist the aid of his informants and if they are willing to help, even anonymously, the task may be possible. If the informants are unable or unwilling to supply any leads, then they should be told courteously but plainly that their information is worthless and their transmission of it harmful.

If verifiable evidence is obtained that some students have, or have seen, advance copies of the examination, the only reasonable course of action is to prepare a new examination, even if it means changing the form of the examination and possibly losing a night of sleep. But if such evidence cannot be obtained even by searching hard for it, the rumor had probably best be allowed to die as quietly as it will.

Problems of this kind are most likely to arise and to cause most serious difficulties on college campuses. They have occurred in high schools, however. Care in safeguarding the examinations before they are given is the best preventative. But it is also helpful to be ready to respond wisely, and vigorously if the situation warrants, when the rumors that a test is out *do* begin to circulate, as they almost surely will sooner or later.

10. Procedures for test scoring

Student answers to objective test items may be recorded either on the test copy itself or on a separate answer sheet. Recording answers in the test booklet has several slight advantages. The student's task is a bit simpler and the danger of error in recording responses is a bit less. The corrected copy of the test is also easier to use for instructional purposes when the answers have been recorded and scored directly in the test booklet. The use of a separate answer sheet, on the other hand, makes the scorer's task much easier. It also makes possible the reuse of the test booklet. If a scoring machine is to be used, the answers must be recorded on an answer sheet which the machine is designed to handle. Exhibit 7.1 illustrates an answer sheet designed for hand scoring.

If the answers are to be recorded on the test booklet, space for the answers should be provided near one margin of the test pages. To speed scoring and minimize the chance for errors, the scorer may record correct answers on the columns of a separate answer key card, using one column for each page of answers and positioning the answers in the column so that they will match the answer spaces on the test copy.

In scoring the answers recorded in test booklets, the scorer may find it helpful to mark the answers, using a colored pencil. A short horizontal line through the student's response can be used to indicate a correct response. Sometimes it is advantageous to mark all responses using, in addition to the horizontal line for correct responses, an "X" through the response for an incorrect response and a circle around the answer space to indicate an omitted response.

Responses are indicated on most separate answer sheets by marking one of the several response positions provided opposite the number of each item. Such answer sheets may be scored by hand, using a stencil key with holes punched to correspond to the correct responses. Alternatively, of course, they may be scored on the machine for which the answer sheet was designed. When a separate answer sheet and a punched key are used, it is possible to indicate incorrect or omitted items by using a colored pencil to encircle the answer spaces that the student did not mark. This kind of marking

STANDARD ANSWER SHEET

Scores
1. ________
2. ________
3. ________
4. ________

Test Title: ____

Name: ____
Last name — first name — initial

Section: ______________________ **Date:** ____________________ 195__.

Directions: Mark a heavy cross (X) in the box corresponding to the answer to each exercise.

	a b c d e		a b c d e		a b c d e		a b c d e		a b c d e
1	☐ ☐ ☐ ☐ ☐	34	☐ ☐ ☐ ☐ ☐	67	☐ ☐ ☐ ☐ ☐	100	☐ ☐ ☐ ☐ ☐	133	☐ ☐ ☐ ☐ ☐
2	☐ ☐ ☐ ☐ ☐	35	☐ ☐ ☐ ☐ ☐	68	☐ ☐ ☐ ☐ ☐	101	☐ ☐ ☐ ☐ ☐	134	☐ ☐ ☐ ☐ ☐
3	☐ ☐ ☐ ☐ ☐	36	☐ ☐ ☐ ☐ ☐	69	☐ ☐ ☐ ☐ ☐	102	☐ ☐ ☐ ☐ ☐	135	☐ ☐ ☐ ☐ ☐
4	☐ ☐ ☐ ☐ ☐	37	☐ ☐ ☐ ☐ ☐	70	☐ ☐ ☐ ☐ ☐	103	☐ ☐ ☐ ☐ ☐	136	☐ ☐ ☐ ☐ ☐
5	☐ ☐ ☐ ☐ ☐	38	☐ ☐ ☐ ☐ ☐	71	☐ ☐ ☐ ☐ ☐	104	☐ ☐ ☐ ☐ ☐	137	☐ ☐ ☐ ☐ ☐
6	☐ ☐ ☐ ☐ ☐	39	☐ ☐ ☐ ☐ ☐	72	☐ ☐ ☐ ☐ ☐	105	☐ ☐ ☐ ☐ ☐	138	☐ ☐ ☐ ☐ ☐
7	☐ ☐ ☐ ☐ ☐	40	☐ ☐ ☐ ☐ ☐	73	☐ ☐ ☐ ☐ ☐	106	☐ ☐ ☐ ☐ ☐	139	☐ ☐ ☐ ☐ ☐
8	☐ ☐ ☐ ☐ ☐	41	☐ ☐ ☐ ☐ ☐	74	☐ ☐ ☐ ☐ ☐	107	☐ ☐ ☐ ☐ ☐	140	☐ ☐ ☐ ☐ ☐
9	☐ ☐ ☐ ☐ ☐	42	☐ ☐ ☐ ☐ ☐	75	☐ ☐ ☐ ☐ ☐	108	☐ ☐ ☐ ☐ ☐	141	☐ ☐ ☐ ☐ ☐
10	☐ ☐ ☐ ☐ ☐	43	☐ ☐ ☐ ☐ ☐	76	☐ ☐ ☐ ☐ ☐	109	☐ ☐ ☐ ☐ ☐	142	☐ ☐ ☐ ☐ ☐
11	☐ ☐ ☐ ☐ ☐	44	☐ ☐ ☐ ☐ ☐	77	☐ ☐ ☐ ☐ ☐	110	☐ ☐ ☐ ☐ ☐	143	☐ ☐ ☐ ☐ ☐
12	☐ ☐ ☐ ☐ ☐	45	☐ ☐ ☐ ☐ ☐	78	☐ ☐ ☐ ☐ ☐	111	☐ ☐ ☐ ☐ ☐	144	☐ ☐ ☐ ☐ ☐
13	☐ ☐ ☐ ☐ ☐	46	☐ ☐ ☐ ☐ ☐	79	☐ ☐ ☐ ☐ ☐	112	☐ ☐ ☐ ☐ ☐	145	☐ ☐ ☐ ☐ ☐
14	☐ ☐ ☐ ☐ ☐	47	☐ ☐ ☐ ☐ ☐	80	☐ ☐ ☐ ☐ ☐	113	☐ ☐ ☐ ☐ ☐	146	☐ ☐ ☐ ☐ ☐
15	☐ ☐ ☐ ☐ ☐	48	☐ ☐ ☐ ☐ ☐	81	☐ ☐ ☐ ☐ ☐	114	☐ ☐ ☐ ☐ ☐	147	☐ ☐ ☐ ☐ ☐
16	☐ ☐ ☐ ☐ ☐	49	☐ ☐ ☐ ☐ ☐	82	☐ ☐ ☐ ☐ ☐	115	☐ ☐ ☐ ☐ ☐	148	☐ ☐ ☐ ☐ ☐
17	☐ ☐ ☐ ☐ ☐	50	☐ ☐ ☐ ☐ ☐	83	☐ ☐ ☐ ☐ ☐	116	☐ ☐ ☐ ☐ ☐	149	☐ ☐ ☐ ☐ ☐
18	☐ ☐ ☐ ☐ ☐	51	☐ ☐ ☐ ☐ ☐	84	☐ ☐ ☐ ☐ ☐	117	☐ ☐ ☐ ☐ ☐	150	☐ ☐ ☐ ☐ ☐
19	☐ ☐ ☐ ☐ ☐	52	☐ ☐ ☐ ☐ ☐	85	☐ ☐ ☐ ☐ ☐	118	☐ ☐ ☐ ☐ ☐	151	☐ ☐ ☐ ☐ ☐
20	☐ ☐ ☐ ☐ ☐	53	☐ ☐ ☐ ☐ ☐	86	☐ ☐ ☐ ☐ ☐	119	☐ ☐ ☐ ☐ ☐	152	☐ ☐ ☐ ☐ ☐
21	☐ ☐ ☐ ☐ ☐	54	☐ ☐ ☐ ☐ ☐	87	☐ ☐ ☐ ☐ ☐	120	☐ ☐ ☐ ☐ ☐	153	☐ ☐ ☐ ☐ ☐
22	☐ ☐ ☐ ☐ ☐	55	☐ ☐ ☐ ☐ ☐	88	☐ ☐ ☐ ☐ ☐	121	☐ ☐ ☐ ☐ ☐	154	☐ ☐ ☐ ☐ ☐
23	☐ ☐ ☐ ☐ ☐	56	☐ ☐ ☐ ☐ ☐	89	☐ ☐ ☐ ☐ ☐	122	☐ ☐ ☐ ☐ ☐	155	☐ ☐ ☐ ☐ ☐
24	☐ ☐ ☐ ☐ ☐	57	☐ ☐ ☐ ☐ ☐	90	☐ ☐ ☐ ☐ ☐	123	☐ ☐ ☐ ☐ ☐	156	☐ ☐ ☐ ☐ ☐
25	☐ ☐ ☐ ☐ ☐	58	☐ ☐ ☐ ☐ ☐	91	☐ ☐ ☐ ☐ ☐	124	☐ ☐ ☐ ☐ ☐	157	☐ ☐ ☐ ☐ ☐
26	☐ ☐ ☐ ☐ ☐	59	☐ ☐ ☐ ☐ ☐	92	☐ ☐ ☐ ☐ ☐	125	☐ ☐ ☐ ☐ ☐	158	☐ ☐ ☐ ☐ ☐
27	☐ ☐ ☐ ☐ ☐	60	☐ ☐ ☐ ☐ ☐	93	☐ ☐ ☐ ☐ ☐	126	☐ ☐ ☐ ☐ ☐	159	☐ ☐ ☐ ☐ ☐
28	☐ ☐ ☐ ☐ ☐	61	☐ ☐ ☐ ☐ ☐	94	☐ ☐ ☐ ☐ ☐	127	☐ ☐ ☐ ☐ ☐	160	☐ ☐ ☐ ☐ ☐
29	☐ ☐ ☐ ☐ ☐	62	☐ ☐ ☐ ☐ ☐	95	☐ ☐ ☐ ☐ ☐	128	☐ ☐ ☐ ☐ ☐	161	☐ ☐ ☐ ☐ ☐
30	☐ ☐ ☐ ☐ ☐	63	☐ ☐ ☐ ☐ ☐	96	☐ ☐ ☐ ☐ ☐	129	☐ ☐ ☐ ☐ ☐	162	☐ ☐ ☐ ☐ ☐
31	☐ ☐ ☐ ☐ ☐	64	☐ ☐ ☐ ☐ ☐	97	☐ ☐ ☐ ☐ ☐	130	☐ ☐ ☐ ☐ ☐	163	☐ ☐ ☐ ☐ ☐
32	☐ ☐ ☐ ☐ ☐	65	☐ ☐ ☐ ☐ ☐	98	☐ ☐ ☐ ☐ ☐	131	☐ ☐ ☐ ☐ ☐	164	☐ ☐ ☐ ☐ ☐
33	☐ ☐ ☐ ☐ ☐	66	☐ ☐ ☐ ☐ ☐	99	☐ ☐ ☐ ☐ ☐	132	☐ ☐ ☐ ☐ ☐	165	☐ ☐ ☐ ☐ ☐

Exhibit 7.1. Standard Answer Sheet

is useful when the answer sheets are returned with copies of the test for class discussion.

Most classroom tests of educational achievement are scored by the instructor. If the test is in essay form, the skill and judgment of the instructor or of someone equally competent are essential. The task of scoring an objective test is essentially clerical and can often be handled by someone whose time is less expensive than an instructor's time and whose skill and energy are less in demand for other educational tasks.

Some school systems and colleges maintain central scoring services. Usually these services make use of small scoring machines, several of which are now available. But even if all the scoring is done by hand, a central service has the value of fostering the development of special skills which make for rapid, accurate scoring. Institutional test scoring services often provide statistical and test analysis services as well. Sometimes they offer test duplication services, providing expert assistance in the special problems of test production and in the maintenance of test security.[4]

Instructors sometimes use the class meeting following the test for test scoring, asking each student to check the answers on the paper of one of his classmates. In some situations this may be a reasonable and rewarding use of class time. But often the process tends to be slow and inaccurate. A difficulty encountered by one student on one test paper may interrupt and delay the whole operation. If the student scorers are concentrating on mechanical accuracy of scoring, as they probably should be, the circumstances will not favor much learning as a by-product of the scoring process.

But students can and usually should have the chance to learn from the mistakes they make on a test. Ordinarily the best occasion for this learning is *after* the tests have been scored and the student's answer sheet has been returned to him. The correct answer to each item can be recorded on the blackboard, on a duplicated hand-out, or best of all, on the student's answer sheet itself. With this information each student can satisfy himself of the accuracy with which his answers have been scored. If he also has a copy of the test, he can discover the nature of his mistakes or ask for an explanation, if

---

[4] Robert L. Ebel, "Improving Evaluation of Educational Outcomes at the College Level," *Proceedings, 1953 Invitational Conference on Testing Problems* (Princeton, N.J.: Educational Testing Service, 1954).

necessary. Protracted arguments over the correctness of the instructor's choice of correct answers can be avoided by asking the protesting student to state his case in writing, with a promise of credit if the case seems to merit it. Discussions of this kind contribute to the student's feeling that he is being treated openly and fairly. They can also contribute enough to an increase of the student's command of knowledge to be well worth the time required.

11. Scoring machines

A number of machines are now available for scoring objective test answer sheets. The first, and still the most widely used, of these machines is the IBM 805 (Figure 7.1). The student marks his re-

Figure 7.1. IBM 805 Scoring Machine (Courtesy of International Business Machines Corporation.)

sponses, using a special pencil whose marks will conduct an electric current, on a special 8½″ × 11″ answer sheet (Exhibit 7.2). This sheet has space for indicating answers to 150 five-response multiple-choice items, or 300 two-choice (true-false) items, on one side. Both

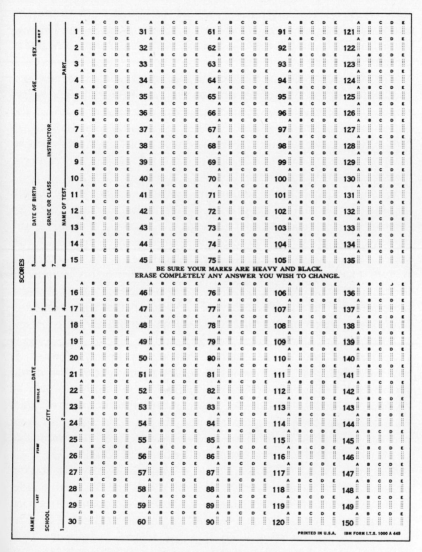

Exhibit 7.2. IBM Answer Sheet (Courtesy of International Business Machines Corporation.)

217

sides of the answer sheet may be used, although both cannot be scored simultaneously. Each side of the answer sheet is divided into ten fields which can be scored separately to obtain scores on different parts of the test.

The machine is set up to score a particular test by means of a cardboard $8\frac{1}{2}'' \times 11''$ key on which holes have been punched to correspond to the correct responses. This key can also be used for the hand scoring of answer sheets. The key controls the positions of 750 pin switches, one opposite each response position, to determine whether a particular mark shall be counted among the right or among the wrong responses.

When an answer sheet is inserted in the machine, the student's graphite pencil marks are pressed against metal contact fingers so that an electric current flows through the mark. The total of the currents through each of the correctly placed marks is fed to a meter which can be adjusted to indicate the number of marks correctly placed. The meter can also be switched to other circuits to indicate the number of wrong responses, the total number of responses, or a score showing the difference between the number of right responses and some fraction of the number of wrong responses.

If the answer sheets have been well and neatly marked, using a proper pencil, and if the machine has been properly adjusted, it will yield highly accurate scores. A skilled operator can obtain and record from 300 to 500 scores per hour. The machine can also be equipped with a special device which records the number of times each response to each question was chosen. The graphic item counter is extremely useful in the analysis of item discriminating power and difficulty, a process to be discussed in Chapter 11.

Recently several other machines designed especially for scoring classroom tests have appeared. One of these, the Burgess Grade-O-Mat, manufactured by Burgess Cellulose Company, Freeport, Illinois, is about the size of a portable typewriter (Figure 7.2). The answer card this machine is equipped to score is a standard IBM precut port-a-punch card like those shown in Exhibit 7.3. The student can mark his answer choices in pencil on the card. Then at the end of the test period he can place the answer card on a cellulose sponge backing and use a plastic stylus to punch out the marked positions. While it is often said that a hole is hard to "erase," these holes can be. If a punched out bit of card is replaced exactly over

Figure 7.2. Burgess Grade-O-Mat

the hole to be "erased" and is then pressed down firmly and rubbed smooth with the round barrel of the stylus, it will stay in place through all ordinary card handling.

The hand-fed Grade-O-Mat optically counts the number of holes in the student's answer card that correspond to holes in the examiner's answer-key card. Counting the wrong responses calls for a separate key and a separate scoring operation. The machine is simple to operate and highly accurate. About 200 answer cards can be scored per hour. A simple card provides about 450 response positions. This means it can accommodate 225 true-false questions, 150 three-response questions, or 90 five-response questions.

A somewhat larger machine is the Grademaster, distributed by Acme Visible Records, Inc., of Crozet, Virginia (Figure 7.3). This machine looks something like a school duplicating machine. It is motor driven and has an automatic answer-sheet feed. The $8\frac{1}{2}''$ × 11″ answer sheet has space for fifty true-false or multiple-choice answers (Exhibit 7.4). A student marks his answer choice by completing or filling in the black rectangle, using a #1 or #2 pencil. He can change his answer by erasing the first mark and making a second.

In scoring, using electrical conductivity, the machine marks each wrong answer, counts the total number of wrong answers, and

NAME _____

TEST NAME _____

SCORE _____ DATE _____

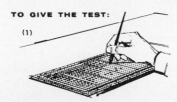

TO GIVE THE TEST:

(1)

Each student is provided with standard port-a-punch answer card, sponge, stylus and test questions. Student punches out hole representing correct answer on each question. Possibility of student copying from neighbor's answer is virtually eliminated.

(3)

The student card is placed directly over the key card. It is scored automatically by the machine in about 11½ seconds.

TO SCORE THE TEST:

(2)

Master or key card, provided by teacher, with correct answers punched out, is placed on carriage of machine by scorer.

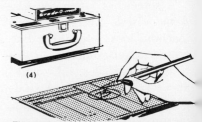

(4)

The scorer removes the student card, notes the score, and goes on to the next. (Actual time studies prove an efficient scorer can process about 200 tests in one hour.)

Exhibit 7.3. Burgess Grade-O-Mat and Port-A-Punch Card

stamps this total on the answer sheet. An omitted answer is counted the same as a wrong answer. It also counts the total number of wrong answers on any set of answer sheets. About 300 sheets can be graded per hour by this machine. Like the Grade-O-Mat, this machine is accurate in scoring and very well constructed.

Other scoring machines, such as those at the State University of

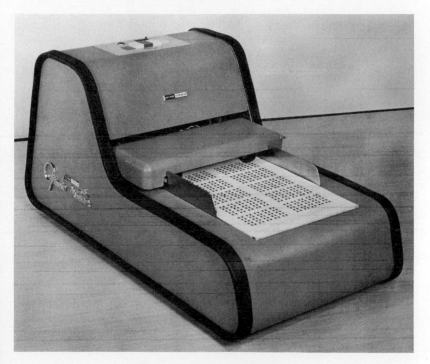

Figure 7.3. Grademaster

Iowa and the Educational Testing Service, are much larger, much faster, and of course, much more expensive. Machines of this kind are specially designed to handle the large volumes and multitest batteries used in large-scale testing programs. They are flexible enough, however, to handle a wide variety of tests. If the number of answer sheets to be scored is large enough to justify the special preparations and programming required, these machines can afford considerable economy in scoring objective tests.

For use with *Grade master* test scoring machine.

Important: Make no marks on this side of sheet except in the blocks below. For complete instructions see reverse side.

	TRUE	FALSE					TRUE	FALSE			
1	a	b	c	d	e	26	a	b	c	d	e
2	a	b	c	d	e	27	a	b	c	d	e
3	a	b	c	d	e	28	a	b	c	d	e
4	a	b	c	d	e	29	a	b	c	d	e
5	a	b	c	d	e	30	a	b	c	d	e

	TRUE	FALSE					TRUE	FALSE			
6	a	b	c	d	e	31	a	b	c	d	e
7	a	b	c	d	e	32	a	b	c	d	e
8	a	b	c	d	e	33	a	b	c	d	e
9	a	b	c	d	e	34	a	b	c	d	e
10	a	b	c	d	e	35	a	b	c	d	e

	TRUE	FALSE					TRUE	FALSE			
11	a	b	c	d	e	36	a	b	c	d	e
12	a	b	c	d	e	37	a	b	c	d	e
13	a	b	c	d	e	38	a	b	c	d	e
14	a	b	c	d	e	39	a	b	c	d	e
15	a	b	c	d	e	40	a	b	c	d	e

	TRUE	FALSE					TRUE	FALSE			
16	a	b	c	d	e	41	a	b	c	d	e
17	a	b	c	d	e	42	a	b	c	d	e
18	a	b	c	d	e	43	a	b	c	d	e
19	a	b	c	d	e	44	a	b	c	d	e
20	a	b	c	d	e	45	a	b	c	d	e

	TRUE	FALSE					TRUE	FALSE			
21	a	b	c	d	e	46	a	b	c	d	e
22	a	b	c	d	e	47	a	b	c	d	e
23	a	b	c	d	e	48	a	b	c	d	e
24	a	b	c	d	e	49	a	b	c	d	e
25	a	b	c	d	e	50	a	b	c	d	e

FORM 368   PRINTED IN U.S.A.   COPYRIGHT 1964   GRADEMASTER DIVISION

Exhibit 7.4. Answer Sheet

12. Correction for guessing

Scores on objective tests are sometimes corrected for guessing. The purpose of such a correction is to reduce to zero the gain in score expected to result from blind guessing. In other words, a guessing correction is intended to give the student who guesses blindly on certain questions no reasonable expectation of advantage in the long run over the student who omits the same questions.

Suppose a student were to guess blindly on 100 true-false test items. Since there are only two possible answers, one of which is certain to be correct, the student has reason to expect that his blind guesses will be right half of the time. Thus his expected score on the 100-item true-false test would be 50. Another student, knowing no less than the first but reluctant to guess blindly, might attempt no answers. His score would be zero. Without correction for guessing, the score of the first student would be higher than that of the second when, in fact, the two scores should be the same.

To correct the first student's score for guessing, it is necessary to subtract from his score an amount equal to his expected gain from blind guessing. Since on a true-false test he can expect to answer one question wrongly for every question he answers rightly, the number of wrong answers is simply subtracted from the number of right answers. If the questions provided three equally likely answers instead of two, the student would expect to give two wrong answers to every right answer. In this case one would subtract one-half of the number of wrong responses from the number of right responses to correct for guessing. If multiple-choice items list five alternative possible answers to each question, only one of which is correct, the expected ratio of wrong to right answers is 4 to 1 and the guessing correction would call for subtracting one-fourth of the number of wrong answers from the number of right answers.

Logic of this kind leads to a general formula for correction for guessing

$$S = R - \frac{W}{N - 1} \qquad\qquad 7.1$$

in which S stands for the score corrected for guessing, R for the number of questions answered rightly, W for the number of questions answered wrongly, and N for the number of possible alternative answers, equally likely to be chosen in blind guessing. It is easy to see that this formula becomes

$$S = R - W \qquad 7.2$$

in the case of two-alternative (true-false) items, or

$$S = R - \frac{W}{4} \qquad 7.3$$

in the case of five alternative multiple-choice test items.

Instead of penalizing the student who guesses, one could correct for guessing by rewarding the student who refrains from guessing. That is, instead of subtracting fifty units from the score of the guesser, we could add fifty units to the score of the nonguesser. This too would eliminate the expected advantage from blind guessing. The assumption in this case is that if the nonguesser had guessed, he would have given the right answer to one-half of the true-false items. On three alternative items he would have been right in his answers to one-third of the items.

Logic of this kind leads to a second general formula for guessing correction

$$S' = R + \frac{O}{N} \qquad 7.4$$

in which S' is the score corrected for guessing on the basis of items omitted, R is the number of items answered correctly, O is the number of items omitted, and N is the number of alternative answers whose choice is equally likely on the basis of blind guessing. Again, it is easy to see that this general formula becomes

$$S' = R + \frac{O}{2} \qquad 7.5$$

in the case of true-false items, or

$$S' = R + \frac{O}{5} \qquad 7.6$$

in the case of five-alternative multiple-choice test items.

If the same set of test scores is corrected for guessing in two different ways, by subtracting a fraction of the wrong answers and by adding a fraction of the omitted answers, two different sets of corrected scores will be obtained. But while the two sets of scores will differ in their average value (with the omit-corrected scores being higher in all cases) and in their variability (with the omit-corrected scores being more variable almost always), the two sets of scores will be perfectly correlated. If student A makes a higher score than student B when the appropriate fractions of their wrong responses are subtracted from the total of their right responses, A will also make a higher score than B when the appropriate fraction of their items omitted is added to the total of their right responses.

Correction for guessing by subtracting a fraction of the wrong responses is sometimes criticized on the ground that it is based on a false assumption—the assumption that every wrong response is the result of blind guessing. But the falseness of that assumption (and usually it is completely false) does not invalidate the correction formula which rests on it, for no such assumption is made in the formula for guessing correction on the basis of items omitted and yet the two formulas yield scores which agree perfectly in their relative ranking of students. Scores corrected by subtraction may be regarded logically as too low in absolute value, just as those corrected by addition may be regarded logically as too high in absolute value. But they are equally sound in relative value. With scores on tests of educational achievement, the absolute value is usually far less significant than the relative value.

It is also worth noting here that if no items are omitted, scores corrected for guessing by subtracting a fraction of the wrong responses correlate perfectly with the uncorrected scores, that is, with the numbers of right responses. This indicates that the magnitude of the effect of a guessing correction depends on the proportion of items omitted. Only if considerable numbers of items are omitted by at least some of the students will the application of either formula for correction for guessing have an appreciable effect.

Correction for guessing is sometimes misunderstood to mean that the effects of chance on the test scores are eliminated or reduced, that the lucky guesser will, after his score is corrected, fare no better than the unlucky guesser. How far this is from truth is illustrated in Table 7.1. To make the illustration as simple as possible we have assumed that thirty-two students attempt all ten items of a true-false test. Each student presumably knew the answers to five of the

ten questions. Hence the true score on this test of each of the
thirty-two students should have been 5, as indicated in the second
column of Table 7.1.

TABLE 7.1

Scores of Thirty-two Students of Equal Ability
on a Ten-item True-False Test

		Frequency Distributions of Scores	
Scale of Test Scores	True	Uncorrected	Corrected
10		1	1
9		5	
8		10	5
7		10	
6		5	10
5	32	1	
4			10
3			
2			5
1			
0			1

But they guess, and as usually befalls those who guess, some are
luckier than others. The laws of probability indicate that one of the
thirty-two would guess right on all five of the remaining questions,
and thus get a total score of 10. Five of the thirty-two would be
lucky on four of the five questions and get scores of 9. One poor
soul would be completely unlucky and guess wrong on all five
questions. His score would remain at 5, reflecting his knowledge
but no luck. These facts are shown in the third column of Table 7.1.

Does the application of a guessing-correction formula improve the
situation? Look at the fourth column of Table 7.1, which displays
the scores obtained by applying Formula 7.2. The differences due
to chance have not been eliminated or even reduced. They have
been magnified. Paraphrasing the words of the Bible: To him that
hath luck a high score shall be given, even after correction for
guessing. From him that hath not luck, even that score which is
rightfully his shall be taken away!

Should the scores on objective tests of educational achievement
be corrected for guessing? Among the considerations that should
influence the instructor's decision are these.

1. *Scores corrected for guessing will usually rank students in about the same relative positions as do the uncorrected scores.*

Almost all experimental studies of the effect of announced correction for guessing on the reliability and validity of test scores have shown slight, if any, improvement attributable to the correction. Usually the correlation between corrected and uncorrected scores from the same test answers is in the high nineties—nearly perfect in terms of the standards of mental tests. Corrected scores may be slightly more reliable or slightly less reliable than uncorrected scores, depending on whether the correlation between number of items omitted and number answered correctly is positive or negative. Corrected scores may be slightly more valid than uncorrected scores if the correlation between number of items omitted and the criterion scores is positive. If not, they may be slightly less valid.

Some interesting, hitherto unpublished data of the effects of guessing instructions and correction for guessing are presented in Tables 7.2 and 7.3. I am indebted to Professors Paul Blommers and E. F. Lindquist for these data from an unpublished study. They were obtained by first administering the tests under instructions not to guess. Then, before the answer sheets were turned in, the students

TABLE 7.2

Effects of Directions Against Guessing and Correction for Guessing, I

Score[a]	A	B	C
Directions	Don't Guess	Guess	Don't Guess
Correction[b]	No	No	Yes
Mean Score	75.6	80.4	79.6
Standard Deviation	19.76	17.41	17.16
Reliability[c]	.936	.898	.920
Intercorrelation			
With Score A		.954	.974
With Score B			.987

[a] Scores for 360 Army Specialized Training Program trainees on a geography test, taken January 28, 1944, at the State University of Iowa.

[b] The correction was made by adding one-fourth of the number of items omitted to the number answered correctly.

[c] The reliability coefficient was the corrected coefficient of correlation between scores on odd numbered and even numbered items.

were given colored pencils and asked to attempt an answer to each item they had omitted. Both sets of responses, the initial incomplete set and the final complete set, were then scored in two ways, with and without correction for guessing.

TABLE 7.3

Effects of Directions Against Guessing and Correction for Guessing, II

Score[a]	A	B	C	D	E
Directions	Don't Guess	Guess	Guess[b]	Don't Guess	Guess
Correction[c]	No	No	No	Yes	Yes
Mean Score	31.2	33.9	34.2	34.1	34.1
Standard Deviation	13.74	12.67	12.58	12.34	12.57
Reliability[d]	.933	.913	.910	.916	.912
Validity[e]			.809	.807	
Intercorrelation					
With Score A			.980	.981	
With Score C				.990	

[a] Scores for 362 Army Specialized Training Program trainees on a mathematics test, taken January 28, 1944, at the State University of Iowa.

[b] An artificial guessing procedure was applied to the items omitted despite instructions to mark every item. No artificial guessing procedure was used to obtain score B.

[c] The correction was made by adding one-fifth of the number of items omitted to the number answered correctly.

[d] Based on the correlation between odd and even numbered items.

[e] Instructor grades were used as the criterion for validity.

The tables show that the students in these groups obtained lower mean scores and more variable scores (i.e., with larger standard deviations) when they refrained from guessing than when they guessed. When the guessing correction, which in this case involved adding a fraction of the omitted items to the number answered correctly, was applied, the mean of the scores obtained under "do not guess" instructions was raised and the standard deviation lowered, as might be expected. But application of the same correction to scores obtained under "answer every item" instructions, as might be expected also, had little effect on the mean and standard deviation.

On both tests the highest reliability was obtained when students were warned not to guess (i.e., when they were told that their scores would be corrected for guessing) but when no guessing correction was actually applied. Obviously such deception could not be practiced in regular test administration and scoring procedures. Of the two feasible alternatives ("do not guess" instructions plus actual correction for guessing, on the one hand, and "answer every item" instructions plus no correction for guessing on the other), there is a slight difference in reliability in favor of the "do not guess" instructions. There is, however, no appreciable difference in validity. In all cases the differences are relatively small and the high inter-correlation between these two alternative scores (B and C in Table 7.2 and C and D in Table 7.3) confirms the impression that guessing and correction for guessing made relatively little difference in a pupil's ranking on these tests. These were expertly constructed tests that yielded scores of good reliability. It seems likely that the data reported in Tables 7.2 and 7.3 are reasonably representative of those that would be obtained under similar instructions with other good classroom tests.

> 2. *The probability of getting a respectable score on a good objective test by blind guessing alone is extremely small.*

Suppose the objective test included 100 multiple-choice items, each of which offered five possible answers. A student who took many of such tests and always guessed blindly on every item in such a test would expect to receive an average score of 20. He could expect a score as high as 24 by blind guessing alone on only one test out of six, as high as 28 on only one test out of 44, and as high as 32 on only one test out of 740.

> 3. *Well-motivated examinees who have time to attempt all items guess blindly on few, if any, items.*

A distinction is being made here between a blind guess and an uncertain response. If an examinee is so poorly motivated that he marks his responses at random, or in a consistent pattern, without paying any attention to the questions, he is guessing blindly. His uncorrected score is likely to be higher than his corrected score but not as high as the score of the poorest student who uses what knowledge he has as a basis for his answers. And if, by unhappy chance, the guesser did make the higher score, his score would still be higher after correction for guessing if both attempted all items, and *might* still be higher if the nonguesser were no better in choosing items to omit than in choosing correct answers.

4. *Ordinarily, no moral or educational evil is involved in the encouragement of students to make the best rational guesses they can.*

Guessing is regarded as an evil by those who see in it an attempt by the examinee either to (1) deceive the examiner into thinking he knows something that he really doesn't know or to (2) get by on the basis of slip-shod learning. If learning were an all-or-none affair, with perfect mastery or total ignorance the only alternatives, these objections to guessing could carry considerable weight.

But in view of the fact that learning is usually a matter of more-or-less, it seems somewhat unreasonable to ask a student to distinguish clearly what he knows from what he does not know and to answer only those questions that he can answer with complete certainty. Schools and colleges prepare for life, and life is seldom like that. Decisions on life's complex problems are seldom beyond question or doubt. Inevitably most of them require some degree of rational guessing, i.e., acting on the basis of insufficient evidence. Decision making cannot be avoided when a question or problem arises since the postponement of choice is itself a decision which may turn out well or badly. The most effective persons in life seem to be those whose informed guesses pay off most frequently.

5. *A student's rational guesses can provide useful information on his general level of achievement.*

Any test is likely to present tasks that some examinees will not be able to handle with complete assurance. If these examinees do the best they can with such questions, then responses should provide the examiner with more information about their abilities than if they were to omit all such uncertain responses entirely.

Even if it were possible to do so, it would probably be undesirable to measure a student's achievements by counting only the things he thinks he knows beyond the shadow of a doubt, or the abilities he thinks he can exercise flawlessly. The number of such things may be quite small and many of them may be quite unimportant. Further, the more successfully a test probes a student's command of knowledge, the more it requires him to go beyond the recitation of facts and phrases committed to memory, the harder it may be for him to avoid some doubts about the correctness of his choices. If a question is complex and difficult enough to challenge a student's command of knowledge, he is unlikely to arrive at an answer he is completely certain is correct. But uncertain responses can provide good evidence of competence, too. Two students may be uncertain to some degree about all the answers they give on a test, but the student of higher achievement is likely to have more of his uncertain answers turn out to be correct.

> 6. *If a test is speeded, a guessing correction removes the incentive for slower students to guess blindly.*

Students who work slowly or who lose track of time when taking a test may be unable to give a considered answer to each question, especially if the test time limits are short. When the test scores are not corrected for guessing, a student who runs out of time can expect a higher score if he guesses blindly than if he does not. Not all students are willing to guess blindly in such circumstances, even when directed to do so. Those who choose not to guess are placed at a disadvantage. Those who do guess blindly make their scores less reliable since the blind guessing adds nothing but random error to their test scores. Correcting test scores for guessing helps solve this problem by removing the incentive to guess blindly on the items the student does not have time to consider.

In some cases a better solution to this problem than correction for guessing may be encouragement of students to work rapidly enough to have time to consider all of the items. Most students could work faster on an examination than they do without serious loss of accuracy in their responses. If they are informed of the passage of time, most will adjust their rates of work so they can finish without guessing. Their scores are then almost certain to be more reliable than if they had guessed blindly on some items, or if a guessing correction had been applied.

7. *Scores corrected for guessing may include irrelevant meas-*
ures of the examinee's test-wiseness or willingness to gamble.

Contrary to what students sometimes seem to believe, the typical correction for guessing applies no special penalty to the one who guesses. It simply tends to eliminate the advantage of the student who guesses blindly in preference to omitting items. The test-wise student knows he has nothing to lose, and perhaps something to gain, by making use of every hunch and scrap of information in attempting an answer to every item. The test-naïve student or the one who tends to avoid taking chances may be influenced by a guessing correction to omit many items on which his likelihood of correct response is well above the chance level. To the degree that scores corrected for guessing give a special advantage to the bold or test-wise student, their validity as measures of achievement may suffer.

8. *Correction for guessing complicates the scoring task some-*
what and tends to lower the accuracy of the scores.

In effect, two scores must be obtained and combined mathematically to yield a single score corrected for guessing. If the tests are scored by hand, as most classroom tests are, both the time required for scoring and the opportunities for error are increased considerably. When machines are used, the speed and accuracy with which formula scores can be obtained depends on the design of the machine and the skill and care with which it is operated. Table 7.4 presents data from a study of scoring accuracy which compared uncorrected with corrected scores when obtained by hand and machine scoring. These data support the general expectation that corrected scores will occasion more errors than uncorrected scores when both are obtained by hand. They indicate that machines can yield corrected scores with the same degree of accuracy as uncorrected scores. The machine used in this study was the Scribe scoring machine of the Educational Testing Service.

It is not easy to make a strong case in favor of correcting test scores for guessing on the basis of these considerations. But if correction for guessing does little good, one can also argue that it does little harm. The truth is that ordinarily it makes little differ-

TABLE 7.4

Errors in Obtaining Corrected and Uncorrected
Test Scores by Hand and Machine Scoring*

Scoring Process	Scoring Formula	Number of Scores Checked	Number of Errors	Per cent Without Error
Hand	R	1,599	1	99.94
Hand	R-KW†	1,403	15	98.93
Machine	R	6,748	29	99.57
Machine	R-KW†	6,558	28	99.57

* The data in this table were obtained from an unpublished document, *Addenda to Report of Recommendations to the Testing Operations Board on the Use of Formula and Rights Scores*, Richard W. Watkins, Chairman, Educational Testing Service, Princeton, N.J., June 21, 1962, 8 pp.

† In these formulas K is a fraction appropriate to the number of alternative answers available in each item, as explained earlier in this chapter. The numerator of the fraction is usually 1. The denominator is usually one less than the number of alternative answers.

ence. If special circumstances seem to require the use of a correction, the instructor can use it with a clear conscience. But his conscience can usually be just as clear, and his life simpler, if he avoids it.

13. Differential scoring weights

All objective test scores are obtained by adding weighted response scores. The simplest system of scoring weights and the one most often used is $+1$ for the correct response to each test item and 0 for any response not correct. Correction for guessing involves a slightly more complex system of scoring weights, such as $+1$ for each correct response, -1, or -2, or -3 etc., for each wrong response, and 0 for each omitted response.

Test constructors sometimes suggest that certain items carry more weight than others because they are thought to be more important items, items of better technical quality, more complex or difficult items, or more time-consuming items. For example, in a test composed of fifty true-false items and twenty-five multiple-choice items, the test constructor may decide that each multiple-choice item should be worth two points and each true-false item only one point.

Reasonable as such differential item weights may seem to be on the surface, they seldom make the test to which they are applied a more reliable or valid measure. Nor do they ordinarily make the test a much worse measure. Like guessing corrections, to which they are closely related, they tend to have relatively small effects. Wilks concluded from a theoretical analysis of the problem that the method of weighting individual items matters little in a long test of intercorrelated items.[5] Guilford and his coworkers reported this finding from an empirical study of weighted scoring.[6] "Our general conclusion is that our logically defensible system of completely weighted scoring did not yield an appreciable gain in either reliability or validity in achievement examinations of from 20 to 100 items." Phillips came to the same conclusion.

> As others have found, the above results show not only that there is little to be gained from weighted scoring, but also that, from the point of view of test construction, weighted scoring is probably not worth the effort. The same advantages can be gained by adding more items or by selecting only the best items from a larger pool. From the administrative point of view, unweighted scoring saves time and offers fewer possibilities for errors in calculating the scores; in addition, the resulting raw scores are probably easier to interpret.[7]

Weighting some of the items in a test more than other items changes the balance of the test but does not ordinarily improve its quality, which depends on the quality of the individual items and on the number of items. Good items are not made any better by giving two points instead of one for a correct response to them. But the poor items, whose contribution to the measurements the test yields is already weak, are weakened still further when they are weighted less than other items. The one case where differential weighting is certain to improve a test occurs if a test includes negatively discriminating items, items which are actually working against the other good items. By weighting such negatively discriminating items negatively, they could be brought over to the side of the

---

[5] S. S. Wilks, "Weighting Systems for Linear Functions of Correlated Variables When There Is No Dependent Variable," *Psychometrika*, III (1938), 23-40.

[6] J. P. Guilford, Constance Lovell, and Ruth M. Williams, "Completely-Weighted versus Unweighted Scoring in an Achievement Examination," *Educational and Psychological Measurement*, II (1942), 15-21.

[7] Alexander J. Phillips, "Further Evidence Regarding Weighted versus Unweighted Scoring of Examinations," *Educational and Psychological Measurement*, III (1943), 151-55.

angels. But a better solution in most cases would be to rewrite the item or at least change the "correct" response.

A test composed of thirty good items and thirty poor (but positively discriminating) items is better than a test of the thirty good items alone. It is not as good as a test of sixty good items would be. Double weighting of the thirty good items makes them no better. The best way of improving such a test is to replace the poor items with good items.

If an achievement test covers two areas, one of which is judged to be twice as important as the other, then twice as many items should be written in relation to the more important area. This will result in more reliable and more valid measures than if an equal number of items is written for each area and those for the more important area are double weighted.

Complex or time-consuming items should be made, if possible, to yield more than one response which can be independently scored as right or wrong. Very difficult items are likely to contribute less than moderately difficult items to test reliability. Giving the difficult items extra weight lowers the average effectiveness of the items and thus lowers the effectiveness of the test as a whole.

It has occurred to some test constructors that differential weighting of responses to test items might be useful in improving test reliability or validity. For example, in a question like the following:

> A child complains of severe pain and tenderness in the lower abdomen, with nausea. What should the child's mother do?
>
> 1. Give the child a laxative.
> 2. Put the child to bed.
> 3. Call the doctor.

Choice of the first response might result in a score of -1, of the second in a score of 0, and of the third in a score of $+1$. In this case the scoring weights were determined a priori. It has also been suggested that they might be determined experimentally, so as to maximize test reliability or validity.

But in this case also the experimental results have been disappointing. Seldom have any appreciable, consistent gains in reliability or validity been found. It seems clear that to gain any real advantage by this means one would need to write items with this purpose specifically in mind. Most item writers, even skilled professionals, have enough difficulty writing items good enough for simple right or wrong scoring. To make them good enough for more finely graded differential weighting seems like a formidable task. Test improvement via additional, good, simply scored items looks more promising to most item writers.

Exceptions will be found, of course, to the generalization that differential weighting of items, or of item responses, is not worthwhile in the scoring of classroom tests of educational achievement. One such exception is described in the chapter on the use of true-false tests in this book. But it is a good general guide to the constructor of an educational achievement test to settle for simple right or wrong scoring of individual items, with each item carrying the same weight as every other item, regardless of its importance, complexity, difficulty, or quality. Increasing the number of scorable units, and making each unit as good as possible, seems better in most situations than differential weighting of items or responses as a means of test improvement.

14. Summary

Some of the principal ideas developed in this chapter are summarized in these twenty statements.

1. Students should be told well in advance when an important test is to be given.
2. Students should be taught essential test-taking skills.
3. The test constructor should avoid clues in the test items that enable an examinee to substitute test-wiseness for command of knowledge.
4. Test anxiety is seldom a major factor in determining a student's score on a test.
5. The test administrator should help the student to adjust his rate of work on a test to the time available for it.
6. The instructor is responsible for the prevention or punishment of cheating on examinations.
7. The development of honor systems does not afford a generally promising solution to the problems of cheating on examinations.
8. The instructor is responsible for preventing any student from

gaining special advance copies of, or advance information about, one of his examinations.

9. The use of separate answer sheets facilitates rapid clerical or machine scoring of objective tests.

10. The machines now available for scoring classroom tests vary widely in speed, complexity, and cost, as well as in capabilities and principles of operation.

11. A guessing correction is sometimes applied to objective test scores to reduce to zero the expected gain from blind guessing.

12. Scores may be corrected for guessing by subtracting a fraction of the wrong responses or by adding a fraction of the omitted responses.

13. Scores corrected for guessing will usually rank the examinees in about the same order as the uncorrected scores.

14. The probability is small of getting a respectable score on a good objective test by blind guessing alone.

15. Well-motivated examinees who have time to attempt all items do little blind guessing.

16. Students should be encouraged to make rational guesses on the answers to objective test items.

17. A guessing correction removes the incentive for slower students to guess blindly on the final items of a speeded test.

18. Scores corrected for guessing may be influenced by the examinee's readiness, or reluctance, to gamble.

19. A guessing correction may complicate the scoring task and may lower scoring accuracy slightly.

20. Giving different weights to different items in a test, or to different correct or incorrect responses in an item, seldom improves score reliability or validity appreciably.

REFERENCES

Anderson, William F., "Attitudes of University Students Toward Cheating," *Journal of Educational Research*, L (April, 1957), 581-88.

Bird, Charles, "The Detection of Cheating in Objective Examinations," *School and Society*, XXV (February 26, 1927), 261-62.

Broen, William E., "Anxiety, Intelligence and Achievement," *Psychological Reports*, V (1959), 701-4.

Cook, Desmond L., "A Comparison of Reading Comprehension Scores

Obtained before and after a Time Announcement," *Journal of Educational Psychology,* XLVIII (November, 1957), 440-46.

Curtis, H. A. and Russell P. Kropp, "A Comparison of Scores Obtained by Administering a Test Normally and Visually," *Journal of Experimental Education,* XXIX (1961), 249-60.

————, *Experimental Analyses of the Effects of Various Modes of Item-presentation on the Scores and Factorial Content of Tests Administered by Visual and Audio-visual Means.* Tallahassee, Florida: Department of Educational Research and Testing, Florida State University, 1962.

Dickenson, H. F., "Identical Errors and Deception," *Journal of Educational Research,* XXXVIII (March, 1945), 534-42.

Ebel, Robert L., "Improving Evaluation of Educational Outcomes at the College Level," *Proceedings, 1953 Invitational Conference on Testing Problems.* Princeton, N.J.: Educational Testing Service, 1954.

————, "Maximizing Test Validity in Fixed Time Limits," *Educational and Psychological Measurement,* XIII (Summer, 1953), 347-57.

Guilford, J. P., Constance Lovell, and Ruth M. Williams, "Completely Weighted versus Unweighted Scoring in an Achievement Examination," *Educational and Psychological Measurement,* II (1942), 15-21.

Hastings, J. Thomas, "Tensions and School Achievement Examinations," *Journal of Experimental Education,* XII (1944), 143-64.

Heston, Joseph C., *How to Take a Test,* p. 47. Chicago: Science Research Associates, 1953.

Huff, Darrell, *Score: The Strategy of Taking Tests,* p. 148. New York: Appleton-Century-Crofts, 1961.

Jackson, Robert A., "Guessing and Test Performance," *Educational and Psychological Measurement,* XV (Spring, 1955), 74-79.

Kieslar, Evan R., "Test Instructions and Scoring Methods in True-False Tests," *Journal of Experimental Education,* XXI (1953), 243-49.

Manual of Instructions for the IBM Test Scoring Machine. Endicott, N.Y.: Department of Education, International Business Machines Corp.

Manuel, Herschel T., *Taking a Test,* p. 77. New York: Harcourt, Brace & World, Inc., 1956.

McNamara, N. J. and Ellis Weitzman, "The Economy of Item Analysis with the IBM Graphic System Counter," *Journal of Applied Psychology,* XXX (1946), 84-90.

Milholland, John E., "The Reliability of Test Discriminations," *Educational and Psychological Measurement,* XV (Winter, 1955), 364-70.

Moore, Robert, "A Comparison of Selected Modifications of a Multiple-choice Examination," *Dissertation Abstracts,* XVI (1956), 1844.

Mueller, Kate (Hevner), "Can Cheating Be Killed?" *The Personnel and Guidance Journal* (April, 1953).

Phillips, Alexander J., "Further Evidence Regarding Weighted versus Unweighted Scoring of Examinations," *Educational and Psychological Measurement*, III (1943), 151-55.

Potthoff, E. F. and N. E. Barnett, "Comparison of Marks Based Upon Weighted and Unweighted Items in New-type Examinations," *Journal of Educational Psychology*, XXXIII (1932), 92-98.

Pressey, Sidney L., "Development and Appraisal of Devices Providing Immediate Automatic Scoring of Objective Tests and Concomitant Self-instruction," *Journal of Psychology*, XXIX, 417-47.

Sarason, Seymour B. and Others, *Anxiety in Elementary School Children*, p. 351. New York: John Wiley and Sons, Inc., 1960.

Saupe, Joe L., "An Empirical Model for the Corroboration of Suspected Cheating on Multiple-choice Tests," *Educational and Psychological Measurement*, XX (Autumn, 1960), 475-89.

Sherriffs, Alex C. and Donald S. Booma, "Who Is Penalized by the Penalty for Guessing?" *Journal of Educational Psychology*, XLV (1954), 81-90.

Stalnaker, John M., "Weighting Questions in the Essay-type Examination," *Journal of Educational Psychology*, XXIX (1938), 481-90.

Swineford, Frances and Peter M. Miller, "Effects of Directions Regarding Guessing on Item Statistics of a Multiple-choice Vocabulary Test," *Journal of Educational Psychology*, XLIV (March, 1953), 129-39.

Troyer, Maurice E. and George W. Angell, *Manual for the SRA Self-Scorer*. Chicago: Science Research Associates, 1949.

Waite, William H., "The Relationships Between Performances on Examinations and Emotional Responses," *Journal of Experimental Education*, XI (1942), 88-96.

Wilks, S. S., "Weighting Systems for Linear Functions of Correlated Variables When There Is No Dependent Variable," *Psychometrika*, III (1938), 23-40.

Woods, Roy C., "Using Students to Score Test Papers," *The Thirteenth Yearbook of the National Council on Measurements Used in Education*, pp. 81-86. East Lansing, Mich.: Michigan State University, 1956.

8 Describing Test Scores Statistically

Let there be n unknown X's
Each with its own special a;
If a_i a b_i annexes,
What is X in terms of b_k?
LEWIS CARROLL

1. Frequency Distributions

Suppose two spelling tests of one hundred words each have been given to a class of twenty-five students. The first test, List A, was dictated on Monday, and the second, List B, composed of entirely different words, on Wednesday. The students' test papers were scored by giving one unit of credit for each word correctly spelled. The scores obtained are shown in Table 8.1. How can these two sets of scores be described statistically? Consider first only the Monday test scores on List A.

Notice that the scores range from a high of 96 for Nathaniel to a low of 61 for Wendell. In order to include all of the scores a *range* of 36 score units ($96 - 60 = 36$, or $97 - 61 = 36$) is required. This range is used as one measure of the variability of the scores. To get a more complete picture of the students' scores on this test, a frequency distribution can be constructed.

Grouping the scores into classes simplifies the frequency distri-

TABLE 8.1

Scores of Twenty-five Pupils on Two Spelling Tests

	List A Monday	List B Wednesday
Aaron	65	67
Barbara	75	72
Ben	66	72
Bud	88	92
Clyde	71	76
Donald	72	72
Dorothy	91	90
Eugene	82	80
Fay	84	80
Frank	76	81
·Gary	69	64
Gladys	67	70
Jack	74	78
Jeff	80	77
Jerry	87	90
Joan	91	85
Melville	65	68
Nadine	77	78
Nathaniel	96	94
Patricia	93	87
Peggy	79	78
Perry	84	89
Richard	76	75
Shirley	73	78
Wendell	61	69

bution with no appreciable loss in accuracy. In this case, since the range of scores is 35, twelve classes of three units each may be used. It is convenient to make the class size an odd number of score units so that the midpoint of the class will be a whole number. On this basis the class intervals shown in the left column of Table 8.2 were set up.

Opposite each class interval the scores which fall in it are recorded. Tally marks could be used instead of scores, but when the number of scores is not large, the use of actual score values is

TABLE 8.2

Frequency Distribution of Twenty-five Scores on List *A*

Class Interval	Scores	Frequency	Deviation
94-96	96	1	6
91-93	91, 91, 93	3	5
88-90	88	1	4
85-87	87	1	3
82-84	82, 84, 84	3	2
79-81	80, 79	2	1
76-78	76, 77, 76	3	0
73-75	75, 74, 73	3	−1
70-72	71, 72	2	−2
67-69	69, 67	2	−3
64-66	65, 66, 65	3	−4
61-63	61	1	−5

$$n = 25$$

convenient and preserves some information which might otherwise be lost. The number of scores falling in each class interval is recorded in the third column headed "Frequency." One can detect in this frequency distribution some signs of the usual tendency for scores to be more concentrated toward the middle of the range. The distribution of scores here is fairly uniform, with some tendency for low scores to be more common than high scores.

The main purpose of the frequency distribution is to give the test constructor an integrated, meaningful picture of the entire distribution of scores. It is also useful in showing how any particular score relates to all the other scores in the group.

2. The median and the mean

One useful statistical summary of a set of test scores is some measure of their typical or average value, usually either the *mean* or the *median*. The "median" is either the middle measure of the group (if the group includes an odd number of measures) or the point halfway between the two middle measures (if the number of measures is even). In the case of this set of scores the median is 76. Because the measures are concentrated more in the bottom half than in the top half of the distribution, the median would be expected to fall somewhat below the mean.

The "mean," or more precisely the "arithmetic mean," of a set of measures is obtained by adding all measures and dividing the sum by the number of measures.

Expressed as a formula

$$M = \frac{\Sigma X}{N} \qquad 8.1$$

In which M stands for the mean, Σ means "the sum of," X represents each score in the group, and N stands for the number of scores in the group. For the group of scores from the Monday spelling test, the sum is 1,942, which makes the mean score 77.68.

If the number of scores is large, if the scores themselves are large, and if a calculating machine is not available, time can sometimes be saved at the cost of only a slight loss in accuracy, by calculating the mean from the frequency distribution.[1] To do this requires a new scale, a deviation scale, whose zero point is located near where we expect the mean to be. The class interval which is expected to contain the mean is designated as zero. If the mean actually does not fall in this interval the calculations will involve larger numbers, but the result will be equally accurate. Successive class intervals above the zero interval are numbered 1, 2, 3, etc. Successive class intervals below the zero interval are numbered −1, −2, −3, etc. These numbers create a new, simpler deviation scale. They are shown in the fourth column of Table 8.2.

On this new, shorter, simpler scale there is one score of 6 (instead of 96), three of 5, one of 4, and so on. There is also one score of −5 (instead of 61), three of −4, two of −3, and so on. The sum of these new deviation scores is 6. Dividing 6 by 25, gives .24 for the mean of the deviation scores.

To translate this deviation score mean to the original score scale one must multiply it by 3, since one deviation score unit is equal to 3 of the original score units, and add 77, since the zero point on

---

[1] Simple hand-operated or more versatile electrically operated desk calculators are available at prices ranging from less than $200 to more than $1,000. The use of such machines can greatly speed up and simplify the statistical calculations described in this chapter. Most schools and colleges have, or should have, one available for faculty use.

the deviation scale corresponds to 77 on the original score scale. These operations yield 77.72 for the estimate of the mean, very close to the value obtained by direct calculation.

A numerical simplification of this kind may not seem worth the mathematical complications it causes and the very slight inaccuracy it introduces in the calculation of the mean. But it can save a great deal of work in the calculation of the standard deviation, as will be illustrated in the next section. Since exactly the same initial steps must be taken in calculating either the mean or the standard deviation by this method, it is advantageous to calculate both of them using the same approach.

Ordinarily the median is easier to determine than the mean. If the set of test scores includes a few extremely high or extremely low scores, the median may give a more reasonable indication of the typical score than does the mean.

> Consider, for example, the set of scores: 8, 9, 10, 11, 22. What is the mean of this set? What is the median? Which best indicates the value of *most* of the scores in the set? Which best indicates the value of *all* of the scores in the set?

Because the value of each score in the set affects the value of the mean, the mean tends to be a more stable measure of the average score level than does the median. That is, the mean is likely to vary less from set to set of scores of the same kind than is the median. Further, the mean is involved, directly or indirectly, in the calculation of many other statistics. Hence the mean is generally regarded by statisticians as a more precise and useful measure than the median of the central tendency of a set of scores.

If an instructor needs no more than an easily obtained estimate of the typical value of a set of scores, the median is probably the measure to be obtained. But if a fully representative estimate is desired and if other statistics are to be calculated, the mean will usually be preferred.

3. The variance and the standard deviation

To provide a concise statistical description of a set of test scores one must take account of variability as well as central tendency.

One measure of variability, the range, has already been mentioned. However, since it is determined by only two scores, the highest and the lowest, it is not a particularly stable measure. The standard deviation is a much more reliable and more generally useful measure.

The standard deviation is defined as the square root of the variance. The variance is the mean of the squared deviations of the measures from their mean. Expressed in formulas,

$$\sigma = \sqrt{\frac{\Sigma d^2}{N}}$$ 8.2

and

$$\sigma^2 = \frac{\Sigma d^2}{N}$$ 8.3

where σ represents the standard deviation, σ^2 the variance, Σ means "the sum of," d is the difference between any score in the group and the mean of all scores in that group, and N represents the number of scores in the group.

For the Monday spelling test scores, the deviation of Aaron's score (65) from the mean of all scores in the group (77.68) is -12.68. The square of -12.68 (-12.68 times -12.68) equals 160.7824. Finding the deviations of all other scores in the group, squaring them, adding the squares, and dividing by the number of scores (25) would give the variance of this set of scores, which is 91.0176. The standard deviation is the square root of the variance, 9.54 in this case.

Some teachers who need to find the standard deviation of a set of test scores may either have forgotten or never have been taught how to find the square root of a number. Various methods are available. The one easiest to explain and to learn how to use is *the guess-and-divide* method. This can be illustrated in finding the square root of 160.7824.

The first problem is to find a number whose square is reasonably close to 160. A table of squares is helpful in this connection. Such a table, or an estimate based on experience, suggests that the square of 12 is 144. This is reasonably close to the number whose square root is needed.

The second step is to divide 160.8 by 12. The quotient is 13.4.

The average (mean) of the quotient and the divisor is 12.7. This becomes the divisor. The process of dividing and averaging divisor and quotient is repeated. With each repetition, the divisor and quotient get to be more nearly alike. If the quotient and the divisor are in good agreement after two divisions, their average is accepted as the needed square root. If not, the process is continued. In this example, the average obtained after two divisions, 12.68, appears to be exactly accurate.

To calculate a standard deviation by converting each score into a deviation from the mean of all scores would be to do the job the hard way. Since the deviation of a score is defined as its difference from the mean, so that

$$d = X - M \qquad\qquad 8.4$$

it is easy to show algebraically that

$$\Sigma d^2 = \Sigma X^2 - \frac{(\Sigma X)^2}{N} \qquad\qquad 8.5$$

so that

$$\sigma^2 = \frac{\Sigma X^2}{N} - \frac{(\Sigma X)^2}{N^2} \qquad\qquad 8.6$$

Expressed in words, this formula indicates that the variance of a set of test scores is equal to the difference between two fractions. The larger is the sum of all the squared scores divided by the number of scores. The smaller is the square of the sum of the scores divided by the square of the number of scores. This is the formula actually used to get the variance of the Monday spelling test scores reported above.

This formula is reasonably convenient if the scores are small and few or if a calculating machine is available. When these conditions do not exist, and often they do not in a classroom testing, the same simplification used earlier in estimating the mean can be applied in calculating the standard deviation. That is, the scores can be grouped in intervals, with the intervals given positive and negative score values from some point near the mean. This amounts to using the deviation values in the fourth column of Table 8.2 as if they were actual scores.

The sum of the squared deviations can be obtained from the data in Table 8.2. There is one score whose deviation is 6, giving a squared deviation of 36. There are four scores (93, 91, 91, 61) whose deviations are 5 or −5, giving a total squared deviation of 100 for this set. (When the deviations are squared, the difference between positive and negative deviations disappears.) There are four scores (88, 66, 65, 65) whose deviations are 4 or −4, giving a total squared deviation for this set of 64. Three deviations of 3 or −3 (total squared deviation = 27), five of 2 or −2 (total = 20), and five of 1 or −1 (total = 5) bring the sum of all twenty-five squared deviations to 252.

The sum of the deviation values themselves (ΣX) is 6. The value of N is 25, and of N^2, 625. These values inserted in Formula 8.6 give

$$[\sigma^2] = \tfrac{252}{25} - \tfrac{36}{625} = 10.0800 - .0576 = 10.0224$$

This $[\sigma^2]$ is not the variance desired, since it is expressed in terms of the deviation score scale. One unit on that scale is equal to three units on the original scale. Since scores must be squared to find their variance, the ratio between the units on the two scales must also be squared to make a proper correction. That is, in this case, $\sigma^2 = 9\,[\sigma^2]$. Hence the variance of these scores, expressed in terms of the original scale, is 90.2016. The square root of this, 9.50, is the value of the standard deviation of these scores.

Lathrop has suggested a short-cut estimate of the standard deviation, assuming a reasonably normal distribution of scores.[2] It is the difference between the sums of the upper and lower one-sixths of the scores, divided by one-half the number of scores. For the List A spelling test scores of Table 8.1, one-sixth of the scores would be 4, to the nearest whole number. The highest four scores are 96, 93, 91, and 91. The lowest four are 61, 65, 65, and 66. Hence the difference between their sums is 371 − 257 = 114. Dividing 114 by 12.5 gives 9.12, a value in fairly good agreement with those obtained from Formulas 8.2 and 8.6. Jenkins has proposed a similar estimate that is slightly less convenient but probably slightly more accurate.[3]

Two other short-cut estimates of the standard deviation of a set of test scores will be suggested later in this chapter, after the scores

---

[2] Robert L. Lathrop, "A Quick but Accurate Approximation to the Standard Deviation of a Distribution," *Journal of Experimental Education*, XXIX (March, 1961), 319-21.

[3] W. L. Jenkins, "A Short-cut Method for σ and r," *Educational and Psychological Measurement*, VI (1946), 533-36.

on which they are based, percentiles and stanines, have been described.

The mean and standard deviation are useful not only in providing a concise description of test scores, but also in judging how well a particular test meets reasonable standards of quality. This process will be described in the next chapter. Score variances, specifically the variances of real test scores, of hypothetical true scores, and of errors of measurement, will be discussed in the chapter on test reliability.

4. The normal distribution

Distributions of test scores frequently approximate the normal distribution. For this reason, and because it is convenient to have a standard, idealized model as a point of reference when estimating the characteristics of actual score distributions, we need to pay attention to the normal distribution here. Some systems of standard scores, such as the stanine scores discussed in this chapter, are based on the properties of the normal distribution of scores.

Some of the essential characteristics of the normal distribution are illustrated in Figure 8.1. It is a symmetrical curve, with the mean and median located in the same central position bisecting the area under the curve. The base line of the curve is marked in standard deviation units.

On Figure 8.1 ordinates (vertical lines from the curve to the base line) have been drawn at intervals of one-half of the standard deviation. Taking a convenient arbitrary length for the central ordinate and calling it 1.00, the other ordinates can be expressed

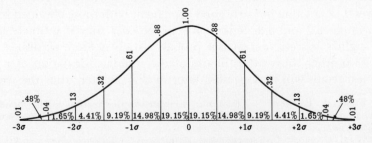

Figure 8.1. The Normal Curve

as decimal values of the central ordinate. It is helpful to refer to the relative lengths of these ordinates when drawing replicas of the normal curve.

Percentages of the total area under the curve are also indicated for the area between each successive pair of ordinates. It is useful to remember that 68.26 per cent of the total area lies between the ordinates located at $+1\sigma$ and -1σ; that 95.46 per cent lies between the ordinates at $+2\sigma$ and -2σ, and 99.72 per cent between the ordinates at $+3\sigma$ and -3σ. Detailed tables of ordinates and areas under the normal curve are available in good statistical references, such as Blommers and Lindquist and Ferguson.[4] Moonan has published frequency distributions that approximate the normal distribution for various numbers of class intervals and for various numbers of measures.[5]

Theoretically, a normal curve extends without limit on either side of the mean. In practice, and for convenience, it is often considered to extend from three standard deviations below to three standard deviations above the mean, since 99.72 per cent of the test scores or other measures comprising the distribution fall within those limits. But the distribution of scores from a class of, say, thirty students will not typically show a range from high score to low of six standard deviations. Hoel's figures indicate that the following ratios of range to standard deviation can be expected for samples of the sizes shown.[6]

Sample Size	Typical Range in Standard Deviation Units
10	3.0
50	4.5
100	5.0
1000	6.5

The typical values shown are averages. In some samples of the

---

[4] Paul Blommers and E. F. Lindquist, *Elementary Statistical Methods* (Boston: Houghton Mifflin Company, 1960); and George A. Ferguson, *Statistical Analysis in Psychology and Education* (New York: McGraw-Hill Book Company, 1959).

[5] William J. Moonan, "A Table of Normal Distribution Frequencies for Selected Numbers of Class Intervals and Sample Sizes," *Journal of Experimental Education*, XXVII (March, 1959), 231-35.

[6] Paul G. Hoel, *Introduction to Mathematical Statistics* (New York: John Wiley & Sons, Inc., 1947).

specified size the observed value of the ratio of range to standard deviation will be considerably more, and in other samples considerably less, than the value indicated. But it may be useful for the instructor to know that in a set of twenty-five test scores the highest score is more likely to be two than three standard deviations above the mean.

Another point worth noting is that the points of inflection of the curve occur at $+1\sigma$ and -1σ. As one follows the curve outward from the mean it is at these points that the slope of the curve stops increasing and starts to decrease. Exactly half of the area under the curve is located between ordinates at $+.6745\sigma$ and $-.6745\sigma$. When the normal curve is used to represent chance fluctuations in test scores due to errors of measurement, the value $.6745\sigma$ is referred to as the probable error of measurement. Half the errors are likely to be larger and half smaller than this value. The standard deviation of the normal curve is referred to as the standard error of measurement when the curve itself is used to indicate the expected distribution of errors of measurement. About 32 per cent of the errors are likely to be larger and 68 per cent smaller than the standard error of measurement.

While it is true, as pointed out at the beginning of this section, that many distributions of test scores do approximate the normal distribution, there is no compelling reason why they ought to. Indeed, to achieve highest reliability with a given number of test items, a flatter score distribution than the normal distribution is advantageous, one which has more scores at the extremes and fewer in the center. Rummel, working with a college-level mathematics test used to exempt some entering freshmen (about 50 per cent) from a course in basic mathematical skills, found that item revisions which flattened the distribution of scores also reduced the errors made in exempting some freshmen and not exempting others.[7]

The test constructor who points with pride to the beautifully normal distribution of scores which his test yields may be using a false standard of quality for his tests. If the scores of his students were determined by their success in matching pennies with him, the distribution of their scores would be approximately normal. Indeed,

---

[7] Josiah Francis Rummel, "The Modification of a Test to Reduce Errors in the Classification of Examinees" (Unpublished dissertation, College of Education, The State University of Iowa, Iowa City, Iowa, 1950).

it is hard to beat pure chance as a generator of normally distributed scores. This does not mean that the normal distributions are always generated by chance errors of measurement. It does mean that such a distribution is not necessarily an indication of quality in a test.

Sometimes tests yield asymmetric or skewed distributions of scores, in which the median score is much nearer the highest score than it is to the lowest, or vice versa. Lord and Cook have reported studies of this characteristic in actual distributions of test scores.[8] If this skewing is not attributable to a few outstandingly capable or incapable students in the group tested, it may be due to excessive ease or excessive difficulty in the test itself. When the test is too easy, students of average achievement may receive scores almost as high as students of outstanding achievement. When it is too hard, students of average achievement may do little better than those of lowest achievement. In either case the distribution of scores is likely to be skewed, or asymmetric. Thus, lack of symmetry in the score distribution may indicate inappropriateness of the test in difficulty. But symmetry is not the same as normality.

5. Percentile ranks

Since the scores on different tests, when taken by different groups, can have widely different means, standard deviations, and distributions, it is useful to have some standard scale to which they all can be referred. One such scale is a scale of percentile ranks. Another is a scale of stanine scores. Since both these scales are useful in interpreting and working with the scores from classroom tests, they will be discussed in some detail.

The percentile rank of a test score indicates what per cent of the scores in a particular set or distribution of scores falls below the midpoint of that score interval. In calculating the percentile rank of any score, half of the persons receiving that score are considered to have scored below, and half of them to have scored above, the midpoint of that score interval.

The calculation of percentile ranks will be first explained and

[8] Frederic M. Lord, "A Summary of Observed Test-score Distributions with Respect to Skewness and Kurtosis," *Educational and Psychological Measurement*, XV (1955), 383-89; and Desmond L. Cook, "A Replication of Lord's Study of Skewness and Kurtosis of Observed Test-score Distributions," *Educational and Psychological Measurement*, XIX (1959), 81-87.

illustrated using the following set of eight test scores: 41, 42, 38, 42, 40, 43, 42, 40. The first step is to prepare an ordered list of consecutive scores, beginning with the score next below the lowest score in the given set and continuing to the score next above the highest score in the set. This list of scores is illustrated in the first column of Table 8.3.

TABLE 8.3

Computation of Percentile Ranks
Given Scores: 41, 42, 38, 42, 40, 43, 42, 40.

List of Scores	Tally of Scores	Cumulative Frequency	Per cent of Frequency	Percentile Rank
44		16	100.00	100
43	/ /	15	93.75	94
42	/// ///	11	68.75	69
41	/ /	7	43.75	44
40	// //	4	25.00	25
39		2	12.50	13
38	/ /	1	6.25	6
37		0	0.00	0

The next column carries a doubled tally of the scores. Each score is tallied twice—once just above and once just below the midpoint of the interval in which it occurs. This double tallying avoids the awkwardness of splitting odd numbers of tallies to show that half of them should be considered to fall below and half above the midpoint of the score interval.

The third column records the cumulative frequency of tally marks up to the midpoint of the interval opposite which the frequency is recorded. The frequency of tally marks up to the midpoint of score interval 37 is 0; to the midpoint of 38 it is 1; to the midpoint of 39 it is 2; and so on. The final figure up to the midpoint of score interval 44 is 16, twice the number of scores since each was tallied twice.

The next step is to convert the cumulative frequencies into per cent of the total frequency. Since 1 divided by 16 and multiplied by 100 is 6.25, that value is recorded opposite score 38 in the column headed "Per cent of Frequency." Other cumulative frequencies are converted into per cent values in the same way. The final step is to round these values to the nearest whole number, rounding border-line values like 12.50 *up* to the next whole number, 13. These rounded values, constituting the percentile ranks, are reported in the fifth column of Table 8.3.

In routing calculations of percentiles it is convenient to use a special 10″ × 10″ chart like that shown in Figure 8.2. This chart was used in the University Examinations Service at the State University of Iowa. Holzinger calls a similar chart a *classifier* and notes that Leonard P. Ayres mentioned it in 1920.[9] Each cell in the chart corresponds to one score. The 100 cells cover scores ranging from 0 to 99. The top row accommodates scores from 0 to 9, the second row from 10 to 19, and so on. Blanks are provided at the top of the chart for identifying the data recorded on it.

The scores for Spelling Test List *A* (Table 8.1) have been entered on the chart of Figure 8.2. Note that on this chart the scores have been tallied only once, in the upper left-hand corner of the appropriate square. The cumulative frequencies are written in the upper right-hand corner of the appropriate square. A special rule is followed for adding the tally marks to get the cumulative frequency.

> *To find the cumulative frequency for any score, add to the cumulative frequency shown in the cell for the next lower score the number of tally marks in that cell and also the number of tally marks in the cell of the score for which the cumulative frequency is desired.*

By this rule each tally mark is added twice, once to contribute to the cumulative frequency for the corresponding score and again to contribute to the cumulative frequency for the next higher score. Thus this rule for addition accomplishes the same result as the double tallying of Table 8.3.

---

[9] Karl J. Holzinger, *Statistical Methods for Students in Education* (Boston: Ginn and Company, 1928), pp. 25-26.

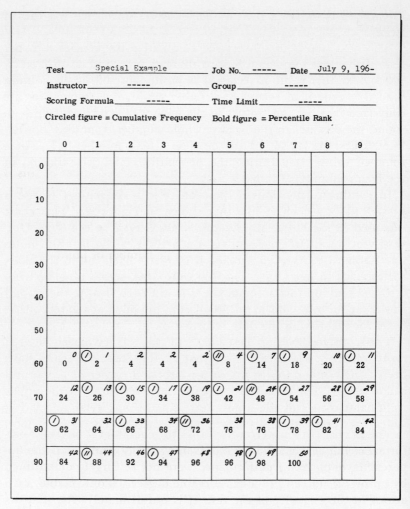

Figure 8.2. Frequency Distribution and Percentile Ranks

If the percentile rank of a score were defined as the per cent of scores falling below a given score, instead of below the midpoint of the score interval, the computation of the percentile ranks would be somewhat simpler. No double tallying or double addition of tallies would be required. But the percentile scale would all be depressed. It would always give some student's score a percentile rank of 0, but never give any student's score a percentile rank of 100. The mean of all the percentile rank equivalents in a given group would not be 50, as it ought to be logically, but something less than 50. If there are gaps in the distribution of scores, more adjacent test scores will be assigned the same percentile rank equivalent. In sum, the advantages of the more precise definition of a percentile rank seem to justify the slight difficulty it adds to the computation.

6. Interpretation of percentile ranks

Test scores expressed as percentile ranks are sometimes confused with test scores expressed as per cent correct. They are, of course, quite different. A per cent correct score is determined by an examinee's performance relative to the content of the test. It expresses the relation between the number of points awarded to a particular examinee's paper and the maximum possible number of points for any paper. Usually the expectation is that few examinees in a group will receive per cent correct scores less than some value near 70 per cent which is often set arbitrarily as the passing score. If the group as a whole does well on an examination, the per cent correct scores will run higher than if the group as a whole does poorly.

A percentile rank, on the other hand, is determined solely by the relation between a particular examinee's score and the scores of other examinees in the group tested. Percentile ranks must necessarily range from near 0 to near 100, regardless of whether the group as a whole does well or poorly on the examination.

The insensitivity of percentile ranks to general level of group performance might seem to be a disadvantage, and would be if the apparent level of group performance were not so largely determined by unintentional, and to a considerable degree uncontrollable, variations in the difficulty of the test. It is unfortunately true that dependable standards of measurement are seldom provided by the examiner's a priori judgments of how difficult a question is likely to be, and, if it requires the exercise of subjective judgment in scoring, his judgments of how well the student has answered it. The typical unreliability of measures obtained by these means has been demonstrated quite convincingly.

Percentile ranks differ from the original or raw test scores, and many other types of scores derived from them, in another respect.

They are rectangularly distributed. Raw score distributions, and those of many other types of scores, generally approximate a normal distribution, more or less. In a normal distribution the scores are concentrated near the middle, with decreasing score frequencies as one moves out to the high and low extremes. In a rectangular distribution the score frequencies are uniform all along the scale. The relation between a normal distribution and a rectangular distribution is illustrated in Figure 8.3.

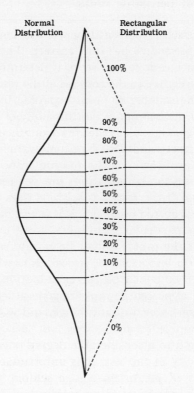

Figure 8.3. Relation Between Normal and Rectangular Distributions

It is clear from this figure that percentile ranks magnify raw score differences near the middle of the distribution but reduce the raw score differences toward the extremes. Stated in other words, a difference of ten percentile rank units near the extremes corresponds to a much larger raw score difference than does the same difference in percentile ranks near the mean. Intuition suggests that the raw score distribution, approximately normal, is a more accurate reflection of the "true" distribution of abilities than is the rectangular distribution. But however plausible such an intuition may seem to be, it is difficult to verify by experiment or logical demonstration.

Because the units on the two scales, raw score and percentile rank, are not equal, averages of the two sets of scores may not give consistent results. This is shown in Table 8.4. To simplify the illustra-

TABLE 8.4

Comparison of Selected Raw Score and Percentile Rank Averages

			Partial Table of Equivalence	
Student A	*Raw Scores*	*Percentile Ranks*	*Raw Scores*	*Percentile Ranks*
Test 1	75	99.4	75	99.4
Test 2	65	93.3	74	99.2
Test 3	70	97.7	73	98.9
			72	98.6
Mean	70	96.8	71	98.2
			70	97.7
Student B			69	97.1
Test 1	68	96.4	68	96.4
Test 2	70	97.7	67	95.5
Test 3	69	97.1	66	94.5
			65	93.3
Mean	69	97.1		

tion it is assumed that raw scores on each of the three tests are normally distributed with a mean of 50 and a standard deviation of 10. A portion of the table of equivalent raw scores and percentile ranks is reproduced on the right side of Table 8.4. Student A is assumed to have received raw scores of 75, 65, and 70 on the three tests. Student B is assumed to have received raw scores of 68, 70, and 69. Note that while Student A has the higher mean raw score, Student B has the higher mean percentile rank.

This example has been chosen purposely to illustrate discrepancies which might arise. Even so, the differences are not very large. In practice, averages based on percentile ranks agree closely with averages based on raw scores. The correlation usually is in the very high nineties.

Can percentile ranks be averaged? Obviously they can, just like any other numbers. We have just done so. But should they be averaged? On this question opinions differ. Those who oppose the practice point out when percentiles are averaged, units that are almost certainly unequal are treated as equal. This, they point out, is mathematically unsound. Others take the position that this logical flaw makes very little difference in practice. Lord, for example, has published a delightful allegory which suggests that even the numbers on football jerseys can be averaged usefully under certain circumstances.[10] One can also note that while raw scores may be less obviously unequal than percentile ranks, neither of them can be shown to be precisely equal in any fundamental sense. Hence any argument on logical grounds against averaging percentiles applies equally, as a matter of principle, to the averaging of raw scores.

If percentile ranks are averaged, it is important to remember that the average of several percentile ranks is not itself a meaningful percentile rank. It is simply a kind of composite score, for which appropriate percentile ranks can be computed. This fact is illustrated by the data in Table 8.5. In the upper section of the table, percentile

TABLE 8.5

**An Illustration of the Relation Between Averages
of Percentile Ranks and Percentile Ranks of Averages**

	Student		
	A	B	C
Test 1	82	54	3
Test 2	97	68	5
Test 3	98	39	2
Test 4	94	79	11
Average of Percentiles	93	60	4
Percentile of Averages	99	60	1

ranks of three students, good, average, and poor, on four tests are reported. These tests were part of an entrance test battery given to all students entering the College of Liberal Arts at the State Uni-

---

[10] Frederic M. Lord, "On the Statistical Treatment of Football Numbers," *American Psychologist,* VIII (1953), 750-51.

versity of Iowa in September 1951. The percentiles of all students were averaged and these averages reconverted into percentile ranks.

Note the difference between the average of the percentiles and the percentile ranks of the averages. These data illustrate a general principle. The percentile rank of the average of several high scores will be higher than the average of the percentile ranks of those scores. The percentile rank of the average of several low scores will be lower than the average of the percentile ranks of those scores. Only with scores whose percentile ranks fall in the midrange is the percentile rank of their average approximately equal to the average of their percentile ranks.

The results observed here are analogous to those observed often in tests of athletic versatility, such as the decathalon. A competitor need not average a first place finish in the ten component contests in order to finish first in the composite. (Obviously he could not *average* a first place finish without actually finishing first in every event.) It could happen, in fact, that a competitor might win the decathalon without finishing first in any of the ten component events. Over-all primacy requires excellence in many of the individual tests but does not require actual primacy in all, or indeed in any, of them.

Once the basic meaning of a percentile rank has been explained, and it is quite easy to explain, scores of this type become extremely useful bases for interpreting a test performance. The scale of percentile ranks is a standard numerical scale, to which the scores from different tests which yield different raw score distributions can all be related. To interpret a raw score on a test one must be familiar with the difficulty level of the tasks composing it. To interpret a percentile rank one must be familiar with the ability level of the group from which the percentile ranks were derived. No test score is wholly self-interpreting, but a simply defined standard scale like that provided by percentile ranks can contribute substantially to test score interpretation.

7. Stanine standard scores

Another convenient and useful basis for score interpretation is provided by the stanine score scale. The term "stanine" was derived from two words, "standard nine," which express its basic meaning.

Stanine scores are normally distributed standard scores which range from 1 to 9. They have the convenience of being single-digit scores, which makes them easy to record and to interpret. While they alter the distribution of raw scores somewhat, forcing it to approximate a normal distribution, the alteration is usually not so radical as that involved in changing raw scores to percentile ranks.

A perfectly normal distribution of stanine scores has a mean of exactly 5 and a standard deviation of approximately 2 stanine score units. Each unit on the stanine scale, except the highest and the lowest unit, is one-half a standard deviation in extent. The middle stanine score unit, 5, extends from one-fourth of a standard deviation below the mean to one-fourth of a standard deviation above it. The limits of other stanine score intervals are shown in Table 8.6. This table also shows what per cent of a group should, theoretically, be assigned each stanine score. These ideal percentages are obtained from a table of areas under the normal curve, using the interval limits shown in Table 8.6.

TABLE 8.6

Percentage of Group Which Should Be Assigned Each Stanine Score Value

Stanine Score	Verbal Translation	Per cent of Group	Interval Limits
9	Highest	4.01	$+1.75\sigma$ to $+\infty$
8	Higher	6.55	$+1.25\sigma$ to $+1.75\sigma$
7	High	12.10	$+.75\sigma$ to $+1.25\sigma$
6	High Average	17.47	$+.25\sigma$ to $+.75\sigma$
5	Average	19.74	$-.25\sigma$ to $+.25\sigma$
4	Low Average	17.47	$-.75\sigma$ to $-.25\sigma$
3	Low	12.10	-1.25σ to $-.75\sigma$
2	Lower	6.55	-1.75σ to -1.25σ
1	Lowest	4.01	$-\infty$ to -1.75σ

When stanine equivalents are assigned to raw scores on typical tests from class groups of typical size, the theoretical percentages required for a perfectly normal distribution of stanine scores can be only approximated. Table 8.7 shows a conversion of the ideal percentages into ideal numbers, or frequencies, of stanine scores for groups of various sizes. However, as will be illustrated shortly, even these approximately ideal numbers can only be approximated in actual assignment of stanine scores.

TABLE 8.7

Number of Scores in Each Stanine for Groups from 20 to 40

Stanine

Size of Group	1	2	3	4	5	6	7	8	9
20	1	1	2	4	4	4	2	1	1
21	1	1	2	4	5	4	2	1	1
22	1	1	3	4	4	4	3	1	1
23	1	1	3	4	5	4	3	1	1
24	1	2	3	4	4	4	3	2	1
25	1	2	3	4	5	4	3	2	1
26	1	2	3	4	6	4	3	2	1
27	1	2	3	5	5	5	3	2	1
28	1	2	3	5	6	5	3	2	1
29	1	2	4	5	5	5	4	2	1
30	1	2	4	5	6	5	4	2	1
31	1	2	4	5	7	5	4	2	1
32	1	2	4	6	6	6	4	2	1
33	1	2	4	6	7	6	4	2	1
34	1	2	5	6	6	6	5	2	1
35	1	2	5	6	7	6	5	2	1
36	1	2	5	6	8	6	5	2	1
37	1	2	5	7	7	7	5	2	1
38	1	2	5	7	8	7	5	2	1
39	1	3	5	7	7	7	5	3	1
40	1	3	5	7	8	7	5	3	1

To convert a set of raw scores to stanines, first arrange them in order from high to low. Then refer to the table to find the ideal frequency distribution of stanines for a group of that size. Because raw scores of the same numerical value must always be assigned the same stanine value, it is not always possible to match the ideal stanine distribution perfectly with the actual distribution. Table 8.8 shows the conversion to stanines of the raw spelling-test scores from List A of Table 8.1. Note that, because of the distribution of raw score values, it was necessary to assign to the List A raw scores one more stanine score of 7, and one less of 8, than called for by Table 8.7.

Transformation of raw scores into stanine scores usually involves some loss of information. That is, some individuals having different raw scores will ordinarily be assigned the same stanine score. Whenever a test yields more than nine different raw scores, and most tests do this, such a loss of differential information will occur. This is the

TABLE 8.8

Conversion of List A Spelling Test Scores
of Table 8.1 to Stanines

Stanine	Ideal Frequency	List A Raw Scores
9	1	96
8	2	93
7	3	91, 81, 88, 87
6	4	84, 84, 82, 80
5	5	79, 77, 76, 76, 75
4	4	74, 73, 72, 71
3	3	69, 67, 66
2	2	65, 65
1	1	61

price one must pay for the convenience of using a simple, single-digit, nine-unit score scale. How serious this loss of information may be depends in part on the reliability of the test and in part on the use to be made of the scores. The more reliable the test, the more serious the loss of information. In reporting test results to students or parents, when one purpose is to discourage overemphasis on small score differences and another to provide easily interpretable scores, stanines have much to recommend them. The second column of Table 8.6 presents some convenient verbal translations of the various stanine scores.

When test scores and other measures of student achievement in a course are being recorded for subsequent combination into a total as a basis for determination of course grades, stanines have two advantages and one disadvantage. The disadvantage is the loss of information just mentioned. One advantage is the single-digit feature which makes them convenient to record. The other is the fact that they provide a uniform scale for all measures. Scores from whatever source carry equal weight in determining a composite if they are converted to stanines before being combined. If some a priori system of differential weighting is desired, stanines provide the uniform basis needed for applying them. In many situations these advantages will seem slight enough, in comparison with the disadvantage, to make the teacher think twice about recording test scores as stanines.

8. Estimating standard deviations from percentiles and stanines

In a normal distribution of scores the difference between scores at the eighty-fourth percentile and the sixteenth percentile is approximately two standard deviations. The difference between scores at the ninety-third percentile and the seventh percentile is approximately three standard deviations. These relations can be obtained from Figure 8.1. If a distribution of scores has been converted into percentile ranks, these facts can be used to obtain an estimate of the standard deviation. The accuracy of the estimate will be greater the closer the distribution of scores approximates the normal distribution and the larger the number of scores in the distribution.

If scores have been converted to stanines, those values can be used similarly to estimate the standard deviation. Table 8.9 indicates that

TABLE 8.9

Estimating the Standard Deviation from Stanine Equivalents

	Average Raw Score	Difference	Estimated σ
Stanine 9	96	$4\sigma = 35$	8.75
Stanine 1	61		
Stanine 8	93	$3\sigma = 28$	9.33
Stanine 2	65		
Stanine 7	89.25	$2\sigma = 21.92$	10.96
Stanine 3	67.33		
Stanine 6	83.33	$\sigma = 10.83$	10.83
Stanine 4	72.50		

$$\frac{39.87}{9.97}$$

Estimated value of $\sigma = 10$.

the difference between the average value of raw scores assigned a stanine value of 9 and those assigned a stanine value of 1 should be about four standard deviations. Similarly, there should be a difference of three standard deviations between the average raw score values equivalent to stanines of 8 and 2, two standard deviations between average raw scores corresponding to stanines of 7 and 3, and one standard deviation between the average of the stanine 6 and stanine 4 raw score values. By using one, or preferably several, of these relations, a reasonably good estimate of the standard deviation should be obtained. Table 8.9 shows this procedure applied to

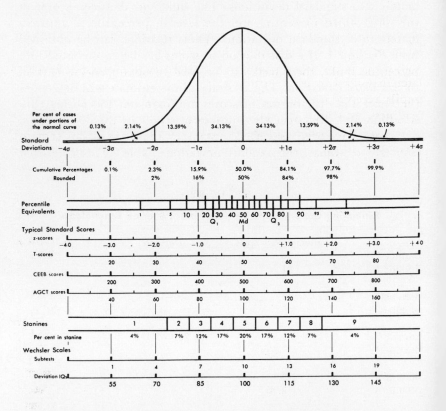

Figure 8.4. Chart Illustrating the Relations of Various Derived Scores to the Normal Distribution and to Each Other (Courtesy of the Psychological Corporation.)

the stanine equivalents shown in Table 8.8. The value obtained is in reasonably good agreement with the values reported previously for the same data.

The Psychological Corporation has published a useful chart based on the normal curve which shows the relations between percentiles, stanines, and other types of standard test scores. That chart is reproduced here as Figure 8.4. Since the main focus of attention in this book is on classroom testing, little attention has been paid to some types of derived scores that are widely used in standardized testing.[11]

9. Coefficients of correlation

In dealing with test scores one frequently has need for an index of their relation to other measures. For example, the relation between scores on a reading readiness test given to pupils in the first grade and scores on a test of reading achievement given a year or two later may need to be determined. If the relation is high and if all pupils received the same kind of instruction regardless of their readiness test scores, the readiness test probably would be judged to be a good test because it accurately forecast later achievement.

Another illustration of the need for an index of the relation between sets of test scores is provided by the determination of some kinds of test reliability. If the same test is given twice to the same group, if two different but equivalent forms are given to the same group, or if a single test is split into two equivalent halves which are separately scored, we use an index of the degree of agreement between the pairs of scores for each person as the basis for estimating the test reliability.

The soundest and most widely used measure of the relation between pairs of measures for individuals in a group is the coefficient of correlation, identified more explicitly as the Pearson product-moment coefficient. This coefficient can be simply, though perhaps not clearly, defined as the "mean z-score product." Expressed as a formula,

$$r = \frac{\Sigma z_x z_y}{N} \qquad 8.7$$

where r is the coefficient of correlation, Σ means "the sum of," z_x

---

[11] Robert L. Ebel, "How to Explain Standardized Test Scores to Your Parents," *School Management*, V, No. 3 (March, 1961), 61-64.

is any individual's score on one of the two measures, expressed in standard (z-score) form, z_y is the same individual's score on the related measure, also expressed in standard form, and N is the number of individuals for whom the relation between the paired scores is to be determined. To convert a raw test score or any other measure to standard score form, divide the difference between that score and the mean of all scores by the standard deviation of all the scores.

Converting each score to standard score form before finding the sum of their products would be a very tedious, time-consuming operation. By applying a little algebra to the formula above, it can be converted to raw score form. The formula then looks more complicated, but it is actually much easier to compute.

$$ r = \frac{N\Sigma XY - \Sigma X \Sigma Y}{\sqrt{[N\Sigma X^2 - (\Sigma X)^2][N\Sigma Y^2 - (\Sigma Y)^2]}} \qquad 8.8 $$

The use of capital letters in this formula indicates that we are dealing here with raw scores rather than standard scores.

What this formula means may be easier to understand if we work through a simple numerical example. Suppose we have the scores of five students on each of two ten-item tests, Test X and Test Y, as shown here.

	Score on	
Student	*Test X*	*Test Y*
A	8	6
B	4	3
C	2	3
D	6	7
E	5	9

The number of pairs of scores to be correlated is five, so $N = 5$. The sum of the five scores on Test X is 25, so $\Sigma X = 25$. The sum of the five scores on Test Y is 28, so $\Sigma Y = 28$. The sum of the products of the scores in each pair, 8×6 plus 4×3, plus 2×3, plus 6×7, plus 5×9, is 153, so $\Sigma XY = 153$. The sum of the squares of the five scores on Test X is 64, plus 16, plus 4, plus 36, plus 25, or 145, so $\Sigma X^2 = 145$. The sum of the squares of the five scores on Test Y is 36, plus 9, plus 9, plus 49, plus 81, or 184, so $\Sigma Y^2 = 184$.

To recapitulate the six basic quantities:

$$N = 5$$
$$\Sigma X = 25$$
$$\Sigma Y = 28$$
$$\Sigma XY = 153$$
$$\Sigma X^2 = 145$$
$$\Sigma Y^2 = 184$$

Now from these six basic quantities we can get, by multiplication (or squaring), the six other quantities called for in the formula.

$$N\Sigma XY = 5 \times 153 = 765$$
$$\Sigma X\Sigma Y = 25 \times 28 = 700$$
$$N\Sigma X^2 = 5 \times 145 = 725$$
$$(\Sigma X)^2 = 25 \times 25 = 625$$
$$N\Sigma Y^2 = 5 \times 184 = 920$$
$$(\Sigma Y)^2 = 28 \times 28 = 784$$

If we now put these six quantities in Formula 8.8 we get:

$$r = \frac{765 - 700}{\sqrt{(725 - 625)(920 - 784)}} = \frac{65}{\sqrt{100 \times 136}}$$

$$r = \frac{65}{\sqrt{13,600}}$$

The square root of 13,600 can be looked up in a table, calculated by the "guess and divide" method described earlier in this chapter, or found in some other way. It turns out to be 116.6. Hence,

$$r = \frac{65}{116.6} = .56$$

Thus the correlation between these five pairs of scores on the two tests is .56.

A work sheet for computing a correlation coefficient on the basis of this formula is shown in Figure 8.5. The data entered on it are from the scores on the two spelling tests presented in Table 8.1. The

-Variable _Scores on List A_

Y-Variable _Scores on List B_

Source of Data _Spelling Test, Table 8.1_

Date _5-13-64_ Job Number _15_ Calculator _Jean_ Checker _Betty_

I. Totals from Calculator

N	ΣX	ΣY	ΣX^2	$2\Sigma XY$	ΣY^2
5	365	379	26,991	55,998	29,097
5	405	403	33,021	65,620	32,645
5	377	379	28,695	57,736	29,109
5	422	412	36,300	70,552	34,338
5	373	389	28,123	58,482	30,475
25	1,942	1,962	153,130	308,388	155,664

II. Operations with Totals

Operation	Calculation	Check
① $= N\Sigma XY - \Sigma X\Sigma Y$	$25 \times 154,194 - 1942 \times 1962 = 44,646$	44,646
② $= \sqrt{N\Sigma X^2 - (\Sigma X)^2}$	$\sqrt{25 \times 153,130 - 1,942 \times 1942} = 238.51$	238.51
③ $= \sqrt{N\Sigma Y^2 - (\Sigma Y)^2}$	$\sqrt{25 \times 155,664 - 1,962 \times 1962} = 205.32$	205.32
④ $= r = \dfrac{①}{② \times ③}$	$\dfrac{44,646}{238.51 \times 205.32} = .9117$	.9117
⑤ $= M_x = \Sigma X \div N$	$1,942 \div 25 = 77.68$	77.68
⑥ $= M_y = \Sigma Y \div N$	$1,962 \div 25 = 78.48$	78.48
⑦ $= \sigma x = ② \div N$	$238.51 \div 25 = 9.54$	9.54
⑧ $= \sigma y = ③ \div N$	$205.32 \div 25 = 8.21$	8.21

Figure 8.5. Computing Worksheet for Correlation

coefficient of correlation between these scores turns out to be .91.

With a reasonably good calculator and with the aid of a systematizing worksheet like that of Figure 8.5, calculation of a product-moment coefficient of correlation is quite simple. When the intercorrelations among several variables must be calculated using a desk calculator, the procedures described by Rummel are convenient.[12]

Other Estimates of Correlation

Another formula for estimating a correlation coefficient is based on differences in rank between the two scores of each pair when the scores from each test have been ranked separately. A different symbol, the Greek letter "rho," is used to indicate that this coefficient of correlation is somewhat different from the Pearson coefficient

$$\rho = 1 - \frac{6\Sigma d^2}{N(N^2 - 1)} \qquad 8.10$$

in which d^2 is the square of the difference between ranks for the scores of any pair and N is the number of pairs of scores.

An example of the application of this formula to the test scores of Table 8.1 is presented in Table 8.10. The first two columns of Table 8.10 reproduce the raw scores from Table 8.1. The next two columns show these scores converted to ranks. Since the highest raw score in List A is 96, it is given a rank of 1 for List A in the third column. The next highest score, 93, is given a rank of 2. There are two of the third highest score, 91. These two scores should occupy positions 3 and 4 in the rank list, but since they are the same in raw score value they should have the same rank value. Instead of giving both a rank of 3, or of 4, we average the two rank positions, 3 and 4, and give the two scores of 91 ranks of 3.5. In general, whenever two or more raw scores in the list are the same they are given the same rank, which is the average of the rank positions they would occupy if they were slightly different. The lowest score in List A, 61, receives the lowest possible rank in a set of 25 scores, namely 25. Note that the correlation obtained by this method agrees well with that obtained by the product-moment method.

A third method of estimating a correlation coefficient involves the ratio of two differences between the sums of scores for high-scoring and low-scoring groups of students.[13] Each group is selected be-

---

[12] J. Francis Rummel, "Procedures for Computation of Zero-order Coefficients Among Several Variables," *Journal of Experimental Education*, XX (March, 1952), 313-18.

[13] John A. Weichelt, "A First Order Method for Estimating Correlation Coefficients," *Psychometrika*, XI (December, 1946), 215-21.

TABLE 8.10

Illustration of Calculation of the Rank Difference Coefficient of Correlation

Raw Scores		Ranks			
List A	List B	List A	List B	d	d^2
65	67	23.5	24	0.5	0.25
75	72	15	19	4.0	16.00
66	72	22	19	3.0	9.00
88	92	5	2	3.0	9.00
71	76	19	16	3.0	9.00
72	72	18	19	1.0	1.00
91	90	3.5	3.5	0.0	0.00
82	80	9	9.5	0.5	0.25
84	80	7.5	9.5	2.0	4.00
76	81	13.5	8	5.5	30.25
69	64	20	25	5.0	25.00
67	70	21	21	0.0	0.00
74	78	16	12.5	3.5	12.25
80	77	10	15	5.0	25.00
87	90	6	3.5	2.5	6.25
91	85	3.5	7	3.5	12.25
65	68	23.5	23	0.5	0.25
77	78	12	12.5	0.5	0.25
96	94	1	1	0.0	0.00
93	87	2	6	4.0	16.00
79	78	11	12.5	1.5	2.25
84	89	7.5	5	2.5	6.25
76	75	13.5	17	3.5	12.25
73	78	17	12.5	4.5	20.25
61	69	25	22	3.0	9.00

$$\Sigma d^2 = 226 \qquad\qquad N(N^2 - 1) = 15,600$$

$$\rho = 1 - \frac{6\Sigma d^2}{N(N^2 - 1)}$$

$$= 1 - \frac{1,356}{15,600}$$

$$= .913$$

cause it constitutes the highest or lowest one-fifth of the total group on one or the other of the measures. For each group we find the sum of the scores of the group on each test separately. The processes are illustrated in Table 8.11, using the data on spelling test scores presented in Table 8.1.

TABLE 8.11

Illustration of Calculation of the Upper-Lower
Difference Coefficient of Correlation

Highest	Scores on		Lowest	Scores on	
List A	List A	List B	List A	List A	List B
Nathaniel	96	94	Wendell	61	69
Patricia	93	87	Aaron	65	67
Dorothy	91	90	Melville	65	68
Joan	91	85	Ben	66	72
Bud	88	92	Gladys	67	70
	459	448		324	346

Highest	Scores on		Lowest	Scores on	
List B	List A	List B	List B	List A	List B
Nathaniel	96	94	Gary	69	64
Bud	88	92	Aaron	65	67
Dorothy	91	90	Melville	65	68
Jerry	87	90	Wendell	61	69
Perry	84	89	Gladys	67	70
	446	455		327	338

$$r = \frac{446 - 327}{459 - 324} = \frac{119}{135} = .882$$
$$r = \frac{448 - 346}{455 - 338} = \frac{102}{117} = .872$$
$$\Bigg\} = .88$$

The five students receiving highest scores on List A: Nathaniel, Patricia, Dorothy, Joan, and Bud are identified. Their scores on both List A and List B are recorded and added. The five students scoring lowest on List A are handled in the same way. Similar data are obtained for the five students scoring highest and the five scoring lowest on List B. These data and the sums are presented in the upper portion of Table 8.11.

From these data two estimates of the coefficient of correlation can be calculated. The first is based solely on scores from List A. In the numerator of the fraction we place the difference in sums of List A scores for the groups scoring highest and lowest on List B. In the denominator we place the difference in sums of List A scores for the groups scoring highest and lowest on List A. Dividing denominator into numerator gives the estimate of the coefficient of correlation, in this case .882. These data and the calculation are shown near the bottom of Table 8.11.

The second estimate is based solely on scores from List B. But this time the numerator contains sums of scores from groups scoring highest and lowest on List A; the denominator is derived from scores on List B.

These somewhat complicated jugglings of numbers can be kept straight if three principles are remembered:

1. Each set of scores on two tests provides data for two estimates of correlation.
2. Each estimate of correlation is based on sums of scores from only one of the two related variables.
3. If the reliability is being calculated using sums of scores on variable x, the groups in the numerator are selected for high or low standing on variable y, those in the denominator for high or low standing on variable x.

10. Interpreting coefficients of correlation

Coefficients of correlation are widely used in the study of test scores. If calculated accurately they provide precise estimates of the degree of relation in the data on which they are based. But when an obtained coefficient of correlation is used as an estimate of the relationship to be expected in other sets of data obtained under similar conditions, note must be made of the large variations that are often found in coefficients of correlation based on small samples, even when the samples are all drawn from the same population.

This is illustrated in Table 8.12, which shows the range in coefficients which can be expected for samples of various size when the true correlation is .30 or .60 or .90. Table 8.12 should be read in this way:

> If one hundred samples of ten pairs of scores each are drawn from a large population of such pairs in which the true correlation is .30 and if the coefficient of correlation is calculated for each pair, fifty of those coefficients would be expected to be more than .05 and less than .51. Ninety-five would be expected to be above $-.41$ and

below .78. The other five would be expected to be even
farther removed from the true value of .30.

As the sample size increases and as the value of the true correlation increases, the range of variation of the sample coefficients

TABLE 8.12

Sampling Errors in Correlation Coefficients*

| True Correlation | Sample Size | Limits of Confidence Intervals | |
		50 Per cent	95 Per cent
.30	10	.05 to .51	−.41 to .78
	30	.18 to .41	−.07 to .60
	100	.24 to .36	.11 to .47
	300	.26 to .34	.19 to ,40
.60	10	.41 to .74	−.05 to .89
	30	.51 to .68	.31 to .79
	100	.55 to .64	.46 to .71
	300	.57 to .62	.52 to .67
.90	10	.84 to .94	.62 to .98
	30	.87 to .92	.80 to .95
	100	.886 to .914	.85 to .93
	300	.893 to .907	.88 to .92

* The confidence limits shown in this table were calculated on the basis of the
Fisher z statistic, using the method described in Section 15.13 of *Elementary Statis-
tical Methods*, by Paul Blommers and E. F. Lindquist, Houghton Mifflin Company,
Boston, 1960.

decreases. Table 8.12 justifies the conclusion that correlation coefficients based on small samples are not very dependable, especially
when the true correlation is moderate or low. A much larger sample
is required to yield a precise estimate of the coefficient of correlation than is required for an equally precise estimate of the mean or
standard deviations.

How much relationship is implied by correlation coefficients of
various values is illustrated in Figure 8.6. The five columns in each
diagram represents scores on one variable (X) of 1, 2, 3, 4, and 5
(reading from left to right). These columns could, of course, repre-

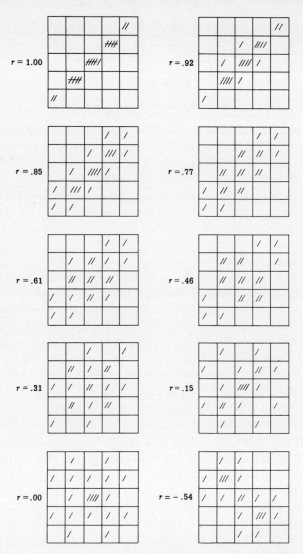

Figure 8.6. Simple Scatter Diagrams Illustrating Various Degrees of Correlation

sent any other set of five equally spaced scores which increase from left to right. The five rows represent similar scores on the other variable, increasing from bottom to top. The distribution of each set of scores is the same in all of the diagrams. That is, there are six scores of middle value, five each of higher and lower scores, and two each of highest and lowest.

The top diagram in the left-hand series illustrates perfect correlation. All the tally marks are in the cells on the diagonal, because the highest scores on one variable are always paired with the highest scores on the other, the second high with the second high, the middle with the middle, and so on. The other diagrams show that, as the tally marks depart increasingly from the diagonal, the correlation decreases correspondingly. When the diagram shows a perfectly balanced or symmetrical distribution of tally marks in each of the columns and rows, as the lower left-hand diagram does, the correlation is zero. When the high scores on one variable tend to be associated with low scores on the other, as in the lower right hand diagram, the correlation is negative.

Another way of interpreting a correlation coefficient is to relate it to the coefficients obtained in other more or less familiar situations. Scores on equivalent forms of a well-constructed educational achievement test, administered separately within a few days of each other, should show coefficients of correlation of .90 or higher. Scores on good tests intended to predict educational achievement correlate with subsequent good measures of achievement to the extent reflected in coefficients which average about .50 and which range from about .30 to about .70, depending on the nature of the achievement, the quality of the measures of promise and of attainment, the interval between the measures, and many other factors. Coefficients or correlation between the scores on individual items of an objective test average about .10 but often range from about −.30 to about .50.

Research workers sometimes refer wryly to the "Irish Coefficients" they often obtain when trying out new tests of elusive mental traits. They mean values like .02 (O'Two), .05, etc. Such coefficients near zero usually mean that the measures bear little or no consistent relation to each other.

Another basis for interpreting a correlation coefficient is to note that it expresses the proportion of independent, equally potent causes influencing performance on the two related tests (or other measures) which are common to both. This principle can be demonstrated using a pair of dice. Both dice are rolled and the total points showing are counted. This gives the first score X of the first pair. Then only one of the dice is picked up and rolled again, leaving the first as it was. Again the total points showing are counted. This gives the second score Y of the first pair. In this case one of two independent, equally potent factors is common to the two scores. The other factor can vary.

If the process above is repeated to yield fifty or one hundred pairs of scores and if the coefficient of correlation between the X and Y scores is calculated, a value near .50 will be obtained. Instead of two dice, four might be used. If only one of the dice was rerolled to obtain the second score of each pair, a correlation of .75 would be expected. If three were rerolled, a correlation of .25 would be expected. Using ten dice and rerolling only one of them should result in an expected coefficient of correlation of .90.

Thus when one encounters a correlation coefficient of, say .83, it is reasonable to make this kind of an interpretation. If the related measures were determined by the combined effects of one hundred independent, equally powerful factors, eighty-three of the one hundred would have to be constant factors. That is, they would have to contribute the same value to each member of the pair of related measures, to yield a coefficient of .83. The other seventeen factors could vary.

This interpretation is suggestive, but it should not be taken too literally as a description of what actually happens. There is usually no evidence to suggest that the performance of students on any test is the result of the combined influence of a number of independent, equally powerful factors.

11. Other references

This chapter has dealt in an introductory fashion with some of the statistics that are useful in dealing with test scores. Many other topics might have been included. Those that were included might have been discussed in more detail. Since they were not, it seems advisable to conclude the chapter with mention of a few other statistical references that the interested student may find useful.

Excellent introductory texts on statistics by Blommers and Lindquist, and by Ferguson, were mentioned earlier in this chapter. A classic in the field, famous for its authoritative and lucid treatment of many problems of test score statistics is Kelley's *Statistical Method*.[14] Peters and Van Voorhis provide clear explanations and mathematical derivations for a great number of useful statistical procedures.[15]

Considerable attention was given to short-cut statistical procedures in the chapter. Diederich has described some of these and other convenient devices in an interesting, well-written leaflet.[16]

There is no lack of other good references on the statistical treatment of test scores, but perhaps these will suffice to get the interested student started along what could become an absorbing and rewarding line of inquiry.

12. Summary

Some of the principal ideas developed in this chapter are summarized in these twenty-five statements.

1. A frequency distribution of scores shows how many scores fall in each group, or at each level, along the score scale.
2. A frequency distribution is useful in showing how any particular score relates to all of the other scores in the group.
3. The median is either the middle measure (if the number of measures is odd) or a point midway between the two middle measures (if the number of measures is even).
4. The mean of a set of scores is found by adding all of the scores and dividing the total by the number of scores.
5. The variance of a set of scores is found by adding the squared deviations of the scores (from the mean of all scores) and then dividing the total by the number of scores.
6. The standard deviation is the square root of the variance.
7. Calculation of the mean and of the standard deviation can sometimes be simplified by starting with the frequency distribution

---

[14] Truman L. Kelley, *Statistical Method* (New York: The Macmillan Company, 1924).

[15] Charles C. Peters and Walter R. Van Voorhis, *Statistical Procedures and Their Mathematical Bases* (New York: McGraw-Hill Book Company, 1940).

[16] Paul Diederich, *Short-cut Statistics for Teacher-made Tests*, Evaluation and Advisory Service Series No. 5 (Princeton, N.J.: Educational Testing Service, 1960), p. 44.

and by making use of a deviation scale whose unit is the class interval and whose zero is the midpoint of an interval near the middle of the distribution.

8. Lathrop's short-cut estimate of the standard deviation is obtained by dividing one-half the number of scores into the difference between the sums of upper and lower one-sixths of the scores.

9. The normal curve is a theoretical, symmetric, bell-shaped curve that provides an idealized representation of the frequency distributions of some kinds of experimental data.

10. The larger the number of scores in a group, the greater the expected range of scores in standard deviation units.

11. Scores in any set can be given a standard relative meaning by converting them into percentile ranks.

12. The percentile rank of a score is approximately equivalent to the percentage of scores lower than it in the set of scores.

13. A complete set of percentile ranks yields a frequency distribution that is rectangular in shape.

14. Conversion of normally distributed scores to percentile ranks increases apparent score differences near the center of the distribution and decreases them near the extremes of the distribution.

15. Percentile ranks may be averaged, but the average is not itself a percentile rank.

16. Stanine standard scores are normally distributed single-digit scores having a mean of 5 and a standard deviation of 2.

17. Stanines have standard relative meaning and single-digit convenience, but their use involves some loss of precision.

18. If the distribution of scores is approximately normal, rough estimates of its standard deviation can be based on the score difference between selected percentile ranks or stanines.

19. The correlation coefficient is a measure of the degree of correspondence between two variables, based on paired values of the variables obtained for each of a number of persons or things.

20. Possible values of the correlation coefficient range from 1.00 expressing perfect positive (direct) relationship, through 0, expressing absence of relationship, to −1.00, expressing perfect negative (inverse) relationship.

21. When scores on two correlated variables are expressed as z scores

(deviations from the mean in standard deviation units), the correlation coefficient is the mean of the z-score products.

22. Correlation coefficients can be calculated from differences in ranks of the paired scores or from a ratio of differences in sums of high and low scores.

23. Correlation coefficients obtained from small or medium-sized samples are subject to large sampling errors.

24. The more closely the tally marks in a two-dimensional scatter diagram are clustered along a diagonal, the higher the correlation.

25. If values of the two variables being correlated can be thought of as the result of influences of a number of independent, equally potent factors, then the correlation coefficient expresses the proportion of those factors making the same (rather than different) contribution to the values in each pair of variables.

REFERENCES

Blommers, Paul and E. F. Lindquist, *Elementary Statistical Methods.* Boston: Houghton Mifflin Company, 1960.

Cook, Desmond L., "A Replication of Lord's Study of Skewness and Kurtosis of Observed Test-score Distributions," *Educational and Psychological Measurement,* XIX (1959), 81-87.

Diederich, Paul, *Short-cut Statistics for Teacher-made Tests,* p. 44. Evaluation and Advisory Service Series No. 5. Princeton, N.J.: Educational Testing Service, 1960.

Ebel, Robert L., "How to Explain Standardized Test Scores to Your Parents," *School Management,* V, No. 3 (March, 1961), 61-64.

Ferguson, George A., *Statistical Analysis in Psychology and Education.* New York: McGraw-Hill Book Company, 1959.

Hoel, Paul G., *Introduction to Mathematical Statistics.* New York: John Wiley & Sons, Inc., 1947.

Holzinger, Karl J., *Statistical Methods for Students in Education,* pp. 25-26. Boston: Ginn and Company, 1928.

Jenkins, W. L., "A Short-cut Method for σ and r," *Educational and Psychological Measurement,* VI (1946), 533-36.

Kelley, Truman L., *Statistical Method.* New York: The Macmillan Company, 1924.

Lathrop, Robert L., "A Quick but Accurate Approximation to the Standard Deviation of a Distribution," *Journal of Experimental Education,* XXIX (March, 1961), 319-21.

Lord, Frederic M., "A Survey of Observed Test-score Distributions with Respect to Skewness and Kurtosis," *Educational and Psychological Measurement,* XV (1955), 383-89.

————, "On the Statistical Treatment of Football Numbers," *American Psychologist,* VIII (1953), 750-51.

Moonan, William J., "A Table of Normal Distribution Frequencies for Selected Numbers of Class Intervals and Sample Sizes," *Journal of Experimental Education,* XXVII (March, 1959), 231-35.

Peters, Charles C. and Walter R. Van Voorhis, *Statistical Procedures and Their Mathematical Bases.* New York: McGraw-Hill Book Company, 1940.

Rummel, J. Francis, *The Modification of a Test to Reduce Errors in the Classification of Examinees.* Unpublished dissertation. Iowa City, Iowa: College of Education, The State University of Iowa, 1950.

Weichelt, John A., "A First Order Method for Estimating Correlation Coefficients," *Psychometrika,* XI (December, 1946), 215-21.

9 How to Judge the Quality of a Classroom Test

I do not believe, however, that inefficient examining can in the long run contribute to good training, and I infer from this the belief that the only course an examining body can properly take is to strive continually to improve its examinations so that they give the maximum support to good training.

R. A. C. OLIVER

What makes a classroom test a good test? This question concerns both students and instructors whenever a test is given. It is one of the most basic questions confronting those who make and use classroom tests. Too often it goes unanswered or is badly answered for lack of sound standards of quality and convenient techniques of applying them.

Some of the important factors which need to be considered in judging the quality of a test are suggested by the ten topics and questions which follow:

1. *Relevance.* Have the types of questions included in the test been selected judiciously to test the desired achievements?
2. *Balance.* Does the proportion of items dealing with each aspect of achievement conform with the test constructor's intent, as expressed in the specifications for the test?
3. *Efficiency.* Does the test make efficient use of the instructor's

limited time for test preparation and grading and of the student's limited time in the examination period?

4. *Objectivity*. Are the questions clear enough and the answers definite enough so that any expert in the field covered by the test would get a perfect or near perfect score?

5. *Specificity*. Do the questions require achievements specific to the field covered by the test so that even intelligent, test-wise novices who have not studied the field would expect scores near the chance level?

6. *Difficulty*. Are the test questions and the test as a whole appropriate in difficulty, neither too hard nor too easy to function effectively with the examinees for which the test is intended?

7. *Discrimination*. Do the individual questions discriminate sharply between examinees of higher and lower achievement and does the test as a whole yield a wide distribution of scores for students who differ in achievement?

8. *Reliability*. Does the test yield scores that agree with those obtained from equally good independent measurements of the same achievement?

9. *Fairness*. Is the test constructed and administered so that each student has a good, and an equal, chance to demonstrate his real achievement in the area covered by the test?

10. *Speededness*. Is the test appropriate in length for the time available, so that good use is made of the examination period without allowing the examinee's rate of work to have an undue influence on the score he receives?

The answers to some of these questions can be obtained by studying the test itself and the written specifications used in developing it, if any are available. The answers to other questions can be obtained from an analysis of test and item scores.

A sample test analysis report is shown as Exhibit 9.1 on the following page. It consists of an outline of qualities or characteristics, paralleled by three columns of data. The first column suggests certain standards. The second reports data for the test under analysis. The third evaluates these data in relation to the standards. (An earlier version of this approach to the analysis of classroom tests was published in 1954.[1])

---

[1] Robert L. Ebel, "Procedures for the Analysis of Classroom Tests," *Educational and Psychological Measurement*, XIV (1954), 352-64.

Test title: *Educational Measurement* Group Tested: *Graduate Students* N = 40

Instructor: *Jones* Date of Test: *5/19/–* Score = *Number right*

Number of Items: *50* Choices per Item: *5* Time Limit: *45 minutes*

	Characteristic	Ideal		Actual	Rating
I.	Relevance and Balance				
	A. Terminology	less than	*20 %*	*20 %*	*High*
	B. Factual Information	less than	*20 %*	*18 %*	*OK*
	C. Generalization	less than	*20 %*	*10 %*	*OK*
	D. Explanation	more than	*10 %*	*14 %*	*OK*
	E. Calculation	more than	*5 %*	*12 %*	*Good*
	F. Prediction	more than	*10 %*	*10 %*	*OK*
	G. Recommended Action	more than	*5 %*	*16 %*	*Good*
II.	Discrimination				
	A. Item				
	1. High (.40 and up)	more than	*25 %*	*18 %*	*Low*
	2. Moderate (.20 to .39)	less than	*25 %*	*26 %*	*OK*
	3. Low (.01 to .19)	less than	*15 %*	*34 %*	*High*
	4. Zero or Negative	less than	*5 %*	*22 %*	*High*
	B. Score				
	1. Mean	about	*30.0*	*32.5*	*Good*
	2. Standard Deviation	more than	*6.67*	*5.84*	*Low*
	3. Reliability	more than	*.80*	*.86*	*Good*
	4. Probable Error	more than		*1.47*	
III.	Speededness				
	Completed Tests	more than	*90 %*	*97 %*	*x Good*

Exhibit 9.1. Test Analysis Report

Subsequent sections of this chapter, where the test characteristics are discussed in some detail, will present justifications for the ideal standards suggested in the sample test analysis report. While these standards are reasonable for most classroom tests, they may not all be appropriate to certain special tests. If an instructor feels that some of the standards are not suitable, he may disregard ratings based on them. Better still, he may work out more appropriate standards, and reevaluate the test in terms of these new standards.

This analysis is applied most easily to objective tests. It is, however, applicable, at least in part, to essay-type tests, such as those used in history and literature, and to problem tests, such as those used in physics, mathematics, and other areas. The only restriction is that individual questions must be separately scored. The analysis is most significant when applied to tests given in large classes, but it can provide useful information in classes as small as ten or fifteen students. Further reference to and explanations of the test analysis report of Exhibit 9.1 will be made in the discussion of the aspects of test quality to which they are related.

1. Relevance

What "relevance" means, as the term is used here, may be suggested by illustrating a set of criteria of relevance for a particular test, such as those presented in Exhibit 9.2. Note that the criteria of relevance are preceded by a brief statement of the purpose of the test. Whether the purpose is a proper purpose or whether these criteria are good criteria, in the sense of specifying the right kind of items for the purposes of this particular test, is not at issue here. For example, the specification that all of the items should be in multiple-choice form is somewhat arbitrary and may not be at all crucial to the over-all quality of the test. At this point in the discussion we are not concerned primarily with the correctness of specified criteria of relevance. The question which should concern us is whether these criteria are clear and definite enough to limit the test to items of the desired type and comprehensive enough not to exclude any such items. Test specifications should be definite and clear enough to provide unambiguous information to the test constructor or the test reviewer.

In the practical construction of classroom tests, criteria of relevance often are not written. They may exist mainly in the mind of the person who is constructing the test. He may not even be conscious of all of them all the time. Hence it would be surprising if

EXHIBIT 9.2

Criteria of Relevance for a Test in Educational Measurement

The purpose of this test is to reveal differences among teachers or prospective teachers in their command of knowledge related to the effective use of educational tests in the classroom.

1. All of the items in the test should be in multiple-choice form.
2. Each of the items should require the examinee to demonstrate that he can answer practical questions or solve practical problems related to effective use of educational tests in the classroom.
3. The idea on which the items is based (i.e., the knowledge or ability it tests) should be discussed in some good textbook on classroom testing.
4. The correctness of the keyed correct answer should be verifiable by reference to an authoritative source other than the textbook which suggested the item.
5. No item should use as its stem and correct response any statements consisting of essentially the same word sequence as found in some sentence in the textbook.

he were to apply them consistently in writing all of the items he puts in the test.

When tests are constructed by committees for wide-scale testing programs, there is usually somewhat greater effort to be explicit about the characteristics desired in the test items. But even in these cases the criteria often are not stated explicitly. To find the work of such committees guided by a collection of explicit statements of the criteria of relevance, similar to those presented in Exhibit 9.2, is probably the exception rather than the rule.

Where several instructors are concerned with teaching the same course, it is quite common for all to share the responsibility for test construction. This practice ought to be extended to single-section courses. Instructors in the same area ought to exchange examinations for review and constructive criticism. While it is true that the best instructors give courses which are unique products of their own special abilities, the important achievements they teach and call for in their tests ought to be things that most of their colleagues would also accept as true and important. No instructor should feel obligated to make all the changes in his test suggested by his colleagues. The ultimate responsibility for its goodness or badness is his. But independent reviews of a test by competent colleagues cost little additional time and often yield large returns in improved quality.

Some specialists in educational testing regard the question of item relevance as inescapably a matter for subjective judgment. The ability to make these judgments soundly, they believe, is what distinguishes the competent from the incompetent test constructor. But relevance is not a purely private affair. It cannot be trusted to wholly subjective (private) decisions. Someone beside the man who makes a test has to believe that it is good. The judgments of the test constructor must eventually pass the test of independent verification. To the extent that they do pass such a test, they cease to be subjective and become objective. For most, if not all, tests of educational achievement it is possible and useful to prepare in advance an explicit statement, comprehensive and concrete, of the qualities desired in the items of the test.

One reason why this task of specifying criteria for desirable test items may not have been more widely attempted is that it can be made to seem hopelessly complex and difficult if one undertakes to specify all the qualities that contribute to the goodness of an item. The degree to which an item lacks some of these qualities will be revealed quite clearly in an item analysis. As an item writer gains skill and experience he gradually learns what to do and what to avoid doing to the end that an increasing proportion of his items will be properly difficult and discriminating. To verbalize all this item writing wisdom and to obtain agreement on the various, sometimes contradictory, principles suggested is indeed a formidable task.

The goal of the criteria of relevance suggested here is much simpler. Their task is only to provide an answer to the question, "Does an item like this belong in a test intended to serve this particular purpose in this particular set of circumstances?" They are not concerned with such things as item difficulty, possible ambiguity, grammatical flaws, semantic weaknesses, or any other characteristics which may affect the discriminating power of the item but do not affect its intent. Criteria of relevance are not intended to guarantee high-quality items, only to increase the probability that the items included in the test will provide tasks appropriate to the purpose of the test.

Perhaps one point will bear repetition. Making the criteria of relevance explicit does not make them valid. What it does accomplish is to make possible more objective consideration of their validity.

Relevance is one of the aspects of quality in a test. In judging relevance it is most helpful to have a clear statement of the characteristics that make certain items, and only those items, relevant to the purposes of the test. Then the relevance of a test is determined by the extent to which the items in it possess the desired characteristics. Relevance is not easy to objectify, but it does need to be judged as objectively as possible.

2. Balance

Balance is a second aspect of quality in a test. The balance of a test is indicated by the extent to which the proportions of items testing each aspect of achievement correspond to those specified for an ideal test of this kind. Balance, like relevance, is not easy to objectify. In order to produce a balanced test, or judge its balance, one must specify distinctly and unambiguously the kind of item which is appropriate to each aspect of achievement. There must be a clear association of each of the aspects of achievement to be tested with each of the types of test items specified.

Most test constructors seek balance in their tests. That is, they hope to make their tests sample representatively all the important aspects of achievement which can be tested effectively. But balance is not always defined clearly or verified specifically. Sometimes, particularly in classroom test construction, it may be left largely to chance.

One of the standard devices of the experienced test constructor who seeks balance in his test is the two-way grid, sometimes called a "test blueprint." The several major areas of content to be covered by the test are assigned to the several rows (or columns) of the grid. The several major kinds of abilities to be developed are assigned to the columns (or rows). Each item may then be classified in one of the cells of the grid. Various numbers of items are assigned to each of the rows and the columns. Knowing the proportions of items specified for a particular row and for a particular column, one can ideally determine the proportion of items appropriate for the cell formed by that row and that column. Travers and Dressel provided an illustration of a test blueprint.[2]

The two-way grid is a good first step toward balance in a test. But it has limitations. For some tests a one-dimensional classification of items may be entirely adequate. Others may require three or four. There is some tendency for content to be related to goals or abilities. Hence the assumption that every cell should be represented by at least one item can be unwarranted. Since the number of cells in the chart equals the number of content areas multiplied by the number of educational goals, there is often a fairly large number of such cells. This leads to a more refined classification of items and a more difficult task of classifying them than may actually be necessary to produce a balanced test.

Another problem in using this device arises from difficulty in providing clear definitions of the categories involved, particularly the goal or ability categories. Content categories, on the other hand, are usually simpler to deal with. In a test for a course in consumer mathematics, for example, it is quite easy to tell whether a given item deals mainly with insurance or with taxation. It is much more difficult to tell whether it deals more with the ability to weigh values than it does with the ability to spend money wisely. Experience suggests that the reliability of a classification of test items in the usual two-way grid may be quite low, especially along the goal or ability dimension.

One way of reducing this difficulty is to classify test items in terms of their overt characteristics as verbal objects instead of on the basis of educational goals to which they seem to relate or mental abilities which they presumably require. Another step toward making the measurement of balance more workable is to forego the fine detail in classification demanded by the two-way grid. Instead, one could settle for separate specifications of the desired weighting on each basis for classifying the items, such as item type or content

---

[2] Robert M. W. Travers, *How to Make Achievement Tests* (New York: The Odyssey Press, Inc., 1950), p. 25; and Paul L. Dressel and Others, *Comprehensive Examinations in a Program of General Education* (East Lansing, Mich.: Michigan State College Press, 1949), pp. 22, 48, 67, 81, 91.

area. Taking these steps might lead to replacement of the two-way grid with separate outlines of categories such as those shown in Exhibit 9.3.

EXHIBIT 9.3

Distribution of Items Among Content Areas and Question Types for a Test in Educational Measurement

Content Areas	Items
Nature of Educational Measurement	2
History of Educational Measurement	2
Statistical Techniques	7
Finding and Selecting Tests	3
Tests and Objectives	3
Teacher Made Tests	4
Test Try-out and Analysis	2
Elementary School Testing	5
Secondary School Testing	4
Educational Aptitude	5
Personality and Adjustment	2
Observational Techniques	2
School Testing Programs	5
Using the Results of Measurement	4
	50

Types of Questions	Items
Terminology	5
Factual Information	10
Generalization	15
Explanation	5
Calculation	5
Prediction	5
Recommended Action	5
	50

Section I of Exhibit 9.1 summarizes some partial evidence on the relevance and balance of a test in educational measurement. A sheet showing the classification of each item in the test with reference to these categories is shown in Exhibit 9.4. The handwritten numbers identify the test items classified in each category. The basis on

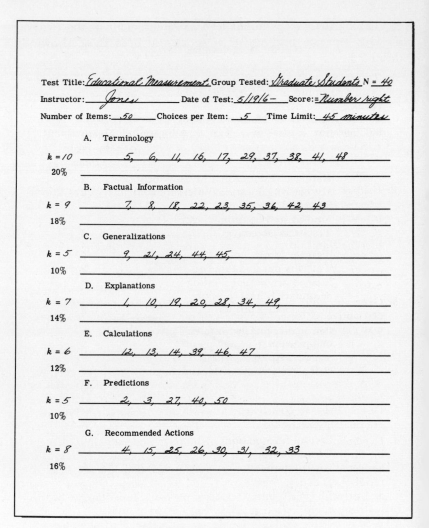

Exhibit 9.4. Relevance Report

which the items were classified is suggested by the Guide to Relevance Categories of Exhibit 9.5. Illustrative examples of items representing each relevance category are provided in Exhibit 9.6.

In general, any course is expected to make some permanent changes in the students who take it—to leave them with new knowl-

EXHIBIT 9.5

Guide to Relevance Categories

1. *Terminology.* A terminology or vocabulary item tests knowledge of one meaning of a particular word or technical term. It may require choice of:
   a. The statement which best defines a given statement
   b. The term which is best defined by a given statement
   c. The best illustration or example of what the term means
   d. The phrases or sentence in which the term is used most appropriately

2. *Factual Information.* A factual information item requires knowledge of a specific fact or a descriptive detail. Often it is answered primarily on the basis of simple recall. It may ask:
   a. Who? and be answered by the name of a person
   b. What? and be answered by a name or a description
   c. When? and be answered by a date or a time
   d. Where? and be answered by the name of a place
   e. How much? and be answered by a numerical quantity

3. *Generalization.* A generalization item requires knowledge of a descriptive statement having general validity. Such a statement may express:
   a. A law or principle
   b. A general description or characterization
   c. A trend or development
   d. A comparison of types or classes, stating their similarities or differences
   Often such statements include words like "generally," "usually," "normally," "often," etc.

4. *Explanation.* An explanation item tests understanding. Except in the cases of stereotyped problems or situations it must be answered on the basis of reasoning rather than on the basis of recall. Explanation items
   a. Deal with causes, effects, reasons, purposes, functions, or factors
   b. Involve application of knowledge of relationships
   c. May call for evidence for or against a statement or procedure
   d. Often include words like "why" or "because"

5. *Calculation.* A calculation item states a mathematical problem whose solution always requires the application of principles of mathematics and may require the application of other laws and principles as well. Often the answer is some numerical quantity. Usually a calculation item must be answered by reasoning rather than by recall.

6. *Prediction.* A prediction item describes a specific situation and asks what will result after a period of time or when certain other factors in the situation are changed. It may specify a novel situation, even an impossible situation, and require reasonable inferences.

7. *Recommended Action.* An item of this type tests knowledge of, or ability to determine by rational processes, the most appropriate action in certain specified circumstances.

edge and understanding, improved and extended abilities, new attitudes, ideals, and interests. But often these long-range goals are neglected when tests are constructed. Instead of being evaluated on

EXHIBIT 9.6

Illustrative Examples of Question Types
(The content area represented by each question is indicated in the parenthesis)

1. Terminology (Statistical Techniques)
   What is meant by the term "error of measurement" as it is used by technically trained specialists?
   a. Any error in test construction, administration, scoring, or interpretation which causes a person to receive different scores on two tests of the same trait.
   b. A test score which is unreliable or invalid as a result of (1) sampling errors in test construction, (2) performance errors on the part of the examinee, or (3) evaluation errors on the part of the scorer.
   *c. The difference between a given measurement and an estimate of the theoretical true value of the quantity measured.
   d. The difference between the obtained score and the predicted score on a trait for a person.

2. Factual Information (Educational Aptitude)
   How is a child's mental age determined on the Stanford-Binet Scale?
   a. By dividing the number of tests passed by the child's age in years.
   *b. By giving a specified number of months of credit for each test passed.
   c. By noting the highest level at which the child answers *all* tests correctly.
   d. By noting the highest level at which the child answers *any* test correctly.

3. Generalization (Educational Aptitude)
   Expert opinion today assigns how much weight to heredity as a determiner of intelligence?
   *a. Less weight than in 1900
   b. More weight than in 1900
   c. All of the weight
   d. None of the weight

4. Explanation (Personality and Adjustment)
   Why is the Rorschach Test regarded as a projective test?
   a. Because scores on the test provide accurate projections of future performance.
   *b. Because the examinee unintentionally reveals aspects of his own personality in the responses he makes.
   c. Because the stimulus material is ordinarily carried on slides which must be projected for viewing.
   d. Because the test is still in an experimental, developmental phase.

5. Calculation (Educational Aptitude)
   What is the I.Q. of an eight-year-old child whose mental age is ten years?
   a. 80
   b. 90
   *c. 125
   d. The answer cannot be determined from the data given.

6. Prediction (Test Try-out and Analysis)
   If two forms of a fifty-item, thirty-minute test are combined to produce a single one hundred-item, sixty-minute test, how variable and reliable will scores from the combined test be (in comparison with those from a single short form)?
   *a. More variable and more reliable
   b. More variable but less reliable
   c. Less variable but more reliable
   d. Less variable and less reliable

7. Recommended Action (Observational Techniques)
   What should a person who constructs a personality rating scale do about defining the traits to be rated?
   *a. He should define them accurately.
   b. He should encourage those who use the scale to develop their own definitions.
   c. He should leave them undefined and encourage those who use the scale to do likewise.
   d. He should limit the scale to traits whose definitions are common knowledge.

the basis of ultimate objectives, the student is sometimes judged on the basis of his memory of what went on from day to day in the class or what he read in preparation for the class sessions.

If a test consists mainly of questions requiring recall of some detail in the process of instruction (e.g., "How did the lecturer illustrate Hooke's Law?") or requiring reproduction of some unique organization of subject matter (e.g., "What were the *three* chief reasons for the failure of the League of Nations?"), it probably does not measure important achievements. If, on the other hand, a majority of the questions deal with applications, explanations, and generalizations, if knowledge of terms and isolated facts is not the sole aim of a large proportion of the questions, and if few questions deal with matters of no consequence outside the classroom, the test probably does measure important achievements.

Considerations such as these are reflected in the so-called ideal standards of relevance and balance in the sample test analysis report shown in Exhibit 9.1 earlier in this chapter. Maximum limits of 20 per cent each are specified for the informational item categories (terms, facts, generalizations). Minimum limits are specified for the item categories which involve application of information. Lower limits (5 per cent) are set for the calculation and action item categories than for the explanation and prediction categories (10 per cent), because the former are often more difficult to devise than the latter.

These limits are all somewhat arbitrary. That is, it would be difficult to demonstrate that any of the percentage values indicated is exactly the right value. But their over-all purpose is to encourage greater use of application-type items and to discourage overemphasis on information-type items.

Unfortunately, the invention and expression of items that demand application of knowledge seems to be a more difficult and exacting task than the construction of informational test items. Cook studied the discrimination and difficulty of objective test items written by ten college instructors.[3] He found their information items to be slightly more discriminating, and slightly easier, than their application items. Perhaps the information items are shorter, simpler, and less subject to ambiguity. However, the differences Cook found

---

[3] Desmond L. Cook, "A Note on Relevance Categories and Item Statistics," *Educational and Psychological Measurement*, XX, No. 2 (Summer, 1960), 321-31.

were small and might be eliminated by using more care and more skill in the item writing.

3. Efficiency

A test that yields a large number of independent scorable responses per unit of time is an efficient test. Sacrificing relevance to gain efficiency would obviously be poor strategy in test construction. But if the difference in relevance is slight or uncertain, there are important advantages in the use of efficient item types. An hour-long test composed of efficient item types is likely to be much more reliable than an hour-long test composed of inefficient item types.

If a large group is to be tested or if the same test can be given repeatedly to successive groups, the most efficient use of an instructor's time may call for him to use objective, machine-scorable questions. Such questions are time-consuming to prepare and many more are required than in the case of problem or essay type questions. Once prepared, however, they can be scored efficiently and can be used repeatedly. But if a unique test must be prepared for each separate small group, the advantage in efficiency is on the side of the problem or essay type.

The essay test tends to be less efficient than the objective test, partly because it requires the student to spend most of his time in writing rather than in reading. The typical examinee can probably read about ten times as fast as he can write. Objective questions based on the interpretation of explanatory materials tend to be less efficient than those testing the student's possession of knowledge. Questions involving situational problems tend to be less efficient than those involving factual information. With problem tests the student spends more time thinking than writing. If provision is made for analytic and partial-credit scoring, not just all-or-none scoring, the problem test can be just as efficient as the objective test in its use of the student's time.

Obviously these different item types are ordinarily used to measure somewhat different aspects of achievement. They are not completely interchangeable. On the other hand, the test constructor who wishes to measure some particular aspect of achievement ordinarily does have some freedom to choose among several types of items that seem suitable. Some studies, such as that by Cook, have shown that quite different types of test items give essentially equivalent measurements of achievement.[4] It seems reasonable to believe that some improvements could be made in tests of educational achievement by paying attention to the efficiency of the item types used. In judging the quality of a classroom test, the matter of efficiency should always be considered.

4. Objectivity

A test question is objective if experts in the field covered by the test all choose the same alternative among the suggested possible answers or if all give essentially the same free-response answer. Casting a question in objective form (i.e., multiple-choice, true-false, etc.) does not automatically produce this kind of objectivity in response since experts sometimes disagree in their choice of the best answer among the possible alternatives. Essay questions, which usually make no claim to objectivity, are nevertheless weakened as devices for measuring educational achievement to the extent that they lack the kind of objectivity (i.e., expert agreement in response) just described. Hence, the objectivity of the items included in a classroom test becomes a fourth basis for judging the quality of the test.

When experts disagree in the answers they give to a test question, the fault usually rests in the question. The supposed truth on which the test constructor based the item may be open to question. Or the item writer may have assumed, but failed to state explicitly, all the conditions necessary to make other experts give the same answer he would give to the question. Most fields of study include, in addition to a body of verified knowledge, some opinions that are not shared by all experts and some hypotheses that have not been fully substantiated. Such opinions and hypotheses often are thought-provoking and provide the stimuli for interesting classroom discussions. But they are less suitable as bases for judging student achievement.

The current trend away from the use of factual or informational

---

[4] Desmond L. Cook, "An Investigation of Three Aspects of Free Response and Choice Type Tests at the College Level" (Unpublished dissertation, State University of Iowa, Iowa City, Iowa, 1955).

types of test questions and toward questions based on generalizations, interpretations, evaluations, and recommended actions seems to increase the room for differences of opinion, even among experts. Though these higher levels of understanding and application may appear to provide more significant bases for judging achievement, they may give less reliable measurements of achievement.

In some cases the question in the item writer's mind may have been quite satisfactory but his expression of it in writing somewhat faulty. Perhaps he used words with too little regard for precise meanings. Perhaps the structure of his sentences obscured or distorted the idea he had in mind. Or perhaps he failed to state all the conditions and qualifications necessary to make one, and only one, answer correct. Some of the criticism that has been directed at multiple-choice test items has been stimulated by deficiencies like these in the choice of ideas for test items or in item writing.

To use objectivity as a basis for judging test quality it is necessary to get two or more experts (preferably five to ten of them and preferably experts who took no part in the test development) to answer the questions in the test. The higher the mean score of these experts, the better. If it is less than 90 per cent of a perfect score, the test may be judged seriously deficient in objectivity. Even if the mean score is much closer to perfection, the test constructor may wish to identify those items on which the experts expressed the greatest disagreement.

5. Specificity

A test shows specificity if a test-wise novice in the field covered by the test receives a near chance score. Specificity is approximately the complement of objectivity.

In the preceding section one consequence of the current preference for questions which emphasize abilities rather than information was mentioned. This was a tendency to reduced objectivity in the test questions. Another consequence is that an examinee's score on such tests may depend to a considerable degree on his general problem-solving or test-taking ability rather than on his specific ability or knowledge. This impairs the test's specificity. Items designed to test interpretations, evaluative judgments and recommended actions may be more relevant to intelligence or general ability than they are to achievement in a specific area of study. To the degree that any test is a test of reading ability or writing ability or general intelligence, it suffers in specificity.

Emphasis on specificity is intended to focus the test constructor's attention on the desirability of limiting his test to items which require special competence in the specific field of study covered by the test. It assumes that an examinee who has not made a special study of the field covered by a test should make a relatively low score on a test of achievement in that field, regardless of how generally able or intelligent he may be.

To use specificity as a basis for judging test quality it is necessary to get several intelligent and test-wise novices to take the test. The lower the mean score of these novices, the better. While it will almost always be well above the expected chance score, it should almost always be less than 20 per cent of the difference between chance and perfect scores above the chance score.

Measures of objectivity and specificity were obtained for individual test items in the course of preparing a collection of 245 multiple-choice items for a test of teacher competence in educational measurement.[5] Nine experts (specialists in educational measurement) and ten novices (bright high school seniors) chose what they considered to be the best answers to each of the questions. The results are shown in Exhibit 9.7.

On this chart each tally represents a test item. The best items are represented by marks in the upper right-hand corner of the chart. The poorest would fall in the lower left-hand corner. Items hardest for the combined group of experts and novices would be found in the upper left-hand corner; those easiest for the combined group in the lower right-hand corner.

The mean score of the nine experts on these 245 items is 208.67, or about 85 per cent of a perfect score. The average score of the ten novices was 73.2. Since 123 of the items were five-choice items, 121 were four-choice items, and one was a three-choice item, the expected chance score on the 245 items is 55.2. Hence the mean score of the novices was 9.5 per cent of the distance between chance

---
[5] National Council on Measurement in Education, *Multiple-choice Items for a Test of Teacher Competence in Educational Measurement* (East Lansing, Mich.: Michigan State University, 1962), p. 35.

and perfect scores. In terms of the standards suggested above, this test is more satisfactory in specificity than in objectivity.

These data suggest that the test could be improved. More novices than experts answered thirteen of the items correctly, and the

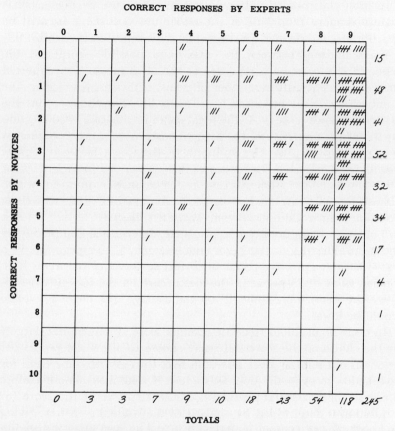

CORRECT RESPONSES BY EXPERTS

Exhibit 9.7. Scatter Diagram Showing the Number of Correct Responses by Nine Experts and Ten Novices to Each of 245 Measurement Test Items

novices ran dead-heats against the experts on seven more items. Twenty-three of the 245 items were answered correctly by more than half of the novices. Twenty-two of the items were missed by more than half of the experts. The test would be considerably improved in objectivity and specificity if about fifty of the items in it were revised or replaced.

6. Difficulty

In most classroom situations a test in which the average score is somewhat more than half of the maximum possible score will be appropriate in difficulty. In the test analysis reported in Exhibit 9.1, a point midway between the maximum possible score and the expected chance score is regarded as the ideal mean. The expected chance score equals the number of items in the test divided by the number of choices per item. Since with fifty five-choice items the expected chance score is 10, the ideal mean in this case is 30 (Section II, B.1 of the analysis). If the average score is very much higher or very much lower than the midpoint of the range between highest possible and expected chance scores the test may be inefficient. That is, it may waste the student's time trying to answer questions which almost no one can answer correctly, or reading and answering questions which almost everyone answers correctly.

The mean score on a test is, of course, determined completely by the mean difficulty of the items composing it. If, for example, in a sixty-item test the proportions of correct response to the items have a mean value of 75 per cent, the mean score on the test must be 45. Were the items more difficult, on the average, the mean test score would be lower.

In essay or problem tests the average score is determined largely by the choice of the scorer. He may choose to allow ten points per question but seldom gives less than five, thus giving some basis for satisfaction to even the poorest student. Or he may choose a more limited range of scores and actually use all of it. If the score for a question is determined by analysis of the student's answer, giving one point for each essential element in the answer, then a question appropriate in difficulty might also show an average score of approximately half of the maximum possible score.

7. Discrimination

The discriminating power of an item is indicated by the difference between good and poor students in proportions of correct response.

For sound statistical reasons, which are explained in Chapter 11, those students in the top 27 per cent on total test score are taken to be "good" students and those in the bottom 27 per cent on total test score are taken to be "poor" students. If the difference in proportions of correct response is .41 or higher, the item is usually said to be highly discriminating. Other categories of discrimination are

---

Test Title: *Educational Measurement*   Group Tested: *Graduate Students*   N = *40*

Instructor: *Jones*   Date of Test: *5/191-*   Score = *Number right*

Number of Items: *50*   Choices per Item: *5*   Time Limit: *45 minutes*

	.95 _____	.90 _____	.85 _____		
High	.80 _____	.75 _____	.70 _____		
$k = 9$	.65 _____	.60 *47, 50*	.55 _____		
18%	.50 *35, 37, 44*	.48 _____	.46 _____		
	.44 *13, 15, 26, 38*	.42 _____	.40 _____		
	.38 _____	.36 *12, 19, 23, 40, 48, 49*	.34 _____		
Fair	.32 _____	.30 _____	.29 _____		
$k = 13$	.28 _____	.27 *3, 4, 6, 7, 39, 43, 46*	.26 _____		
26%	.25 _____	.24 _____	.23 _____		
	.22 _____	.21 _____	.20 _____		
	.19 _____	.18 *1, 9, 10, 11, 22, 24, 29, 36, 41*	.17 _____		
Low	.16 _____	.15 _____	.14 _____		
$k = 17$	.13 _____	.12 _____	.11 _____		
34%	.10 _____	.09 *2, 5, 8, 15, 16, 31, 42, 45*	.07 _____		
	.05 _____	.03 _____	.01 _____		
	.00 _____	.00 *14, 17, 20, 25, 27*	.00 *32, 33*		
Zero	-.01 _____	-.03 _____	-.05 _____		
or					
Neg.	-.07 _____	-.09 *21, 34*	-.11 _____		
$k = 11$	-.15 *28*	-.20 _____	-.25 *30*		
22%	-.30 _____	-.40 _____	-.50 _____		

Exhibit 9.8. Discrimination Report

similarly identified on the report form (Section II, A–Exhibit 9.1). The more items classified as highly or moderately discriminating, the better the test. The sample test left something to be desired in this respect. Too many of the items were low in discriminating power.

In addition to the summary of item discrimination provided on the test report, a separate sheet may be prepared to identify by number the items falling at each level of discriminating power. Such a sheet is shown in Exhibit 9.8. Here again, the handwritten numbers identify items in the test. For tests composed of multiple-choice or true-false items, a copy of the test can be prepared showing the frequency with which good and poor students chose each alternative. This information is particularly useful in item revision.

If the items in a test tend to discriminate clearly between good and poor students, the test scores will tend to vary widely. This permits the total test scores to discriminate clearly, as they are ordinarily intended to do, between students at different levels of ability.

Score variability is measured by the standard deviation (Section IIB, Exhibit 9.1). The larger it is, under ordinary conditions, the better the test. A standard deviation of one-sixth the range between highest possible score and the expected chance score is quite satisfactory. For some good tests the standard deviation is more than one-fourth of the available range. For poorer tests it may be less than one-tenth of the available range. If a test is too hard, too easy, or composed of too many poorly discriminating items, it will yield scores having a small standard deviation. The size of the standard deviation of a set of test scores is an important factor in their reliability. Other things equal, the larger the standard deviation, the higher the reliability.

8. Reliability

The index of reliability reported in Section IIB of the test analysis of Exhibit 9.1 represents the estimated correlation between the scores on the test and scores on another equivalent test composed of different items but designed to measure the same kind of achievement. A high reliability coefficient indicates that a student's score was not influenced much by the chance selection of certain items rather than other items for inclusion in the test or by the student's luck or lack of luck in guessing correct answers. Some good objective tests have reliability coefficients of .90 or more. This level is difficult to achieve consistently with homogeneous class groups and with items which had not previously been tried out, analyzed, and revised. The standard for reliability on this analysis is set somewhat lower at .80. The sample test exceeds this minimum standard, with a coefficient of .86.

The probable error, shown as 1.47 for the sample test of Exhibit 9.1, is calculated from the reliability coefficient (r) and the standard deviation of the test scores (σ) using the formula:

$$\text{Probable error} = .67\sigma\sqrt{1 - r} = 1.47$$

The probable error indicates the degree of accuracy that can be expected in the test scores. In the case of the sample test, half the scores will be in error (that is, will differ from the theoretical true score values) by less than 1.47 score units. This concept of errors of measurement is discussed more completely in Chapter 10.

No ideal value is specified in Exhibit 9.4 for the probable error, and no evaluative rating is given. This is because the probable error of scores from a good test is not necessarily smaller than that of scores from a poor test, since a good test may yield scores that are more variable (i.e., having a larger standard deviation) than the scores from a poor test. Hence good tests may have larger probable errors of measurement than poor tests.

Reliability is often the most significant *statistical* measure of the quality of a classroom test. While validity is generally considered to be more important than reliability, the statistical validity of a classroom test cannot ordinarily be determined. To determine it one needs an external criterion of achievement that is a better measure of true achievement than the test scores themselves. This is seldom available. If the items are highly relevant and well balanced and if the scores are highly reliable, the test will necessarily be highly valid as a measure of the achievement covered.

The reliability of a test depends on how sharply the items discriminate between good and poor students, how many items there are, how similar the items are with respect to the ability measured, and how much the students differ from one another in the ability being measured. Thus, it is easier to get a higher reliability of scores in one subject than in another, and with one group of students than with another. The other two factors of reliability, quality and number of items, are under the instructor's control. If the coefficient is too low it can almost always be raised by improving the items used or adding more items, or both. The subject of test reliability is discussed much more fully in Chapter 10.

While the type of reliability just described can also be calculated for essay tests, there is another type which is also important on such tests. It is the degree of agreement between independent scorers or even between independent scorings by the same scorer. Essay tests can be reliably scored, but they often are not. Those who use such tests extensively owe it to their students to demonstrate that the scores assigned were not largely the result of chance judgments of the moment or of the unique opinions of the person scoring them. If an instructor can arrange for competent independent scoring of his essay test papers, scoring reliability can be estimated by calculating a correlation coefficient by one of the methods described in Chapter 8.

9. Fairness

A test is fair to students if it emphasizes the knowledge, understanding, and abilities which were emphasized in the actual teaching of the course. Occasionally a test includes questions which ought to be covered in the course but which were somehow omitted in the instruction of the group being tested. Again, an instructor may evaluate student achievement in a course on the basis of skills, such as ability to spell correctly, which the instructor regards as important but which he made no attempt to teach in the course. Such tests are not entirely fair to the students.

Instructors are in the best position to judge the fairness of a test to their students. A student's opinion on this matter is often biased by his success or lack of success with the test. Probably no effective test has ever been given that was regarded as perfectly fair by all persons taking it. On the other hand, student comments on a test's fairness are often worth securing and considering. If it does nothing more, the request for comments will show the instructor's concern for fairness. And often it can do much more. A student may call attention to ambiguity in a question, to the presence of questions dealing with matters not covered in class, or to omission of questions on matters which were stressed. There are few classroom tests so good that they cannot be improved on the basis of student comments and suggestions.

The administration of a test also affects its fairness. It should be handled efficiently and quietly, with no confusion or disturbance that might interfere with effective performance or give some examinees special advantages. All examinees should be on an equal footing so far as prior knowledge of the examination is concerned. They should have enough advance information about it to be able to prepare properly. The physical environment of heat, light, and space should be comfortable and convenient.

The judgment of the instructor who gave the test provides the best basis for evaluating this aspect of its quality. But here again student comments can be revealing and helpful.

10. Speededness

A test is unspeeded to the degree that the scores of examinees on it are unaffected by increases in the time allowed for work on it. While there is by no means unanimous agreement on the issue of speededness, the current preference in achievement testing is to remove the pressure of time limitations, at least insofar as it can be done without seriously lowering over-all efficiency in examining. That is, the student's score is made to depend more on what he can do than on how fast he can do it.

Speed obviously is quite important in repetitive, clerical-type operations. Ordinarily, however, it is much less important in critical or creative thinking or in decision making. The fact that good students tend to be quicker than poor students is not in itself a sufficient reason for penalizing the occasional good but slow student. Hence, it is sometimes recommended that test time limits be generous enough for at least 90 per cent of the students to attempt an answer to the last question in the test. In the sample test of Exhibit 9.1, 97 per cent of the examinees attempted the last item.

If the time limits are made too liberal in an attempt to free all examinees from pressure to hurry, significant parts of the examination period will be wasted by a large proportion of the examinees who work more quickly. Something less than 100 per cent completion will ordinarily be considered ideal for most achievement tests. For tests in some courses in which speed of production is one of the goals of instruction and in which speed practice is provided, it may be desirable to minimize rather than to maximize the number of students who complete the test. In such cases there is little waste of examination *time* but there may be much waste of examination *questions* that some of the examinees never reach.

11. Concluding statement

Ten aspects of test quality have been identified and discussed in this chapter. For most of them evaluations of the test can be based on evidence gained by studying the test itself or by analyzing the data that it provides. This study and analysis does not itself improve the test. What it does is to provide some stimulus and some more adequate basis for test improvement. The relevance and balance of the test can be improved. Weak questions identified in the analysis can be revised or discarded. Systematic test analysis provides one of the best available means for the progressive improvement of classroom tests.

12. Summary

Some of the principal ideas developed in this chapter are summarized in these twelve statements.

1. A good classroom test is relevant, balanced, efficient, objective, specific, difficult, discriminating, reliable, fair, and unspeeded.
2. Test analysis can reveal the extent to which a test possesses the qualities it ought to have.
3. Specific criteria of relevance ought to be written as a basis for determining what kinds of items are appropriate for inclusion in a test.
4. To balance the proportions of items used to test each aspect of achievement, it is helpful to outline categories of content, item type, etc., and to specify the number or proportion of items desired in each category.
5. An efficient test includes as many independently scorable responses per unit of testing time as is possible without sacrifice of relevance.

6. The extent to which experts agree on the correct answer to a test question is a measure of its objectivity.

7. If a test question is properly specific, it will not be answered correctly by a significant number of novices who lack special competence in the field covered by the test.

8. A test is appropriate in difficulty if the mean score on it is about midway between the maximum possible score and the expected chance score.

9. The greater the difference between proportions of correct response among students of high and low achievement, the higher the discrimination (discriminating power) of the item.

10. The most significant statistical measure of the quality of a classroom test is its reliability coefficient.

11. A classroom test is fair (or valid) to the extent that it actually demands of students the command of knowledge that the course was intended to develop.

12. Most classroom tests should be essentially unspeeded, so that nearly all examinees have time to attempt all items.

REFERENCES

Cook, Desmond L., *An Investigation of Three Aspects of Free-response and Choice-type Tests at the College Level.* Unpublished dissertation; Iowa City, Iowa: State University of Iowa, 1955.

————, "A Note on Relevance Categories and Item Statistics," *Educational and Psychological Measurement,* XX (Summer, 1960), 321-31.

Dressel, Paul L. and Others, *Comprehensive Examinations in a Program of General Education,* pp. 22, 48, 67, 81, 91. East Lansing, Mich.: Michigan State College Press, 1949.

Ebel, Robert L., "Procedures for the Analysis of Classroom Tests," *Educational and Psychological Measurement,* XIV (1954), 352-64.

National Council on Measurement in Education, *Multiple-choice Items for a Test of Teacher-Competence in Educational Measurement,* pp. 35. East Lansing, Mich.: Michigan State University, 1962.

Travers, Robert M. W., *How to Make Achievement Tests,* p. 25. New York: The Odyssey Press, Inc., 1950.

IO How to Estimate, Interpret, and Improve Test Reliability

A very convenient conception is that of the "reliability coefficient" of any system of measurements for any character. By this is meant the coefficient between one half and the other half of several measurements of the same thing.

C. SPEARMAN

1. The importance of reliability

For most tests of educational achievement the reliability coefficient provides the most revealing statistical index of quality that is ordinarily available. If the scores yielded by any educational achievement test were all perfectly accurate, true scores with no errors attributable to the particular sample of questions used, to the particular conditions of alertness, anxiety, fatigue, or other factors which might affect examinee performances, to lucky guesses or unlucky slips, and with no errors caused by the mistakes or biases of the person scoring the test, then the test would have perfect reliability, reflected by a reliability coefficient of 1.00. No educational achievement test, no other type of mental test, and indeed no physical measurement has ever achieved this degree of perfection. Error is unavoidably involved in any measurement, but the goal of measurement specialists in all fields is to reduce these inevitable errors of measurement to a reasonable minimum.

Expertly constructed educational achievement tests often yield reliability coefficients of .90 or higher. In contrast, the achievement tests used in many elementary, secondary, and college classrooms often show reliability coefficients of .50 or lower. One of the ways of making test scores more reliable is to lengthen the test on which they are based, that is, to include more questions or items in it and to allow more time for it. But a test having a reliability coefficient of .50 would need to be increased to nine times its original length to bring its reliability up to .90. (The basis for this statement is provided by formula 10.1 on page 314.) Hence, from this point of view, a test having a reliability coefficient of .90 is nine times as good as a test having a reliability coefficient of .50.

Reliability is a necessary condition for quality in an educational achievement test, but it is not a sufficient condition. The author of a test which yields highly reliable scores may only have succeeded in measuring something irrelevant or trivial with very great precision. On the other hand, the author of a test which yields only unreliable scores has clearly not succeeded in measuring anything very precisely. If a test does not yield reliable scores, whatever other potential merits it may have are blurred and may be largely lost. Only to the degree that test scores are reliable can they be useful for any purpose whatsoever.

Reliability is important to students whose grades are often heavily dependent on the scores they make on educational achievement tests. If they were clearly aware of the importance of test reliability to them, it is likely that they would ask for evidence that the tests used to measure their achievement are not only fair in terms of the purposes of the course, but also are of sufficient technical quality to yield reliable scores.

Reliability is important also to the teacher who is aware that his examinations have shortcomings and who seeks to improve them. Estimates of the reliabilities of his tests would provide the essential information for judging their technical quality and for motivating efforts to improve them. Lengthening an unreliable test is not the only way, and may not be the best way, to improve its reliability. If modern knowledge and techniques of test construction are applied, most educational achievement tests can be made to yield scores having reliability coefficients that at least approach .90.

2. The concept of test reliability

One way of clarifying the concept of reliability is to contrast it with validity. These two definitions point up the contrast.

1. The term "reliability" means the consistency with which a set of test scores measure whatever they do measure.
2. The term "validity" means the accuracy with which a set of test scores measure what they ought to measure.

If the perforations on a target made by successive shots from a rifle are all clustered closely, the rifle is performing reliably. If those perforations are all clustered in the bull's-eye, the rifle is also performing validly.

The number of words in a poem can be measured with high reliability. Such a measure would be readily accepted as a valid measure of the length of the poem. It would not, however, be accepted by most poets or literary critics as a valid measure of the literary merit of the poem.

For most tests of educational achievement no good statistical measure of validity is ordinarily obtainable. To estimate its validity, we must look at the test itself, and, if they are available, at the principles used by the test constructor in deciding what kind of tasks to include in the test. On the other hand, a good estimate of the reliability of the test can be obtained quite simply. Since a test must be reliable if it is to be valid, the statistical analysis of the quality of educational achievement test scores ordinarily places primary emphasis on the reliability of those scores. A test yielding reliable scores is not necessarily valid. But an educational achievement test composed of questions which seem pertinent and significant to expert teachers or professors is very likely to be as valid as it is reliable. This is especially likely if those instructors also have some expertness in educational measurement.

At least three factors contribute to the reliability or unreliability of a set of test scores. One is the appropriateness and definiteness of the task. Tasks which are too easy or too difficult or which permit students to make widely divergent interpretation of what is expected of them are not likely to yield highly reliable scores.

Another is the constancy or stability of a student's ability to perform the tasks presented in the test. Human beings vary from hour to hour and from day to day in their alertness, energy, emotional balance, and other characteristics. If these personal variables affect a student's test performance appreciably, they will reduce the reliability of the scores. A third is the consistency and objectivity of the person who scores the test. To the extent that the scores he assigns depend upon his notions of the moment rather than on consistent standards, uniformly applied to all the papers he reads, the scores he records will lack reliability.

3. An operational definition of test reliability

The reliability coefficient for a set of scores from a group of examinees is the coefficient of correlation between that set of scores and another set of scores on an equivalent test obtained independently from the members of the same group.

Three aspects of this definition deserve comment. First, it implies that reliability is not a property of a test by itself but rather of a test when applied to a particular group of examinees. The more appropriate a test is to the level of abilities in the group, the higher the reliability of the scores it will yield. The wider the range of talent in a group, the higher the reliability of the scores yielded by a test of that talent.

Second, the operational definition specifies the use of a correlation coefficient as a measure of reliability. One of the properties of the correlation coefficient is that it provides a relative, rather than an absolute, measure of agreement between the pairs of scores for the same persons. If the differences between scores for the same person are small relative to the differences between scores for different persons, then the test will tend to show a high reliability. But if the differences between scores for the same person are large relative to the differences between persons, then the scores will show low reliability.

Third, the operational definition calls for two or more independent measures, obtained from equivalent tests of the same trait for each member of the group. This is the heart of the definition.

The different means by which sets of independent measurements of the same achievement are obtained provide the differences between the various methods for estimating test reliability.

4. Methods of obtaining independent scores on equivalent tests

At least five methods have been used for obtaining the independent measurements necessary for estimating test reliability. These methods yield reader reliability, test-retest, equivalent forms, split halves, Kuder-Richardson, or analysis of variance coefficients.

4.1 Reader reliability

Tests like essay tests whose scores depend appreciably on the expert judgment of a reader are sometimes scored independently by two or more readers. The correlation between, or among, the multiple sets of ratings for a single set of student examination papers provides a measure of the reliability with which the papers were read.[1] Scorer reliability coefficients are seldom calculated for objective tests, not because scoring errors are never made, but because it is simpler and more meaningful to report the number and sizes of the errors than to report a scoring reliability coefficient. An objective test would have to be scored very carelessly indeed to show anything but a very high coefficient of scoring reliability. Even if over half of the answer sheets in a set of thirty-five were scored wrongly, with errors like those shown below, the coefficient of scoring reliability would still be closer to .99 than to .98.

Size of Scoring Error	Number of Errors
4	2
3	2
2	5
1	11
0	15
	35

Coefficients of *reader* reliability should not be confused with

[1] Robert L. Ebel, "Estimation of the Reliability of Ratings," *Psychometrika*, XVI (December, 1951), 407-24.

coefficients of *examinee* reliability or coefficients of *test* reliability. A coefficient of reader reliability indicates how closely two or more readers agree in rating the same set of examination papers. A coefficient of examinee reliability indicates how consistently the examinees perform on the same set of tasks. A coefficient of test reliability indicates how similarly the examinees perform on different, but supposedly equivalent, tasks. Sometimes the reliability of reading an essay test can be quite high, though its test reliability might be quite low. The test-retest reliability coefficient, next to be described, is essentially a measure of examinee reliability. All of the others are essentially measures of test reliability.

4.2 Test-retest

Perhaps the simplest obvious method of obtaining repeated measures for the same individuals of the same ability is to give the same test twice. This would provide two scores for each individual tested. The correlation between the set of scores obtained on the first administration of the test and that obtained on the second administration yields a test-retest reliability coefficient.

A number of objections have been raised to the test-retest method. One is that the same set of items is used in both sets. Since this set of items represents only one sample from what is ordinarily a very large population of possible test items, the scores on the retest provide no evidence on how much the scores might change if a different sample of questions were used. Another is that the students' answers to the second test are not independent of their answers to the first. Their responses to the test items on their second presentation may be influenced by memory of the responses they gave the first time. Their responses may also be influenced by discussions of the questions among students between the first and second testings or by other kinds of efforts to learn how to answer the questions that proved troublesome when the test was first administered. A third is that if the interval between the test and the retest is long, errors of measurement may get confused with real changes in student ability as a result of learning. Finally, readministration of the same test simply to determine how reliable it is does not appeal to most students or teachers as a very useful way of spending educational time. Lack of interest on the student's part may sometimes make the second test a much poorer measure than the first, even though the actual test is the same in both cases.

4.3 Equivalent forms

If two or more parallel forms of a test have been produced in such a way that it seems likely that the scores on these alternate forms will be equivalent and if each student in the group is given both forms of the test, then the correlation between scores on the two forms provides an estimate of their reliability. The major drawback to this approach is that educational achievement tests, particularly those prepared for use in classrooms, are usually produced singly. Parallel alternate forms are not ordinarily available. Even when they are there would be some valid objections from students to duplicate testing simply to obtain an estimate of the reliability of the first test.

4.4 Split-halves

The difficulties associated with determination of test-retest and equivalent-forms reliability coefficients encouraged the search for more practical alternatives. In one of these, a single test was split into two reasonably equivalent halves. These independent subtests were then used as a source of the two independent scores needed for reliability estimation. One common method of splitting a test has been to score the odd-numbered items and the even-numbered items separately. Then the correlation between scores on the odd- and even-numbered items is calculated. Of course, splitting a test in this way means that the scores whose reliability is determined have been obtained from half-length tests. To obtain an estimate of the reliability of the total test it is necessary to correct or step up the half-test correlation to the expected full-length value. This is done with the help of the Spearman-Brown formula.

The general Spearman-Brown formula, which may be used to predict the increase in reliability resulting from lengthening a test by the addition of items like those in the original test, is:

$$r_n = \frac{nr_s}{(n-1)r_s + 1} \qquad 10.1$$

This formula should be read as follows: "The Reliability, r_n, of a test n times as long as a shorter test of known reliability, r_s, is equal to n times the reliability of the shorter test, divided by $(n - 1)$ times the reliability of the shorter test, plus 1." If, for example, a given test has a reliability of .50 and if its length is increased to nine times the original length, by the addition of equivalent items, then the formula indicates that the reliability of the lengthened test may be found by dividing 4.50 by 5.00, which gives .90 as the reliability of the lengthened test.

When we need only to predict the reliability of a test twice as long as a given test, as in the case of reliability estimation by the split-half method, the formula is somewhat simpler.

$$r_l = \frac{2r_s}{r_s + 1} \qquad 10.2$$

If, for example, the correlation between the odd-numbered items and the even-numbered items in a particular test should be .82, then the formula indicates that the reliability of the total test should be given by 1.64 divided by 1.82, which is approximately .90.

A short-cut method for estimating test reliability from scores on split halves of a test has been proposed by Rulon.[2] The formula he gives is equivalent to this:

$$r = 1 - \frac{\sigma_d^2}{\sigma_s^2} \qquad 10.3$$

Where σ_d^2 is the variance of the differences between the half test scores and σ_s^2 is the variance of the sum of the half test scores. Stanley suggested a further simplification, using the following formula.[3]

$$r = 1 - \frac{D_d^2}{D_s^2} \qquad 10.4$$

In this case D_d^2 represents the squared difference between the sum of difference scores on the 27 per cent of papers having largest half test difference scores and the sum of difference scores on the 27 per cent of papers having smallest half test difference scores. D_s^2 represents the squared difference between the sums of total scores on the

---

[2] P. J. Rulon, "A Simplified Procedure for Determining the Reliability of a Test by Split-halves," *Harvard Educational Review*, IX (January, 1939), 99-103.

[3] Julian C. Stanley, "A Simplified Method for Estimating the Split-half Reliability Coefficient of a Test," *Harvard Educational Review*, XXI (Fall, 1951), 221-24.

27 per cent of papers having largest total scores and the sum of total scores on the 27 per cent of papers having smallest total scores.

Does this seem confusing? Consider the example shown in Table 10.1, which has been kept small and simple. Eleven students are identified by letters in the first column of the table. Their scores on odd and even items of a forty-item test are reported in the second and third columns. The sums of and the differences between these eleven pairs of half test scores are shown in the fourth and fifth columns.

TABLE 10.1

Split Half Reliability Calculation (Stanley's Procedure)

Student	Odd	Even	Sum	Difference
A	11	8	19	3 H
B	8	0	8 L	8 H
C	9	8	17	1
D	14	11	25 H	3
E	12	14	26 H	−2 L
F	7	6	13 L	1
G	18	11	29 H	7 H
H	6	8	14	−2
I	6	9	15	−3 L
J	6	3	9 L	3
K	5	10	15	−5 L
	Sum of three highest		80	18
	Sum of three lowest		30	−10
	Difference	$D_s =$	50	$D_d =$ 28
	Difference Squared	$D_s{}^2 =$	2,500	$D_d{}^2 =$ 784

$$r = 1 - \frac{784}{2,500} = .69$$

Notice that some of the differences in the fourth column are negative. It makes no difference whether odd scores are subtracted from even or even from odd, but all the subtractions in any one calculation must be in the same direction and negative differences must be indicated.

Since 27 per cent of 11 is very nearly 3, we look for the three highest sums and the three lowest sums in the fourth column. These are identified by the letters "H" and "L" respectively. The sum of the highest three is 80, of the lowest three is 30, so the difference between these sums is 50. The squared difference is 2,500. By a similar process the value 784 is obtained for the squared difference between the sum of the three highest difference scores and the three lowest difference scores.

Note that the largest negative values are treated as the lowest differences. Note, too, that ties in rank on the difference scale create no problems. In this calculation, to get the three lowest differences needed, one of the −2 values but not the other is included in the sum. The quotient of 784 divided by 2,500 is nearly .31. This value subtracted from 1.00 gives the reliability coefficient of .69 as indicated.

The values used in Table 10.1 were taken from a table in which the over-all odd-even correlation was known to be .50. By use of the Spearman-Brown formula, the whole test reliability can be estimated to be .67. The results obtained from Stanley's formula are in good agreement with this value, even though a sample of 11 cases is rather small as a basis for estimating a reliability coefficient. Hence the method seems accurate enough for classroom use in estimating test reliability coefficients.

There are many ways in which a test may be split into two approximately equal parts. Some of these ways are likely to yield more nearly equivalent tests than others. Hence, the particular estimate of test reliability obtained may be to some degree a function of the particular split that is chosen. Lord has shown how wide the variations may be under certain conditions.[4] But if reasonable care is taken in splitting the test into equivalent halves and if the test is reasonably long and homogeneous, these errors are not likely to be serious.

When test scores are corrected for guessing or when special response weighting such as that suggested in Chapter 5 is used, the split-halves technique probably affords a better combination of accuracy and convenience than any other method of estimating test reliability. While other formulas, such as those described in the next

---

[4] Frederic M. Lord, "Sampling Error Due to Choice of Split in Split-half Reliability Coefficients," *Journal of Experimental Education*, XXIV (March, 1956), 245-49.

section, may be advantageous when simple unit-weight rights-only scoring is employed, they become more difficult to handle when applied to tests using multiple scoring weights.

4.5 Kuder-Richardson

In the September 1937 issue of *Psychometrika*, Kuder and Richardson published an article, "The Theory of the Estimation of Test Reliability." [5] Included in this paper were a series of formulas, two of which have become widely accepted as a basis for estimating test reliability. Their Formula 20 is:

$$r = \frac{k}{k-1}\left[1 - \frac{\Sigma pq}{\sigma^2}\right] \qquad 10.5$$

In this formula k represents the number of items in the test, Σ means "the sum of," p stands for proportion of the responses to one item which is correct, and q the proportion of the responses which are not correct (so that p plus q always equals 1), and σ^2 represents the variance of the scores on the test. This formula requires that the proportion of correct responses to each item be determined and in each case multiplied by the proportion of responses which are not correct. These p times q values for each item are then added for all items. That sum, divided by the variance (square of the standard deviation of the test scores and subtracted from 1, is then multiplied by the fraction k over k minus 1 (the number of items in the test divided by 1 less than the number of items) to obtain an estimate of the reliability of the test scores. Kuder-Richardson Formula 20 is applicable only to tests in which the items are scored by giving one point if answered correctly and nothing if not answered correctly. If the scores of the tests are corrected for guessing or if other forms of weighted scoring are used, more complex variations of the formula must be employed.

Use of Kuder-Richardson Formula 20 requires information on the difficulty (proportion of correct response) of each item in the test. If the items do not vary widely in difficulty, a reasonably good approximation of the quantity Σpq can be obtained from information on the mean test score, M, and the number of items in the test, k.

---

[5] G. F. Kuder and M. W. Richardson, "The Theory of the Estimation of Test Reliability," *Psychometrika*, II (September, 1937), 151-60.

For example, if the mean score on a test (on which each correct response counts one score unit and no other response or lack of response counts anything) is half the number of items in the test, the average proportion of correct response per item must be .50. In general, the average value of p (which we will designate $\bar{p}$) is

$$\bar{p} = \frac{M}{k}$$

Since $q = 1 - p$, the average value of q (designated $\bar{q}$) must be:

$$\bar{q} = 1 - \frac{M}{k}$$

Thus the average value of $\overline{pq}$ will be:

$$\frac{M}{k}\left(1 - \frac{M}{k}\right)$$

The sum of these values for all items, since there are k items, will be:

$$\Sigma \overline{pq} = k \times \frac{M}{k}\left(1 - \frac{M}{k}\right) = M\left(1 - \frac{M}{k}\right) \qquad 10.6$$

Substituting this value for pq in our Formula 10.5 gives:

$$r = \frac{k}{k-1}\left(1 - \frac{M\left(1 - \frac{M}{k}\right)}{\sigma^2}\right) \qquad 10.7$$

This is the Kuder-Richardson Formula 21.

One limitation of this formula is that it always gives an underestimate of the reliability coefficient when the items vary in difficulty, as they almost always do. If a test includes many items or questions on which the average score is near perfect or near zero, this underestimate could be quite large. If most of the items have average scores of more than 30 per cent but less than 70 per cent of the maximum possible score, the underestimate is much smaller.

These relations are illustrated in Table 10.2, using hypothetical data for a test of one hundred items. In Test A, all items are at the same 50 per cent level of difficulty. In Test B the items vary moderately, and in Test C they vary widely in difficulty. The mean scores of all tests are the same, but the standard deviations differ. It is generally true that tests whose items vary widely in difficulty yield less variable scores than tests whose items are more uniform in difficulty.

The reliability estimates at the bottom of the table were obtained by applying formulas 10.5 and 10.7 to these data.

TABLE 10.2

**Influence of Variations in Item Difficulty on the Accuracy
of Kuder-Richardson 21 Reliability Estimates**

Proportion of Correct Response	Number of Items		
	Test A	Test B	Test C
1.00			5
.90			10
.80			10
.70		10	10
.60		25	10
.50	100	30	10
.40		25	10
.30		10	10
.20			10
.10			10
.00			5
Mean Test Score	50	50	50
Standard Deviation	15	12	8
Reliability Coefficient			
K. R. 20	.898	.844	.749
K. R. 21	.898	.835	.615

If the Kuder-Richardson 20 estimates are taken as the more accurate values, it is apparent that Kuder-Richardson 21 gives a perfectly accurate estimate when all items are of the same level of difficulty, as they are in Test A. When the items vary somewhat in difficulty, as in Test B, the Kuder-Richardson 21 coefficient is only slightly under the Kuder-Richardson 20 coefficient. But when the items vary widely, as in Test C, the underestimate is much greater. Hence, before accepting a Kuder-Richardson 21 coefficient as a good estimate of reliability, one would need to be satisfied that few of the items in the test are extremely easy or extremely difficult.

5. Derivation of a general Kuder-Richardson formula

It is not necessary for a person to be able to derive a formula in order to use it in calculations. For this reason, and because the derivation of formulas is often mathematically complex and difficult for students to follow, derivations are seldom presented in introductory texts in measurement. On the other hand, to know where a formula comes from is to understand it better and perhaps to be able to use it more effectively. Because a fairly simple derivation of these two formulas is possible and because working through it should add considerably to the student's understanding of the formulas, and of the whole concept of reliability, the derivation will be developed here.

We begin by defining test reliability as the correlation between scores on equivalent forms of a test. Equivalent forms, for our purposes, include equal numbers of items selected at random from the same pool of items. In practice we would seldom actually select the items at random because of our desire to cover the same areas of achievement in both forms of the test. But since we do not know the statistical characteristics of these items—their difficulties, discriminating powers, and correlations with other items—in advance, we may be almost selecting them at random so far as their statistical properties are concerned.

Let us suppose then that we have scores on two equivalent forms of a test for each of a group of students. To keep the problem simple we'll consider a small group of students, only five of them. Their names and their scores on forms A and B of the test are presented in the first three columns of Table 10.3. Burton's score on Form A was 12 and on Form B 15. Kathy's scores were 13 and 11, and so on. Our problem is to calculate the correlation between these five pairs of scores.

TABLE 10.3

Scores of Five Students on Two Forms of a Test

| | Original Scores | | Deviation Scores | | Deviation Products | | |
	A	B	A	B	A²	B²	AB
Burton	12	15	3	6	9	36	18
Kathy	13	11	4	2	16	4	8
Alberta	11	9	2	0	4	0	0
Glenn	5	7	−4	−2	16	4	8
Jerry	4	3	−5	−6	25	36	30
Mean	9	9	0	0	14	16	12.8

One way of calculating this correlation is to divide their covariance by the square root of the product of their variances. As we shall see directly, their covariance is 12.8. The variance of scores on Form A is 14. The variance of scores on Form B is 16. The square root of the product of 14 and 16 is 15, approximately. Dividing this into 12.8 gives .86 for the correlation between these five pairs of scores. Hence the equivalent forms reliability coefficient for this test is .86.

The values for covariance and variance used in computing the reliability coefficient were obtained from Table 10.3. The variance of a set of scores is defined as the mean of their squared deviations from their own mean. These squared deviations for the five pairs of scores in our example are shown in columns six and seven of Table 10.3. Their mean values, i.e., the variances in each case, are shown at the bottom of those columns.

Covariances are similar to variances except that two variables are involved. Instead of squaring each deviation, we multiply the deviation of one variable by the deviation of the other in a pair of values. For example, the deviation of Burton's score on Form A, 3, is multiplied by the deviation of his score on Form B, 6, to obtain the deviation product of 18 shown in the last column of Table 10.3. The mean of these products for all students, 12.8 as shown at the bottom of the last column, is the covariance of scores on the two forms of this test for the five students.

Can a similar estimate of reliability be obtained from only one form of the test? Consider that the estimate we just obtained was based on sets of items drawn from the same general pool and that the numerical value of the estimate depended on the relation between scores on these two sets of items. Could we not obtain a similar estimate by studying the relation between scores on the items in just one set? Perhaps we can.

As a start, let us see how the relation between total scores on Forms A and B of our test depends on the relations between scores on the items composing them. To keep the illustration simple we have used only three items in each form of the test. The scores of the five students on these six items, their total scores on each form of the test, and their mean scores on each item and on each form are shown in Table 10.4. These scores, expressed as deviations from the mean scores, are shown in Table 10.5. The bottom line of this table shows the variance of each set of scores.

TABLE 10.4

Original Item and Test Scores of Five Students on Two Forms of a Test

	Form A				Form B			
Name	1	2	3	Total	1'	2'	3'	Total'
Burton	4	3	5	12	5	5	5	15
Kathy	5	4	4	13	4	3	4	11
Alberta	3	5	3	11	3	4	2	9
Glenn	2	2	1	5	2	2	3	7
Jerry	1	1	2	4	1	1	1	3
Mean	3	3	3	9	3	3	3	9

TABLE 10.5

Deviation Item and Test Scores of Five Students on Two Forms of a Test

	Form A				Form B			
Name	1	2	3	Total	1'	2'	3'	Total'
Burton	1	0	2	3	2	2	2	6
Kathy	2	1	1	4	1	0	1	2
Alberta	0	2	0	2	0	1	−1	0
Glenn	−1	−1	−2	−4	−1	−1	0	−2
Jerry	−2	−2	−1	−5	−2	−2	−2	−6
Variance	2	2	2	14.0	2	2	2	16.0

Having all of these scores in deviation form, we are prepared to calculate the covariance of item and total scores for Form A with the item and total scores for Form B. These are shown in Table 10.6. These covariances have the interesting and useful property of being additive. That is, the sum of the covariances of Item 1 of Form A with Items 1', 2', and 3' equals the covariance of Item 1 with total scores on all three items. The same is true of the other rows and columns of Table 10.6. The sum of the nine interitem covariances is 12.8, exactly the same as the interform covariance we used in the earlier computation. This relationship is the basis for our method of estimating test reliability when only a single form of the test is available.

To see how this is possible consider the interitem variances and covariances, the item-test covariances, and the test variance shown

TABLE 10.6

Two Form Item and Test Covariances

Form A	1'	2'	3'	Total'
1	1.8	1.4	1.6	4.8
2	1.2	1.4	.6	3.2
3	1.8	1.6	1.4	4.8
Total	4.8	4.4	3.6	12.8

Form B (header spanning 1', 2', 3', Total')

in Table 10.7. The item variances, 2, 2, and 2, and the test variance, 14, are shown on a diagonal of the table. The interitem covariances are 1.4, 1.6, and 1.0. Again as in Table 10.6, the sum of all the item variances and interitem covariances equals the test variance. Likewise, the sum of all the item-test covariances equals the test variance.

TABLE 10.7

One Form Item and Test Variances and Covariances

Form A	1	2	3	Total
1	2	1.4	1.6	5.0
2	1.4	2	1.0	4.4
3	1.6	1.0	2	4.6
Total	5.0	4.4	4.6	14.0

Form A (header spanning 1, 2, 3, Total)

Now compare Table 10.6, showing the covariances of items in two forms of a test, with Table 10.7, showing the variances and covariances of items in one form of a test. The main difference is that variances along the diagonal of Table 10.7 take the place of covariances along the diagonal of Table 10.6.

Our problem is to get a good estimate of the interform covariance (shown as 12.8 in Table 10.6) from the data given in Table 10.7. Let us assume that the average values of the interitem covariances should be the same in both tables, since the items were all drawn from the same pool. That average value in Table 10.7 is 1.4 plus 1.6 plus 1.0 divided by 3, or 1.333. Since nine such interitem covariances are added in Table 10.6 to give the intertest covariance, we multiply 1.333 by 9 to get 12.0 for our single test estimate of the intertest covariance. The variance of the single test (and presumably of its hypothetical equivalent form also) is 14.0. So to get an estimate of the reliability we divide 12.0 by the square root of 14 times 14 (which is, of course, 14) and get .86 for our single form estimate of the equivalent forms reliability of the test. This is the same value we got before. (The data in the sample problem we started with were selected to make this happen. It wouldn't ordinarily come out that neatly with such small samples of items and students.)

Can what we just did be expressed in a general formula, applicable to tests having more than three items and involving different numerical values? We said that the equivalent forms reliability could be found by dividing the intertest covariance by the square root of the product of their variances, or

$$r_{AB} = \frac{C_{AB}}{\sqrt{\sigma_A{}^2 \cdot \sigma_B{}^2}} \qquad 10.8$$

If $\sigma_A{}^2 = \sigma_B{}^2$, as it should if B is a hypothetical test equivalent to A, then

$$r_{AB} = \frac{C_{AB}}{\sigma_A{}^2} \qquad 10.9$$

We obtain our estimate of C_{AB} from Table 10.7 by finding the average value of the interitem covariances. But in a long test, finding all of the interitem covariances would be a tedious job. There is an easier way.

We start with the variance of the test scores (14 in Table 10.7), subtract the sum of the item variances (6 in Table 10.7), and divide the result by the number of interitem covariances (6 in Table 10.7) to get the average value of the interitem covariance (1.333 in Table 10.7). If there are k items in a test there will always be k item variances and $k^2 - k$ interitem covariances. Hence if we designate the sum of the item variances by the symbol $\Sigma\sigma_i{}^2$, the average interitem covariance is

$$\frac{\sigma_A{}^2 - \Sigma\sigma_i{}^2}{k^2 - k} \qquad 10.10$$

But in Table 10.6, with a test of k items, there are k^2 interitem covariances. Hence the value of the inter test covariance C_{AB} we are seeking is

$$C_{AB} = k^2 \left(\frac{\sigma_A{}^2 - \Sigma\sigma_i{}^2}{k^2 - k} \right) \qquad 10.11$$

which can be simplified to

$$C_{AB} = \frac{k}{k - 1} (\sigma_A{}^2 - \Sigma\sigma_i{}^2) \qquad 10.12$$

To find the test reliability, the intertest covariance estimate must be divided by the test variance. Hence

$$r_{AB} = \frac{k}{k - 1} \frac{(\sigma_A{}^2 - \Sigma\sigma_i{}^2)}{\sigma_A{}^2} = \frac{k}{k - 1} \left(1 - \frac{\Sigma\sigma_i{}^2}{\sigma^2} \right) \qquad 10.13$$

This is a general expression for the basic Kuder-Richardson formula. It indicates that if the ratio of the sum of the item variances to the test variance is subtracted from unity and if the resulting difference is multiplied by $\frac{k}{k - 1}$, the single-form reliability estimate will be obtained.

6. Derivation of Kuder-Richardson Formula 20

The formula just developed is not limited, as is the Kuder-Richardson Formula 20, to items scored 1 if correctly answered and zero if not correctly answered. But since many tests are scored in that way, and since the Formula 20 version is probably the better known, we should show that the two are equivalent when items are scored 1 or 0. What we will actually undertake to show is that $\sigma_i{}^2 = p \cdot q$, where p is the proportion of correct response and q is $1 - p$.

Our starting point is the general formula for variance given as Formula 8.6 in Chapter 8.

$$\sigma^2 = \frac{\Sigma X^2}{N} - \frac{(\Sigma X)^2}{N^2} \qquad 8.6$$

Since a correct answer is scored 1 and any other answer 0, the number of correct answers R is equal to X. Also, since $1^2 = 1$ and $0^2 = 0$, the number of correct answers R is equal to X^2. That is,

$$R = \Sigma X = \Sigma X^2$$

Then, too, the proportion of correct answers, p, is R divided by n, so that

$$p = \frac{R}{n} = \frac{\Sigma X}{n} = \frac{\Sigma X^2}{n}$$

Accordingly

$$\sigma_i{}^2 = p - p^2 = p(1 - p)$$

But since $1 - p = q$,

$$\sigma_i{}^2 = pq \quad \text{and} \quad \Sigma\sigma_i{}^2 = \Sigma pq$$

in case the items are scored either 1 or 0. This relationship when substituted in formula 10.13 gives the usual Kuder-Richardson Formula 20, shown earlier in this chapter as Formula 10.5.

$$r = \frac{k}{k - 1} \left(1 - \frac{\Sigma pq}{\sigma^2} \right) \qquad 10.5$$

7. Derivation of the Spearman-Brown formula

The approach used here to derive the Kuder-Richardson formula for test reliability can also be used to derive the Spearman-Brown formula. Our problem is to obtain a reasonable estimate of r_n, the reliability of a test n times as long as a given shorter test, Test S, whose reliability is r_s. Tables 10.6 and 10.7 offer the key, if we consider the interitem covariances of these tables to represent instead the covariances of short tests equivalent to Test A, and the intertest covariance of Table 10.6 and the test variance of Table 10.7 to represent instead the covariance and variance of the lengthened test.

Under these considerations the reliability of the lengthened test is obtained by dividing the covariance of the lengthened test by its variance, or

$$r_n = \frac{C_{nn'}}{\sigma_n{}^2} \qquad 10.14$$

But $C_{nn'}$ is the sum of n^2 short-test covariances, or

$$C_{nn'} = n^2 C_{ss'} \qquad 10.15$$

and $\sigma_n{}^2$ is the sum of $n(n - 1)$ short-test covariances $C_{ss'}$ and n short-test variances $\sigma_s{}^2$, or

$$\sigma_n{}^2 = n(n - 1)C_{ss'} + n\sigma_s{}^2 \qquad 10.16$$

Hence the reliability of the lengthened test is

$$r_n = \frac{n^2 C_{ss'}}{n(n - 1)C_{ss'} + n\sigma_s{}^2} = \frac{nC_{ss'}}{(n - 1)C_{ss'} + \sigma_s{}^2} \qquad 10.17$$

But the short-test covariance $C_{ss'}$ is equal to the short-test reliability r_s multiplied by the short-test variance σs^2, or

$$C_{ss'} = r_s \sigma_s^2 \qquad 10.18$$

Accordingly, by substitution,

$$r_n = \frac{nr_s\sigma_s^2}{(n-1)r_s\sigma_s^2 + \sigma_s^2} = \frac{nr_s}{(n-1)r_s + 1} \qquad 10.1$$

This is the general Spearman-Brown formula, given earlier in this chapter as Formula 10.1.

8. Computation of Kuder-Richardson reliability coefficients

Typical reliability calculations, involving larger numbers of students and items than the simplified illustrations used in these explanations, are facilitated by desk calculators or other computing aids. If the calculation is to be based on the general Kuder-Richardson formula (Formula 10.13), a form somewhat more convenient for routine calculation is

$$r = \frac{k}{k-1}\left(1 - \frac{n\Sigma Q^2 - \Sigma T^2}{n\Sigma X^2 - (\Sigma X)^2}\right) \qquad 10.19$$

in which:

k is the number of items
n is the number of students
ΣQ^2 is the sum of the squares of the k times n individual question scores
ΣT^2 is the sum of the squares of the k question total scores
ΣX^2 is the sum of the squares of the n student total scores
ΣX is the sum of the n student total scores

Perhaps the best way to explain this method for estimating a reliability coefficient is to carry through a computation on the basis of a specific example. Table 10.8 displays the scores of ten students on five questions. Harry's score on question 1 was 7 points; on question 2, 8 points; on question 3, 6 points; and so on. This test might have been a five-item essay test in which each question was scored on the basis of a ten-point scale with no points for no answer at all and ten points for an ideal answer. Alternatively, these data might represent

TABLE 10.8

Scores of Ten Students on Five Questions

Question

Student	1	2	3	4	5	Total
Harry	7	8	6	10	10	41
Joseph	5	10	10	9	6	40
Ruth	3	6	5	3	4	21
Charles	5	3	5	6	4	23
Gary	2	4	6	1	2	15
Violet	9	8	5	9	5	36
Esther	4	3	3	1	2	13
Marion	3	1	3	5	0	12
Joan	4	5	4	8	4	25
Roy	7	6	5	7	5	30
Total	49	54	52	59	42	256

scores on a ten-problem test in physics or engineering, again with each problem scored on a ten-point scale. Or the five scores might have been obtained from a fifty-item multiple-choice test in which the first ten items contribute to the score on question 1, the next ten to question 2, the next ten to question 3, and so on. Thus, the same kind of data would be generated regardless of whether the test involved had been essay, problem, or objective. The method is not limited, of course, to a test composed of five questions. Nor is it limited to a group of ten students. This particular example has been kept simple to enable the reader to follow the explanation more easily. For the scores of ten students on five questions shown in Table 10.8

$$k = 5 \qquad \Sigma X^2 = 7,610$$

$$n = 10 \qquad \Sigma T^2 = 13,266$$

$$\Sigma X = 256 \qquad \Sigma Q^2 = 1,638$$

When these are substituted in Formula 10.19, the result is

$$r = \frac{5}{4} \left(1 - \frac{10 \times 1,638 - 13,266}{10 \times 7,610 - 256 \times 256} \right) = .88$$

The computations involved in this example are similar to, but not identical with, those employed in the statistical procedures known as "analysis of variance." In a typical analysis of the variance of the scores of n pupils on k test items, three components would be extracted:

1. variance attributable to differences among the students in ability
2. variance attributable to differences among the test items in difficulty
3. variance attributable to inconsistency in the behavior of examinees from item to item, often referred to as the interaction, residual, or error variance

A number of writers, including Hoyt, Jackson and Ferguson, Ebel, and Lindquist, have discussed the use of analysis of variance in the estimation of test reliability.[6]

9. The interpretation of reliability coefficients

A reliability coefficient, as has been said, is an estimate of the coefficient of correlation between one set of scores on a particular test for a particular group of examinees and an independent set of scores on an equivalent test for the same examinees. The higher this coefficient, the more consistently the test is measuring whatever it does measure. Perfect reliability, never actually obtained in practice, would be represented by a coefficient of 1.00. While reliability coefficients of .96 or higher are sometimes reported, most test constructors are reasonably well satisfied if their tests yield reliability coefficients in the vicinity of .90. The reliability coefficients ordinarily obtained for teacher-made tests tend to fall considerably short of this goal.

Another way of interpreting a reliability coefficient is to say that it is an expression of the ratio of the variance of true scores to the variance of obtained scores. The variance of a set of scores is obtained by finding how much each score differs from the mean of the set of scores, squaring those differences, adding them, and dividing

---

[6] Cyril Hoyt, "Test Reliability Obtained by Analysis of Variance," *Psychometrika*, VI (1941), 153-60; R. W. B. Jackson and George A. Ferguson, *Studies on the Reliability of Tests*, Department of Educational Research Bulletin 12 (Toronto, Canada: University of Toronto, 1941); Robert L. Ebel, "Estimation of the Reliability of Ratings," *Psychometrika*, XVI (December, 1951), 407-24; and E. F. Lindquist, *Design and Analysis of Experiments in Psychology and Education* (Boston: Houghton Mifflin Company, 1953), pp. 357-82.

by the number of scores. By the "hypothetical true score" of an individual on a test is meant the average of a very large number of scores that might be obtained on similar tests, under similar conditions, for the same individual. The difference between the true score and an obtained score is called an "error of measurement." It is assumed that, in a very large number of obtained scores for the same person, the errors of measurement will tend to cancel each other, so that the average of a very large number of obtained scores closely approximates the true score for that person.

The definition of reliability just given can be expressed in a formula as follows:

$$r = \frac{\sigma_t^2}{\sigma_o^2} \qquad 10.20$$

in which r stands for the coefficient of reliability, σ_t^2 represents the variance of the true scores, and σ_o^2 represents the variance of the obtained scores.

The relation between obtained scores, true scores, and errors of measurement can also be expressed in the formula:

$$x = \bar{x} + e \qquad 10.21$$

in which x stands for any test score, $\bar{x}$ for the average of a very large number of similar scores, and e for an error of measurement.

It is ordinarily assumed that errors of measurement are uncorrelated with true scores. In other words, the size of the error of measurement is assumed to be unrelated to the size of the true score. If this is true, the variance of the obtained scores equals the variance of the true scores plus the variance of the errors of measurement. This can be expressed in a formula as follows:

$$\sigma_o^2 = \sigma_t^2 + \sigma_e^2 \qquad 10.22$$

in which σ_o^2 stands for the variance of the obtained scores, σ_t^2 for the variance of the true scores, and σ_e^2 for the variance of the errors of measurement.

Some of these relations are illustrated numerically in Table 10.9, where the true scores, the errors of measurement, and the obtained scores for five students are displayed. Note that for each student, the obtained score equals the true score plus the error of measurement. The mean of the true score is 15, of the errors of measurement 0, which makes the mean of the obtained scores also 15. The vari-

TABLE 10.9

Reliability and Errors of Measurement

Students	True Scores	Errors of Measurement	Obtained Scores
Arline	18	−2	16
Dan	9	+1	10
Jean	15	+2	17
John	21	+1	22
Victor	12	−2	10
Mean	15	0	15
Variance	18	2.8	20.8

$$\text{Reliability} = \frac{18}{20.8} = .865$$

$$\sigma_e = \sqrt{2.8} = 1.67 \quad \text{(Direct calculation)}$$

$$\sigma_e = 20.8 \sqrt{1 - .865}$$

$$= 4.56 \times .367$$

$$= 1.67 \quad \text{(From formula)}$$

ances of true scores, errors of measurement, and obtained scores, calculated as described previously, are given in the next line of the exhibit. The ratio of the variance of the true scores to that of the obtained scores, in this case .865, is the reliability of this set of obtained scores.

In almost all practical measurement situations, the only information available is the obtained scores of the persons measured. Their true scores are unknown and the error of measurement associated with each obtained score is also unknown. However, given the standard deviation of the distribution of obtained scores and the reliability coefficient of those scores, one can estimate the standard deviation of the errors of measurement. This quantity is called the "standard error of measurement." By combining equations 10.9 and 10.11 above to eliminate the expression for the variance of the two true scores and then by solving the resulting combined equation for the variance of errors of measurement and taking the square root of both sides, this expression is obtained for the standard error of measurement.

$$\sigma_e = \sigma_o \sqrt{1 - r} \qquad\qquad 10.23$$

When the values for σo and r shown in Table 10.9 are substituted in this formula, the value $\sigma_e = 1.67$ is obtained. Note that this is identical with the value obtained when the standard deviation of the errors of measurement is calculated directly. This shows that an estimate of the standard deviation of the errors of measurement can be obtained from the standard deviation and reliability of the obtained scores, without any information about the individual errors of measurement.

The standard error of measurement provides an indication of the absolute accuracy of the test scores. If, for example, the standard error of measurement for a set of scores is 3, then for slightly more than two thirds of the obtained scores (about 68 per cent of them) the errors of measurement will be three points or less. For the remainder of scores, of course, the errors of measurement will be greater than three score units.

Another way of expressing the absolute accuracy of test scores is to use the probable error of measurement. For half of the scores in any set of scores, the errors of measurement will be no greater than the probable error of measurement for that set. The other half, of course, will have errors greater than the probable error of measurement. The probable error of measurement is somewhat smaller than the standard error of measurement. It is, in fact, .6745 times the standard error of measurement.

One of the shortcomings of the reliability coefficient is that its magnitude is not solely dependent upon the quality of the test. It depends also on the variability of the group to which the test is applied. Since the standard error of measurement is affected very little by the variability of the group tested, it is sometimes proposed as a measure of reliability that would be superior to the ordinary reliability coefficient. Unfortunately, the standard error of measurement has shortcomings of its own. For tests using a given type of item, the standard error of measurement is almost entirely dependent upon the number of items in the test and hardly at all upon their quality. This point has been demonstrated by Lord and supported by Swineford.[7]

---

[7] Frederic M. Lord, "Do Tests of the Same Length Have the Same Standard Error of Measurement?" *Educational and Psychological Measurement,* XVII (1957), 501-21; F. M. Lord, "Tests of the Same Length Do Have the Same

Since a reliability coefficient looks like a proportion, some users are tempted to interpret it as the proportion of scores which agree, i.e., are identical. This is not correct. However, it is possible to derive from a correlation coefficient an expression for a proportion or per cent of agreement under certain specified conditions. Suppose, for example, a group of individuals is divided into two equal parts on the basis of their scores on some test. Those in the half making the higher scores are placed in one group, and the others in the half making the lower scores are placed in the other group. What per cent of the individuals in this group would remain in the same half if their true scores were known? The answer is suggested by Table

TABLE 10.10

**Interpreting Reliability Coefficients
in Terms of Per cent of Agreement**

Correlation Coefficient	Per cent of Agreement	
	By Halves*	By Thirds**
1.00	100	100
.96	95	79
.90	90	73
.85	87	69
.81	85	65
.76	83	62
.64	80	55
.49	74	49
.25	66	40
.00	50	33

* Robert L. Ebel, "The Frequency of Errors in the Classification of Individuals on the Basis of Fallible Test Scores," *Educational and Psychological Measurement*, Winter, 1947, pp. 725-34.
** Joshua A. Fishman, *1957 Supplement to College Board Scores No. 2*, The College Entrance Examination Board, New York, 1957, p. 206.

10.10. If the reliability coefficient were .96, then 95 per cent of the individuals in the group would stay in the same half on the basis

Standard Error of Measurement," *Educational and Psychological Measurement*, XIX (1959), 233-39; and Frances Swineford, "Note on 'Tests of the Same Length Do Have the Same Standard Error of Measurement,'" *Educational and Psychological Measurement*, XIX (1959), 241-42.

of their scores as that to which they were originally assigned on the basis of their fallible scores. Only 5 per cent would be transferred from the lower half to the upper or from the upper half to the lower. On the other hand, dividing a group into two equal parts on the basis of totally unreliable test scores would be expected to result in 50 per cent wrong assignments.

The third column in Table 10.10 illustrates somewhat similar data where the group is divided into thirds. In this case, however, the per cent of agreement estimated is between obtained scores on two equivalent forms of a test, each of which yields scores that are somewhat unreliable. It is not, as was true of the per cents in the second column, estimated agreement between obtained scores for one test and estimated true scores for the same test.

The relation between the reliability of the test scores or other bases used in assigning course marks and frequency of error in marking is a topic of special interest. An "error in marking" is any course mark awarded which differs from the mark that would have been awarded on the basis of a perfectly reliable measure of course achievement. Table 10.11 illustrates these errors for a five-letter

TABLE 10.11

Accuracy in Assigning 1,000 Marks on the Basis of Measures
Whose Reliability Coefficient Is .90*

True Marks

Assigned Marks	A	B	C	D	F
A	38	12	0	0	0
B	12	193	45	0	0
C	0	45	310	45	0
D	0	0	45	193	12
F	0	0	0	12	38

* Underlined figures are frequencies of accurately assigned marks.

marking system when the reliability of the basis for marking is .90. This table assumes that 5 per cent of the marks assigned are A's, 25 per cent are B's, 40 per cent are C's, 25 per cent are D's, and 5 per cent are F's. The table includes 1,000 marks. The first column of this table should be read as follows: "Of the fifty students who should have received marks of A, thirty-eight actually did receive A's and twelve received B's." Since 228 of the marks assigned differ from the true mark that should have been assigned, the per cent of incorrect marking is approximately 23 per cent. Table 10.12 shows the per cent of incorrect marking under a similar marking system when the reliability of the marking basis varies from 1.00 to .00.

TABLE 10.12

Estimated Percentages of Incorrect Marking
on the Basis of Measures of Differing Degrees
of Reliability, Assuming a Five-Category
(5-25-40-25-5) Distribution

Reliability of Measures	Per cent Incorrect
1.00	0
.99	5
.98	9
.95	15
.90	23
.80	33
.70	40
.50	50
.00	70

10. Improving test reliability

The coefficient of reliability of a set of test scores is related to a number of other characteristics of the test and of the group tested. Typically the reliability coefficient will be greater for scores:

1. from a longer test than from a shorter test
2. from a test composed of more homogeneous items than from a more heterogeneous test
3. from a test composed of more discriminating items than from a test composed of less discriminating items
4. from a test whose items are of middle difficulty than from a test composed mainly of quite difficult or quite easy items
5. from a group having a wide range of ability than from a group more homogeneous in ability

6. from a speeded test than from one which all examinees can complete in the time available

The Spearman-Brown formula, discussed earlier in this chapter (Formula 10.1), indicates the theoretical relation between test reliability and test length. The effect of successive doublings of the length of an original five-item test, whose reliability was assumed to be .20, is shown in Table 10.13. The same data are shown graphically in Figure 10.1.

TABLE 10.13

Relation of Test Length to Test Reliability

Items	Reliability
5	.20
10	.33
20	.50
40	.67
80	.80
160	.89
320	.94
640	.97
∞	1.00

As the table and the figure indicate, the higher the reliability of the test, the smaller the increase in reliability with added test length. Adding sixty items to a twenty-item test could increase its reliability from .50 to .80. But adding eighty more items to the eighty-item test would raise its reliability only from .80 to .89. To achieve perfect reliability, an infinite number of items would have to be used, which of course means that perfect reliability is unattainable by lengthening any unreliable test.

Two assumptions, one statistical the other psychological, are involved in the use of the Spearman-Brown formula. The statistical assumption is that the material added to the original test to increase its length has the same statistical properties as the original test. That is, the added items should have the same average difficulty as the original items and their addition to the test should not change the average intercorrelation among the test items. The psychological assumption involved is that lengthening the test should not change the way in which the examinees respond to it. If practice on items

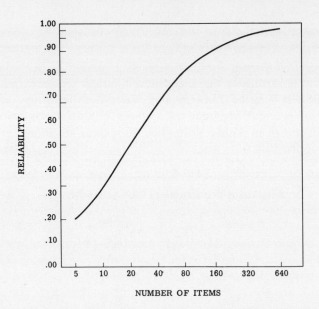

Figure 10.1. Relation of Test Length to Test Reliability

like those in the test facilitates correct response, if fatigue or bore-dom inhibits it, or if any other factors make the examinees respond quite differently to the lengthened test, reliability predictions based on the Spearman-Brown formula could be erroneous.

Homogeneity of test content also tends to enhance test reliability. A one hundred-item test in American history is likely to be more reliable than a one hundred-item test covering all aspects of achieve-ment in high school. Also the subject matter in some courses, such as mathematics and foreign languages, is more tightly organized, with greater interdependence of facts, principles, abilities, and achievements, than is the subject matter of literature or history. This is another aspect of test content homogeneity which makes high reliability easier to achieve in tests of mathematics and foreign lan-guages than in some other tests of educational achievement.

The items in homogeneous tests tend to have higher indices of discrimination than items in tests covering more diverse content and abilities. But item discrimination is also heavily dependent on the technical quality of the item—on the soundness of the idea underly-ing the item, the clarity of its expression, and in the case of multiple-choice items, the adequacy of the correct response and the attractiveness of the distracters to examinees of lower ability. The nature and determination of indices of discrimination and their relation to test reliability will be discussed in greater detail in the next chapter. For the present it will be sufficient to say that the relation is close and important. Working to improve the discrimination of the individual items in most classroom tests is probably the most effective means of improving test reliability and, hence, of test quality.

The difficulty of a test item affects its contribution to test reliability. An item which all examinees answer correctly, or all miss, contributes nothing to test reliability. An item which just half of the examinees answer correctly is potentially capable of contributing more to test reliability than any other item that is more difficult or less difficult. But such an item could also be totally nondiscriminating, in which case it would contribute nothing to the reliability of the test. Items of middle difficulty, that is, from 25 to 75 per cent correct response, are all capable of contributing much to test reliability. Items which more than 90 per cent or fewer than 10 per cent of the examinees answer correctly cannot possibly contribute as much. Contrary to popular belief, a good test seldom needs to include items which vary widely in difficulty. This point will be discussed in more detail in the next chapter.

The reliability coefficient for a set of test scores depends also on the range of talent in the group tested. If an achievement test suitable for use in the middle grades of an elementary school is given to pupils in the fourth, fifth, and sixth grades, the reliability of the complete set of scores will almost certainly be higher than the reliability of the scores for pupils of any one grade.

The reliability coefficient, as we have said, reflects the ratio of true score variance to observed score variance. The wider the range of talent, the greater the true score variance. If the variance of the errors of measurement is unaffected by the range of talent, as should be expected, then the observed score variance will not increase as fast, i.e., in the same proportion, as the true score variance. Thus increasing the range of talent, and hence the true score variance, tends to increase the reliability coefficient.

The relation of reliability to score variability can be illustrated further by a research study that failed. The study was intended to find out how the reliability of a test might differ for students at different levels of ability. The investigator divided 1,000 answer sheets from the test into ten groups of one hundred each, putting the one hundred answer sheets having highest scores into one group, the one hundred next high in a second, and so on. Then he calculated an odd-even reliability coefficient for each of the ten sets. Much to his surprise, the coefficients he obtained were all negative. He had expected them to be low, but not negative.

The explanation was not hard to find. All the papers in any one group had total scores of nearly the same value. Hence a student who got *more* than half of his total score on the odd-numbered items necessarily got *less* than half of his total score on the even-numbered items. A student whose score on the odd-numbered items was lower than that of other students in his group had to get a score on the even-numbered items that was higher—hence the negative odd-even correlation and the resulting negative reliability coefficients. The same results would have been obtained if the Kuder-Richardson formulas had been used, although the explanation is a bit more complicated.

What the investigator should have done was to use as a basis for selecting the different ability groups some measure other than (and independent of) the score on the test he was analyzing. He probably should have included 500 or more answer sheets in each group, too, since the reliabilities he got would probably be quite low and hence subject to large errors unless based on very sizable samples.

Classroom tests are sometimes constructed and scored so that the range of scores obtained is much less than that which is theoretically available. For example, an essay test with a one hundred-point maximum score may be graded with a view to making 75 a reasonable passing score. This usually limits the effective range of scores to about thirty points. A true-false test, scored only for the number of items answered correctly, has a useful score range of only about half the number of items. A multiple-choice test, on the other hand, may have a useful score range of three-fourths or more of the number of items in the test. Hence a one hundred-item multiple-choice test is usually more reliable than a one hundred-item true-false test.

The dependence of test reliability on score variability is illustrated with hypothetical data for three kinds of tests in Figure 10.2. The essay test was assumed to consist of ten questions, each worth a maximum of ten points, with a score of 75 on the entire test set in ad-

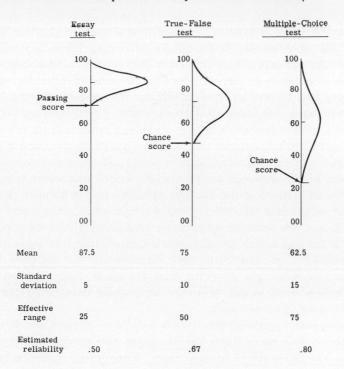

	Essay test	True-False test	Multiple-Choice test
Mean	87.5	75	62.5
Standard deviation	5	10	15
Effective range	25	50	75
Estimated reliability	.50	.67	.80

Figure 10.2. Hypothetical Score Distributions for Three Tests

vance as the minimum passing score. The other two tests consist of one hundred items each and are scored by giving one point of credit for each correct answer. There is no "correction for guessing" by a subtraction of a fraction of the wrong answers. Each multiple-choice answer is assumed to offer four alternative answers, so that the expected chance score on it is 25. The expected chance score on the true-false test is, of course, 50.

The data at the bottom of Figure 10.2 show the expected difference among the tests in average score (mean), in variability (standard deviation), in effective range, and in reliability. While these are hypothetical data, based on deductions from certain assumptions, they are reasonably representative of the results teachers typically achieve in using tests of these types.

It is possible to construct a one hundred-item multiple-choice test whose reliability will yield scores above .90, but it is not easy to do and relatively few instructors succeed in doing it. Again, one hundred-point essay tests can be handled so that their reliability will be as satisfactory as that of a one hundred-item multiple-choice test. But this also is not easy to do, and few of those who prepare and score classroom tests succeed in doing it without taking special pains.

Scores from a test given to a group under highly speeded conditions will ordinarily show a higher reliability coefficient than would be obtained for scores from the same test given to the same group with time limits generous enough to permit all examinees to finish. But most of the increased reliability of speeded test scores is spurious. It is an artifact of the method of estimating reliability. If, instead of estimating reliability from a single administration of the speeded test, we were to administer separately timed equivalent forms of the test under equally speeded conditions, the correlation between scores on these equivalent forms would be less than that estimated from a single administration. Hence the apparent increase in reliability which results from speeding a test is usually regarded as being a spurious increase.

Here is what causes the trouble. Scores on a speeded test depend not only on how many items the examinee can answer, but also on how fast he can work to answer them. Thus to estimate the reliability of scores on a speeded test one must estimate both ability and speed. By splitting a test into halves or into individual items, one can get two independent estimates of ability. But there is no way of getting independent estimates of speed, short of timing separately the responses to individual items or parts of the test. When this is not done, the estimates of speed are not only independent, they are forced to appear almost identical. The apparent reliability of the measurements of speed is very high. When this is combined with a valid estimate of the reliability of the measurements of ability, the composite is spuriously inflated. The implication of this is that dependable estimates of test score reliability can be obtained from a single administration of a test only if the speed at which an examinee works is not an important factor in determining his score.

The importance of test reliability as a factor in test quality has been stressed in this chapter. How can the test constructor make more reliable tests? By taking advantage of the factors affecting reliability which are under his control. This means writing, revising, and selecting test items so that they will discriminate as clearly as possible between much and little of the achievement the test is intended to measure. Choosing items of high discrimination will result automatically in choosing items of middle difficulty if the index of discrimination recommended in the next chapter is used. This means also including as many items as possible in the test, so as to make the test as long as possible. When the time available for testing is limited, as it usually is, the test constructor will tend to favor items which are least time consuming individually.

11. Summary

Some of the principal ideas developed in this chapter are summarized in these seventeen statements.

1. Educational tests always are less than perfectly reliable because of item sampling errors, examinee performance errors, and scoring errors.

2. A test must be reliable to be valid, but reliability does not guarantee validity.

3. "Test reliability" may be defined operationally as the "coefficient of correlation between scores on two equivalent forms of a test for a specified group of examinees."

4. Separate coefficients of test reliability, examinee reliability, and scoring reliability may be obtained.

5. The coefficient of correlation between scores on two reasonably equivalent halves of a test can be corrected by using the Spearman-Brown formula to obtain a good estimate of test reliability.

6. Short-cut estimates of test reliability can be obtained from the sums and the differences of the half-test scores.

7. The Kuder-Richardson formulas yield estimates of test reliability from data on the variability of test scores and item scores and the number of items in the test.

8. The more widely the items in a test vary in difficulty, the more seriously the Kuder-Richardson formulas, particularly Formula 20, may underestimate reliability.

9. A reliability coefficient may be interpreted as a ratio of the variance of true (error-free) scores to the variance of obtained (error-affected) scores.

10. The standard error of measurement is an estimate of the general magnitude of errors expressed in test score units.

11. The standard error of measurement is found by multiplying the standard deviation of the scores by the square root of the difference between the reliability coefficient and one.

12. From the reliability coefficient it is possible to estimate the percentage of agreement between independent measurements when used to classify persons into groups of high, medium, and low achievement.

13. Longer tests composed of more discriminating items are likely to be more reliable than shorter tests composed of less discriminating items.

14. Homogeneous tests are likely to be more reliable than heterogeneous tests.

15. Scores obtained from heterogeneous groups are likely to be more reliable than scores obtained from homogeneous groups.

16. The more variable the scores obtained from a test, the higher its reliability is likely to be.

17. Reliability coefficients obtained from speeded tests tend to be spuriously high.

REFERENCES

Ebel, Robert L., "Estimation of the Reliability of Ratings," *Psychometrika,* XVI (December, 1951), 407-24.

———, "The Frequency of Errors in the Classification of Individuals on the Basis of Fallible Test Scores," *Educational and Psychological Measurement,* VII, No. 4 (1947), 725-35.

Fishman, Joshua, *1957 Supplement to College Board Scores No. 2,* p. 206. New York: The College Entrance Examination Board, 1957.

Hoyt, Cyril, "Test Reliability Obtained by Analysis of Variance," *Psychometrika,* VI (1941), 153-60.

Jackson, R. W. B. and George A. Ferguson, *Studies on the Reliability of Tests,* Department of Educational Research Bulletin 12. Toronto, Canada: University of Toronto, 1941.

Kuder, G. I. and M. W. Richardson, "The Theory of the Estimation of Test Reliability," *Psychometrika,* II (September, 1937), 151-60.

Lindquist, E. F., *Design and Analysis of Experiments in Psychology and Education,* pp. 357-82. Boston: Houghton Mifflin Company, 1953.

Lord, Frederic M., "Do Tests of the Same Length Have the Same Standard Errors of Measurement?" *Educational and Psychological Measurement,* XVII (1957), 501-21.

———, "Sampling Error Due to Choice of Split in Split-half Reliability

Coefficients," *Journal of Experimental Education,* XXIV (March, 1956), 245-49.

————, "Tests of the Same Length Do Have the Same Standard Error of Measurement," *Educational and Psychological Measurement,* XIX (1959), 233-39.

Rulon, P. J., "A Simplified Procedure for Determining the Reliability of a Test by Split-halves," *Harvard Educational Review,* IX (1939), 99-103.

Stanley, Julian C., "A Simplified Method for Estimating the Split-half Reliability Coefficient of a Test," *Harvard Educational Review,* XXI (Fall, 1951), 221-24.

Swineford, Frances, "Note on 'Tests of the Same Length Do Have the Same Standard Error of Measurement,' " *Educational and Psychological Measurement,* XIX (1959), 241-42.

II How to Improve Test Quality
Through Item Analysis

The construction of solid and reliable tests requires consideration of quantitative information regarding the difficulty and discriminating power of each test exercise, or item, that is proposed for use. Such information is provided by item-analysis data.

FREDERICK B. DAVIS

1. The value of item analysis data

The analysis of student response to objective test items is a powerful tool for test improvement. Item analysis indicates which items may be too easy or too difficult and which may fail for other reasons to discriminate clearly between the better and the poorer examinees. Item analysis sometimes suggests why an item has not functioned effectively and how it might be changed to improve it. A test composed of items revised and selected on the basis of item analysis data is almost certain to be a much more reliable test than one composed of an equal number of untested items. Finally, the teacher who tests his tests through item analysis is likely to improve his skills in test construction much more rapidly than one who does not.

346

2. The process of item analysis

Item analysis begins after the test has been administered and scored. Many different processes of item analysis and many different indices of item quality have been developed.[1] A procedure simple enough to be used regularly by classroom teachers but complete and precise enough to contribute substantially to test improvement has been chosen for detailed discussion in this chapter. It requires the six steps outlined below.

1. Arrange the scored tests or answer sheets in order of score, from high to low.
2. Separate two subgroups of test papers, an upper group, consisting of approximately 27 per cent of the total group, who received highest scores on the test, and a lower group consisting of an equal number of papers from those who received lowest scores.
3. Count the number of times each possible response to each item was chosen on the papers of the upper group. Do the same separately for the papers of the lower group.
4. Record these response counts opposite the responses they refer to on a copy of the test.
5. Add the counts from the upper and lower groups to the keyed correct response. Divide this sum by the maximum possible sum, i.e., the sum of the number of papers in upper and lower groups. Express the quotient as a percentage, i.e., multiply the decimal fraction by 100. The result is an index of item difficulty.
6. Subtract the lower group count of correct responses from the upper group count of correct responses. Divide this difference by the maximum possible difference, i.e., the number of papers in the upper (or lower) group. This quotient, expressed as a decimal fraction, is the index of discrimination.

3. An example of item analysis

An illustration of the data obtained by this process for one item is presented in Exhibit 11.1. This item was constructed for a test

---

[1] Frederick B. Davis, "Item Analysis in Relation to Educational and Psychological Testing," *Psychological Bulletin*, XLIX (1952), 97-121; and William W. Turnbull, "A Normalized Graphic Method of Item Analysis," *Journals of Educational Psychology*, XXXVII (1956), 129-41.

EXHIBIT 11.1

Illustration of Item Analysis Data

74% What change in life expectancy (number of years a person is
.48   likely to live) has been occurring?
  *(1) It has been increasing (47-24)
   (2) It has been declining due to rising rates of cancer and
       heart disease (0-10)
   (3) It has increased for young people but decreased for older
       people (0-5)
   (4) It has remained about the same (1-7)
       (Omits 0-2)

of understanding of contemporary affairs in 1946. Answer sheets
were available for 178 students, so the upper and lower groups con-
sisted of the forty-eight papers having highest and the forty-eight
having lowest scores. The best answer is marked with an asterisk.
The figures in the parentheses following each response indicate
how many of the upper group students (first figure) and how many
of the lower group students (second figure) chose each response. Of
the forty-eight upper group students, forty-seven chose the first
(correct) response and one chose the fourth response. Of the forty-
eight lower group students, twenty-four chose the first response,
ten the second, five the third, and seven the fourth. Evidently two
of the lower group students failed to respond to the item.

The moderate degree of difficulty of the item is indicated
by the 74 per cent of correct response in the two groups combined [100 (47 + 24) ÷ 96 = 74 per cent]. The reasonably good
level of discrimination is indicated by the difference of .48 in proportions of correct response between upper and lower groups
[(47 − 24) ÷ 48 = .48]. Each of the distracters functioned well since
each attracted some responses, largely from students in the lower
group.

4. Selection of the criterion groups

Step 3 in the process of item analysis called for the counting of
responses in upper and lower 27 per cent groups. Why 27 per cent?
Why not upper and lower fourths (25 per cent) or thirds (33 per
cent) or even halves (50 per cent)? The answer is that 27 per cent

provides the best compromise between two desirable but inconsistent aims (1) to make the extreme groups as large as possible and (2) to make the extreme groups as different as possible. Truman Kelley demonstrated that when extreme groups, each consisting of approximately 27 per cent of the total group are used, the ratio of the difference in average abilities of the groups to the standard error of their difference, i.e., the degree of uncertainty about the size of the real difference, is maximum.[2] By the term "real difference" in the preceding sentence is meant the difference which would be observed in a very large population of students like those in the limited sample whose responses we actually can study.

What Kelley showed was that by taking upper and lower groups of 27 per cent of the total group, one can say with the greatest confidence that those in the upper group are superior in the ability measured by the test to those in the lower group. If we were to take upper and lower 10 per cent groups the difference in average levels of ability should be greater than with the 27 per cent groups, but the 10 per cent groups are also much smaller. This means that we can be less sure what their average levels of ability in the two groups really are, and, indeed, less certain that the upper group is really superior to the lower. If we were to take upper and lower 50 per cent groups we would have groups of maximum size, but because our basis for classifying them is not perfectly accurate, some students in the upper group probably belong in the lower, and vice versa. This also would reduce our certainty that the upper group is really superior to the lower.

While upper and lower groups of 27 per cent are best, they are not really much better than groups of 25 or 33 per cent would be. If one likes to work with simple fractions like one-fourth or one-third, instead of an odd percentage like 27 per cent, he should feel free to use upper and lower fourths or thirds. However, he should guard against the intuitive feeling that 33 per cent is better than 27 per cent because in involves groups of larger size or that 25 per cent is better than 27 per cent because the difference between the groups is greater. In each case the supposed advantage is slightly more than offset by the opposing disadvantage. The optimum value is 27 per cent.

---

[2] Truman L. Kelley, "The Selection of Upper and Lower Groups for the Validation of Test Items," *Journal of Educational Psychology*, XXX (1939), 17-24.

5. Special criterion groups

The larger the number of papers included in the upper and lower 27 per cent groups, the more reliable the analysis data will be. In the analysis of classroom tests it is desirable, where possible, to base the analysis on the answers of several class groups that have taken the same test. Seldom will one who analyzes a classroom test have more data at his disposal than he can use conveniently. But in wide-scale testing programs it sometimes happens that 27 per cent of the total group tested will include several hundred students. The work involved in counting responses varies directly with the number of students in the high and low groups, but the reliability of the indices of discrimination and the other item analysis data obtained does not. Increasing the size of the upper and lower groups beyond one hundred students each is usually considered to be unprofitable since the improvement in the precision of the item statistics is small in relation to the effort required to obtain it.

If taking 27 per cent of the total group gives more answer sheets than can be handled conveniently, a smaller percentage may be taken. However, it is better to take all of the highest and lowest x per cent of the total group than to choose x per cent at random from each of the extreme 27 per cent groups. In terms of our original purpose, the greater the difference between the groups in average level of ability, the better, so long as groups of reasonable size are obtained.[3] A study by Aschenbrenner demonstrated that the reliability of discrimination indices obtained from extreme 10 per cent upper and lower groups tended to be greater than that obtained from extreme 27 per cent upper and lower groups when the extreme groups included one hundred students each.

It is true, of course, that discrimination indices of this type computed from different upper and lower group proportions are not exactly comparable. That is, if indices of discrimination were calculated for items in the same test first from upper and lower 27 per cent groups and then from upper and lower 10 per cent groups, one would not expect exactly the same indices for a particular item from the two different proportions. Those from the 10

---

[3] Robert L. Ebel, "The Reliability of an Index of Item Discrimination," *Educational and Psychological Measurement* (1951), pp. 403-9.

per cent groups would tend to be larger than those for the 27 per cent groups. But since the test constructor is seldom faced with the problem of comparing indices of discrimination based on different proportions, the influence of the proportion used on the size of the index obtained seldom induces any errors in item selection. Further, in almost all situations, the use of 27 per cent for the upper and lower groups will be convenient as well as logically most defensible.

In ordinary item analyses, no distinction is made between upper-group students having different criterion (total test) scores. The student with the highest criterion score is treated just like the student whose score falls just below the top quarter. Nor is any distinction made among students whose scores place them in the lower group, even though the best of those students may be considerably better than the poorest.

Flanagan has suggested that item response counts, and the discrimination indices obtained from them, could be made more reliable if added weight were given to the responses of students whose criterion scores were extremely high or extremely low.[4] One of several suggestions he offered is that responses on the top 9 per cent and bottom 9 per cent of the papers be counted twice, with responses on the next 20 per cent down from the top and up from the bottom be counted only once. This has the effect of (1) increasing the size of the upper and lower criterion groups and (2) increasing the difference between them in average levels of ability, both of which are desirable. This procedure is likely to be especially helpful in the analysis of classroom tests where the criterion groups usually are quite small at best. Flanagan has demonstrated the effectiveness of this procedure.[5] He has also prepared tables to assist in the determination of correlation coefficients by this weighting procedure.

6. Counting the responses

The counting of responses to the items is likely to be the most tedious and time-consuming part of the analysis. However, for

---

[4] John C. Flanagan, "The Effectiveness of Short Methods for Calculating Correlation Coefficients," *Psychological Bulletin*, XLIX (July, 1952), 342-48.

[5] John C. Flanagan, *Calculating Correlation Coefficients* (Pittsburgh, Pa.: American Institute for Research, 1962).

many classroom tests the number of papers in each group will be less than ten, which makes the task seem less formidable. If paid clerical help is not available, student volunteers may do the work. It is quite possible to obtain the response counts by a show of hands in class, as Diederich has suggested, or to circulate tally sheets within upper, middle, and lower thirds of the class and have the students record their own responses.[6] An attachment on the IBM 805 scoring machine, called the "graphic item counter," will obtain item analysis data conveniently from tests whose answers have been recorded on IBM answer sheets. Of course, the student's responses can also be key-punched into IBM cards and the counts obtained by machine. Diamond has suggested that a typewriter may be used to help secure item response counts.[7]

7. The index of discrimination

The index of discrimination which results from Step 6 was first described by Johnson.[8] Since then it has attracted considerable attention and approval. It is usually designated by the capital letter "D." It is simpler to determine and to explain than such other indices of discrimination as the biserial coefficient of correlation, the tetrachoric coefficient of correlation, Flanagan's coefficient, and Davis' coefficient.[9] It has the very useful property, which most of the correlation indices lack, of being biased in favor of items of middle difficulty. This bias is illustrated in the second column of Table 11.1. If 100 per cent of the examinees respond to an item correctly, there can be no difference between the upper and lower groups in proportions of correct response. But if only 50 per cent of the examinees respond correctly, it is possible that all of those in the upper group

---

[6] Paul Diederich, "Short-cut Statistics for Teacher-made Tests," *Evaluation and Advisory Service Series No. 5* (Princeton, N.J.: Educational Testing Service, 1960), p. 44.

[7] Solomon Diamond, "The Typewriter as an Aid in Item Analysis," *American Journal of Psychology*, L (1939), 111-13.

[8] A. Pemberton Johnson, "Notes on a Suggested Index of Item Validity: The U-L Index," *Journal of Educational Psychology*, LXII (1951), 499-504.

[9] John C. Flanagan, "General Considerations in the Selection of Test Items and a Short Method of Estimating the Product-Moment Coefficient from the Data at the Tails of the Distributions," *Journal of Educational Psychology*, XXX (1939), 674-80; and Frederick B. Davis, "Item Analysis Data," *Harvard Education Papers No. 2*, Graduate School of Education, Harvard University, 1946.

TABLE 11.1

Relation of Item Difficulty Level to Maximum Value of *D* and to Bits of Differential Information Provided

Percentage of Correct Response	Maximum Value of D	Bits of Differential Information*
100	.00	0
90	.20	36
80	.40	64
70	.60	84
60	.80	96
50	1.00	100
40	.80	96
30	.60	84
20	.40	64
10	.20	36
0	.00	0

* In a group of twenty examinees.

and none of those in the lower group responded correctly. In this case the difference in proportion of correct responses would be 1.00 minus 0.00, so that *D* would be 1.00.

Note that the values in the second column of the table are maximum values. They would not be expected to occur often in practice. But the expected value of *D* for items of 50 per cent difficulty is usually greater than that for items of 40 or 60 per cent difficulty, and much greater than that for items of 0 to 100 per cent difficulty. Exactly what the expected value of *D* would be for any level of item difficulty depends on other characteristics of the item and the test.

The third column of Table 11.1 reports the number of bits of differential information that an item of a given level of difficulty can supply. An item that one examinee answers correctly and one examinee misses supplies one bit of differential information for that group of two examinees. If both answered it correctly or missed it, the item would supply no differential information. An item that A, B, C, and D answer correctly but that E and F miss supplies eight bits of differential information. So far as that item is concerned, A shows more ability than E and more than F (two bits of differential information). B shows more than E and more than F (two more bits). Similar statements, four in all, can be made about the relative abilities of C, D, E, and F. Clearly the number of bits of differential information an item can yield is the product of the number who pass and the number who fail it. The figures in the third column were derived by applying this rule, assuming a class of twenty examinees.

If the primary goal of item selection is to maximize test reliability, as it probably should be for most classroom tests, the items having highest discrimination in terms of this index should be chosen. Item difficulty need not be considered directly in item selection, since no item which is much too difficult, or much too easy, can possibly show good discrimination when the Upper-Lower-Difference Index is used.

The second column of Table 11.1 indicates the bias of D in favor of items of middle difficulty. The third column suggests why such a bias may be desirable. Items of middle difficulty have the *potential* of supplying more differential information than do those of extreme ease or difficulty. Note that items in the middle range of difficulty, from 25 to 75 per cent, all have at least three-fourths of the maximum potential discrimination.

Of course, not all the discriminations an item affords are likely to be correct discriminations. An item answered correctly by 50 per cent of the good students and 50 per cent of the poor students provides exactly as many "incorrect" and "correct" discriminations. In the context of item discrimination analysis, the discriminations between good students who answer an item correctly and poor students who miss it are regarded as "correct" discriminations. But discriminations between good students who miss an item and poor students who answer it correctly are regarded as "incorrect" discriminations.

Findley has demonstrated that the index of discrimination D is exactly proportional to the difference between the numbers of correct and incorrect discriminations an item makes.[10] This relationship is illustrated in Table 11.2. The table is based on an examinee group of thirty-seven, so that ten students make up the high scoring 27 per cent and ten students the low scoring 27 per cent.

The second row of figures in Table 11.2 may be interpreted in

---

[10] Warren G. Findley, "Rationale for the Evaluation of Item Discrimination Statistics," *Educational and Psychological Measurement*, XVI (1956), 175-80.

TABLE 11.2

Illustration of the Relation of D
to the Net Number of Correct Discriminations

Correct Responses		Number of Discriminations			Net	Index of
High	Low	Correct	Neutral	Incorrect	Correct	Discrim-inations
10	7	30	70	0	30	.30
9	6	36	58	6	30	.30
8	5	40	50	10	30	.30
8	4	48	44	8	40	.40
7	3	49	42	9	40	.40
6	2	48	44	8	40	.40
4	2	32	56	12	20	.20
3	1	27	66	7	20	.20
2	0	20	80	0	20	.20

this way. If nine good students answer an item correctly and four poor students $(10 - 6 = 4)$ miss it, the number of correct discriminations is $9 \times 4 = 36$. But one good student missed the item and six poor students answered it correctly. Hence there were six incorrect discriminations. The net number of correct discriminations is $36 - 6 = 30$. The item, however, fails to discriminate between the nine good and six poor students who gave correct answers, and between the one good and four poor students who gave incorrect answers. Thus the item missed fifty-eight $(9 \times 6$ plus $1 \times 4)$ opportunities to discriminate. These are designated as "neutral" discriminations in Table 11.2.

Note that the proportion of net correct discriminations $(30 \div 100 = .30)$ is exactly equal to the value of the index of discrimination D for an item that nine of ten good students and six of ten poor students answer correctly. The two columns to the right of Table 11.2 illustrate this exact proportionality between D and the net number of correct discriminations, or the exact identity of D and the proportion of correct discriminations. Findley proved that this relationship is direct and completely general. The index of discrimination D thus provides an excellent measure of how much useful information about differences in achievement a test item can contribute.

Item discrimination indices of all types are subject to considerable sampling error. The smaller the sample of answer sheets used in the analysis, the larger the sampling errors. An item which appears highly discriminating in one small sample may appear weak or even negative in discrimination in another sample. The values obtained for achievement test items are also sensitive to the kind of instruction the students received relative to the item. Hence the use of refined statistics to measure item discrimination seldom seems to be warranted.

But even though the discrimination indices of individual items cannot be determined reliably without using large samples of student responses, item analysis based on small samples is still worthwhile as a means of over-all test improvement. How much better the test composed of most discriminating items can be expected to be will depend on how large the samples and how small the sampling errors are.

8. The criterion for item analysis

The item analysis described in this chapter, like most item analyses, makes use of an internal criterion for the selection of groups of high and low achievement. That is, the total score on the test whose items are to be analyzed is used as the criterion rather than some other independent (external) measure of achievement. In order to conclude that an item showing high discrimination is a good item, one must assume that the entire test, of which that item is a part, is a good test.

Such an assumption is ordinarily quite reasonable. That is, the test constructor comes close enough to the mark on his first attempt to make the total score on his test a fairly dependable basis for distinguishing between students of high and low achievement. However, it must be conceded that item analysis using an internal criterion can only make a test a better measure of whatever it does measure. To make the test a better measure of what it *ought* to measure (if that should be different from what it *does* measure) one would need to use some better criterion than the total score on the test itself. Obviously this would be an external criterion. However, one should guard against the error of thinking that being external *makes* it better. An external criterion has no real advantage over the internal criterion unless it is a better measure than the test of whatever the test is supposed to measure. Ryans found the available external criteria to be of limited value in validating the items of a professional information test.[11]

The use of total test score as a basis for selecting upper and lower groups for item analysis has two important advantages. The first is relevance. Within limits set by the wisdom and skill of the test constructor, the score on his test does come closer than any other measure is likely to come to measuring what he wished to measure. The second is convenience. The total score on the test whose items are being analyzed is always readily available.

The selection of highly discriminating items, using total test score as the criterion, results in a test whose items are valid measures of what the whole test measures. In this sense, item analysis is a technique of item validation. But the kind of analysis and selection we have been considering does not demonstrate, and might not even improve, the validity of the test as a whole. What it can do to the test as a whole, and this is no small thing, is to make the test more reliable, and thus probably more valid too.

The fact that the score on an item being analyzed contributes to the total score on the test, the criterion against which the item is being tested, makes the index of discrimination somewhat greater than it would be if the item score did not contribute to the test score.

The total score on a comprehensive test does not always appear to provide the ideal criterion for judging the discriminating power of a particular item in the test. Consider a complex test of English composition, for example, in which various subsets of items test grammar, diction, spelling, punctuation, and organization. Should the students be placed in upper or lower criterion groups on the basis of total score on the entire complex test or would it be better to use as a criterion the score on the spelling test items alone?

When the items in a test can be grouped in fairly distinct subsets or types, as in the English test just mentioned, a subset score provides a more clearly relevant criterion for the items in that subset than does the total test score. Unfortunately, the subset score, based on fewer items, provides a less reliable criterion. Also, on the practical side, the use of different criterion groups complicates the process of analyzing the items in a test.

---

[11] David G. Ryans, "The Results of Internal Consistency and External Validation Procedures Applied in the Analysis of Test Items Measuring Professional Information," *Educational and Psychological Measurement*, XI (1951), 549-60.

Finally, if the test is considered to be homogeneous enough so that a single score is adequate for reporting student achievement, then a single score should also be adequate for selecting the upper and lower groups for item analysis.

All things considered, the best procedure for general use seems to be that of using the total test score as the basis for selecting the criterion groups. Only in special circumstances, as when separate scores are to be reported on subsets of items, should consideration be given to the use of criterion scores from more clearly relevant subsets of items.

9. Must all items discriminate?

In an educational achievement test whose principal function is to distinguish different levels of achievement as clearly as possible, it is desirable for each item to have as high an index of discrimination as possible. Since an item which is answered correctly by all examinees, or incorrectly by all, cannot discriminate at all, such an item has no place in the kind of achievement test we have been considering.

But items of this sort may be appropriate in another kind of achievement test whose function is to report how many tasks the examinee can perform of some meaningful, clearly defined collection of tasks. For example, such a test might be given to determine how many words on a certain list the individual can spell correctly or how many words on a list of technical terms he can define correctly. Let us refer to this kind of test as a test of "content mastery" to distinguish it from the test of "relative achievement" referred to in the preceding paragraph.

Most tests of educational achievement are and probably should be tests of relative achievement rather than tests of content mastery. It is often difficult to make the score on a test of content mastery clearly meaningful. To achieve this goal, the tasks relevant to an area of content must be defined and described clearly and the process of item writing must be standardized so that irrelevant variations in item difficulty are minimized. Further, scores on tests of content mastery tend to be considerably less reliable than tests of relative achievement, for equivalent numbers of items. This is a result of including items in the content mastery test regardless of their discriminating power and hence regardless of their contribution to reliability. For these reasons the prevailing emphasis on tests of relative achievement rather than on tests of content mastery seems reasonably well justified.

The preference for items which show a high index of discrimination should not be pushed to the point of excluding from the test those items which are clearly relevant to some aspect of the achievement to be measured by the test, but which cannot be made to yield a high index of discrimination. Suppose, for example, that the test specifications call for an item covering some information or skill but that all the items written to test this aspect of achievement turn out to have indices of discrimination under .20. Suppose, further, that careful examination of the items reveals no serious technical flaws, such as ambiguous or misleading wording, unintended clues, or absence of one clearly defensible best answer. What should the test constructor do?

If the low discrimination is due to the extreme ease or extreme difficulty of the items, they should, if possible, be revised to make them more appropriate in difficulty. If such attempts at revision prove unsuccessful or seem certain to fail, the items should be dropped. However defensible their inclusion may be in principle, they will make in practice little difference in the relative scores of the students.

If the low discrimination is not due to technical weakness in the item or to inappropriate difficulty, the test constructor should review the reasons for including items of this kind in the test. If he remains convinced that they do belong, he should include them regardless of their low discrimination. In fact, he may wish to include more items of this kind than originally planned, so that the relative weakness of each item's contribution to the total score can be offset by the weight of a greater number of such items.

10. The index of item difficulty

The measure of item difficulty obtained in Step 5 is, in a sense, an inverse measure. It expresses difficulty as the per cent of responses which are correct. The higher the numerical value of this index of difficulty, the easier the item. This inverse relation between what is ordinarily meant by difficulty and the index used to measure it is illogical, but the convention has become so firmly established that to attempt a change would be only to contribute to confusion.

The index of difficulty of a test item is not solely the property of that item. It reflects also the ability of the group responding to the item. Hence instead of saying, "The index of difficulty for this item is 56 per cent," it would be better to say, "When this item was administered to that particular group, its index of difficulty was 56 per cent."

The estimation of item difficulty from the responses of only the upper and lower groups, disregarding the middle group, involves some bias. Omitting the information provided by the middle group also has the effect of reducing the size of sample on which the difficulty index is based. This, in turn, tends to increase sampling errors somewhat. However, the use made of difficulty indices in classroom testing is seldom crucial enough to justify high precision in their determination.

It is sometimes suggested that item-difficulty indices should be corrected for chance success (or guessing) so that the per cent reported would indicate what proportion of the group *knew* the answer, instead of including also those who just luckily happened to get it right. Even if such a correction were logically defensible, which is by no means clear, the refinement might be hard to justify in consideration of the use typically made of item-difficulty indices in classroom test construction.

This use will ordinarily involve mainly items of low discrimination and will suggest whether the low discrimination can be attributed to extreme ease or difficulty of the item. Of course, if the results of the test are used for diagnosis of pupil difficulty or of inadequate teaching, the indices of item difficulty will have added significant uses.

11. Distribution of item difficulty values

It is quite natural to assume, and many test constructors do assume, that a good test intended to discriminate well over a fairly wide range of levels of achievement must include some easy items to test the poorer students and some difficult items to test the better students. But the facts of educational achievement testing seldom warrant such an assumption. The items in most achievement tests are not like a set of hurdles of different heights, all of which present essentially the same task and differ only in level of difficulty. Achievement test items do differ in difficulty, but they differ also in the kind of task they present.

Suppose a class of twenty students takes a test on which twelve of the students answer Item 6 correctly but only eight answer Item 7 correctly. A reasonable assumption is that any student who answered the harder question (Item 7) correctly should also answer correctly the easier question (Item 6). Anyone who missed the easier question would also be expected to miss the harder. But such assumptions and expectations are often mistaken when applied to educational achievement tests.

Table 11.3 presents data on the responses of eleven students to

TABLE 11.3

Responses of Eleven Students to Six Test Items

Student	A	B	C	D	E	F	G	H	I	J	K
Item 1	+	+	+	+	+	+	+	+	+	0	0
Item 2	+	+	+	+	+	+	0	+	0	0	+
Item 3	+	0	+	0	0	+	+	+	+	0	0
Item 4	+	+	0	+	0	0	+	0	0	+	0
Item 5	+	+	+	+	+	0	0	0	0	0	0
Item 6	+	+	0	0	+	0	0	0	0	+	0

six test items. A plus (+) in the table represents a correct response, a zero (0) an incorrect response. In this exhibit the students have been arranged in order of ability, and the items in order of difficulty. Note that the item missed by good student B was not one of the most difficult items. Poor student J missed all of the easier items but managed correct answers to two of the more difficult items.

It is possible to imagine a test which would give highly consistent results across items and across students when administered to a particular group. Results would be called consistent if success by a particular student on a particular item practically guaranteed success on all other items in the test which were easier for the group than that item. Correspondingly, failure on a particular item would almost guarantee failure on all harder items if the student responses were highly consistent. But a test showing such a degree of consistency among the responses would also be characterized by much higher reliability than ordinarily obtained with the same number of items. Such tests can be imagined but are seldom met with in practice. This is another reason why specifications requiring that the test include items ranging widely in difficulty are seldom warranted.

Most item writers produce some items which are ineffective (nondiscriminating) because they are too difficult or too easy. Efforts to improve the accuracy with which a test measures, that is, to improve its reliability, usually have the effect of reducing the range of item difficulties rather than of increasing it. The differences in difficulty that remain among items which are highest in discrimination are usually more than adequate to make the test effective in discriminating different levels of achievement over the whole range of abilities for which the test is expected to be used.

Some data from a simple experimental study of the relation between spread of item difficulty values, on the one hand, and spread of test scores and level of reliability coefficients, on the other, are presented in Figure 11.1.

Three synthetic tests of sixteen items each were "constructed" by selecting items from a sixty-one-item trial form of a Contemporary Affairs test. This trial form had been administered to over 300 college freshmen and an item analysis performed to yield indices of difficulty and discrimination for each item. The items constituting the three sixteen-item tests were selected so as to yield tests differing widely in difficulty distributions.

> In test C, the items selected were *concentrated* in difficulty values as near the middle of the entire distribution of difficulty values as possible.

> In test D, the items selected were *distributed* in difficulty values as uniformly as possible over the entire range of available difficulty values.

> In test E, the items were selected for *extreme* difficulty values, including the eight easiest and the eight most difficult items.

When these three sixteen-item "tests" were scored on a set of 253 answer sheets for the sixty-one-item tryout form, the distributions of scores displayed in the histograms of Figure 11.1 were

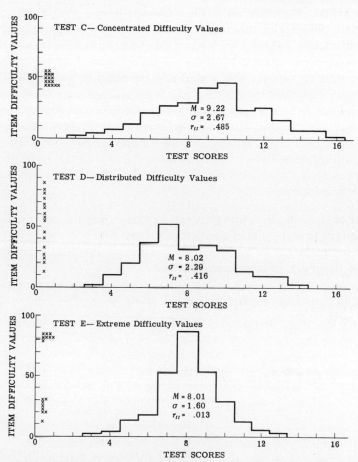

Figure 11.1. Relation of Distribution of Test Scores to Distribution of Item Difficulty Values

obtained. The distributions of item difficulties are indicated by the tally marks along the vertical scales to the left of each histogram.

Note the inverse relation between the spread of item difficulties and the spread of test scores. The wider the dispersion of difficulty values, the more concentrated the distribution of test scores. Note, too, the very low reliability of scores on the test composed only of very easy or very difficult items and the somewhat higher reliability of the scores when items are concentrated near the midpoint in difficulty than when they are distributed in difficulty. In short, the findings of this study support the recommendation that items of middle difficulty be favored in the construction of achievement tests.

The relation between the spread of item difficulty values and the reliability and validity of a test has been studied analytically and experimentally by a number of other investigators including Cronbach and Warrington, Lord, and Richardson.[12] Their articles will shed additional light on the nature of the problem and on its optimum solution.

12. Item selection

One of the two direct uses that can be made of indices of discrimination is in the selection of the best (i.e., most highly discriminating) items for inclusion in an improved version of the test. How high should the index of discrimination be?

Experience with a wide variety of classroom tests suggests that the indices of item discrimination for most of them can be evaluated on these terms:

Index of Discrimination	Item Evaluation
.40 and up	Very good items
.30 to .39	Reasonably good but possibly subject to improvement
.20 to .29	Marginal items, usually needing and being subject to improvement
Below .19	Poor items, to be rejected or improved by revision

It probably goes without saying that no special effort should be made to secure a spread of item discrimination indices. The higher the better. Of two tests otherwise alike, the one in which the average index of item discrimination is the highest will always be the better, i.e., the more reliable.

A fairly simple and direct relationship exists between the mean

[12] Lee J. Cronbach and Willard G. Warrington, "Efficiency of Multiple-choice Tests as a Function of Spread of Item Difficulties," *Psychometrika*, XVII (1952), 127-47; Frederic M. Lord, "The Relation of the Reliability of Multiple-choice Tests to the Distribution of Item Difficulties," *Psychometrika*, XVII (1952), 181-94; and Marion W. Richardson, "The Relation Between the Difficulty and the Differential Validity of a Test," *Psychometrika*, I (1936), 33-49.

value of D, the number of items in a test, and its probable reliability coefficient. Suppose that a test is composed of one hundred items whose mean index of discrimination D is .40. Suppose that a class of thirty-seven students took this test, so that ten students each constitute the top and bottom 27 per cent groups. Then for a typical item whose value of D is .40, the ten good students must have given four more correct responses than the ten poor students. Taking all one hundred items into account, the ten good students must have given 400 more correct responses than the ten poor students. Then the difference between good and poor groups in mean test score must have been 40.

The good and poor groups constitute the top 27 per cent and bottom 27 per cent, respectively, of the total group. Assuming the scores of the total group to be normally distributed, the difference between the mean scores of the top 27 per cent and the bottom 27 per cent should be 2.45 times the standard deviation of the scores in the total group. Kelley showed that the mean deviation of the scores in the tail of a normal distribution is equal to $y\sigma/q$, where y is the height of the ordinate of a unit normal distribution at the point of truncation, σ is the standard deviation of the distribution, and q is the proportion of the total area under the curve that is included in the tail.[13] If $q = .27$, the point of truncation must be .61 σ from the mean, so that y equals .33. Hence the mean score of the upper group is .33 $\sigma/.27$, or 1.225 σ above the mean. Since the mean score of the lower group is also 1.225 σ below the mean, the difference in these group means must be 2.45 σ.

In the example described earlier, the difference in group means was .40. Hence in this case, assuming a normal distribution of scores, the standard deviation of scores would be expected to be 16.35 and the variance of the scores 267. If we assume further that the mean score on the test is 50 and all items equally difficult, the reliability formulas KR20 (10.5) or KR21 (10.7) give the value .915 for the coefficient of reliability of the test scores.

Using various other values for D, but otherwise the same assumptions, the values for the standard deviation and the reliability coefficient of a one hundred-item test can be calculated. These are shown in Table 11.4, which indicates that a mean index of discrimination of near .40 is needed in order to achieve a reliability of

---
[13] Kelley, *op. cit.*

TABLE 11.4

Relation of Item Discrimination to Test
Reliability for a One Hundred-item Test

Mean Index of Discrimination	Standard Deviation of Scores	Reliability of Scores
.1225	5.0	.00
.16	6.53	.42
.20	8.16	.63
.30	12.25	.84
.40	16.32	.915
.50	20.40	.949

more than .90 in a one hundred-item test. It shows, also, that even in a test of zero reliability the items would show a mean index of discrimination D, of about .12. This is due to the fact that the item whose discrimination is being measured contributes itself to the total test scores used as a basis for measuring discrimination.

The fewer the items in the test, the larger this spurious element in the index of discrimination is likely to be. Table 11.5 shows, for

TABLE 11.5

Values of D Indicating Zero Reliability
for Tests of Various Length

Number of Items* in the Test	Mean Index of Discrimination D
6	.50
9	.40
17	.30
37	.20
67	.15
150	.10
600	.05

* Used to determine upper and lower groups, including the item whose discrimination is to be measured.

tests of various lengths, how large the mean index of discrimination might be for tests of zero reliability. These are essentially minimum values of D for tests of the length indicated. An index of discrimination determined for an item in a short test has a larger spurious element than one for an item in a longer test. These minimum values need to be kept in mind in the interpretation of indices of discrimination of this type.

It is easier to write items which show high discrimination in some fields, like mathematics and foreign languages, than in others, like reading or social studies. Part of the explanation may be that the difference between truth and error, between right and wrong is wider and more distinct in the former. Part of the explanation may also be that the subject matter of mathematics and foreign languages is more tightly organized and dependent on step-by-step mastery. Deficiencies in learning some of the preliminaries are hard to compensate for by extra efforts subsequently. This has the effect of widening the spread of levels of achievement and making the difference between upper and lower groups much greater in the case of mathematics and foreign languages than it is in the case of reading and social studies. Whatever the explanation, the fact of generally higher levels of item discrimination in some tests than in others seems quite clear and probably should be recognized in evaluating item-discrimination indices in different fields of testing.

13. Item revision

The second, and perhaps the more constructive, of the two direct uses which can be made of indices of item discrimination, in conjunction with other analysis data, is in the revision of the test items. Five items illustrating this process of revision on the basis of analysis data are presented and discussed here. These items were written for a test of background knowledge in the natural science area and were intended for use by high school students. They were administered to a representative group of students in a preliminary tryout. The responses of good and poor students to these items were analyzed, and those items whose analysis data were most satisfactory were selected for the final form of the test. Among the items which were rejected there appeared to be some which might be salvaged by revision. When revisions had been made, the items were tried out with another representative group of students and reanalyzed. Results of the tryouts before and after revision for five selected items are indicated in the following paragraphs.

The first item deals with the distinction between the terms "climate" and "weather."

37%   What, if any, is the distinction between climate
.13   and weather?
          1. There is no important distinction. (1-6)
          2. Climate is primarily a matter of temperature and rainfall, while weather includes many other natural phenomena. (33-51)
      *3. Climate pertains to longer periods of time than weather. (43-30)
          4. Weather pertains to natural phenomena on a *local* rather than a *national* scale. (23-13)

This item is somewhat too difficult for the group tested (only seventy-three correct responses among 200 students) and does not discriminate well (only thirteen more good than poor students answered it correctly). Examination of the response counts indicates that the second response was attractive to a considerable number of good students and that the fourth response was more attractive to good students than to poor. Since the stem of the question seemed basically clear and since the intended correct response seemed reasonable, efforts in revision were concentrated on changing distracters 2 and 4. It appeared that response 2 could be made less attractive by making it simpler and somewhat more specific. Since response 4 seemed much too plausible to the better students in the group being tested, it was "spoiled" by substituting a more obviously incorrect response. The revised item (revisions in upper-case letters) reads:

62%   What, if any, is the distinction between climate
.58   and weather?
          1. There is no important distinction. (2-22)
          2. CLIMATE IS PRIMARILY A MATTER OF RAINFALL, WHILE WEATHER IS PRIMARILY A MATTER OF TEMPERATURE. (3-25)
      *3. Climate pertains to longer periods of time than weather. (91-33)
          4. WEATHER IS DETERMINED BY CLOUDS, WHILE CLIMATE IS DETERMINED BY WINDS. (4-20)

Analysis data of the revised item reveal that the revisions were effective. The changed item is much easier and much more highly discriminating than the original. Only nine of the good students chose distracters. Equally important is the fact that these revisions did not appreciably increase the number of poor students choosing the correct response. It is interesting to note that on the second try-out the number of poor students who chose response number 1 increased markedly, even though this response had not been altered.

The next item deals with the common misconception that meteors are "falling stars."

36%   Do stars ever fall to the earth?
.35   1. Yes. They may be seen often, particularly dur-
          ing certain months. (12-28)
       2. Yes. There are craters caused by falling stars in
          certain regions of the earth. (30-43)
       3. No. The earth moves too rapidly for its gravita-
          tional force to act on the stars. (5-11)
     *4. No. The falling of a single average star would
          destroy the earth. (53-18)

This item again is somewhat too difficult, though its discriminating power is fairly good. The item might be made somewhat easier by revising the second response. This response can be legitimately criticized as "tricky" because there are *meteor* craters. Hence in the revision, this response alone was changed.

42%   Do stars ever fall to the earth?
.56   1. Yes. They may be seen often, particularly dur-
          ing certain months. (20-68)
       2. NO. PLANETS LIKE THE EARTH HAVE
          NO ATTRACTION FOR STARS. (1-4)
       3. No. The earth moves too rapidly for its gravita-
          tional force to act on the stars. (9-14)
     *4. No. The falling of a single average star would
          destroy the earth. (70-14)

The change obviously spoiled the attractiveness of the second response. Again it is interesting to note that this change did not increase the proportion of poor students choosing the correct answer but apparently shifted most of their choices to the first response, which had not been changed in the revision.

The next item attempted to get at the notion, important in "dry farming," that cultivation of the soil surface helps to conserve soil moisture.

23%   Under which of the following conditions is sub-
.09   soil moisture most likely to come to the surface
        and evaporate during dry weather?
        1. When the temperature of the soil is high. (12-26)
        2. When the soil is cultivated regularly. (56-40)
        3. When the air pressure is high. (5-16)
     *4. When the soil is closely packed. (27-18)

This item is much too difficult and is low in discrimination. The chief offender is response 2. Not only was it attractive to a great many students, but it was even more attractive to the good students than to those of low ability. Since this response to the stem of the items reveals acceptance of an idea which is exactly opposite to the idea for which we were testing, the data should probably have been interpreted to mean that the item could not be salvaged. However, an attempt was made by writing a new second response.

13%   Under which of the following conditions is subsoil
.02   moisture most likely to come to the surface and
        evaporate during dry weather?
        1. When the temperature of the soil is high. (59-25)
        2. WHEN THE AIR ABOVE THE SOIL IS
            MOTIONLESS. (15-33)
        3. When the air pressure is high. (12-30)
     *4. When the soil is closely packed. (14-12)

This revision improved the performance of the second response but resulted in no improvement in the item as a whole. In fact, the item is even more difficult and less discriminating than it was before. The notion that closely packed soil facilitates capillary action and thus hastens the loss of soil moisture apparently is not widely enough held to make possible the construction of a discriminating item on this point for this population of students.

The next item deals with cause of shortage in the ground water supply.

48%   Water shortages in many localities have been caused
        by which, if any, of these factors?

.17   1. Removal of natural plant cover allowing faster
          run-off into streams. (17-13)
       2. Increased demands for water in homes, busi-
          nesses, and industry. (15-26)
       3. Neither 1 or 2. (12-22)
    *4. Both 1 and 2. (56-39)

This item is of appropriate difficulty but is not highly discriminating. In this case it appeared that the fault might lie with the
design of the item itself. The question was framed in such a way
that there were two important correct answers, and hence it was
necessary to include each of these as a single, supposedly incorrect
response and to make "both" the correct response. This approach
is apparently somewhat confusing. Furthermore, no opportunities
are provided for the use of bona fide distracters. In the revision one
of the correct responses was placed in the stem of the item and
three bona fide distracters were provided as follows:

53% WHAT FACTOR, OTHER THAN INCREASED
.62   WATER USE, HAS BEEN RESPONSIBLE FOR
      WATER SHORTAGES IN MANY LOCALI-
      TIES?
      1. RESTRICTION OF STREAM FLOW BY
         HYDROELECTRIC DAMS. (3-22)
      2. DISTURBANCE OF NORMAL RAINFALL
         BY ARTIFICIAL RAINMAKING. (3-18)
      3. INTENSIVE FARM CULTIVATION,
         WHICH PERMITS MOST RAINFALL TO
         SOAK INTO THE GROUND. (10-38)
    *4. REMOVAL OF NATURAL PLANT COVER
         ALLOWING FASTER RUN-OFF INTO
         STREAMS. (84-22)

The item was made somewhat easier and much more discriminating. In this case, the revision process worked in a way that
gladdened the heart of the item writer.

The final item in this illustrative series deals with mechanical
advantage of a single fixed pulley.

12% What is the maximum mechanical advantage ob-
.21   tainable with a single fixed pulley and a rope which
      will break under a load of 500 pounds?
    *1. 1 (22-1)   3. 500 (38-40)
     2. 2 (20-30)   4. 1,000 (20-29)

While this item appeared to discriminate marginally, it was far too difficult. The item writer assumed that the principal difficulty lay in the abstract nature of the concept of the mechanical advantage. Hence he attempted to rephrase the item using a concrete situation.

39% A WORKMAN LIFTS PLANKS TO THE TOP
−.07 OF A SCAFFOLD BY PULLING DOWN ON A ROPE PASSED OVER A SINGLE FIXED PULLEY ATTACHED TO THE TOP OF THE SCAFFOLD. THE ROPE WILL BREAK UNDER A LOAD OF 500 POUNDS, AND THE WORKMAN WEIGHS 200 POUNDS. WHAT IS THE HEAVIEST LOAD THE WORKMAN CAN LIFT WITH THE PULLEY?

  1. 100 pounds (1-6)   3. 400 pounds (32-23)
*2. 200 pounds (35-42) 4. 500 pounds (32-29)

The item in this form was considerably easier, but it turned out to have negative discriminating power. The correct response to the revised item was much more obvious to the poor students than was the correct response in the original item and only somewhat more obvious to the good students. It appears that the problem situation, though completely defensible scientifically, is just complex enough to mislead the good students, while being fairly simple on a superficial basis to the poor students.

The foregoing items do not illustrate all the possible ways in which item analysis data may be interpreted to aid in item revision. What they do is to illustrate the general nature of the process and to indicate that it *may* be highly successful.

14. Summary

Some of the principal ideas developed in this chapter are summarized in these sixteen statements.

1. Item analysis is a useful tool in the progressive improvement of a teacher's classroom tests.
2. Item analysis begins with the counting of responses made by good and poor students to each of the items in the test.
3. It is convenient and statistically defensible to consider as "good"

students those whose scores place them in the upper 27 per cent of the total group and to consider as "poor" students those whose scores place them in the lower 27 per cent of the total group.

4. Using extreme groups smaller than 27 per cent of the total or giving extra weight to the responses on very high-score and very low-score papers may improve the precision of item analysis data.

5. Responses may be counted by hand tally, by show of hands in class, or by machine.

6. A convenient and satisfactory index of discrimination D is simply the difference between upper and lower 27 per cent groups in the proportion of correct responses.

7. The value of D can be as great as 1.00 only if the item is of 50 per cent difficulty. For extremely easy or extremely difficult items its maximum value will be much lower.

8. The value of D is exactly proportional to the net number of correct discriminations an item makes.

9. While logical objections can be made to the use of the total score on a test as a criterion for analyzing the items in the test, the practical effect of these shortcomings is usually small, and the practical convenience of disregarding them is great.

10. In exceptional circumstances, as when content mastery alone is to be tested or when some essential aspect of achievement is difficult to measure, the inclusion of items of low discrimination in a test may be justified.

11. The proportion of correct response to an item in upper and lower 27 per cent groups combined provides a satisfactory measure of item difficulty.

12. For most classroom tests it is desirable that all of the items be of middle difficulty, with none of them extremely easy or extremely difficult.

13. In general, the wider the distribution of item difficulty values in a test, the more restricted the distribution of test scores and the lower the reliability of those scores.

14. Good classroom test items should have indices of discrimination of .30 or more.

15. The reliability coefficient of a test can be predicted from the number of items in the test and the mean index of discrimination.

16. Data on the response choices of good and poor students can be used as a basis for item revision and improvement.

REFERENCES

Cronbach, Lee J. and Willard G. Warrington, "Efficiency of Multiple-choice Tests as a Function of Spread of Item Difficulties," *Psychometrika,* XVII (1952), 127-47.

Davis, Frederick B., "Item Analysis Data," *Harvard Education Papers No. 2,* Graduate School of Education, Harvard University, 1946.

———, "Item Analysis in Relation to Educational and Psychological Testing," *Psychological Bulletin,* XLIX (1952), 97-121.

Diamond, Solomon, "The Typewriter as an Aid in Item Analysis," *American Journal of Psychology,* L (1939), 111-13.

Diederich, Paul, "Short-cut Statistics for Teacher-made Tests," *Evaluation and Advisory Service Series No. 5,* p. 44. Princeton, N.J.: Educational Testing Service, 1960.

Ebel, Robert L., "Procedures for the Analysis of Classroom Tests," *Educational and Psychological Measurement,* XIV (1954), 352-64.

———, "The Reliability of an Index of Item Discrimination," *Educational and Psychological Measurement* (1951), pp. 403-9.

Feldt, Leonard S. and Alfred E. Hall, "Stability of Four Item Discrimination Indices over Groups of Different Average Ability," *American Educational Research Journal,* Vol. I, (1964) pp. 35-46.

Findley, Warren G., "Rationale for the Evaluation of Item Discrimination Statistics," *Educational and Psychological Measurement,* XVI (1956), 175-80.

Flanagan, John C., *Calculating Correlation Coefficients.* Pittsburgh, Pa.: American Institute for Research, 1962.

———, "The Effectiveness of Short Methods for Calculating Correlation Coefficients," *Psychological Bulletin,* XLIX (July, 1952), 342-48.

———, "General Considerations in the Selection of Test Items and a Short Method of Estimating the Product-Moment Coefficient from the Data at the Tails of the Distributions," *Journal of Educational Psychology,* XXX (1939), 674-80.

Johnson, A. Pemberton, "Notes on a Suggested Index of Item Validity: The U-L Index," *Journal of Educational Psychology,* LXII (1951), 499-504.

Kelley, Truman L., "The Selection of Upper and Lower Groups for the Validation of Test Items," *Journal of Educational Psychology,* XXX (1939), 17-24.

Lord, Frederic M., "The Relation of the Reliability of Multiple-choice

Tests to the Distribution of Item Difficulties," *Psychometrika*, XVII (1952), 181-94.

Richardson, Marion W., "The Relation Between the Difficulty and the Differential Validity of a Test," *Psychometrika*, I (1936), 33-49.

Ryans, David G., "The Results of Internal Consistency and External Validation Procedures Applied in the Analysis of Test Items Measuring Professional Information," *Educational and Psychological Measurement*, XI (1951), 549-60.

Turnbull, William W., "A Normalized Graphic Method of Item Analysis," *Journal of Educational Psychology*, XXXVII (1946), 129-41.

I2 The Validity of Classroom Tests

Examinations comprise a crucial aspect of the whole educational process, since they represent willy-nilly what all the fine words have been about. Moreover examinations furnish practically the only objective evidence of the value of a course of instruction. A published examination (and examinations are always published, whether officially or unofficially) presents a fair statement of the course objectives. All else that is said about the course may be summarily classified in the category of "pious hopes."

M. W. RICHARDSON

1. The concept of validity

A recent radio news item reported results of a scientific investigation of human anxiety. After paying his respects briefly to the elaborate and esoteric methods by which psychologists attempt to measure anxiety, the commentator came to the point that justified his report. How anxious are the people of the United States, in comparison with those in other countries? Expressing pleased surprise he reported that, despite our restlessness, we are less anxious than the people of India, Italy, Japan, England, and several other countries.

One may guess that many of those who heard the report accepted it as true without much question. It was, after all, the result of a scientific investigation, done by an eminent psychologist, using higher mathematics and electronic computers. Anxiety is a familiar experience. It does not seem unreasonable in this age of scientific marvels that anxiety should be measured precisely enough to justify the conclusion that the people of India are, on the whole, more anxious than the people of the United States.

But some specialists in the measurement of human traits would be less inclined to accept the report unquestioningly. They would remember that anxiety is a subjective sensation and that the problems of measuring subjective sensations have proved very difficult to solve in many cases.[1] No standard, generally accepted method of measuring anxiety exists. Some of the different measures that have been proposed and tried out yield quite different results. So the specialists might be more inclined than the layman to ask, "What *kind* of anxiety do Italians have more of than Englishmen?" or "What kind of *evidence* supports the view that Indians show more anxiety than Japanese?" They would, in short, raise questions about the validity of the measures of anxiety on which the conclusions in the news report were based.

Validity has been defined in different ways by different authors. Lindquist has said, "The validity of a test may be defined as the accuracy with which it measures that which it is intended to measure, or as the degree to which it approaches infallibility in measuring what it purports to measure." [2] This definition suggests that to determine how valid a test is, one must compare the reality of what it *does* measure with some ideal conception of what it *ought* to measure. Cureton has expressed a somewhat narrower, but more operationally oriented version of essentially the same idea. "The validity of a test is an estimate of the correlation between the raw test scores and the 'true' (that is, perfectly reliable) criterion scores." [3] Most of the widely accepted, basic definitions of validity tend to follow this same general pattern.

---

[1] Henry K. Beecher, *Measurement of Subjective Responses* (New York: Oxford University Press, Inc., 1959).

[2] E. F. Lindquist, *A First Course in Statistics* (rev. ed.; Boston: Houghton Mifflin Company, 1942), p. 213.

[3] E. E. Cureton, "Validity," in *Educational Measurement,* ed. E. F. Lindquist (Washington, D.C.: American Council on Education, 1951), p. 625.

While there is merit in this conception of validity, it also has shortcomings.[4] To say that a test is valid in so far as it measures what it ought to measure leaves a very difficult question unanswered in many cases. That is the question, "What should the test measure?" Criterion scores that measure exactly the same thing as the test is intended to measure are seldom available, even in unreliable form, for most classroom tests of educational achievement.

It is not surprising, therefore, that few classroom tests can claim verified validity in terms of this conception. What may be surprising is that physical scientists, who probably do a better job of measuring, on the whole, than psychologists and educators, seem to worry very little about this kind of validity. They tend to worry more about how accurate and how useful their measurements are than about essentially unanswerable questions which ask whether they are measuring what they *intend* to measure or what their procedures *purport* to measure.

Consider this question, "Which is the more valid measure of central tendency, the mean or the median?" Surely this question has much in common with the question, "Which is the more valid measure of intelligence, the Stanford-Binet or the Wechsler scale for children?" Why is it that the first question is almost never asked, whereas the second is asked frequently? Neither question, it may be pointed out, has ever been answered conclusively. In neither case do we have any independent external criterion to which we can appeal for a decision.

With respect to the first question, our behavior is more like that of the typical scientist; that is, we define the measurements, develop their properties, and use whichever is more appropriate or convenient in a particular situation. With respect to the second, we withhold full confidence in either test in the hope that someone will find an answer to the essentially unanswerable question we have asked. Neither central tendency nor intelligence is a meaningful quantitative concept apart from some specific operations for calculation or some specific testing procedures.

There are, of course, other definitions of validity than the two

---

[4] Robert L. Ebel, "Must All Tests Be Valid?" *American Psychologist*, XVI (October, 1961), 640-47.

quoted earlier in this chapter. Edgerton has said: "By 'validity' we refer to the extent to which the measuring device is useful for a given purpose." [5] Cronbach explains: "The more fully and confidently a test can be interpreted, the greater its validity." [6] Guilford suggested that, "In a very general sense, a test is valid for anything with which it correlates." [7] And a good dictionary suggests that a test, or anything else, is valid if it is "Founded on truth or fact; capable of being justified, supported or defended; well grounded; sound." [8] Such definitions as these broaden the concept of validity considerably and permit a formulation that may be of more practical value in classroom testing.

2. Types of validity

One approach to this alternative conception is to consider some of the different types of validity that have been identified by various writers. *Technical Recommendations for Achievement Tests*, formulated and published by a number of specialists in educational and psychological measurement, mentions four types of validity: content, predictive, concurrent, and construct.[9] Anastasi discusses face validity and factorial validity in addition to content validity and various types of empirical validity.[10] Ross and Stanley mention curricular validity.[11] Gulliksen has discussed intrinsic validity.[12] And Mosier differentiated four types of face validity: validity by assumption,

[5] H. A. Edgerton, "The Place of Measuring Instruments in Guidance," in *The Measurement of Student Adjustment and Achievement*, eds. Wilma T. Donahue, C. H. Coombs, and R. M. W. Travers (Ann Arbor, Mich.: University of Michigan Press, 1949), p. 52.

[6] L. J. Cronbach, "Validity," in *Encyclopedia of Educational Research*, ed. C. W. Harris (New York: The Macmillan Company, 1960).

[7] J. P. Guilford, "New Standards for Test Evaluation," *Educational and Psychological Measurement*, VI (Winter, 1946), 427-38.

[8] *Webster's New Collegiate Dictionary* (Springfield, Mass.: G. and C. Merriam Company, 1951), p. 940.

[9] American Educational Research Association, *Technical Recommendations for Achievement Tests* (Washington, D.C.: AERA, 1955), p. 16.

[10] Anne Anastasi, *Psychological Testing* (New York: The Macmillan Company, 1954), p. 127.

[11] C. C. Ross and Julian C. Stanley, *Measurement in Today's Schools* (Englewood Cliffs, N.J.: Prentice-Hall, Inc., 1954), p. 101.

[12] Harold Gulliksen, "Intrinsic Validity," *The American Psychologist*, V (October, 1950), 511.

validity by definition, the appearance of validity, and validity by hypothesis.[13] Here are brief characterizations of several of these types of validity.

"*Concurrent validity* is concerned with the relation of test scores to an accepted contemporary criterion of performance on the variable which the test is intended to measure." [14]

Construct validity is concerned with "what psychological qualities a test measures" and is evaluated "by demonstrating that certain explanatory constructs account to some degree for performance on the test." [15]

"*Content validity* is concerned with the adequacy of sampling of a specified universe of content." [16]

"*Curricular validity* is determined by examining the content of the test itself and judging the degree to which it is a true measure of the important objectives of the course, or a truly representative sampling of the essential materials of instruction." [17]

Empirical validity "refers to the relation between test scores and a criterion, the latter being an independent and direct measure of that which the test is designed to predict." [18]

"*Face validity* refers, not to what a test necessarily measures, but to what it appears to measure." [19]

"The *factorial validity* of a test is the correlation between that test and the factor common to a group of tests or other measures of behavior. . . . such validity is based on factor analysis." [20]

Intrinsic validity involves the use of experimental techniques other than correlation with a criterion to provide objective, quantitative evidence that the test is measuring what it ought to measure.[21]

"*Predictive validity* is concerned with the relation of test scores

---

[13] Charles I. Mosier, "A Critical Examination of the Concepts of Face Validity," *Educational and Psychological Measurement,* VII (Summer, 1947), 192.

[14] American Educational Research Association, *op. cit.,* p. 16.

[15] American Psychological Association, Inc., *Technical Recommendations for Psychological Tests and Diagnostic Techniques* (Washington, D.C.: APA, 1954), p. 14.

[16] American Educational Research Association, *op. cit.,* p. 16.

[17] Ross and Stanley, *op. cit.,* p. 101.

[18] Anastasi, *op. cit.,* p. 127.

[19] *Ibid.,* p. 121.

[20] *Ibid.,* p. 123.

[21] Gulliksen, *op. cit.,* p. 511.

to measures on a criterion based on performance at some later time." [22]

"Validity by definition: For some tests the objective is defined solely in terms of the population of questions from which the sample comprising the test was drawn, e.g., when the ability to handle the one hundred number facts of addition is tested by sampling of those number facts." [23]

These types of validity are not all distinctly different from each other. In fact, one or two of them are practically identical with one or two others. But enough major differences appear to justify grouping them into two major categories: those concerned with primary or direct validity and those concerned with secondary or derived validity. A test has direct, primary validity to the extent that the tasks included in it represent faithfully and in due proportion the kinds of tasks that provide an operational definition of the achievement or the trait in question. A test has derived, secondary validity to the extent that the scores it yields correlate with criterion scores which possess direct, primary validity. Thorndike and Hagen suggest a similar dichotomy of types of validity: those which depend primarily on rational analysis and professional judgment (here identified as *direct* validity) and those which depend on empirical and statistical evidence (which are designated here as *derived* validity).[24]

Some types of validity that seem appropriate for each category are listed below:

Direct	*Derived*
Validity by Definition	Empirical Validity
Content Validity	Concurrent Validity
Curricular Validity	Predictive Validity
Intrinsic Validity	Factorial Validity
Face Validity	Construct Validity

The distinction between the two categories is not sharp in all cases. For example, it can be argued that factorial validity and construct validity, despite their involvement of multiple measurements and

---

[22] American Educational Research Association, *op. cit.,* p. 16.

[23] Charles I. Mosier, "A Critical Examination of the Concepts of Face Validity," *Educational and Psychological Measurement,* VII (Summer, 1947), 192.

[24] Robert L. Thorndike and Elizabeth Hagen, *Measurement and Evaluation in Psychology and Education* (New York: John Wiley & Sons, Inc., 1955), pp. 109-10.

coefficients of correlation, do represent a basic (primary) kind of validity. Still, a distinction seems warranted between primary validity, which must be built into a test and which can be evaluated only by examining critically the decisions of the test constructor, and derived validity, which always involves correlation with some real or hypothetical criterion.

3. Derived validity

There are two kinds of derived validity that are of principal interest to constructors of classroom tests—concurrent and predictive. Correlations between scores on a test and criterion measures available at the time the test is given indicate concurrent validity. Correlations between prior test scores and subsequent measures of achievement indicate predictive validity.

Efforts are sometimes made to determine the concurrent validity of educational achievement tests by correlating the test scores of pupils with the grades teachers assign to the same pupils. If the test scores *were* used to determine grades the correlation would have to be high, whether the test were any good or not. Part of the trouble is that teachers' grades often are not highly reliable. Another part is that the grades usually do, and usually ought to, reflect pupil achievements which the test could not or was not intended to measure. One could reasonably expect students who get grades of A in a biology course to make a higher average score on a biology achievement test than the students who get grades of B. But it would be unreasonable to expect every A student to make a higher score on the test than any B student. Further, one could probably show that the average score of A students in biology on an intelligence test was higher than the average score of the B students. Would this then validate the intelligence test as a biology test?

Predictive validity applies more to aptitude tests than to classroom tests of educational achievement. A case can be made for the contention that all measurement is for the purpose of prediction, but this does not alter the fact that there is a great difference between the way aptitude test scores and achievement test scores are typically used. The validities of classroom tests of educational achievement are seldom judged on the basis of how well they predict subsequent achievement.

4. Operational definitions

For many achievement tests the most important type of validation, sometimes the only possible type, is direct validation. Rulon has stressed the primary role of direct intrinsic validity for classroom tests in these words.

> What we need is to be able to choose between available test techniques on the basis of what operations we are trying to teach the learner to perform, and what materials we are trying to teach him to perform these operations upon. Both these materials and these operations should be represented in the test situation if the test is to be "obviously valid."
>
> Such a test must always be the criterion by which any not obviously valid test is validated.
>
> The "obviously valid" test is its own criterion.[25]

All types of direct validation require explicitly or by implication a definition of the achievement or trait to be measured. An essential characteristic of a measurable property, as Cook has pointed out, is that it must be clearly defined and unambiguous.[26] "So long as we stick to operational definitions in discussing and thinking about the abstract concepts used in educational measurements," says Cureton, "we will be on safe ground." [27] To be operationally defined, an achievement must be defined in terms of tasks that will differentiate between those having more and those having less of that achievement.

There is no better way of making clear what one means by achievement in algebra or chemistry or psychology than by describing how one would measure the amounts of those achievements that other persons possess. Much thinking and writing about educational goals and outcomes is vaguer than it ought to be because words like "intelligence," "motivation," and "creativity" are used freely without definite specification, and probably without any definite conception, of their operational definitions. Good tests of human traits can provide useful operational definitions of those traits.

[25] P. J. Rulon, "On the Validity of Educational Tests," *Harvard Educational Review*, XVI (1946), 290-96.

[26] Walter W. Cook, "Tests: Achievement," in *Encyclopedia of Educational Research*, ed. Walter S. Monroe (rev. ed.; New York: The Macmillan Company, 1950), p. 1464.

[27] Cureton, *op. cit.*, p. 641.

But many classroom tests do not provide very clear or authoritative definitions of the qualities they measure. They reflect the understandings and values and limitations of a single test author. Even though this test constructor has carefully thought out the basic rationale for the test (and many constructors of classroom tests fail to do this, unfortunately), this rationale may not be clearly evident to one who looks at the test. Thus while one can say that every test does define the trait it measures in some fashion, most classroom tests do not define what they measure very authoritatively or clearly. Usually they would be better tests if their authors would try to make them better operational definitions of what they ought to measure.

Many of the problems of validation that perplex test constructors are really problems of operationally defining the achievement or the trait to be tested. If anxiety, for example, were defined authoritatively, comprehensively, and unequivocally, in terms of the responses to standard test situations that differentiate more anxious from less anxious persons, there would be far less concern about the validity of an anxiety test. The same statement can be made about practically all other traits or achievements that instructors would like to test. The persistent difficulties that plague our efforts to measure some outcomes of education are less attributable to limitations of measurement than to uncertainty about what is to be measured.

Well, then, why not get busy defining in operational terms these traits and achievements in which we are interested? We should, but we should not look for quick, easy success. Two obstacles, at least, may be expected. One is the persistent belief that what a word (or a concept) like "anxiety" or "intelligence" or creativity means can somehow be discovered by research or by the analysis of data. But language is always invented, and what a term means is always determined by some consensus among past and present users of the term. Research can discover what people *do* mean by the term "anxiety." It cannot reveal what anxiety *ought* to mean. Tests cannot reveal what intelligence *really* is; they can only illustrate what certain test constructors believe that the term "intelligence" ought to mean.

But different tests thus imply different definitions of intelligence or of almost any other trait or achievement for which tests have ever been made. This suggests the second obstacle—the difficulty of reaching substantial agreement on the operational definition of a trait or an achievement. If agreement is not reached, if each test constructor projects his own unique perceptions and values and theories in each test he constructs, without regard for the perceptions and values and theories of others who build similar tests, nothing of general value has been defined and no test of general validity is likely to be produced.

Fortunately, our inability to discover in nature what a term should mean or the absence of any revelation of ultimate criteria for our tests does not condemn us to an endless Babel of competing operational definitions. Not all possible operational definitions of an achievement are likely to be equally reasonable. They are not likely to yield tests that prove equally useful. They are not likely to be publicized with equal vigor and skill. If the concept to be defined is necessary and useful, a consensus on its meaning will emerge in time. The process can be hastened if enough of those concerned with using the concept will dedicate enough of their time and energies to developing a rational consensus. Substantial progress has already been made in defining some traits and achievements in these terms. A great deal more would be useful.

5. The role of judgment

The dependence of direct intrinsic validity on human judgment makes some test specialists quite uneasy. Human judgment is fallible. Competent judges, as has been implied, may disagree. What these specialists would like to find is a way of determining test validity that does not involve fallible human judgments. Empirical test validation might provide this way if it were not for the problem of finding a valid criterion. But the difficulties and uncertainties involved in getting directly valid criterion measures are exactly as serious and troublesome as those of obtaining directly valid test scores. In fact, the two problems are almost identical, as Anastasi has indicated.[28] There is no means of test validation which is com-

[28] Anne Anastasi, "The Concept of Validity in the Interpretation of Test Scores," *Educational and Psychological Measurement*, X (Spring, 1950), 67-78.

pletely empirical, which is completely impersonal and objective, and which avoids the vagueness and uncertainty of human judgments altogether.

To say that the exercise of judgment is unavoidable in constructing valid tests or determining their validity is not to say that one man's judgment is as good as the next or that any man's judgment is above rational and corrective criticism. The decisions of the test constructor reflect his knowledge and those values. The knowledge may be incomplete. The reasoning may be faulty. Even the values may reflect faulty knowledge or reasoning. Assumptions which have not been, but could be, tested may be involved in the test constructor's decisions.

There is no simple, uniform, wholly objective procedure for determining the validity of a test or of a test item. The judgment of the test constructor is inevitably involved in the process of test construction. But his judgment is not beyond criticism and improvement. It can be refined and given a sounder basis, as Gulliksen has argued persuasively.[29] Not all the differences of opinion among test constructors with respect to questions of relevance are likely to be resolved quickly and surely by rational consideration and further experimental evidence. It is unlikely that a majority of the teachers of any subject will ever agree on one particular test as the ideal test of achievement in that subject. What can be expected is increasing awareness of, and agreement on, the essentials for validity in items purporting to test achievement in that subject. Capable, conscientious teachers are likely to make progressively better tests as they think and discuss what their tests ought to measure and as they invent and try out new tasks for their tests.[30]

6. Tasks and traits

This chapter has suggested that the validity of a test can be judged, in part at least, by studying the test itself. But does a test really measure what it appears to measure? Is this a test of scientific understanding, as its title claims, or is it really an intelli-

---

[29] Gulliksen, *op. cit.*

[30] Robert L. Ebel, "Obtaining and Reporting Evidence on Content Validity," *Educational and Psychological Measurement,* XVI (1956), 269-82.

gence test? Is that a test of intelligence, or is it really only a reading test?

If one is willing to accept as a definition of what a test is measuring a simple description of the tasks that the test requires a student to perform, then what a test appears to measure and what it really does measure will be practically identical. For example, the question, "What is the sum of $\frac{1}{5}$ and $\frac{1}{6}$?" appears to measure, and really does measure (beyond his ability to read), the student's ability to add two particular common fractions. The tasks in most classroom tests of educational achievement can be described as obviously and sensibly as this if one is willing to settle for an obvious, common-sense description.

But some are not. Some prefer to name their tests and describe what their tests are measuring, not in terms of the tasks they present, but in terms of the traits they presumably measure. So we have tests of intelligence, persistence, empathy, rigidity, creativity, anxiety, tolerance, perceptiveness, reasoning, and many other traits. For tests like these, the question of whether the test really measures what it claims to measure does arise, as indeed it should. Does the task of completing a figure analogy measure intelligence? Does ability to suggest unconventional uses for a brick measure creativity? Does ability to repeat a series of digits in reverse order measure memory?

Unfortunately, when such questions do arise, it is usually impossible to find satisfactory answers to them. For the traits these tests are supposed to measure are so highly generalized and so variable from one situation to another that a primary, intrinsically valid trait-defining test is seldom available for them. In the absence of such direct measures of the traits in question it is well nigh impossible to establish the validity of tests which claim to measure the traits indirectly.

Whenever measures of magnitude A, obtained by operations which define magnitude A, correlate with measures of magnitude B, obtained by operations which define magnitude B, then A measures B to some degree, and B measures A. But if we have no measures that define magnitude A, it is impossible to answer the question, "Do the operations we used to obtain measures B really measure A?" For reasons like these we can not always tell for sure whether test B does in fact measure trait A.

The generality of meaning of many trait names and the variability of the behavior attributed to such traits, depending on the specific circumstances, have caused much trouble for those who try to construct tests of these traits. It is not uncommon to find that the scores on three different tests, all purporting to measure the same trait, show intercorrelations of near zero. Further, there is a dangerous tendency to overgeneralize behavior predictions on the basis of trait names. Here is an example.

Applicants for positions on the police force in one city were shown this sign

```
Throw trash
in the
the trash cans.
```

and asked to comment on it. If they noticed the repetition of the word "the," they were given credit for perceptiveness and their chances of acceptance were improved.

All would agree that policemen need to be perceptive, to notice and remember important details like the license numbers of certain cars and descriptions of certain people. But there is little evidence, and really not much reason to expect, that people who are good at noticing printing errors in signs will also be good at noticing essential details at the scene of a crime.

Test items like the misprinted sign, which have only a verbal claim to direct relationship to the trait to be measured, do call for empirical validation. But perhaps they should be validated not as measures of perceptiveness, but as predictors of effectiveness on the police force. The trouble is that to do a good job of that kind of empirical validation is extremely difficult. The primary, directly valid measures of effectiveness are hard to design and harder still to use effectively. Fortunately, classroom tests can usually avoid most of these quicksands of trait measurement. If they are built carefully and skillfully enough they can have direct, primary validity.

7. Validity and reliability

The term "validity," as noted earlier in this chapter, is sometimes defined as the "accuracy with which the test measures what it is intended to measure." This is in contrast with "reliability," which can be defined as the "accuracy with which the test measures whatever it does measure." Clearly, a test which measures accurately what it is intended to measure also measures with equal or greater accuracy whatever it does measure. Hence to the degree that a test is valid it must also be reliable. Further, a test cannot measure more accurately what it is intended to measure than the accuracy with which it measures what it *does* measure.[31] Hence in order to be valid a test must be reliable.

The converse of the relation just stated between reliability and validity is not necessarily true, however. That is, a reliable test— one which measures accurately whatever it does measure—is not necessarily a valid test—one which measures accurately what it is intended to measure. Reliability is a necessary condition for validity, but it is not a sufficient condition.

Indeed, there is at least the possibility that a test constructor, working to improve the reliability of his test, might actually lower its validity. Some types of ability, like knowledge of word meanings or ability to solve numerical problems, are easier to measure reliably than other things, such as understanding of principles or ability to suggest appropriate action in a practical problem situation. If the test constructor concentrates on the types of ability that can be measured easily, to the neglect of others that also ought to be measured, his test could become more reliable but less valid.

Again, a homogeneous test is likely to be more reliable than a heterogeneous test. But if a course of instruction aims to develop a variety of different abilities or relatively unrelated understandings, an appropriate test of achievement for that course must show corresponding variety, or heterogeneity, in the items it includes. Making the test valid in this case may interfere somewhat with making it reliable.

The selection of items for high indices of discrimination, as

---

[31] This statement is not contradicted by the fact that it is theoretically possible for a test to yield a validity coefficient that is numerically larger than its reliability coefficient for the same examinees. For the validity coefficient can reach its theoretical maximum only if the criterion for validity is a perfectly accurate measure of whatever the test does in fact measure. In that case the difference between what a test is intended to measure and what it does measure has disappeared. If error-free criterion measures are assumed for both reliability and validity, the index of validity can never be larger than the index of reliability.

pointed out in Chapter 11 on item analysis, tends to make the test more reliable. If the rejected items are low in discrimination because of low technical quality, the reliability is gained at no sacrifice in validity. But if they show low indices of discrimination because they are measuring something different from the majority of items in the test and if that something is an essential part of what the whole test ought to measure, then the elimination of those items from the test would increase reliability at the expense of validity.

None of these possibilities of opposition or interference between reliability and validity justify any devaluation of high reliability as a goal in test construction. Reliability is essential to validity. While the test constructor is not justified in taking shortcuts to reliability by measuring only those things that can be easily measured with high reliability or by making his test more homogeneous than is warranted by the complexity of what he is testing, he is not justified either in settling for an unreliable test. He must try to measure what needs to be measured as reliably as possible. If he does not, the validity of his test will suffer.

8. Validity and relevance

Reliability is clearly an important component of validity. Another component is relevance. A test which measures with a high degree of accuracy what it is intended to measure is highly valid because it is both highly relevant and highly reliable. But a test could be highly reliable, in theory at least, without being highly valid if it lacked a high degree of relevance.

For almost all classroom tests of educational achievement, relevance is a matter of logical analysis and expert judgment. Unlike reliability, it ordinarily cannot be measured statistically, on the basis of experimental data, after the test has been given. Relevance must be built into the test.[32] What a test actually does measure is determined by the test constructor as he works, step by step, to build the test. The cumulative effect of the decisions he makes at each step in the process determines the relevance of the test. If the indi-

---

[32] Edith M. Huddleson, "Test Development on the Basis of Content Validity," *Educational and Psychological Measurement*, XVI (Autumn, 1956), 283-93.

vidual items in the test are relevant, that is, if they require demonstration of mastery of some essential aspect of the course and if they sample proportionally all those essential aspects, then the test as a whole will be relevant.[33]

Much of what this book has had to say about test construction has related to the problem of building relevance into the tests. This is especially true of the chapters on what can be measured, on test planning, and on the writing of true-false and multiple-choice items. But it may be useful to restate here some of the factors which are most likely to affect the relevance of classroom tests of educational achievement.

Chapter 2 suggested that the principal objective of all classroom instruction is to develop in the students a command of useful knowledge. To measure a student's achievement of this objective, a classroom test should present tasks that require a student to demonstrate his command of the knowledge, that is, his ability to use it. It should not reward sheer verbal memory. It should include novel, practical problems which require the application of knowledge. It should not present problems which can be solved by logical reasoning alone. The tasks in the test should require demonstration of achievement of the unique goals of instruction in the particular course. They should not be answerable successfully on the basis of general intelligence alone. The items in the test should be free of irrelevant clues which play into the hands of the sophisticated test taker. Above all, the tasks selected should relate to the most fundamental, the most central, and hence the most useful concepts and principles developed by the course.

The kind of validity we have been discussing, based on relevance and reliability, is the kind most classroom tests of educational achievement ought to have, and indeed the only kind they ordinarily can have. It is primary, direct, intrinsic validity. Sometimes it is referred to as "content validity" or "curricular validity." How much of this kind of validity a test possesses cannot be determined by looking at the scores the test yields. Instead one must look at the test itself, at the rationale and specifications for the test, if they are available, and at directions for administering and scoring it.

---

[33] Roger T. Lennon, "Assumptions Underlying the Use of Content Validity," *Educational and Psychological Measurement,* XVI (Autumn, 1956), 294-304.

9. Characteristics of validity

The validity of any test is clearly a matter of degree, not an all-or-none quality. Tests are not valid or invalid. They are more or less valid. Further, the validity of a test is not completely determined by the test itself. It depends on the purpose for which the test is used, the group with which it is used, and the way it is administered and scored. Instead of asking, "How valid is this *test?*" it would be more precise to ask, "How valid are the *scores* from this test when it is used in a specified way for a specified purpose with a specified group?" Most classroom tests are constructed with a very specific group and purpose in mind. Flaws in test administration might adversely affect the reliability of the scores but are not likely to affect relevance appreciably.

How long does the validity of a classroom test last? If copies of the test are returned to the students for discussion and remedial instruction after the test was given and if the students who take the same course in successive years have frequent contacts with each other, the validity of a test may be abraded rapidly. Or if the teacher begins to use test content for teaching purposes, i.e., to teach for the test directly, then its validity will also suffer. The tasks in any test are only a sample. At best they are a sample of a population of tasks any one of which the student would meet for the first time were it to be included in the test. Direct teaching for any of the tasks in a test tends to spoil the test as a representative sample from a population of novel tasks.

On the other hand, where no extensive use is made of the test for teaching and where contacts between members of successive classes are likely to be few and casual, the same test may retain its validity for a long time. Good tests are hard enough to build to make a teacher or professor consider carefully the pros and cons of using test items for teaching purposes.

10. Summary

The main conclusions to be drawn from the discussions presented in this chapter can be summarized in the following nineteen propositions.

1. A test may not, in fact, measure what its title suggests that it measures.

2. Validity is a complex concept that has been interpreted variously by different writers. Many different types of validity have been described.

3. Physical scientists show less concern than psychologists for the validity of their measurements.

4. It is often difficult and seldom essential to secure a conclusive answer to questions asking which of two procedures provides the more valid measure of a particular characteristic.

5. Validity may be determined directly by critical analysis of the test's specifications and contents or indirectly by analysis of its correlations with a criterion or with other intrinsically valid measures.

6. Course grades usually do not provide satisfactory criteria for the empirical validation of classroom tests of educational achievement.

7. The best procedures for establishing the validities of tests of educational achievement are usually those involving direct validation.

8. Many of the problems of test validation arise from lack of clear and generally accepted definitions of the thing to be measured.

9. The clearest definitions of quantitative concepts are those that specify the operations involved in measuring the concept.

10. Not all operational definitions of a trait or an achievement will prove to be equally rational or equally useful.

11. What a trait name, an educational achievement, or any other concept means can be determined better by looking for a consensus in the way competent people use the term than by analyzing the correlations among test scores.

12. The exercise of judgment is inescapable in the construction of valid tests. No wholly empirical processes of test validation are available.

13. Test validity can be defined more meaningfully in terms of the tasks the test samples than in terms of the traits it is presumed to measure.

14. To be valid a test must be both relevant and reliable.

15. A test can often, though not always, be made more valid by making it more reliable.

16. Validity can be built into a test of educational achievement by

giving careful attention to the relevance of the tasks included
in it.

17. Validity is a matter of degree. Tests are not valid or invalid.
They are more or less valid.

18. Validity depends on the purposes for which a test is used, the
group with which it is used, and the skill with which it is used.

19. Test validity may deteriorate as the test is used repeatedly.

REFERENCES

American Educational Research Association, *Technical Recommendations
for Achievement Tests,* p. 16. Washington, D.C.: AERA, 1955.

American Psychological Association, Inc., *Technical Recommendations
for Psychological Tests and Diagnostic Techniques,* p. 14. Washington,
D.C.: APA, 1954.

Anastasi, Anne, "The Concept of Validity in the Interpretation of Test
Scores," *Educational and Psychological Measurement,* X (Spring, 1950),
67-78.

Bechtoldt, Harold, "Construct Validity: A Critique," *The American Psychologist,* XIV (October, 1959), 619-29.

Beecher, Henry K., *Measurement of Subjective Responses.* New York:
Oxford University Press, Inc., 1959.

Campbell, Donald T. and Donald W. Fiske, "Convergent and Discrimi-
nant Validation by the Multi-trait Multi-method Matrix," *Psychological
Bulletin,* LVI (March, 1959), 81-105.

Cook, Walter W., "Tests: Achievement," in *Encyclopedia of Educational
Research* (rev. ed.), p. 1464, ed. Walter S. Monroe. New York: The Macmillan Company, 1950.

Cronbach, L. J., "Validity," in *Encyclopedia of Educational Research,* ed.
C. W. Harris. New York: The Macmillan Company, 1960.

———— and P. E. Meehl, "Construct Validity in Psychological Tests," *Psychological Bulletin,* LII (1955), 281-302.

Cureton, E. E., "Validity," in *Educational Measurement,* ed. E. F. Lindquist. Washington, D.C.: American Council on Education, 1951.

Ebel, Robert L., "Must All Tests be Valid?" *American Psychologist,* XVI
(October, 1961), 640-47.

————, "Obtaining and Reporting Evidence on Content Validity," *Educational and Psychological Measurement,* XVI (1956), 269-82.

Edgerton, H. A., "The Place of Measuring Instruments in Guidance," in
The Measurement of Student Adjustment and Achievement, p. 52, eds.
Wilma T. Donahue, C. H. Coombs, and R. M. W. Travers. Ann Arbor,
Mich.: University of Michigan Press, 1949.

Guilford, J. P., "New Standards for Test Evaluation," *Educational and Psychological Measurement,* VI (Winter, 1946), 427-38.

Gulliksen, Harold, "Intrinsic Validity," *The American Psychologist,* V (October, 1950), 511.

Huddleston, Edith M., "Test Development on the Basis of Content Validity," *Educational and Psychological Measurement,* XVI (Autumn, 1956), 283-93.

Lennon, Roger T., "Assumptions Underlying the Use of Content Validity," *Educational and Psychological Measurement,* XVI (Autumn, 1956), 294-304.

Lindquist, E. F., *A First Course in Statistics* (rev. ed.), p. 213. Boston: Houghton Mifflin Company, 1942.

Mosier, Charles I., "A Critical Examination of the Concepts of Face Validity," *Educational and Psychological Measurement,* VII (Summer, 1947), 192.

Ross, C. C. and Julian S. Stanley, *Measurement in Today's Schools,* p. 101. Englewood Cliffs, N.J.: Prentice-Hall, Inc., 1954.

Rulon, P. J., "On the Validity of Educational Tests," *Harvard Educational Review,* XVI (1946), 290-96.

Spiker, C. C. and B. R. McCandless, "The Concept of Intelligence and the Philosophy of Science," *Psychological Review,* LXI (1954), 255-66.

Thorndike, Robert L. and Elizabeth Hagen, *Measurement and Evaluation in Psychology and Education,* pp. 109-10. New York: John Wiley & Sons, Inc., 1955.

I 3   Marks and Marking Systems

*The findings of the study strongly support the con-
clusion that scholastic achievement is a substantial predictor of progress in management in the Bell System.
There can be no question but that college recruiting
efforts will succeed more in their objective of bringing
capable future managers into the business the more they
emphasize rank in college graduating class as a criterion
of employment.*

DONALD S. BRIDGMAN

1. The problem of marking

The problem of marking student achievement has
been persistently troublesome at all levels of education. Hardly a
month goes by without the appearance in some popular magazine
or professional journal of an article criticizing current practices or
suggesting some new approach. Progressive schools and colleges are
constantly experimenting with new systems of marking, or sometimes of not marking. And still the problem seems to remain.

One of the reasons why it remains is that marking is a complex
and difficult problem. From some points of view it is even more
complex and difficult than the problem of building a good test and
using it properly. In an early classic of educational measurement,
Thorndike explained some of the reasons why educational achievement often is difficult to measure.

Measurements which involve human capacities and acts are subject to special difficulties due chiefly to:

1. The absence or imperfection of units in which to measure.
2. The lack of constancy in the facts to be measured, and
3. The extreme complexity of the measurements to be made.[1]

Marks are, of course, measurements of educational achievement.

A second reason why problems of marking are difficult to solve permanently is because marking systems tend to become issues in educational controversies. Odell noted that research on marking systems did not become really significant until after the beginning of the present century.[2] At about the same time, the development of objective tests was ushering in the somewhat controversial "scientific movement" in education. The rise of progressive education in the third and fourth decades of this century, with its emphasis on the uniqueness of the individual, the wholeness of his mental life, freedom and democracy in the classroom, and the child's need for loving reassurance, led to criticisms of the academic narrowness, the competitive pressures, and the common standards of achievement for all pupils, implicit in many marking systems. In the sixth and seventh decades renewed emphasis on what is called "basic education" and on the pursuit of academic excellence, has been accompanied by pleas for more formal evaluations of achievement and more rigorous standards of attainment.[3]

Standards! That is a word for every American to write on his bulletin board. We must face the fact that there are a good many things in our national life which are inimical to standards—laziness, complacency, the desire for a fast buck, the American fondness for short cuts, reluctance to criticize slackness, to name only a few. Every thinking American knows in his heart that we must sooner or later come to terms with these failings.[4]

The shifting winds of educational doctrine blow unsteadily even at the same time. Some educational leaders espouse one philosophy,

---

[1] E. L. Thorndike, *Mental and Social Measurements* (2d ed.; New York: Teachers College, Columbia University, 1912), Chap. 2.

[2] C. W. Odell, "Marks and Marking Systems," in *Encyclopedia of Educational Research*, ed. Walter S. Monroe (New York: The Macmillan Company, 1950), pp. 711-17.

[3] Nelson A. Rockfeller and Others, *The Pursuit of Excellence* (Garden City, N.Y.: Doubleday & Company, Inc., 1958), p. 49.

[4] John W. Gardner, *Excellence* (New York: Harper and Row, Publishers, 1961), pp. 158-59.

some another. Some teachers find it easy to accept one point of view, some another, even when they teach in the same educational institution. Since somewhat different marking systems are implied by each of these different philosophical positions, it is not surprising that differences of opinion, dissatisfaction, and proposals for change tend to characterize instructor reactions to marking systems.

A third reason why marking systems present perennial problems is that they require teachers, whose natural instincts incline them to be helpful guides and counsellors, to stand in judgment over some of their fellow men. This is not the role of friendship and may carry somewhat antisocial overtones.

"Forbear to judge, for we are sinners all," said Shakespeare, echoing the sentiments of the Sermon on the Mount: "Judge not, that ye be not judged." It is never difficult to give a student a good mark, particularly if it is higher than he really expected. But since the reach of many students exceeds their grasp, there are likely to be more occasions for disappointment than pleasure in marks.

For all these reasons, no system of marking is likely to be found that will make the process of marking easy and painless and generally satisfactory. This is not to say that present marking practices are beyond improvement. It is to say that no new marking system, however cleverly devised and conscientiously followed, is likely to solve the basic problems of marking. The real need is not for some new system. Good systems already exist. Odell observed in 1950 that, "Most of the writings since 1938 are so similar to earlier published material that little has been added to either research or opinion in this area." [5] Reviewing articles on marking problems and practices that were written a half century ago, one is struck by their pertinence to the present-day. The same problems that were troublesome then are still troublesome. Some of the same remedies that were being proposed then are still being proposed.

Marking procedures, Hadley has pointed out, are about as good or as weak as the teachers who apply them.[6] Few teachers mark as well as they could, or should. Palmer has discussed candidly, but kindly, some of the failures of English teachers in marking the

---

[5] Odell, *op. cit.*

[6] S. Trevor Hadley, "A School Mark—Fact or Fancy?" *Educational Administration and Supervision*, XL (1954), 305-12.

achievements of their students.[7] The more confident a teacher is that he is doing a good job of marking, the less likely he is to be aware of the difficulties of marking, the fallibility of his judgments, and the personal biases he may be reflecting in his marks. Most teachers' marks, says Hadley, are partly fact and partly fancy. The beginning of wisdom in marking is to recognize these shortcomings. The cultivation of wisdom is to work to improve them. For measurements and reports of achievement are essential in education, and no better alternative to marks seems likely to appear.

2. The need for marks

Most instructors, at all levels of education, seem to agree that marks are necessary. Occasionally a voice is raised to cry that marks are educationally vicious, that they are relics of the dark ages of education.[8] But, as Madsen has pointed out, the claim that abolition of marks would lead to better achievement is, by its very nature, impossible to demonstrate.[9] If we forego measurements of relative achievement, what basis remains for demonstrating that one set of circumstances produces better educational results than another? Comparison of achievements between persons or between methods of teaching is inevitable, Madsen suggests. He concludes that it is the misuse of marks, not their use, that is in need of censure.

The uses made of marks are numerous and crucial. They are used to report a student's educational status to him, to his parents, to his future teachers, and to his prospective employers. They provide a basis for important decisions concerning his educational plans and his occupational career. Education is expensive. To make the best possible use of educational facilities and student talent, it is essential that each student's educational progress be watched

---

[7] Orville Palmer, "Seven Classic Ways of Grading Dishonestly," *The English Journal,* October, 1962, pp. 464-67.

[8] Dorothy De Zouche, " 'The Wound Is Mortal': Marks, Honors, Unsound Activities," *Clearing House,* XIX (1945), 339-44; and H. B. Brooks, "What Can Be Done About Comparative Marks and Formal Report Cards?" *California Journal of Secondary Education,* X (1935), 101-6.

[9] I. N. Madsen, "To Mark or Not to Mark," *Elementary School Journal,* XXXI (June, 1931), 747-55.

carefully and reported as accurately as possible. Reports of course marks serve somewhat the same function in education that financial statements serve in business. In either case, if the reports are inaccurate or unavailable, the venture may become inefficient.

Marks also provide an important means for stimulating, directing, and rewarding the educational efforts of students. This use of marks has been attacked on the ground that it provides extrinsic, artificial, and hence undesirable stimuli and rewards. Indeed, marks are extrinsic, but so are most other tangible rewards of effort and achievement. Most workers, including professional workers, are grateful for the intrinsic rewards that sometimes accompany their efforts. But most of them are even more grateful that these are not the only rewards. Few organized, efficient human enterprises can be conducted successfully on the basis of intrinsic rewards alone.

To serve effectively the purpose of stimulating, directing, and rewarding student efforts to learn, marks must be valid. The highest marks must go to those students who have achieved to the highest degree the objectives of instruction in a course. Marks must be based on sufficient evidence. They must report the degree of achievement as precisely as possible under the circumstances. If marks are assigned on the basis of trivial, incidental, or irrelevant achievements or if they are assigned carelessly, their long-run effects on the educational efforts of students cannot be good.

Some students and instructors minimize the importance of marks, suggesting that *what* a person learns is more important than the *mark* he gets. This conception rests on the assumption that there generally is not a high relationship between the amount of useful learning a student achieves and the mark he receives. Others have made the same point by noting that marks should not be regarded as ends in themselves, and by questioning the use of examinations "merely" for the purpose of assigning marks.

It is true that the mark a student receives is not in itself an important educational outcome—by the same token, neither is the degree toward which the student is working, nor the academic rank or scholarly reputation of the professors who teach him. But all of these symbols can be and should be valid indications of important educational attainments. It is desirable, and not impossibly difficult, to make the goal of maximum educational achievement compatible with the goal of highest possible marks. If these two goals are not closely related, the fault would seem to rest with those who teach the courses and who assign the marks. From the point of view of students, parents, teachers, and employers there is nothing "mere" about the marking process and the marks it yields. Stroud has underscored this point.

> If the marks earned in a course of study are made to represent progress toward getting an education, working for marks is *ipso facto* a furtherance of the purposes of education. If the marks are so bad that the student who works for and attains them misses an education, then working for marks is a practice to be eschewed. When marks are given, we are not likely to dissuade pupils from working for them: and there is no sensible reason why we should. It simply does not make sense to grade pupils, to maintain institutional machinery for assembling and recording the gradings, while at the same time telling pupils marks do not amount to much. As a matter of fact they do amount to something and the pupil knows this. If we are dissatisfied with the results of working for marks we might try to improve the marks.[10]

Marks are necessary. If they are inaccurate, invalid, or meaningless, the remedy lies less in deemphasizing marks than in assigning them more carefully so that they more truly report the extent of important achievements. Instead of seeking to minimize their importance or seeking to find some less painful substitute, perhaps instructors should devote more attention to improving the validity and precision of the marks they assign and to minimizing misinterpretations of marks by students, faculty, and others who use them.

3. Shortcomings of marks

The major shortcomings of marks, as they are assigned by many instructors and recorded in many institutions, are twofold: (1) the lack of clearly defined, generally accepted, scrupulously observed definitions of what the various marks should mean and (2) the lack of sufficient relevant, objective evidence to use as a basis for assigning marks. One consequence of the first shortcoming is that marking standards and the meanings of marks tend to vary from instruc-

---

[10] James B. Stroud, *Psychology in Education* (New York: David McKay Co., Inc., 1946), p. 632.

tor to instructor, from course to course, from department to department, and from school to school. Another consequence is that instructor biases and idiosyncrasies tend to reduce the validity of the marks. A consequence of the second shortcoming is that the marks tend to be unreliable.

Variability in marking standards and practices have been reported by many investigators. Travers and Gronlund, for example, found wide differences of opinion among the members of a graduate faculty on what various marks should mean and the standards that should be followed in assigning them.[11] Odell reported,

> Where a typical five-letter system is used, the per cents of the highest letter are likely to vary from 0 or near 0 to 40 or more; of the next to the highest from about 10 to 50 or more; and of the failure mark from 0 up to 25 or more.[12]

Some schools and colleges publish, for internal guidance and therapy, periodic summaries of the marks assigned in various courses and departments. In one such unpublished study, instructors in one department were found to be awarding 63 per cent A's or B's, whereas those in another awarded only 26 per cent A's or B's. Course X in one department granted 66 per cent A's and B's, whereas Course Y in the same department granted only 28 per cent. Each of these two courses, incidentally, enrolled more than fifty students.

Lack of stability in the assignment of grades from year to year is also apparent. Specifically, there appear to be long-run tendencies in many institutions to increase the proportion of high grades issued and to decrease the proportion of low grades. For example, during the years 1936 to 1939 one large institution issued 33 per cent A and B grades. From 1951 to 1954 the corresponding proportion of A's and B's had increased to 44 per cent. In the same two periods the proportion of D's and F's dropped from 30 to 18 per cent.

The lack of clearly defined, uniform bases for marking and standards for the meanings of various marks tends to allow biases to lower the validity of marks. Often a student's mark has been influenced by the pleasantness of his manner, his willingness to partici-

---

[11] Robert M. W. Travers and Norman E. Gronlund, "Meaning of Marks," *Journal of Higher Education*, XXI (1950), 369-74.

[12] Odell, *op. cit.*

pate in class discussions, his skill in expressing ideas orally or in writing, or his success in building an image of himself as an eager, capable student. Some of these things should not ordinarily be allowed to influence the mark he receives.

Carter found that girls are somewhat more likely to get higher marks than boys of equal ability and achievement.[13] Hadley reported that pupils well liked by teachers tended to get higher marks than pupils of equal ability and achievement who were less well liked.[14] These findings tend to support the accusations of students, and the guilt-feelings of instructors, that accomplishment is not the pure and simple basis on which marks are assigned. Indeed, as Palmer has noted, some instructors deliberately use high marks as rewards and low marks as punishments for behavior quite unrelated to the attainment of the objectives of instruction in a course.[15]

The studies of Starch and Elliott on the unreliability of teachers' marks on examination papers are classic demonstrations of the instability of judgments based on presumably absolute standards.[16] Identical copies of an English examination paper were given to 142 English teachers, with instructions to score it on the basis of 100 per cent for perfection. Since each teacher looked at only one paper, no relative basis for judgment was available. The scores assigned by the teachers to the same paper ranged all the way from 98 to 50 per cent. Similar results were obtained with examination papers in geometry and in history.

Evidently marks such as Starch and Elliott collected for single examination papers are not highly reliable. How is it for composite semester marks? After surveying the evidence, Odell concluded that "the usual reliability of semester marks is indicated by a coefficient of from .70 to .80, perhaps even of from .80 to .90." With respect to the validity of marks, and on the basis of admittedly indirect and inadequate evidence, he suggested that "the degree of validity as

---

[13] Robert S. Carter, "How Invalid Are Marks Assigned by Teachers?" *Journal of Educational Psychology*, XLIII (1952), 218-28.

[14] Hadley, *op. cit.*

[15] Palmer, *op. cit.*

[16] Daniel Starch and E. C. Elliott, "Reliability of Grading Work in History," *School Review*, XXI (1913), 676-81; "Reliability of Grading Work in Mathematics," *School Review*, XXI (1913), 254-59; "Reliability of the Grading of High School Work in English," *School Review*, XX (1912), 442-57.

a measure of mastery of subject matter is fairly high, probably on the average at least not below that represented by a coefficient of correlation of .70 and in many cases much higher." [17]

In assessing these estimates of reliability and validity it may be helpful to keep two things in mind. One is that semester marks are based on much more extensive and comprehensive observations of pupil attainments, perhaps as much as or more than eighty hours of observation. One hour of intensive "observation" under the controlled conditions of a well-standardized test of achievement can yield measurements whose reliability may exceed .90.

The other thing to keep in mind is that a coefficient of correlation even as high as .70 does not reflect very pure and precise measurements of the thing to be measured. In fact, if only half of the observations summarized in the mark are completely relevant to the attainment being marked and if the other half are completely irrelevant, the validity of the mark would be about .70 (assuming that each observation carries equal weight and that all observations are perfectly reliable). Hence if the summary values for the reliability and validity of semester marks reported by Odell do not suggest utter chaos, they do suggest that considerable room for improvement remains.

4. Institutional marking systems

An obvious method for dealing with one of the major shortcomings of marks—the lack of a clearly defined, scrupulously observed definition of what the various marks should mean—is for a school faculty to develop, adopt, and enforce an institutional marking system. Ruch has stressed the point that marking schemes are essentially matters of definition.[18] Any marking system, he suggests, is somewhat arbitrary. "The adopted marking scheme must be defined. Its sole meaning and value rest upon its definition to pupils, teachers and parents alike."

Travers and Gronlund also emphasize the importance to an institution of clear definition of its marking system.[19] And Odell observes,

---

[17] Odell, *op. cit.*

[18] G. M. Ruch, *The Objective or New-type Examination* (Chicago: Scott, Foresman & Company, 1929), pp. 369-402.

[19] Travers and Gronlund, *op. cit.*

> . . . when serious attention has been given to the matter
> and the general principles that should govern marking are
> agreed upon by a group of teachers, the marks the members
> of the group assign tend to form distributions much more
> similar than if this had not been done and their reliability is
> somewhat improved.[20]

If an institution lacks a clearly defined marking system or if instructors do not assign marks in conformity with the policies that define the system, then the marks will tend to lose their meaning and the marking system will fail to perform its essential functions adequately. A marking system is basically a system of communication. It involves the use of a set of specialized symbols whose meanings ought to be clearly defined and uniformly understood by all concerned. Only to the degree that the marks do have the same meaning for all who use them is it possible for them to serve the purposes of communication meaningfully and precisely.

The meaning of a mark should depend as little as possible on the teacher who issued it or the course to which it pertains. This means that the marking practices of an instructor, of a department, or indeed of an entire educational institution are matters of legitimate concern to other instructors, other departments, and other institutions. It means that a general system of marking ought to be adopted by the faculty and the administration of a school or college. It requires that the meaning of each mark must be clearly defined. General adherence to this system and to these meanings ought to be expected of all staff members. Such a requirement would in no way infringe the right of each instructor to determine which mark to give to a particular student. But it would limit the right (which some instructors have claimed) to set his own standards or to invent his own meanings for each of the marks issued.

An educational institution that sets out to improve its educational effectiveness by improving its marking practices and to improve its marking practices by developing an institutional marking system is likely to encounter a number of questions such as these on which opinions will differ.

1. Should marks report absolute achievement, in terms of content mastery, or achievements relative to those of other comparable students?

---

[20] Odell, *op. cit.*

2. Should marks be regarded as measurements or as evaluations?
3. Should marks simply indicate achievement in learning or should they be affected by the student's attitude, effort, character, and similar traits?
4. Should marks report status achieved or amount of growth in achievement?
5. Should a student receive a single composite mark or multiple marks on separate aspects of achievement?
6. Should the marking system report few or many different degrees of achievement?
7. Should letters or numbers be used as the marking symbols?

Each of these questions will be discussed in turn in the sections that follow.

5. Absolute versus relative marking

Two major types of marking systems have been in use in the United States since 1900. In the early years of the century almost all marking was in per cents. A student who learned all that anyone could learn in a course, whose achievement could therefore be regarded as flawless, could expect a mark of 100 (per cent). A student who learned nothing at all would, theoretically, be given a mark of zero. A definite per cent of "perfection" usually between 60 and 75 per cent was ordinarily regarded as the minimum passing score. Because a student's per cent mark is presumably independent of any other student's mark, per cent marking is sometimes characterized as "absolute marking."

The second major type of marking system is based on the use of a small number of letter marks, often five, to express various levels of achievement. In the five-letter A-B-C-D-F system, truly outstanding achievement is rewarded with a mark of A. A mark of B indicates above average achievement; C is the average mark; D indicates below average achievement; and F is used to report failure (i.e., achievement insufficient to warrant credit for completing a course of study). Because a letter mark is intended to indicate a student's achievement relative to that of his peers, letter marking is sometimes characterized as relative marking.

A popular term for one variety of relative marking is "grading on the curve." The "curve" referred to is the curve of normal distribution. One method for grading or marking on the curve, using five letter marks, is to determine from the ideal normal curve what proportion of the marks should fall at each of five levels and to follow these proportions as closely as possible in assigning marks. For example, the best 7 per cent might get A's, the next best 23 per cent get B's, and so on. Another process is to define the limits of the score intervals corresponding to various marks in terms of the mean and standard deviation of the distribution of achievement scores. Those whose scores are more than 1.5 standard deviations above the mean might get A's, those between .5 and 1.5 standard deviations above the mean get B's, and so on. This second process does not guarantee in advance that 7 per cent of the students must get A's and 7 per cent must fail. If the distribution of achievement is skewed, as it may be, or irregular, as it often is, these characteristics will be reflected in variations in the proportions of each mark assigned.

In the early decades of this century letter marking began to supersede per cent marking. A clear majority of educational institutions now uses letter marks. But per cent marking is by no means dead. Some schools still use per cents instead of letters in their marking systems. Others indicate per cent equivalents of the various letter marks they issue. Official examining bodies still prefer to define passing scores in terms of per cent, though they often transform test scores, or control the scoring process, to avoid any significant change in the ratio of failures to passes. The controversy that began when per cent marking was first seriously attacked, and when the movement to substitute letter marks gained support, continues today. The issue of absolute versus relative marking is still a live one, particularly when relative marking is identified as "grading on the curve."

Ruch has criticized per cent marking on the ground that it implies a precision that is seldom actually attainable.[21]

> . . . a large body of experimental evidence points to the fact that from but five to seven levels of ability are ordinarily recognizable by teachers in marking pupils. . . . The difference between an "85" and an "86" is a difference at least five times as fine as the human judgment can ordinarily distinguish.

[21] Ruch, *op. cit.*

There is substantial basis for this criticism, but it should not be taken too literally. How many levels of ability can be recognized depends on how much good information the teacher has available. No doubt an attempt to decide whether to give a pupil an 85 or an 86 has seemed ridiculous to many teachers. Seldom is a teacher in a position to say, "I am 100 per cent certain that this pupil's true mark is 85, not 86 or 84." But given more information as a basis for judgment, the teacher's task might seem less ridiculous. And if a teacher recognizes that he will always have to settle for less than 100 per cent confidence in the accuracy of his marks, he may be willing to trade a little of that confidence for a little more precise indication of his best guess at a student's level of achievement. As pointed out elsewhere in this chapter, the use of broad categories in marking tends to reduce the number of wrong marks, but it always sacrifices so much precision in the process that the overall reliability of the marks declines.

The widespread initial use of per cent marking and its persistence in modern times suggest that there must be things to be said in its favor. Two advantages are mentioned most often. The first is that per cent marking clearly relates achievement to degree of mastery of what was set out to be learned. It does not give high marks to incompetent students simply because they happen to be the best of a bad lot. It does not require that some students receive low marks when they and all their classmates have done well in learning what they were supposed to learn. To know what proportion a student has mastered of a defined set of learning objectives is to know something more, and something less, than to know that he was outstanding, or average, or poor, compared with some other students, in mastering the same set of learning objectives. Achievement cannot be reported fully without reference to what (i.e., command of knowledge and utilizable skill) has been achieved.

A second reputed advantage of per cent marking is that it provides fixed, standard measures of achievement. This is in contrast to relative grading, where the achievements of the group set standards for what is excellent, average, or very poor in individual achievement. A student whose achievements result in his designation as valedictorian in one school might be regarded as only average in another school. Relative standards are likely to be variable standards.

Unfortunately, per cent marking often fails to live up to its promise of providing truly meaningful and stable measures of achievement. To calculate a meaningful per cent, two quantities must be measured in common units with reasonable accuracy: (1) the amount available to be learned in a course and (2) the part of that amount which a particular student did, in fact, learn. These things are so difficult to measure that they are almost never measured. In what units can the material available to be learned be measured? On what basis can an instructor estimate how much might be learned in a particular course?

It is sometimes asserted that standards for marking are inherent in the subject matter itself. But no one ever learns all there is to know about a subject, nor is it possible to ascertain reliably by any known operations what proportion of the theoretical sum total of knowledge in a field any student possesses. It is equally difficult to set any rational minimum standard for passing, in terms of subject matter alone. Educational achievement does not come in separate and equal units which are easy to count and which are learned on an all-or-none basis.

A mark of 90 used to be thought to mean that the student who received it had learned 90 per cent of what he was expected to learn in a given course. But it takes very little analysis to discover how little meaning there is in such a statement. In what units does one measure amount of knowledge? On what basis can an instructor say how much *should* be learned in a given course? By what operations can one measure the total to be learned and the part the student did learn?

Sometimes those who defend so-called absolute standards argue that the experienced teacher knows what these standards are and that the inexperienced teacher can quickly learn them if he will only try. But this is obviously just a roundabout way of saying that the standards are derived from the observed performances of the students themselves, which means that they are relative and are not absolute measures of subject matter achievement at all. In spite of the arguments in favor of absolute, teacher-determined, marking standards, no one has ever described in concrete, operational terms exactly how such standards could be defined and applied.

Few per cent marks are ever calculated by division of a measurement of the part learned by a measurement of the total available to be learned. Instead, per cent marks almost always reflect a highly subjective judgment, against a somewhat vague and individualistic standard, of the *relative* quality of student's performance. If he is very good, relative to other students the instructor has, has had, or can imagine having, his per cent mark is likely to be high. If not, it is likely to be lower.

The studies by Starch and Elliott, mentioned earlier in this chapter, clearly demonstrated how variable from teacher to teacher these presumably absolute standards of achievement might be. Ruch has illustrated how much this variability can be reduced when relative marks, based on rankings, are substituted for absolute marks, based on per cent.[22] Evidence of these kinds was largely responsible for the shift away from percentage marking and toward letter marking early in this century. Relative standards, based on the average performances of groups of typical students, turn out to be more stable than presumably absolute standards, based on the idiosyncratic judgments of individual instructors.

But not all class groups to which marks must be assigned are typical. Some are above and others are below average in general ability and achievement simply because of sampling fluctuations. There may be almost as much chance variation in potential learning ability from one class of twenty-six students to another class of twenty-six students as there is in trick-taking potential from one hand of thirteen bridge cards to another. Some differences may be the result of self-selection, as when students with special talent or interest elect courses in music, advanced mathematics, or creative writing. Further, able students may tend to elect academically oriented college preparatory courses, while less able students may try to get into vocational training courses. Finally, some class differences may be planned deliberately by school officials in the interests of more effective instruction, as when students studying the same subject are grouped on the basis of ability in different classes. Does "grading on the curve" make sense in such atypical classes (which probably constitute a large majority of all classes)?

From one point of view it is absurd to give an A for the best achievement in a low ability group if identical achievement would have received a mark of C in a group of higher ability. But from

---

[22] Ruch, *op. cit.*

another point of view it is equally absurd to deny the possibility of recognizing outstanding achievement among low-ability students with a mark of A, or of recognizing, with marks of C, D, or even F, that students of high ability can do what is for them mediocre, poor, or even failing work.

In many colleges students enrolling to study a foreign language such as German are placed in different classes on the basis of how much German they already know. A student in beginning German has almost the same chance at an A mark as a student in intermediate or advanced German. In some of these same colleges students enrolling in freshman English are also placed in different classes on the basis of how much English they already know. But the student enrolled in the "remedial" course usually has much less likelihood of receiving an A than the student placed in the advanced course. This kind of differential marking, as between beginning German and remedial English, makes sense to those who believe that it is more appropriate to study the one than the other at the college level. But it does not make sense to those who feel that a college can and should teach any college student what he most needs to know, provided only that he is willing to study hard to learn it.

Granting the generalizations that most classes in schools and colleges are atypical and that seriously atypical classes can put serious strains on systems of relative marking, one can still make a case for the advantages in reliability and meaningfulness of a marking system that places more emphasis on relative than on absolute achievement. Absolute standards seem much too difficult to define clearly and with general acceptability to provide in themselves an adequate basis for reliable, meaningful marks.

Variations from class to class in ability and achievement do not preclude reasonable marking on a relative basis. Allowances can be made for the sampling fluctuations in small classes by not insisting on rigorous adherence to a designated ideal distribution in each small, atypical class, but only in the composite distribution of marks for many such classes. One can make provision for a somewhat different "curve" in classes of high ability than in classes of lower ability. But such differences should be public knowledge and should be sanctioned by the whole faculty. Ordinarily they should not be extreme differences. It is unrealistic and psychologically unwise to foster the belief that capable students are entitled to higher marks simply because they are capable. It is equally unrealistic and unwise to create conditions that predestine some students to do below average work and to receive below average marks in every course they undertake to study. Human beings, fortunately, exhibit a diversity of talents. A good school or college makes provision for developing diverse special talents and for recognizing and rewarding them.

Teachers of subjects like art, music, or physical education sometimes report difficulty in distinguishing reliably as many as five levels of achievement among their students. In such cases the tendency is to use only the top marks of the scale, giving few if any D's or F's. In a few cases where the classes are small and highly selected this practice may be justified. But in others, especially where the problem is lack of reliable measures of achievement rather than sectioning by ability, the practice is not justified. If only three levels of achievement can be distinguished in a large, unselected group, the marks assigned to these levels probably should be B's, C's, and D's rather than A's, B's, and C's.

A basic principle of relative marking is that a student's achievement should be marked by comparing it with the achievement of the student's peers. But who, for example, are the peers of a talented girl studying vocal music? Are they all the girls of her own age in the country, in school and out? Or are they only those girls specializing in vocal music at the same stage in their training as she is? One way, perhaps the best way, to give marks clearly defined operational meaning, is to mark a student's performance relative to the performance of other students who are interested in and capable of taking the same course. It is not wholly feasible or reasonable to compare the vocal performance of a girl who is trying to learn to sing exceptionally well with the vocal performance of other girls who are not trying to learn to sing at all. Hence it seems somewhat unreasonable to insist that students with special talents should never be given average marks.

One common criticism of relative marking is that it permits the students rather than the teachers to set the standards. This is true. There is the further implication that student-set standards are likely to be low—lower, at least, than those most teachers would set. But this appears not to be true. For when the teachers depart from the proportions of marks recommended in a system of relative marking, they usually seem to do it by giving too many high marks rather than too many low marks.

Another way of stating essentially the same criticism is to claim that relative marking encourages a general slow-down of student effort. The argument is that under a relative system the members of a class can earn just as good marks on the average by taking it easy as by putting forth maximum effort. There is nothing wrong with the abstract logic of this argument, but there is something wrong with its practical psychology. How can any student who agrees to this slow-down be sure that some other student may not work just a bit harder and wind up receiving a higher mark?

Yet another criticism of relative marking is that it requires an instructor to give some low marks and some average marks, even if most of the students in the class learn practically all that he was trying to teach them. Do they not all deserve high marks in such a case? How frequently this hypothetical situation of nearly universal, nearly maximum achievement can be expected to occur is not specified. Some good instructors claim they have never encountered such a case. But even if purely hypothetical, the issue it raises is important and deserves an answer. Actually, two answers can be offered.

The first is that if a high mark implies outstanding, and hence unusual, achievement and if an average mark implies normal, and hence typical, achievement, it is logically inconsistent to give most of the class members a high mark. They should all get average marks since their achievements are about average for the group. None of them have shown outstanding achievement.

The second is that if the students in a class differ appreciably in abilities, preparation, and interests, as they almost always do, the only way that nearly all of them can achieve all that is asked of them is to ask much less than the best could achieve. To equalize achievement by minimizing it deprives some students of the education they could get and may deprive society of the benefits of their fully developed talents. Most good teachers prefer to challenge and to help each pupil to learn as much as he can.

Some instructors have expressed fear that relative marking would lead to such a slow-down. A few students have claimed to know of classes where it happened. But there seems to be little evidence that it ever actually did happen. If it did, the blame might lie more with uninspiring course content or with poor student motivation than with relative marking. Ordinarily the personal competition implicit in relative marking will stimulate as much or more effort to achieve than the impersonal stimulus of an absolute standard of achievement.

In most areas of human activity awards go to individuals who are outstanding in relative, not absolute, terms. There are no absolute standards for speed in running the mile or for distance in throwing the javelin. The winner in any race is determined on a relative basis. Runners on a starting line seldom agree to loaf along simply because there is no absolute standard of speed they have to meet. From the point of view of the individual runner in the 100-yard dash, as well as from that of the individual student majoring in history or chemistry, the best way to achieve outstanding success is to put forth outstanding effort.

A marking system cannot be all things to all men. A single symbol cannot represent low achievement from one point of view (i.e., actual degree of content mastery) and high achievement from another (i.e., progress in relation to reasonable expectation). What it can and should have is one clearly defined and jealously guarded kind of meaning. School and college faculties have the opportunity and the obligation to establish and maintain clearly defined meanings for the symbols used in their marking systems.

6. Measurement or evaluation

As the term is used here, a measurement in education is a quantitative description of how much a student has achieved. A measurement is objective and impersonal, and it can be quite precisely defined in operational terms. An evaluation, on the other hand, is a qualitative judgment of *how good* or *how satisfactory* the student's performance has been. Evaluations tend to be subjective, quite highly personal, and difficult to define precisely. Evaluations are often based in part on measurements of achievement, but they are also based on many other kinds of evidence. Measurement can describe how much of this ability or that characteristic an individual possesses. But to tell how well educated he is or how well prepared for a particular job, an evaluation is required.

There are several advantages in treating a marking system as a means of reporting measurements of achievement rather than as a means of reporting evaluations. In the first place, evaluations are complex, involving many variables and many considerations that are unique to a particular student. This makes it difficult to report evaluations adequately in a standardized marking system. Judgments of how good a student's educational achievement has been depend not only on how much he has achieved, but also on his opportunity for achievement, the effort he has put forth, and the need that this achievement is likely to serve in his educational and vocational future. It is not easy to make marks valid as *measures* of achievement, but it is next to impossible to make them valid as *evaluations*.

In the second place, because of the many poorly defined and highly individual factors which must be considered in making an evaluation, few teachers have a sufficient basis for making fair evaluations. Some teachers may be well informed about the home background and the personal problems of many of their students and hence can judge quite accurately each student's opportunity to learn and the real effort he has made to learn. But many teachers lack some of this background essential to sound evaluations. Such teachers can help a student to make an honest evaluation of his own achievements, but the teacher can seldom do the whole job alone. And perhaps the teacher should not, even if he could. Imposed evaluations may not only be less accurate than self-evaluations. They may be less effective also. If students and teachers regard marks as objective measurements of achievement rather than as subjective evaluations, there is greater likelihood that the teachers will assign fair and accurate marks, and there is less likelihood that students will react emotionally so that the relations between student and teacher are damaged.

Consider this analogy. If the scale shows that a man weighs 210 pounds, it is reporting a measurement. The fact may be unpleasant, but there is nothing personal about it and no good cause for anger at the scale. But if a tactless acquaintance suggests that he is getting too fat, the acquaintance is making an evaluation. It can be taken as a personal affront, and a natural reaction is to resent it. The fact that the heavy man may have been thinking the same thing himself does not soothe his feelings very much. In somewhat the same way, the interpretation of marks as evaluations rather than as measurements may have been responsible for some of the tension and unpleasantness associated with their use.

Finally, there may be less need or justification for making a formal report and a permanent record of an evaluation than there is for recording a measurement. Usually it is less important for a future teacher or employer to know that Henry did as well as could be expected of him or that he failed to live up to expectations than to know that he was outstanding in his ability to handle language or mediocre in his mathematical ability. Evaluations are instrumental to particular decisions. Once the decision has been made, there is little to be gained by basking in a favorable evaluation or in agonizing over an unfavorable one. To be successful and to maintain emotional stability, a person must not cherish too long the evaluations, favorable or unfavorable, that others have made of him or that he has made of himself. Measured achievement, on the other hand, often represents a more permanent foundation on which future education and success depend. The more accurately it is reported and the more completely it is recorded, the more soundly a student and his advisors can judge which choices he should make.

A teacher may thus be well advised to regard the marks he assigns in a course as objective, impersonal measures of achievement rather than as subjective, personal evaluations. He may even be able, happily, to persuade his students to accept them on this basis.

7. Achievement or attitude and effort

Studies such as those by Carter, Hadley, Travers and Gronlund, and others indicate that teachers often base the marks they issue on factors other than degree of achievement of the objectives of instruction. No doubt they will continue to do so, since marks can be useful instruments of social control in the classroom and since some degree of such control is essential to effective teaching. But the use of marks for these purposes must be limited, for it can easily be abused and tends to distort the intended meaning of the mark.

One of the important requirements of a good marking system is that the marks indicate as accurately as possible the extent to which the student has achieved the objectives of instruction in the particular course of study. If improving the student's attitude toward something or improving his willingness to put forth effort for educational achievement is one of the specific objectives of the course and if the instructor has planned specific educational procedures in the course to attain this goal, then it is quite appropriate to consider these things in assigning marks. But often this is not the case. When it is not, attitude and effort probably should be excluded from consideration in determining the mark to be assigned.

Involving judgments of character and citizenship in marking is even more hazardous. Such judgments tend to be impressionistic evaluations rather than objective descriptions. If we like the behavior we call it straightforward, or perhaps thoughtful. If not, we are more likely to call it tactless, or perhaps indecisive. The countercharges of political leaders suggest that what looks like intelligent and courageous statesmanship to those in one party looks like incompetent bungling or spineless expedience to those in the other. Seldom are the traits of good character or good citizenship defined objectively, without the use of value-loaded and question-begging modifiers like "good," "desirable," "effective," "appropriate," etc.

The result of these difficulties is that valid assessments of character and citizenship are not easy to secure and not often secured. As Odell remarked, in reference to marks reflecting character or citizenship, "In general, the conclusion seems justified that when a mark of this sort is given, it is not highly valid." [23]

8. Status or growth

Some instructors, seeking to improve the fairness of the marks they issue, attempt to base them on the amount of improvement the student has made rather than on the level of achievement he has reached. Scores on a pretest, and other preliminary observations, are used to provide a basis for estimates of initial status. The difference between these and subsequent test scores and other indications of achievement permits estimates of the amount of change or growth.

---

[23] Odell, *op. cit.*

Unfortunately these growth measures usually are quite unreliable. Each test score or observation includes its own error of measurement. When these are subtracted from other measurements, the errors tend to accumulate instead of to cancel out. Consequently the difference scores sometimes consist mainly of errors of measurement. Lord, Diederich, and others have pointed out some of the difficulties in using this approach.[24] If his tests are appropriate and reliable, an instructor may safely use the difference between mean pretest and post test scores as one measure of the effectiveness of his instruction. But few educational tests are good enough to reliably measure short-run gains in educational achievement for individual students.

From some points of view it may seem fairer to use growth rather than final status as a measure of achievement. But, apart from the characteristic unreliability of growth scores just mentioned, there are other problems. One is that for many educational purposes, knowledge that a student is good, average, or poor when compared with his peers is more important than knowledge that he changed more or less rapidly than they did in a certain period of time. Another is that students who get low scores on the pretest have a considerably greater likelihood of showing subsequent large gains in achievement than their classmates who earned higher initial scores. Students are not slow to grasp this fact when their achievement is judged on the basis of gains. The course of wisdom is for them to make sure that their pretest performance is not so good as to constitute a handicap later on.

One rather strong incentive for marking students on the basis of growth rather than status is to give all students a more nearly equal chance to earn good marks. A student who makes good marks, on the basis of status, in one course is likely to make good marks in other courses.[25] A student whose marks are high one semester is likely to get high marks the next semester.[26] The other, darker side of this picture is that status marking condemns some students

[24] Frederic M. Lord, "The Measurement of Growth," *Educational and Psychological Measurement,* XVI (1956), 421-37; and Paul B. Diederich, "Pitfalls in the Measurement of Gains in Achievement," *School Review,* LXIV (1956), 59-63.

[25] David Ohlson, "School Marks versus Intelligence Rating," *Educational Administration and Supervision,* XIII (1927), 90-102.

[26] L. W. Ferguson and W. R. Crooks, "Some Characteristics of the Quality Point Ratio," *Journal of General Psychology,* XXVII (1942), 111-18.

to low marks in most subjects, semester after semester. Low marks discourage effort. Lack of effort increases the probability of more low marks. So the vicious cycle continues, bringing dislike of learning and early withdrawal from school.

The debilitating effect of low marks on educational interest and effort is probably sufficient to constitute a major educational problem. But whether marking on the basis of growth rather than status provides an effective solution to the problem may be open to question. For one thing, growth measures are usually of rather low reliability, as already indicated. Few students, even poor students, would really favor the substitution of more or less randomly distributed (and hence rather meaningless) praise or blame for consistently dependable measures of status, however discouraging that status might seem to be.

Another limitation of growth measures as an antidote to the discouragement sometimes brought by low-status measures is that they don't really conceal or offset differences in status very effectively. The poor reader knows he is a poor reader, and so do his classmates, even if he gets a good mark for growth in reading. A student who has a hard time with arithmetic is not encouraged very much by the report that, for him, a mediocre score on an arithmetic test represents rather commendable achievement. Students are not likely to forget, nor should they, that in the long run it is competence achieved that will count and that rate of growth is important only as it contributes to status.

What, then, is the answer? Success is important to all of us. None of us should expect it all of the time, but we should not expect it to be denied all of the time either. Fortunately we do differ in what we can do well. This student is a whiz at mathematics. That one has a talent for languages. This girl is a beauty. That one can act. This boy is a fine athlete. That one is a supersalesman. One trick to successful, happy living, as Robert Frost pointed out, is to "Get up something to say for yourself." What this means, he made clear, is that each person needs to find something he can do better than most other people, if only because he works harder than they to learn how to do that particular thing. And, as John Gardner has pointed out, there are many varieties of excellence.

If students are taught to dislike school by constant reminders of their low achievement, the remedy probably is not to try to persuade them that rate of growth toward achievement is more important than status achieved, for that is a transparent falsehood. The remedy probably is to provide varied opportunities to excel in various kinds of worthwhile achievement. Certainly this can be done within a comprehensive school. It may even be done within a single classroom by an alert, versatile, dedicated teacher. When it is done, marking on the basis of status achieved will no longer mean that some students always win and others always lose. Each can enjoy, as he should, some of the rewards of excellence in his own specialty.

Finally, when reasonable care is taken to enroll students in courses appropriate for their levels of ability and preparatory training, differences in initial status can be limited. In such cases the need to measure achievement in terms of change is also greatly reduced.

9. Single or multiple marks

Achievement in most subjects of study in schools and colleges is complex. There are knowledges to be imparted, understandings to be cultivated, abilities and skills to be developed, attitudes to be fostered, interests to be encouraged, and ideals to be exemplified. Correspondingly, the bases used for determining marks include many aspects or indications of achievement: homework, class participation, test scores, apparent attitude, interest and effort, and even regularity of attendance and helpfulness to the teacher. How can a single symbol do justice to these various aspects of achievement?

The answer of some observers is that it cannot. A mark, they say, is a hodgepodge of uncertain and variable composition. They suggest that the essential step in improving marks is to make them more analytical and descriptive. Multiple marks or written reports have been proposed as improvements over the traditional single letter or number. Bolmeier recommends that marks be analytical enough to be meaningful.[27] Two trends in marking noted by Smith and Dobbin are (1) increased comprehensiveness in the areas of

[27] Edward C. Bolmeier, "Principles Pertaining to Marking and Reporting Pupil Progress," *School Review*, LIX (1951), 15-24.

student development being marked and (2) greater specificity in what is marked.[28]

There is considerable merit in these suggestions, and under favorable conditions they can improve marking considerably. But they do involve problems. For one thing, they multiply considerably the already irksome chores of marking. For another, they create additional problems of defining precisely what is to be marked and of distinguishing clearly among the different aspects of achievement. An even more serious problem is that of obtaining sufficient evidence, specific to each aspect of achievement, on which to base a reliable mark. Finally, and largely as a result of the preceding difficulties, the multiple marks exhibit considerable "halo effect." That is, they seem to be determined more by the instructor's overall impression of the student than by his successful analysis and independent measurement of various components of achievement.

Multiple marking is no panacea for the ills of marking. It may well call for more information than the instructor can readily obtain and more effort than the improvement it yields seems to warrant. It may try to tell the student and his parents more than can be told clearly, perhaps even more than they really care to know. Multiple marking is not the only road to improvement in marking and probably not the best road currently available. Much can be done to make single marks more meaningful and more reliable. Perhaps those possibilities should be exploited before the more complex problems of multiple marking are tackled.

10. Few marks or many?

A major difference between two systems of marking is that letter marks are usually few in number (five, most commonly) whereas per cent marks provide up to one hundred different values, of which about thirty are commonly used. Those who advocated letter marks when they were first introduced suggested that the bases on which marks are usually determined are not reliable enough to justify the apparent precision of per cent marking. They claimed

---

[28] Ann Z. Smith and John E. Dobbin, "Marks and Marking Systems," in *Encyclopedia of Educational Research*, ed. Chester W. Harris (3rd ed.: New York: The Macmillan Company, 1960), pp. 783-91.

that the best that most instructors can do is to distinguish about five different levels of achievement. Many instructors seemed to agree with this view.

Some proposals for improving marks have gone even farther than the five-letter system in reducing marking categories. The use of only two marks such as "S" for "satisfactory" and "U" for "unsatisfactory," "P" for "pass" and "F" for "fail," or "credit"—"No Credit" has been suggested and adopted by some institutions. Two-category marking has not become popular, however. Indeed, there is some pressure from instructors and students to refine the presently popular five-letter system of marking by adding plus and minus signs to the basic letters.

The notion that marking problems can be simplified and marking errors reduced by using fewer marking categories is an attractive one. Its weakness is exposed by carrying it to the limit. If only one category is used, if everyone is given the same mark, all marking problems vanish, but so does the value of marking. A major shortcoming of two-category marking, and to some degree of five-category marking as well, is this same kind of loss of information. To trade more precisely meaningful marks for marks easier to assign may be a bad bargain for education.

The use of fewer, broader categories in marking does indeed reduce the frequency of errors in marking. That is, with a few broad categories more of the students receive the marks they deserve because fewer wrong marks are available to give them. But each error becomes more crucial. The apparent difference between satisfactory and unsatisfactory, or between a B and a C, is greater than the difference between 87 and 88 on a per cent marking scale. If a fallible instructor (and all of them, being human, are fallible) gives a student a per cent mark of 86 when omniscient wisdom would have assigned a mark of 89, the error has less consequence than if the instructor assigns a C when a B should have been given, or an "unsatisfactory" mark when the mark should have been "satisfactory." Hence the use of fewer categories is no royal road to more reliable marking. And, as noted previously, reducing the number of categories reduces the information conveyed by the mark.

The more reliable the information on which marks are based, the greater the value of a large number of marking categories. But

no matter how unreliable that information may be, it is *never* true
that few categories report the information more accurately than
many categories. This is illustrated in Table 13.1, which may be

TABLE 13.1

Loss of Reliability from Use of Broad Categories in Marking

Reliability of Marking Basis	RELIABILITY OF MARKS Number of Categories			
	2	5	10	15
.95	.63	.85	.92	.94
.90	.60	.80	.87	.89
.80	.53	.71	.78	.79
.70	.47	.62	.68	.69
.50	.33	.45	.48	.49

read as follows: "If marks are based on information having a
reliability of .95, the use of two categories in marking would reduce
the reliability to .63, of five categories to .85, and of ten categories
to .92. In the case of fifteen categories the reduction is very slight,
only from .95 to .94." Other rows in the table may be read similarly.
The data in Table 13.1 were prepared from formulas derived and
explained by Peters and Van Voorhis.[29] Values in the table assume
equally spaced categories and normal distributions of scores and
marks.

It is apparent from Table 13.1 that the use of fewer marking
categories is not required by unreliability of the basis for marking.
On the contrary, the use of very few categories aggravates the
problem of unreliability. If maximum reliability of information is
the goal, a five-letter system is better than a two-letter system, and
the use of ten categories in marking is better than five. The main
arguments for fewer categories in marking must be on grounds of
convenience and simplicity, not on grounds of the unreliability of
the basis for marking. A system using nine single digits, the stanine

[29] Charles C. Peters and Walter R. Van Voorhis, *Statistical Procedures and Their Mathematical Bases* (New York: McGraw-Hill Book Company, 1940), pp. 393-99.

system described later in this chapter, seems to offer a reasonable compromise between precision and convenience.

11. Letters or numbers

The successful revolt against per cent marking was aided by the substitution of letter marks for numbers. Letters helped to emphasize the contrast between clearly relative marking and supposedly absolute per cent marking. But the use of letters creates at least two problems. One is that the letters must always be transformed to numbers before they can be added or averaged. The other is that letters imply evaluations of achievement, rather than measurements.

For both these reasons the return to numerical symbols in marking would be advantageous. This advantage must be weighed against the confusion likely to result from introduction of a new set of symbols, with new and unfamiliar meanings. If an educational institution sets out with vigor to improve its marking system, a change in the set of symbols used may help to dramatize and reinforce other, more subtle changes. Since the stanine system of marking seems to afford substantial advantages over the five-letter system, it should receive serious consideration if a change is contemplated.

12. Quality control in a marking system

What a mark means is determined not only by how it was defined when the marking system was adopted, but also, and perhaps more importantly, by the way it is actually used. If an instructor assigns some A's, many B's, some C's, and very few lower marks, then B has become his average mark, not C, as the marking system may have specified. Thus institutional control of marking requires surveillance of the results of the marking process and may require corrective action.

The temptations for instructors to depart from institutional policy in marking are many, and the rationalizations for doing so are not hard to find. Some instructors regard marking as the personal prerogative of the instructor. They may not distinguish between their very considerable freedom to determine which mark a particular student shall receive and their very considerable responsibility to make the meaning of their marks consistent with those of other instructors. To rationalize deviations from overall institutional policy in distribution of marks, they may claim unusual ability or disability in their students, special interest or aptitude in the subject of study, or (usually only by implication) exceptionally fine teaching.

Some instructors yield to the subtle pressures to give more high and fewer low marks. Perhaps they feel inclined to temper justice with mercy. Perhaps they wish to avoid controversy. An instructor seldom has to explain or justify a high mark or to calm the anger of the student who received it. Some instructors may feel that the favorable reputations of their courses among students depend on their generosity with high marks. Many good instructors like their students so much as persons that they find it difficult to disappoint any of them with a low mark, particularly if the student seems to have been trying to learn. These temptations to depart from standard marking practices are understandable as temptations, but most of them do not carry much weight as reasonable justifications. There are indeed some situations that do warrant departure from general institutional policies in marking. But the determination of which situations those are probably cannot be left to the individual instructor concerned if uniformly meaningful marks are desired.

There are several things an educational institution can do to maintain the meaningfulness of the marks issued by its instructors. One is to publish each semester summary distributions of the marks issued in each course by each instructor. This is done systematically by some colleges and has been found quite effective. Another is to record alongside each mark reported to a student or his parents a set of numbers showing the distribution of marks to the student's classmates. The purpose of this is to make the relative meaning of the mark immediately apparent to all concerned.

A somewhat simpler variant of the procedure just described is to accompany each marking symbol by a fraction, the numerator of which shows what per cent of the class received higher marks, while the denominator shows what per cent received lower marks.

These fractional interpretations may be required only when the instructor has exceeded or fallen short of specified limits for the proportion of marks above or below each category. Such a requirement tends to encourage observance of institutional regulations without preventing necessary exceptions.

Finally, an institution can return to the instructor a set of marks whose distribution among the marking categories is unsatisfactory and ask him to resubmit a revised set of marks.

13. A method of marking[30]

This section will describe a method of converting test scores, or composite numerical measures of achievement, into marks. The method is built around the five-unit scale of letter marks that most schools and colleges use currently, though as will be shown it can be adapted to the nine-unit stanine system quite easily.

One of the purposes of any systematic method of assigning marks is to establish greater uniformity among instructors in their marking practices, and hence in the meaning of the marks they issue. A school or college faculty that adopts such a system and requires all faculty members to conform to it in issuing marks will almost certainly improve the uniformity of marking practices and hence make the marks issued much more consistently meaningful. Another purpose is to make the systematic conversion of numerical measures into course marks simple enough to compete successfully with the unsystematic, hit-or-miss procedures that some instructors actually do use. To this end the procedures make use of statistics which are easy to determine or which can be estimated with sufficient accuracy by short-cut methods.

One basic assumption of the method is that the five-letter marks should represent equal intervals on the score scale. This is an alternative to strict *grading on the curve,* which disregards numerical score values, considers only the rank order of the scores, and gives the top 7 per cent A's, the next 23 per cent B's, and so on. It is also an alternative to the use of unequal numerical intervals which usually result when the end points of these intervals are located at gaps or natural breaks in the distribution of scores. Most such gaps are chance affairs, attributable largely to chance errors of

---

[30] This method was developed in cooperation with Dean Dewey B. Stuit at the State University of Iowa. It was described in *Technical Bulletin No. 8* of the University Examinations Service, distributed to staff members of the College of Liberal Arts with the approval of the Educational Policy Committee in November, 1954.

measurement. Hence they seldom reflect natural points of division between discrete levels of ability.

Acceptance of this assumption means that there can be no a priori certainty that expected per cents of A's, B's, or any other mark will be assigned. Indeed, in a particular class group there might be no A's or no F's at all. However, in large class groups (and, in the long run, in small class groups) the distribution of letter marks will ordinarily approximate a normal distribution.

The method makes use of the median score as the basic reference point or origin of the letter mark scale. Since there is seldom a meaningful *absolute zero* on any scale of academic achievement, it is almost always necessary to use some other reference point in setting the scale. The median or middle score provides a reference point that is reasonably easy to determine and reasonably stable from one sample to another. If the distribution of scores is skewed, the median is a more typical or representative measure than the mean.

When a five-unit scale is used for measuring achievement, the standard deviation of the test scores provides a unit of convenient size. The usual range of scores in a distribution of twenty to forty scores equals about four or five standard deviation units. While the standard deviation is tedious to calculate without machine assistance, it can be estimated quite simply, with reasonable accuracy, for purposes of assigning marks.

Finally, the method of mark assignment here described makes provision for different distributions of marks in classes having different levels of average academic ability. The method does not require such differences, but it does allow for them if the faculty decides in favor of them. Mention was made earlier in the chapter of the differences of opinion which exist in school and college faculties on this question. Probably most faculties would favor giving more high marks in classes of high ability. But when they vote for this policy they also vote, whether explicitly or not, for giving lower than average marks in some other classes. There are both advantages and disadvantages in differentiating levels of marking to correspond with ability levels in various classes.

Differentiating levels of marking requires uniform ability measures for the pupils in various classes. This could be provided either by scores on some test of academic aptitude or by grade-point averages in previous courses. Of course the mark a particular student receives should not be directly affected by his aptitude test score or his previous grade-point average. Few instructors would argue that one student should get a higher mark than another simply because he is thought to have more ability. His achievement should determine the mark he gets. But since there is a substantial correlation between prior measures of ability and subsequent measures of achievement, it seems reasonable that the average mark in a class of more able students should be higher than the average mark in a class of less able students.

Four steps are involved in this process of assigning marks.

1. Select from Table 13.2 a distribution of marks appropriate to the level of ability of the class being graded.
2. Calculate the median and the standard deviation of the scores on which the marks are to be based.
3. Determine the lower score limits of the A, B, C, and D mark intervals, using the median, the standard deviation, and the appropriate lower limit factor from Table 13.2.
4. Assign the designated marks to the students whose scores fall in intervals determined for each mark.

Table 13.2 presents mark distribution statistics for classes at seven different levels of academic ability. The first column lists descrip-

TABLE 13.2

Letter Mark Distribution Statistics for Classes at Seven Levels of Ability

Ability Level	Ability Measures		Lower Limit Factor	Per cent of Marks				
	GPA	Percentile		A	B	C	D	F
Exceptional	2.80	79	0.7	24	38	29	8	1
Superior	2.60	73	0.9	18	36	32	12	2
Good	2.40	66	1.1	14	32	36	15	3
Fair	2.20	58	1.3	10	29	37	20	4
Average	2.00	50	1.5	7	24	38	24	7
Weak	1.80	42	1.7	4	20	37	29	10
Poor	1.60	34	1.9	3	15	36	32	14

tive labels of the ability levels. The next two columns, headed "ability measures," provide means for deciding which level is appropriate for a particular class. If the grade-point averages (GPA) of the class members in their previous course work is known, the mean of these GPA's indicates which ability level is appropriate for the class. If, for example, the class mean of those GPA's was found to be 2.24, the teacher could conclude that this class is slightly above average in ability, so that the level designated "fair" would be appropriate.

If grade-point averages are not available, inconvenient to use, or undesirable for some other reason, average aptitude test scores can be used in place of the grade-point averages. For this purpose, all students in the school or college must have taken the same test or battery of tests which yields a measure of the academic ability of each student. If the scores of those students are available in the form of local school percentile ranks, then the average of those percentile ranks could also be used to select the appropriate ability level. If, for the hypothetical class we have in mind, that average turned out to be 45, the instructor could conclude that it is below average in ability and that the mark distribution for a *weak* class would be appropriate.

The five columns on the right of Table 13.2 indicate, for each ability level, what per cent of the marks would be A's, B's, and so on if the distribution of numerical measures being converted to grades were perfectly normal. Since few distributions are likely to be perfectly normal, the per cent of each mark assigned in any actual case will usually differ somewhat from the per cent indicated in Table 13.2. One could, of course, arrange the numerical measures in rank order and convert them to letter marks on the basis of the "ideal" percentages for a class of the specified level of ability. But, as suggested earlier, this process is open to more of the criticisms of grading-on-the-curve than is the process being described here.

The second step in the process requires calculation of the median and the standard deviation. To calculate the median, follow the steps outlined below.

1. Arrange the scores in order from high to low.
2. If the number of scores is odd, the middle score is the median. The middle score in an odd number of scores is the score whose rank order is represented by the whole number just larger than half the number of scores. For example, in a set of twenty-five scores the median is the thirteenth score (13 is just larger than 12.5).

3. If the number of scores is even, the median is the average of the two scores closest to the middle of the distribution. For example, in a set of twenty-six scores the median is the average of the thirteenth and fourteenth scores.

To estimate the standard deviation this short-cut approximation is recommended.

Divide the difference between the sums of scores in the upper and lower one-sixths of the distribution of scores by one-half of the number of scores in the distribution.

Suppose we have twenty-six scores. The sum of the top four scores (upper one-sixth of the distribution) might be 137. The sum of the bottom four scores (lower one-sixth) might be 69. Then the estimated standard deviation would be

$$\frac{137 - 69}{13} = \frac{68}{13} = 5.23$$

The third step in the process, determining the lower score limits, makes use of the fourth column of Table 13.2, headed "Lower Limit Factor." The values in this column show how far the lower limit of the score interval for A marks lies above the median, in standard deviation units. In the case of a class of "fair" ability, the A mark interval begins 1.3 standard deviations above the median of the score distribution. In the case of a class of weak ability, the A mark interval begins 1.7 standard deviations above the median. Since the score interval that corresponds to each mark is one standard deviation in extent, once the lower limit of the A interval is determined, the lower limits of the B, C, and D intervals can be found by successive subtractions of the standard deviation from the lower limit of the A's.

As an example of this process consider a set of scores having a median value of 66.2 and a standard deviation of 6.5 for a class whose ability level is regarded by the teacher as "good." Table 13.2 indicates that the lower limit of the A mark interval should be 1.1 standard deviations (6.5) above the median (66.2). Hence this lower limit is 73.35. The lower limit of the B mark interval is one standard deviation less, or 66.85. Similarly, the lower limit of the C marks is found to be 60.35, and of the D marks, 53.85.

The fourth step, assigning the marks, is facilitated by recording the score intervals for each letter grade in whole score units. In the example above, A marks would be assigned to all scores of 74 or higher. B marks to scores from 67 to 73, C marks to scores from 61 to 66, D marks to scores from 54 to 60, and F marks to scores of 53 or lower.

Table 13.3 illustrates the application of this method of mark assignment to a sample problem. The previous grade-point aver-

TABLE 13.3

Sample Problem in Letter Mark Assignment

A. Data for the problem
1. Class ability level measures
   a. Mean GPA on previous years' courses   2.17
   b. Mean percentile on aptitude test   56.3
   c. Appropriate grade distribution (Table 13.2)   *Fair*
2. Achievement scores   (number of students = 38)

112	100	93	84	78	72	66	51
109	97	91	83	75	71	62	47
106	97	90	82	75	70	59	44
105	95	89	81	75	69	59	
104	95	84	80	74	68	58	

B. Calculations from the data

1. Median $\dfrac{81 + 80}{2} = 80.5$

2. Standard deviation $\dfrac{636 - 318}{19} = 16.7$

Marks	Lower Limits			Intervals	Number	Per cent
A	80.5 + 1.3 × 16.7	=	102.2	103-112	5	13
B	102.2 − 16.7	=	85.5	86-102	9	24
C	85.5 − 16.7	=	68.8	69-85	15	39
D	68.8 − 16.7	=	52.1	53-68	6	16
F				44-52	3	8
					38	100

ages of the students in this class, as well as their aptitude test percentiles, indicate that the grade distribution for a class slightly better than average, designated in Table 13.2 as "fair," would be appropriate. Since there are thirty-eight students in the class, the median is the average of the nineteenth and twentieth scores. The top and bottom sixths in a class of thirty-eight include six scores each. Hence the six highest scores, from 100 to 112, are added to obtain the sum of 636. The sum of the six lowest scores, from 44 to 59, is 318. The difference between 636 and 318, divided by half the number of scores, gives the estimated standard deviation.

Using the lower limit factor of 1.3 (obtained from Table 13.2 for a "fair" class) in conjunction with a standard deviation of 16.7 and a median of 80.5, it is determined that the lower limit of the A mark interval is 102.2. Successive subtractions of the standard deviation give the lower limits of the other mark intervals. From these lower limits the whole number score intervals are easily determined and the appropriate letter mark can be assigned to each numerical score. Note that the actual per cent of scores to which each mark was assigned differs somewhat from the ideal values of Table 13.2, reflecting the fact that the distribution of scores given in Table 13.3 was not perfectly normal.

A system of mark assignment similar to the one just described has also been developed for use with stanine marks. As mentioned earlier in the chapter, a stanine system of marking has some advantages over the five-letter system. Like the method for assigning letter marks, the method for assigning stanines uses the median as a reference (or starting) point. But since the stanine scale has nine intervals instead of five, it is necessary to use half of the standard deviation, instead of the standard deviation as the scale unit. The usual range of a distribution of twenty to forty scores extends for approximately nine of these semistandard deviation units.

TABLE 13.4

Stanine Distribution Statistics for Classes at Seven Levels of Ability

Ability	Ability Measures			Distribution of Stanine Marks								
	GPA	Percen-tile	Lower Limit Factor	9	8	7	6	5	4	3	2	1
Exceptional	2.80	79	1.90	17	16	19	19	14	9	4	1	1
Superior	2.60	73	2.30	13	13	18	20	16	11	6	2	1
Good	2.40	66	2.70	9	11	16	20	18	13	8	3	2
Fair	2.20	58	3.10	6	9	14	19	19	16	10	4	3
Average	2.00	50	3.50	4	7	12	17	20	17	12	7	4
Weak	1.80	42	3.90	3	4	10	16	19	19	14	9	6
Poor	1.60	34	4.30	2	3	8	13	18	20	16	11	9

Table 13.4 presents stanine distribution statistics for classes at seven different levels of ability. The first three columns of Table 13.4 are identical with those of Table 13.2. The lower-limit factors differ because they are expressed in semistandard deviation units rather than full-standard deviation units and because they define the lower limit of the top one-ninth rather than the top one-fifth of the score scale. The remaining nine columns indicate expected percentages of each stanine score (if the distribution of scores to be converted is normal) in classes at each level of ability.

The use of the term "stanine" to describe these scores is open to criticism on two grounds.

1. True stanines are determined from a rank order of scores, not from the median and half standard deviation of the distribution of scores.
2. True stanines always show the same distribution of scores, not differing distributions depending on the ability level of the class, as indicated in Table 13.4.

But since the scale used is basically a "standard nine" scale, it seems better to use the familiar term "stanine" somewhat imprecisely than to invent some new term. One can, of course, assign stanines on the basis of the percentage distributions shown in Table 13.4. This process is somewhat simpler than to determine stanine intervals from the median and semistandard deviation. The only drawback is that use of the percentage distributions involves the questionable assumption that the distribution of achievements in a small class is perfectly normal, or at least that the departures from normality are of no consequence. If one prefers to assume that the irregularities observed in the distribution of raw scores are not due to chance errors of measurement or to peculiarities of the test, but do, in fact, reflect with reasonable accuracy the differences among the students in true achievement, then the linear conversion of raw scores to stanines will be preferred. In most cases either approach will give substantially the same results.

The process of transforming scores to stanines is very much like that of transforming scores to letter marks, as illustrated in Table 13.5. A distribution that is appropriate to the level of ability of the class is selected from Table 13.4. The median score is calculated. Instead of estimating the standard deviation, however, half of the standard deviation is estimated when stanines are involved. The rule for this estimation is:

Divide the difference between the sums of scores in the upper and lower one-sixths of the distribution of scores by the number of scores in the distribution.

From the median, the semistandard deviation, and the appropriate lower-limit factor from Table 13.4, calculate the exact values of the lower limits of each stanine score interval. This process is illustrated in the lower section of Table 13.5. Rounding these exact

TABLE 13.5

Sample Problem in Stanine Assignment

A. Data for the problem
  1. Class ability level measures
     a. Mean GPA on previous year's courses   2.17
     b. Mean percentile on aptitude test   56.3
     c. Appropriate grade distribution (Table 13.2)   *Fair*
  2. Achievement scores   (number of students = 38)

112	100	93	84	78	72	66	51
109	97	91	83	75	71	62	47
106	97	90	82	75	70	59	44
105	95	89	81	75	69	59	
104	95	84	80	74	68	58	

B. Calculations from the data

1. Median $\dfrac{81 + 80}{2} = 80.5$

2. Semistandard Deviation $\dfrac{636 - 318}{38} = 8.37$

Stanines	Lower Limits		Intervals	Number	Per Cent
9	80.5 + 3.1 × 8.37 =	106.45	107-112	2	5
8	106.45 − 8.37 =	98.08	99-106	4	11
7	98.08 − 8.37 =	89.71	90-98	7	18
6	89.71 − 8.37 =	81.34	82-89	5	13
5	81.34 − 8.37 =	72.97	73-81	7	18
4	72.97 − 8.37 =	64.60	65-72	6	16
3	64.60 − 8.37 =	56.23	57-64	4	11
2	56.23 − 8.37 =	47.86	48-56	1	3
1			44-47	2	5
				38	100

values upward to integral values, the raw score limits of each stanine interval can be determined and the stanine marks assigned.
Note that since these stanine marks were assigned on the basis of
equal score intervals, the per cents of each stanine mark do not correspond exactly to those anticipated in a normal distribution of
scores or marks.

14. The basis for marks

When a course mark is determined, as it usually is, by combining marks on daily recitations, homework, term papers, and scores
on quizzes and tests, each of the components carries more or less
weight in determining the final mark. To obtain marks of maximum validity, the instructor must give each component the proper
weight, neither too much nor too little. How can he determine
what those weights ought to be? How can he determine what they
actually are? If what they are does not correspond to what they
should be, what can he do?

It is not easy to give a firm, precise answer to the question of
how much influence each component ought to have in determining the final mark. But several guiding principles can be suggested.

In general, the use of several different kinds of indicators of competence is better than use of only one, provided each of the indicators is relevant to the objectives of the course and provided also
that it can be observed or measured with reasonable reliability.

Exclusive reliance on tests, for example, may give an unfair advantage to students who have special test-taking skills and may unfairly handicap students who give the best account of their achievements in discussions, on projects, or in other situations. But irrelevant accomplishments, such as mere glibness, personal charm, or
self-assurance, should not be mistaken for solid command of knowledge. Nor should much weight be placed on vague intangibles or
subjective impressions that cannot be quantified reliably.

If measures of each component aspect of achievement are highly
correlated, the problem of weighting them properly is far less critical
than if they are quite unrelated. For most courses the various measurable aspects of achievement are related closely enough so that

proper weighting is not a critical problem. The natural "un-weighted" weighting will give marks almost as valid as those resulting from more sophisticated statistical procedures.

The actual weight that a component of the final mark does carry depends on the variability of its measures and the correlations of those measures with measures of the other components. This makes the precise influence of a component quite difficult to determine. As a first approximation to the weight of a component, the standard deviation of the measures of that component serves quite well. If one set of scores is twice as variable as another, the first set is likely to carry about twice the weight of the second.

When the whole possible range of scores is used, score variability is closely related to the extent of the available score scale. This means that scores on a forty-item objective test are likely to carry about four times the weight of scores on a ten-point essay test question, provided that scores extend across the whole range in both cases. But if only a small part of the possible scale of scores is actually used, the length of that scale can be a very misleading guide to the variability of the scores.

In view of the difficulty of determining precisely how much weight each component ought to carry, the difficulty of determining precisely how much weight each component does, in fact, carry seems less serious as an obstacle to valid marks. Further, as we have noted, if the components are quite highly related, the difference between optimum and accidental weighting may be hard to detect, as it affects the validity of the marks. But if the instructor finds a serious discrepancy between what he thinks the component weights ought to be and what they in fact are, two courses are open to him.

One is to multiply the underweighted components by some weighting factor to increase their variability and hence increase the weight they carry. The other is to increase the number of observations of the underweighted component, or the precision with which it is measured, and hence also to increase the weight it carries. Of the two methods, the first is likely to be more convenient. The second is likely to yield the more reliable, and in this case the more valid, marks.

If an instructor has promised his class, for example, that the final mark will be based on five components, weighted as follows:

Contributions in class   15%
Daily assignments   20%
Term paper or project   15%
Midterm test   20%
Final test   30%

then he should plan to obtain enough independent scores on "contributions in class" so that the variability of the total of those scores is about half the variability of the scores on the final test. By the same token, the final test should be half again as long (or include half again as many items) as the midterm test.

A wise instructor will warn his students that the actual weight of each component may differ somewhat from the intended weight. But he can assure them, and rest assured himself, that if he has planned carefully to make the weights what he intended, the inevitable deviations of the actual from the ideal weights will not affect the validity of his marks appreciably.

One final admonition. It is a mistake to convert test scores to letter marks, record these in the grade book, and then reconvert the letter marks to numbers for purposes of calculating the final average. A better procedure is to record the test scores and other numerical measures directly. These can be added, with whatever weighting seems appropriate, to obtain a composite score which can then be converted into the final mark.

Not only does the recording of scores rather than letters usually save time in the long run, it also contributes to accuracy. Whenever a range of scores, some higher, others lower, is converted to the same letter mark, information is lost. Usually this information is not retrieved when the letter marks are changed back to numbers so they can be added or averaged. Each B, whether a high B or a low B in terms of the score on which it was based, is given the same value in the reconversion. Hence to avoid the loss of score information it is usually desirable to record the raw scores, not the scores after conversion to letter marks.

15. Illustration of mark determination

The process of combining quantitative estimates of achievement on the basis of written work, class observations, quizzes, and tests

TABLE 13.6

Class Record Data and Mark Assignment

Subject: *Test Construction*   Date: *First Semester, 1963-64*

Names	Dates	Multiple-Choice Items (20) 10-2	True-False Items (20) 10-14	Discrimination Item (15) 10-25	Article Reports (10) 11-6	Mid-Term Test (150) 11-13	Mean and Sigma (35) 11-28	Percentile Ranks (30) 12-10	Discrimination Indices (30) 12-16	Test Project (75) 1-15	Take-Home Test (150) 1-20	Final Test (175) 1-23	Sum (710)	Stanine	Mark
Beck, Charles		9	7	7	5	80	21	17	16	53	91	83	389	6	C
Beebe, Paul		16	8	12	9	100	18	19	29	66	133	125	535	9	A
Bell, Marion		3	1	2	1	69	12	20	16	47	88	73	332	4	C
Blinn, Lula		13	18	7	6	102	31	15	16	61	111	125	505	8	A
Bruno, Alice		7	13	10	6	62	14	12	18	43	85	75	345	5	C
Colgan, Mary		10	5	2	7	115	25	25	17	67	86	113	472	8	B
Hooper, Martha		12	5	6	4	70	8	8	14	29	87	23	266	3	D
Horton, Elizabeth		16	16	11	7	124	18	28	22	68	134	135	579	9	A
Kopp, Martha		9	12	6	5	99	15	19	21	55	92	94	427	6	B
Kruse, Theodore		17	16	14	4	108	30	14	20	63	90	120	496	8	A
Merlin, Dawn		14	9	10	6	144	20	18	22	70	125	137	585	9	A
Murphy, Edward		10	5	8	2	75	17	20	20	60	79	97	396	6	C
Peterson, Sandra		5	5	1	2	83	22	13	11	41	69	64	311	4	D
Potter, Marilyn		6	2	3	2	78	21	15	25	62	94	103	412	6	B
Randall, Peggy		4	6	2	7	134	18	24	26	70	145	157	596	9	A
Roman, Mary		8	8	7	2	118	20	18	24	60	136	123	519	9	A
Sautos, Betty		4	2	6	1	83	19	17	30	66	90	86	413	6	B
Shelby, Marilyn		5	7	3	3	104	24	10	18	47	98	70	376	5	C
Silver, Enid		4	4	6	5	98	18	15	24	62	100	104	446	7	B
Snell, Daniel		6	10	3	2	117	16	16	17	50	81	117	437	7	B
Spooner, Janet		9	8	3	4	121	18	14	30	60	93	105	463	7	B
Sweeney, Nancy		5	10	7	1	104	20	19	22	59	107	110	462	7	B
White, Shirley		7	3	4	3	91	20	14	12	45	87	94	381	5	C
Williams, Roberta		3	5	5	5	85	15	10	16	41	109	97	391	6	C
(Standard Deviations)		4.08	4.58	3.33	2.08	20.58	5.58	4.75	5.17	10.08	19.5	27.0	86.75		

438

is illustrated in Table 13.6. This table is intended to represent excerpts from a teacher's class record book showing all the measurements combined to determine the final course mark. In this case all test scores and measures of quality of work on special assignments and projects were recorded numerically. These numerical scores, added together without special weighting, yield the sums which were then converted into letter marks (and in this case, for purposes of illustration, to stanines as well). The median value of these sums is 432.

The distributions appropriate for a class of exceptional ability were selected, for both marks and stanines, because these were graduate students for whom, according to college rules, any mark below C carries no credit. The names, of course, are fictitious. Values in the bottom row of the table are estimates of the standard deviation of each set of scores. These figures indicate that the final test carried greatest weight, about one-fourth of the total, while the "article reports" assignment carried least weight, about one-fiftieth. The figures in parentheses near the titles for each set of scores indicate the maximum possible value of those scores. Thus the maximum possible total score would have been 710.

It is interesting to note that application of Kuder-Richardson Formula 21 to these scores yields an estimate of about .98 for the reliability of the composite scores. Hence whatever other failings these marks may have, they cannot be regarded as seriously unreliable. On the other hand, it is probably unusual for marks in a class to be based on eleven different measures as highly sensitive to student differences and as highly related from measure to measure as these are.

16. Summary

Some of the principal ideas developed in this chapter are summarized in these twenty-seven statements.

1. Marking systems are frequent subjects of educational controversy because the process is difficult, because different educational philosophies call for different marking systems, and because the task is sometimes disagreeable.
2. Measurements and reports of achievement are essential in education, and no better means than marks seem likely to appear.

3. To serve effectively their purposes of stimulating, directing, and rewarding student efforts to learn, marks must be valid and reliable.

4. There is nothing wrong with encouraging students to work for high marks if the marks are valid measures of achievement.

5. The major shortcomings of marks are attributable to frequent lack of clearly defined and scrupulously observed meanings for the marks and to frequent lack of sufficient good evidence to use as a basis for assigning marks.

6. Marking standards often vary from instructor to instructor and from institution to institution.

7. Girls usually get higher marks than boys of equal ability and achievement.

8. Marks will tend to lose their meaning if the institution lacks a clearly defined marking system or does not require instructors to mark in conformity with the system.

9. Relative marking systems, which make use of letter marks such as A, B, C, D, and F, have, in a majority of the educational institutions in this country, replaced presumably absolute marks, which make use of per cents.

10. It is extremely difficult to determine per cent marks so that they do, in fact, express absolute levels of achievement.

11. Evidence of the unreliability of per cent marks, obtained by Starch and Elliott early in this century, was largely responsible for the shift toward letter marking.

12. Variations from class to class in ability and achievement complicate but do not preclude reasonable marking on a relative basis.

13. Relative marking is as likely as absolute marking to stimulate student efforts to achieve.

14. Some marking problems can be simplified by regarding a mark as a measurement rather than as an evaluation.

15. Marks should ordinarily be based exclusively on achievement and should not attempt to indicate attitude, effort, or deportment.

16. Marks measuring status tend to be more reliable, more meaningful, and educationally more constructive than marks measuring growth.

17. The discouraging effect of consistently low marks can be coun-

teracted better by providing students with diverse opportunities to excel than by basing marks on growth.

18. The use of multiple marks on various aspects of achievement can improve marking but may cost more in extra effort than the improvement is worth.

19. The more marks available in the system to indicate different levels of achievement, the more reliable the marks will be, but the less convenient the system may be to use.

20. A return to numerical marks would emphasize their use as measurements and would simplify the calculation of grade-point averages.

21. Publication of distributions of marks, course by course, is essential to quality control of the marketing system.

22. Relative marking that divides the score scale into equal intervals is an alternative to strict marking on the "curve."

23. A system of relative marking that makes provision for different distributions of marks in classes having different levels of average academic ability is possible.

24. An equal-interval relative marking system may require calculation of some average measure like the median and some measure of variability like the standard deviation.

25. In general, the numerical basis for assigning marks should include diverse components, such as contributions in class, homework, projects, and test scores.

26. The weight carried by each component toward determination of the composite depends on the variability of the component scores.

27. Precise weighting of the components of a numerical basis for assigning marks is not crucial to the quality of the marks assigned.

REFERENCES

Bangs, Cecil W. and Harry A. Greene, *Teachers' Marks and the Marking System,* Extension Bulletin No. 244. Iowa City, Iowa: State University of Iowa, 1930.

Bolmeier, Edward C., "Principles Pertaining to Marking and Reporting Pupil Progress," *School Review,* LIX (1951), 15-24.

Brooks, H. B., "What Can Be Done about Comparative Marks and Formal

Report Cards?" *California Journal of Secondary Education,* X (1935), 101-6.

Carter, Robert S., "How Invalid Are Marks Assigned by Teachers?" *Journal of Educational Psychology,* XLIII (1952), 218-28.

Crooks, A. D., "Marks and Marking Systems: A Digest," *Journal of Educational Research,* XXVII (1933), 259-72.

Davis, J. DeWitt, "The Effect of the 6-22-44-22-6 Normal Curve System on Failures and Grade Values," *Journal of Educational Psychology,* XXII (November, 1931), 636-40.

De Zouche, Dorothy, " 'The Wound Is Mortal': Marks, Honors, Unsound Activities," *Clearing House,* XIX (1945), 339-44.

Diederich, Paul B., "Pitfalls in the Measurement of Gains in Achievement," *School Review,* LXIV (1956), 59-63.

Elsbree, Willard S., *Pupil Progress in the Elementary School.* New York: Bureau of Publications, Teachers College, Columbia University, 1943.

Ferguson, L. W. and W. R. Crooks, "Some Characteristics of the Quality Point Ratio," *Journal of General Psychology,* XXVII (1942), 111-18.

Fine, Benjamin, "ABC of Grading Puzzles Parents," *New York Times Magazine,* November 18, 1957, p. 33.

Gardner, John W., *Excellence,* pp. 158-59. New York: Harper and Row, Publishers, 1961.

Hadley, S. Trevor, "A School Mark—Fact or Fancy?" *Educational Administration and Supervision,* XL (1954), 305-12.

Jones, John A., "Grading, Marking and Reporting in the Modern Elementary School," *Educational Forum,* XIX (1954), 45-54.

Kelley, Truman L., "Use of Literal Grades," *Journal of Educational Psychology,* XLI (1950), 488-92.

Lord, Frederic M., "The Measurement of Growth," *Educational and Psychological Measurement,* XVI (1956), 421-37.

Madsen, I. N., "To Mark or Not to Mark," *Elementary School Journal,* XXXI (June, 1931), 747-55.

McNemar, Quinn, "On Growth Measurement," *Educational and Psychological Measurement,* XVIII (1958), 47-55.

Norsted, R. A., "To Mark or Not to Mark," *Journal of Education,* CXXI (1938), 81-84.

Odell, C. W., "Marks and Marking System," in *Encyclopedia of Educational Research,* pp. 711-17, ed. Walter S. Monroe. New York: The Macmillan Company, 1950.

Ohlson, David, "School Marks versus Intelligence Rating," *Educational Administration and Supervision,* XIII (1927), 90-102.

Palmer, Orville, "Seven Classic Ways of Grading Dishonestly," *The English Journal* (October, 1962), pp. 464-67.

Perry, Winona M., "Are Grades and Grading Systems Comparable from One Institution to Another?" *American Association of College Registrars Journal*, XVIII (1943), 159-65.

Peters, Charles C. and Walter R. Van Voorhis, *Statistical Procedures and Their Mathematical Bases*, pp. 393-99. New York: McGraw-Hill Book Company, 1940.

Rockefeller, Nelson A. and Others, *The Pursuit of Excellence*, p. 49. Garden City, N.Y.: Doubleday & Company, Inc., 1958.

Rothney, John W. M., "What Research Says to the Teacher," *Evaluating and Reporting Pupil Progress*, p. 33. National Education Association, 1955.

Ruch, G. M., *The Objective or New-type Examination*, pp. 369-402. Chicago: Scott, Foresman & Company, 1929.

Smith, Ann Z. and John E. Dobbin, "Marks and Marking Systems," in *Encyclopedia of Educational Research* (3rd ed.), pp. 783-91, ed. Chester W. Harris. New York: The Macmillan Company, 1960.

Starch, Daniel and E. C. Elliott, "Reliability of the Grading of High School Work in English," *School Review*, XX (1912), 442-57.

———, "Reliability of Grading Work in History," *School Review*, XXI (1913), 676-81.

———, "Reliability of Grading Work in Mathematics," *School Review*, XXI (1913), 254-59.

Strang, Ruth M., "Reporting Pupil Progress," *School Executive*, LXXII (1953), 47-50.

Stroud, James B., *Psychology in Education*, p. 632. New York: David McKay Co., Inc., 1946.

Thorndike, E. L., *Mental and Social Measurements* (2d ed.), Chap. 2. New York: Teachers College, Columbia University, 1912.

Travers, Robert M. W. and Norman E. Gronlund, "Meaning of Marks," *Journal of Higher Education*, XXI (1950), 369-74.

Vaughn, Kenneth W., "Planning the Objective Test," in *Educational Measurement*, pp. 167-70, ed. E. F. Lindquist. Washington, D.C.: American Council on Education, 1951.

Wesman, Alexander G. and G. K. Bennett, "Multiple Regression versus Simple Addition of Scores in Prediction of College Grades," *Educational and Psychological Measurement*, XIX (Summer, 1959), 243-46.

Wrinkle, William L., *Improving Marking and Reporting Practices*, p. 120. New York: Holt, Rinehart & Winston, Inc., 1947.

Appendix
Glossary of Terms Used
in Educational Measurement

Vague and insignificant forms of speech, and abuse of language, have so long passed for mysteries of science; and hard or misapplied words with little or no meaning have, by prescription, such a right to be taken as deep learning and height of speculation, that it will not be easy to persuade either those who speak or those who hear them, that they are but the covers of ignorance and hindrance of true knowledge.

JOHN LOCKE

This glossary of 150 terms used in educational measurement is intended primarily to aid the reader who encounters an unfamiliar term. It can also be used profitably as the subject of direct, intensive study. In educational measurement as in other special fields, study of the meaning of technical terms helps to increase understanding of the concepts they represent. It is thus an important aspect of achievement.

The explanations in this glossary have been made somewhat more detailed than usual in the hope of increasing their contributions to understanding. An effort has been made, too, to make them conform to general usage by specialists in educational measurement. However, since usage varies and since many of these terms have not been given precise, authoritatively sanctioned definitions, no claim can be made that these are the only correct descriptions of the meanings of each term listed. Other useful glossaries of measurement terms by Gerberich, Lyman, Lennon, and by the California Test Bureau are available.[1]

1. An *achievement quotient* is calculated by dividing a student's achievement age by his mental age. Hence it is essentially a ratio of scores on two kinds of tests, achievement and aptitude. Presumably it shows how his actual achievement compares with his potential achievement. However, most test specialists now agree that achievement quotients present a greatly oversimplified and often misleading basis for judging achievement. Achievement quotients are sometimes referred to as "accomplishment quotients."

2. An *achievement test* is one designed to measure a student's grasp of some body of knowledge or his proficiency in certain skills. Such tests are often used to measure achievement in arithmetic, chemistry, English composition, typing, medical diagnosis, and other subjects of study. Most tests made by teachers for classroom use are achievement tests.

3. An *age norm* is the average score on an aptitude or achievement test for pupils of a particular age group. Age norms are usually reported in tables showing the average scores of students in a series of different age groups.

4. An *age scale* is a test in which the items are arranged in groups on the basis of the earliest age at which a group of typical, normal pupils can answer those items correctly. Binet's intelligence test scale is an age scale.

5. An *analogies test* requires the examinee to supply the missing term necessary to yield two pairs of terms having the same relationship within each pair. It is a test designed to measure ability to perceive similarities and differences, as well as relationships, among words, figures, or ideas.

6. An *aptitude test* is one given to determine the potential of an individual for development along a special line or the extent to which he is likely to profit from instruction along that line. Tests

---

[1] J. Raymond Gerberich, *Specimen Objective Test Items* (New York: David McKay Co., Inc., 1956), pp. 392-412; Howard B. Lyman, *Test Scores and What They Mean* (Englewood Cliffs, N.J.: Prentice-Hall, Inc., 1963), pp. 194-205; Roger T. Lennon, "A Glossary of 100 Measurement Terms," *Test Service Notebook, No. 13* (New York: Harcourt, Brace & World, Inc.); *A Glossary of Measurement Terms,* Los Angeles, Calif.: California Test Bureau, pp. 1-16.

of academic aptitude, scientific aptitude, music aptitude, clerical aptitude, and other special aptitudes are available.

7. *Attenuation* is the reduction of a coefficient of correlation from its theoretical true value due to errors of measurement in the variables being correlated. Errors of measurement could by chance make a coefficient of correlation higher than it ought to be, but the more common effect of such errors is to lower the coefficient obtained. Formulas are available for estimating the "true correlation" when the reliabilities of correlated measures are known.

8. An *average* is a number, not always an actual score, which represents the most typical or representative value in a group of scores. "Average" is a generic term designating any measure of a central tendency, such as the mean, median, or mode. In ordinary speech, the term "average" often means the same thing as the term "arithmetic mean."

9. *Basic skills* are tool skills such as those involved in reading, language, and arithmetic. Their development is regarded as essential to the further study of content subjects, and they tend to be emphasized in the elementary grades.

10. The *battery of tests* is a set of several tests intended to be administered in succession to the same subjects. The tests in a battery are usually designed to yield comparable scores and are provided with norms on the same or comparable groups of subjects.

11. The *best answer item* is a multiple-choice item in which the incorrect responses are not totally wrong. The examinee's task is to select the best response, even though it may not be a perfectly correct response. In a best answer item the difference between the correct answer and the incorrect alternatives is a difference in degree of correctness.

12. In a *bimodal distribution* the measures tend to concentrate or pile up at two distinct points or regions along the score scale. The frequency distribution curve for a bimodal distribution has two pronounced humps or peaks, though these may not be of the same height.

13. In a *classification exercise* the examinee's task is to assign each item or specimen given to the appropriate category or class. Or this task may be to decide whether a particular item does or does not belong in a particular class. The items to be classified may consist of names, descriptive phrases, pictures, statements, etc. The categories or classes the examinee is to use may be defined for him,

or he may.be required to infer the appropriate definition from the examples of items belonging in the class.

14. *Comparable scores* are expressed on the same scale, and have the same mean and the same variability. If scores on several tests are truly comparable for a group of subjects, the distributions of their scores on each test would be identical, though the scores of any one student on the several tests might differ.

15. A *completion test* requires a subject to supply the missing part of a sentence, a series, or a graphic pattern. The most typical form of a completion exercise is that based on a complex sentence or a unified paragraph.

16. *A composite score* is a single value used to express the result of combining scores on several different tests. It may be some average of the scores of the individual tests or a summation of their weighted scores. Often the average or sum is converted to the appropriate value on some different standard score scale.

17. The *content validity* of an educational achievement test is determined by the extent to which the items in the test adequately sample the areas of subject matter and the abilities which a course of instruction has aimed to teach.

18. A *control group* in an educational experiment is not subject to the experimental treatment but is otherwise as nearly as possible like the experimental group or groups. Tests given before the experimental treatment are used to establish the similarity of the control and experimental groups. Tests given to all groups after the experimental treatment are used to indicate the influence of that treatment on the experimental groups.

19. A *correlation coefficient* is a pure number, limited by the values plus 1 and minus 1, that expresses the degree of relationship between two sets of test scores or other measurements of each of the individuals in a group. The letter "r" is ordinarily used to represent the correlation coefficient. The most widely used coefficient of correlation is obtained from the Pearson product-moment formula, though a number of other formulas are also used.

20. *Credit by examination* involves the use of approved examinations for the granting of academic credit. Credit by examination may be used to shorten the time required for a capable student to earn an academic degree. It also provides a means for recognizing and rewarding an individual's achievement resulting from informal learning experiences or independent study.

21. A *criterion* is a standard of judging. In test development it usually refers to a characteristic or a combination of characteristics used as a basis for judging the validity of a test or some other measurement procedure. The criterion for the validity of scores from an aptitude test is ordinarily some measure of academic achievement, perhaps obtained from a good achievement test.

22. A *critical incident* is the description of some occurrence involving a person which is taken to indicate unusual competence or lack of competence on his part. The term "critical incident" has been popularized by the work of John Flanagan and his associates. It has been used by them as a basis for defining job requirements and for developing proficiency tests.

23. A *critical score* separates those which are satisfactory in terms of some purpose or criterion from those which are unsatisfactory. A minimum passing score on a test is a critical score.

24. *Cross validation* is a process of testing the quality of a test item, a test, or a test battery using data independent of that used originally to select or revise the items for the test. If the test is not cross-validated, that is, if the same data are used to test its quality as were used to develop it, the validity coefficients obtained are likely to be spuriously high.

25. A *culture-free test,* usually an intelligence test, is presumably insensitive to the effects of an individual's cultural background or environment on his score. Hence it is intended to provide valid measures of the individual genetic equipment for learning. It is now generally agreed that no culture-free test is possible, and that even a culture-fair test, on which examinees from different cultural backgrounds may expect to do equally well, may be almost impossible to achieve.

26. A *cumulative frequency* is a number obtained from a frequency distribution of scores that shows for any given score interval the number of the scores in the distribution that lie below and in that interval. Cumulative frequencies are useful in the computation of percentile ranks.

27. A *decile* is any one of nine points that divide the score scale into ten intervals, each of which includes one-tenth of the total frequency. Normally the score differences between successive deciles are unequal.

28. A *derived* score is obtained by converting a score from one system of measurement into another. Raw scores on a test, consisting of the number of correct responses, with or without correction for

guessing, are frequently converted into such derived scores as percentile ranks, z-scores, or T-scores. Some derived scores are quantitatively proportional to the original scores; some are not.

29. The *deviation* of a test score is the difference between that score and some point of reference such as the mean, the median, or an arbitrary reference point. An average of the measures of deviation of the scores in the distribution provides a measure of the variability of those scores.

30. A *diagnostic test* is designed to reveal specific weaknesses or failures to learn in some subject of study such as reading or arithmetic. In a diagnostic test the main interest is in scores on individual items or on small groups of highly similiar items.

31. A *differential aptitude battery* is a group of diverse tests, yielding comparable scores and intended to show an individual's relative chances of success in each of a variety of activities. Differential aptitude batteries are sometimes developed on the basis of factor analysis studies.

32. The *difficulty index* of a test item is usually based on the proportion of examinees in a group who answer the test item correctly. The most common index of difficulty is the per cent of correct response, though difficulty indices on other scales are sometimes encountered. When per cent of correct response is used as the difficulty index, the higher the numerical value of the index, the lower the difficulty of the item.

33. A *discrimination index* is a measure of the extent to which students who are judged to be good in terms of some standard succeed on the item and those who are judged to be poor on the same standard fail it. A commonly used index of discrimination is simply the difference in a proportion of correct response between the group of those scoring in the top 27 per cent on the total test and the group scoring in the bottom 27 per cent on the same test. Other indices of discrimination are based on the coefficient of correlation between success on the item and total score on the test.

34. *Dispersion* refers to the scatter, variability, or spread of a distribution of scores around some central value such as the mean or median. The terms "dispersion" and "variability" are practically synonymous. Dispersion may be measured by the average deviation, the standard deviation, the variance, or the range.

35. The *distracter* is any of the incorrect answer options in multiple-choice test items. A good distracter is chosen by many of the poorer students but few of the good students.

36. A *distribution of scores* is a tabulation or enumeration of the frequency of occurrence of each score in a given set of scores. A distribution of scores may be indicated graphically by a frequency polygon or by a histogram.

37. An *empirical key* to the correct answers of a test is based not on the judgments of the test constructor, but on the differences between the answers actually given by individuals belonging to different criterion groups, such as good or poor students, friendly or hostile students, and so on. In an empirical key the responses are often weighted so as to maximize the difference between the chosen criterion groups.

38. The items in *equivalent forms* of a test are the same in type, cover the same content, have the same distribution of difficulty values, and yield scores having the same mean, variability, and reliability. The existence of equivalent forms is particularly useful when the same characteristic of a student must be measured more than once. Test theorists have developed precise specifications for the statistical equivalence of alternate forms of a test.

39. An *error of measurement* is the difference between an obtained score and the corresponding true score. Any actual test score may be regarded as the sum of a true score and an error of measurement which may be either positive or negative. The median value of the numerical size of the errors of measurement in a particular set of test scores is called the probable error.

40. The *error variance* in a set of test scores is the mean of the squared errors of measurement for each score in the set. The reliability of a set of test scores is sometimes defined as the "proportion of the total score variance which is not error variance."

41. An *essay examination* consists of questions or instructions which require the examinee to compose a more or less extensive original written response. Essay test questions frequently begin with words like "discuss," "explain," or "describe." The examinee is allowed relative freedom in composing his response. This requires that its quality must be judged subjectively by one skilled and informed in the subject.

42. An *evaluation* is a judgment of merit, sometimes based solely on measurements such as those provided by test scores but more frequently involving the synthesis of various measurements, critical incidents, subjective impressions, and other kinds of evidence.

43. An *examination* is any process for testing the ability or achievement of students in any area. Often this process is based

primarily on a particular instrument, such as a paper-and-pencil test. In ordinary speech, the terms "examination" and "test" are frequently used as synonyms. If a distinction between the two is to be made, "examination" should be regarded as more comprehensive and complex than "test."

44. In an *expectancy table* the rows ordinarily correspond to score intervals on some predictor of achievement and the columns correspond to score intervals on some measure of actual achievement. The figures in each cell of such a double-entry table indicate the relative frequency with which an individual having a given score on the predictor will receive a given score on the criterion of achievement. Expectancy tables serve somewhat the same function as validity coefficients for tests but provide more detailed information.

45. An *external examination* is one chosen or prepared by someone other than the classroom teacher for administration to the students in that classroom. The tests used in state-wide or nation-wide testing programs, and sometimes those used in local testing programs, are external examinations.

46. A test possesses *face validity* if the questions in it appear to measure the knowledge or ability the test is intended to measure. Psychologists tend to discount face validity on the ground that appearances may be deceiving. However, if the observer is perceptive and experienced, his judgment that a test possesses face validity may carry considerable weight as an indication that it is valid.

47. *Factor analysis* involves the use of a variety of mathematically sophisticated techniques to identify a small number of hypothetical characteristics that will account for the correlations between scores on a much larger number of tests for the individuals in a particular group.

48. The *forced-choice technique* makes use of multiple-choice items in which the examinee is required to select one of several choices, regardless of how much he may like all of them or how little he may like any of them. The forced-choice technique is used mainly with items intended to measure personality characteristics. In an ideal form of forced-choice item, the alternatives are equally acceptable and equally often chosen by members of a typical group. However, the choice of one alternative over another is more frequently made by persons having a particular personality characteristic than by those having its opposite.

49. A *frequency distribution* consists of a sequence of score inter-

vals opposite each of which is recorded the number of scores in the total group falling in that interval. The terms "frequency distribution" and "distribution of scores" are nearly synonymous.

50. A *grade norm* is the mean or median achievement of pupils in a particular school grade on a given standardized test. Grade norm tables usually present these mean scores for several adjacent grades. The practice of fractionating intervals between grades into tenths and of reporting estimated mean scores for each tenth of an interval is quite common.

51. *Graphic item counter* is a device that may be attached to the IBM test scoring machine to count the number of times any response to a multiple-choice test item is marked in a particular set of test papers.

52. A *graphic rating scale* is a line whose ends represent contrasting extremes of a trait. The rater places a check mark at a point along the line corresponding to his judgment of how much or how little of the trait the particular individual possesses. Sometimes the line is divided into segments, each of which is accompanied by a brief verbal description of how much of the trait it represents.

53. A *guessing correction* is a factor that is added to or subtracted from the number of items correctly answered. The purpose of this correction is to make the score a student could expect to get by guessing blindly on certain questions no higher than the score of a student who omits those items in preference to guessing blindly on them. If the correction is effected by subtraction, the factor subtracted is the number of wrong responses divided by one less than the number of options per item. If the correction is effected by addition, the factor added is the number of items omitted divided by the number of options per item. A guessing correction, however, does not correct for a particular student's luck, or lack of it, in blind guessing.

54. *Halo effect* describes a bias in ratings arising from the tendency of a rater to be influenced in his rating of specific traits by his general impression of the person being rated.

55. *Heterogeneity*, when applied to the individuals in a group or the items in a test, refers to the degree to which they are different or unlike. The individuals or items in a highly heterogeneous group are very unlike.

56. *Homogeneity*, as applied to the individuals in a group or the items in a test, refers to similarity. The items in a highly homo-

geneous test or the individuals in a highly homogeneous group are all very much alike. A highly homogeneous group of students or set of test items is low in heterogeneity.

57. The *honor system,* as applied to the administration of tests, requires students to be individually responsible for their own honesty and avoidance of cheating. To emphasize this responsibility, instructors and proctors are ordinarily absent from a room in which an examination is being given under the honor system. Some honor systems make students responsible for reporting any cheating on the part of their classmates.

58. An *IBM scoring machine* is an electrical device for counting the number of correct or incorrect answers to the items in a multiple-choice or true-false test. The machine requires the use of a specifically designed answer sheet. It is capable of producing part scores, weighted scores, and scores corrected for guessing.

59. A test possesses high *internal consistency* if it is composed of items which all measure much the same thing and which are therefore highly intercorrelated. A measure of internal consistency provides one measure of test reliability.

60. An *internal criterion* is applied in judging the discriminating power of a test item when the score on the total test containing that item is used as a basis for choosing students for the high and low achievement groups. Although indices of discrimination based on the use of an internal criterion are always inflated somewhat, the degree of inflation is not large in moderately long tests. Further, good external criteria are seldom available.

61. In an *interpretative test,* the questions are based on background material supplied in the test itself. The background material may consist of excerpts of prose, poetry, statistical tables, pictures, or diagrams.

62. An *inventory* consists of a number of questions, tasks, or other stimuli, designed more to provide a comprehensive description of some aspect of an individual's characteristics than to provide a quantitative measurement of one of those aspects. Inventories are more commonly used in the description of interest, attitudes, or personality traits than in the measurement of intellectual achievements.

63. *IQ* stands for "intelligence quotient," originally a ratio of the individual's mental age to his chronological age. (On modern intelligence tests it may be a standard score whose mean is 100 and standard deviation 16 in the appropriate reference population.)

The IQ is the most commonly used index of brightness, or rate of mental development.

64. The *item stem* of a multiple-choice test item is the introductory question or incomplete statement. The examinee chooses an answer to or a completion of the item stem from among the options provided in the remainder of the item. A complete multiple-choice item consists of the item stem and the answer options.

65. An *item-test correlation* is the coefficient of correlation between scores on the item and scores on the test as a whole. If the item test correlation is calculated directly, the formulas for the biserial coefficient or the phi coefficient are ordinarily used. More commonly, however, item-test correlations are read from specially prepared tables designed to give estimates of the Pearson product-moment coefficient of correlation.

66. The *Kuder-Richardson formulas* provide estimates of the reliability of a single test from a single administration. The information ordinarily required is the number of items in the test, the standard deviation of the test scores, and the difficulty of each item in the test, or the average difficulty of all items as reflected in the mean test score. Because of their convenience and their statistical soundness, the Kuder-Richardson formulas are now widely used in the estimation of test reliability.

67. A *mark* is a rating of achievement assigned on the basis of some scale such as the five-letter A-B-C-D-F scale, the percentage scale, the stanine scale, or some other. Marks are widely used in reporting pupil achievements in various subjects to parents and in recording them on cumulative school records.

68. A *matching exercise* consists of two lists of statements, terms, or symbols. The examinee's task is to match an item in one list with the one most closely associated with it in the other.

69. A *mastery test* is not intended to indicate how much a student has achieved relative to other students, but only whether or not he has achieved enough to satisfy the minimum requirements of the teacher or the examining agency. The items of the mastery test are typically easier than those in the test intended to discriminate among different levels of achievement.

70. The *mean* is a measure of the central tendency or of the average numerical value of a set of scores. It is calculated by adding all of the scores and dividing the sum by the number of scores.

71. *Measurement* is a process of assigning numbers to the individual members of a set of objects or persons for the purpose of

indicating differences among them in the degree to which they possess the charactcristic being measured. If any characteristic of persons or things can be defined clearly enough so observed differences between them with respect to this characteristic can be consistently verified, the characteristic is measurable. A more refined type of measurement involves comparison of some characteristic of a thing with a preestablished standard scale for measuring that characteristic.

72. The *median* is the point in a score distribution which divides it into two parts containing equal numbers of scores. If the number of scores in the distribution is odd, the median is the middle score. If the number is even, the median is a point midway between the two scores nearest the middle. The median is identical with the fifth decile or the fiftieth percentile.

73. A person's *mental age* is his score on a test of mental ability expressed in terms of the chronological age in months of persons whose average test score is the same as his. Thus, if a child's mental test score is equal to that of the average eight-year-old on the same test, he has a mental age of eight years (ninety-six months) regardless of his actual chronological age.

74. The *mode* is the most frequently occurring value in a frequency distribution. If the frequency distribution is displayed graphically, the mode is the score corresponding to the highest point on the curve.

75. A *multiple-choice item* has two parts: the stem, consisting of a direct question or an incomplete statement, and two or more options, consisting of answers to the question or completions of the statement. The examinee's task is to choose the correct, or the best, answer option in terms of the question posed by the item stem.

76. A *nonverbal test,* usually an intelligence test, aims to minimize the importance of language skills as a factor determining the test score. In the purest form of nonverbal test there is no use of words, written or spoken, either by the examiner giving the test or by the subjects responding to it. More commonly, a nonverbal test is one in which no written directions are employed and to which the subject responds without using language. Such tests are commonly used in testing small children, illiterates, and others with language deficiencies.

77. A *norm,* as the term is used in relation to test scores, is the average or typical test score (or other measure) for members of a specific group. Norms are often presented in tables giving the

typical score values for a series of different homogeneous groups such as students in a given grade or students of a given age.

78. A *normal distribution* is an ideal frequency distribution defined by a mathematical formula. It is represented by a symmetrical, bell-shaped curve characterized by scores concentrated near the middle and tapering toward each extreme. Tables have been prepared to show the height of the ordinate at various points along the base line (score scale) and for showing areas under the curve in various intervals along the base line. The heights of the ordinates indicate the relative frequencies of each score in the distribution. The areas under the curve over various score intervals indicate what proportion of the total number of scores fall in that interval.

79. *Normalized standard scores,* like other standard scores, have a predetermined mean and standard deviation. In addition they are derived in a way that makes the distribution of standard scores approximately normal, regardless of the shape of the distribution of raw scores on which they were based.

80. An *objective test* is one which can be provided with a simple predetermined list of correct answers, so that subjective opinion or judgment in the scoring procedure is eliminated. The scoring of true-false, multiple-choice, or matching exercises is completely objective. The scoring of short-answer or completion items is partly objective.

81. During an *open book test,* the examinee may consult his textbook, reference books, or, sometimes, notes he has brought with him. The purpose of the open book test is to emphasize command of knowledge, as distinguished from recall of factual information. Examinations of this type seem to be most popular in mathematics, engineering, and the sciences.

82. The *percentile rank* of a particular score in a given distribution of scores is a number indicating the percentage of scores in the whole distribution which fall below the point at which the given score lies. Percentile ranks are sometimes also called "centile ranks," reflecting the fact that there are one hundred units on the scale of such scores. Distribution of percentile (or centile) ranks is approximately rectangular, whereas most raw score distributions from which the percentile ranks are derived are roughly normal.

83. In a *performance test* the subjects ordinarily respond by overt action, that is by motor or manual behavior. In a performance

test the subject is required to demonstrate his skill by manipulating objects or instruments.

84. The *phi coefficient* is an index of relationship between two variables, each of which yields only two different values. For example, one could calculate a phi coefficient between the scores of a group of students on two items in a test. In this case the two variables to be related are scores on the two items for each of a number of students. The phi coefficient is relatively simple to compute.

85. On a *point scale* the examinee's score is the sum of the points awarded for each of the tasks in the test. The scores on most aptitude and achievement tests are reported on a point scale. However, the term is ordinarily used to distinguish intelligence tests which use this type of scoring from those like the Binet on which scores are expressed in terms of age levels.

86. A *power test* is one on which the examinee's score depends on how much he is able to do, not how rapidly he is able to do it. Hence, in a power test there is either no time limit at all or a very generous time limit. The tasks in a power test are sometimes arranged in order of increasing difficulty, with the expectation that the examinee will stop when he reaches tasks of a level of difficulty beyond his capabilities.

87. *Practice effect* is a term used to explain part of a change, usually an increase in the score of an individual when he takes the same test or essentially the same test, more than once. The magnitude of these practice effects depends on the nature of the test involved, the interval between testings, and motivation of the student being tested.

88. The *probability* of an occurrence is a decimal fraction expressing the ratio of actual occurrences to opportunities for occurrence. The analysis and computation of probabilities make up a special branch of mathematics.

89. The *probable error* of a set of test scores is the median error of measurement, in absolute value. Half of the errors of measurement are larger and the other half smaller than the probable error of measurement. The probable error is usually calculated from the standard error and is equal to 0.6745 times the standard error of measurement. The probable error is a good measure of the estimated accuracy of a test score but not of its reliability, since a longer and more reliable test may have a larger probable error of measurement than a shorter less reliable test.

90. A *profile* is a graphic representation of the relative magnitude of a student's scores on several tests. In order for such a profile to be meaningful, the scores on all of the tests must be comparable scores, based on the same standard scale. Peaks on the profile represent those areas of ability or achievement in which the individual exceeds his own average. Valleys in the profile indicate those areas where he is weak relative to his achievement in other areas. The general level of the profile on the chart indicates the general level of his ability or achievement relative to those from which the test norms were obtained.

91. A *projective test* is intended to stimulate free expression by the examinee, guided and restricted as little as possible by directions from the examiner. The problems in a projective test are often intentionally ambiguous. The examinee's responses are analyzed for the purpose of revealing his interests, motivations, perceptions, problems, values, and modes of adjustment. The stimulus material for projective tests may consist of such things as ink blots, pictures, incomplete sentences, and so on. The examinee may be asked to describe what he sees in the stimulus material or to indicate what sense he can make out of it. Projective tests are used largely in the study of personality. The task presented by a projective test item is frequently said to be unstructured because of the examinee's relative freedom of response.

92. The *purity* of a test is the degree to which it measures only one factor of mental ability. In factor analysis, the saturation or purity of a test is defined as the percentage of the reliable portion of test score variance that is accounted for by the most prominent factor in that variance. In a battery of different pure tests, the objective of the test constructor is to make each test as reliable as possible but to make the correlation between the scores on the different tests as low as possible.

93. *Q sort* is a technique for standardizing the measurement of the relevance or applicability of descriptive statements to a particular subject. The judge making the Q sort is given a set of cards on each of which a different descriptive statement is written. He is directed to sort these statements into a given number of piles with the statements most applicable to the person being rated placed in the pile at one extremity and those least applicable in a pile at the other extremity. Not only the number of piles to be used, but also the number of statements to be placed in each pile is often prescribed in advance. By this means the appropriateness of each statement to a given individual can be measured. If the rating is

repeated for another individual, it is possible to correlate these statement scores for the two persons as the measure of the similarity of their personalities.

94. A *quality scale* consists of a series of typical specimens of such things as handwriting, composition, or drawings of a particular subject, arranged in an order of merit, usually with a numerical value assigned to each. Such a scale is then used as a standard of comparison for rating the quality of work of other examinees. The Thorndike Handwriting Scale is a familiar example of a quality scale.

95. A *quartile* is one of three points along the score scale of a frequency distribution which divide the distribution into four parts of equal frequency. The first quartile corresponds to the twenty-fifth percentile, the second to the median, or fiftieth percentile, and the third to the seventy-fifth percentile.

96. A *questionnaire* is a list of planned written questions relating to a particular topic, usually intended to gather descriptive information from a number of selected respondents. An important difference between a questionnaire and a test is that in a questionnaire the responses are ordinarily summarized question by question, whereas in a test they are summarized respondent by respondent.

97. In a table of *random numbers* there is no observable system or order in the sequence of the digits. That is, one cannot predict with better than chance success which digit will occur at a given point in the table or which digit is likely to follow some other digit.

98. A *random sample* is a sample selected in such a way as to guarantee equal probability of selection to all possible samples of this size that could be formed from the members of the universe involved. It is also true that each element in the universe has equal probability of being included in a random sample. The problem of selecting a truly random sample from any population is not simple.

99. A *range of scores* is the smallest interval on the score scale which will include all of the measures in the distribution. It is sometimes defined, more simply but somewhat inaccurately, as the difference between the highest and the lowest scores in the distribution. The range of scores provides a simple measure of the variability of the scores of the distribution.

100. A *rate score* is the measure of an individual's speed of performance of tasks of a particular type, stated either in terms of the

number of units of work done in a given time or the number of units of time required to complete a given amount of work.

101. A *raw score* is the number first obtained in scoring the test, before any transformation to a standard score or other derived score. For objectively scorable tests, the raw score usually consists of the number of right answers, the number right minus some fraction of the number wrong, the time required for performance, the number of errors, or some other directly defined measure. On an essay test the raw score is often the scorer's estimate of the quality of the response, relative to some quantitative standard of perfection.

102. A *rectangular distribution* is a frequency distribution in which successive equal intervals along the score scale include the same frequency or number of scores. A distribution of percentile ranks is rectangular, not bell-shaped, as in the case of a normal distribution.

103. *Regression* in statistics refers to the tendency for predicted scores to lie closer to the mean than the predictor scores when the two are correlated and expressed on the same standard score scale. If the two measures were perfectly correlated, there would be no regression. Since height and weight are correlated positively, but not perfectly, the tallest individual in a group is likely to be heavier than the average individual but is unlikely to be the heaviest individual. The heights of fathers and sons are correlated, but not perfectly correlated. The fact that the sons of tall fathers tend to be taller than the average of their generation reflects this correlation. But the fact that the sons of tall fathers tend to be not as tall relative to the whole population as their fathers is an illustration of regression. Regression accounts for some of the findings that high-aptitude students seem to be underachievers and low-aptitude students overachievers.

104. The *relevance* of a task in a test is the extent to which it contributes to the purposes of the test by virtue of the abilities it calls into play. For example, a question that asks students to give the dates of birth and death of several English poets may have low relevance in a test of poetic appreciation. On the other hand, a question asking a student to calculate the standard deviation of a set of scores might have high relevance in a test of ability to use statistical techniques. Relevance is one of the major aspects of quality in tests of educational achievement.

105. The *reliability coefficient* is the estimate of the coefficient of correlation between the scores for students in a particular group

on two equivalent forms of the same test. If equivalent forms of the same test are not available, the reliability of a single form can be estimated by splitting it into equivalent halves and using the correlation between scores on equivalent full-length tests. The reliability of a test may also be estimated on the basis of the variance of the test scores and of the item scores. Reliability is sometimes defined also as the proportion of total score variance which is not error variance, i.e., attributable to errors of measurement.

106. The *representative sample* is one chosen in such a way as to make it more likely than a random sample to exhibit the same characteristics as the population. Representative samples are often stratified samples, with predetermined numbers of cases chosen randomly from different geographical areas, different age groups, or other subgroups which are thought to differ systematically with respect to the characteristic being measured.

107. A *response count* for an objective test item indicates the frequency with which one or more of the answer options were chosen by examinees in a particular group. Response counts are the bases for estimating the difficulty and discriminating power of the test items. They may be obtained by counting hands or, in some cases, by special counting or tabulating equipment.

108. A *response set* is a predisposition on the part of an examinee to differ systematically from other examinees in his handling of uncertain responses to a test item. For example, willingness to guess may be a response set. If two examinees have the same limited amount of information about the answer to a question, one of them may be willing to guess, the other may not. Some examinees may be systematically less reluctant to mark true-false statements false than other examinees. Response sets may or may not affect the reliability and validity of the measurements yielded by a test.

109. *Rote learning* is memorization of a sequence of words or other symbols by repeated utterance or observation. Material learned by rote may or may not be meaningless to the person who has learned it, but the process of learning does not rely on meaningfulness as an aid to learning.

110. A *Rorschach test* consists of a series of standardized ink blots to which the examinee responds by describing what he "sees" in them. The Rorschach test is a projective test used in the study of personality.

111. A *sampling error* is the difference between the value of some statistic, such as the mean or the standard deviation calculated from a sample, and that which would have been obtained if it had been

calculated on the basis of the entire population. If, for example, the score of one fourth-grade pupil in arithmetic were used as an indication of the level of achievement of the entire fourth grade, the difference between his score and the average score on the same test for all pupils in the grade would be a sampling error. Samples are seldom perfectly representative of populations. If they were, there would be no sampling error.

112. A *scale* is a sequence of numbers whose use is defined and limited so they will have special significance in indicating various degrees of some trait or characteristic. For example, the scores obtainable from any test constitute a scale. Scales are sometimes represented graphically by intervals and subdivisions of intervals along a line.

113. A *scatter diagram* is a device for displaying the relationship between scores on two tests for the individuals in a particular group. Scores on one test are represented on the vertical dimension, those on the other along the horizontal dimension. A dot, tally mark, or other symbol is entered on the diagram at such a position with reference to the horizontal and vertical scales as to reflect the pair of scores for a particular individual. If the scores on the two variables are highly correlated, the tally marks on the scatter diagram tend to fall close to a straight line. A scatter diagram is sometimes used as the starting point in the calculation of a coefficient of correlation. Because each tally mark represents scores on two variables, a scatter diagram is sometimes referred to as a "double-entry table."

114. A *score* is a number assigned to an examinee to provide a quantitative description of his performance on a particular test. The original raw score is often converted into a standard score or some other derived score to facilitate comparison or interpretation.

115. A *scoring formula* indicates how the raw score on the test is to be obtained from the number of correct, incorrect, or omitted responses. The simplest scoring formula is "Score equals number right." If scores corrected for guessing are desired, the number of wrong responses divided by one less than the number of answer options per item is frequently subtracted from the number of correct responses. Alternatively, the number of omitted items divided by the number of answer options per item can be added to the number of right responses.

116. A *scoring key* indicates the correct answer to each item. The term "scoring key" is also applied to devices, such as stencils

punched in positions corresponding to the correct answers or cut strips of paper with answers written on them, that facilitate the scoring of objective tests.

117. In a *self-marking test* a student records his answers in such a way as to facilitate the counting of correct responses. Sometimes this involves automatic replication of the student's response mark by the use of carbon paper on the back of an answer sheet. If the mark falls within a preprinted box hidden from the examinee during the test, it is scored as a correct response. A self-marking test does not require the use of a separate key in scoring.

118. *Sigma* is a character in the Greek alphabet corresponding to the Roman letter "s" which, in lower-case form (σ), is used as the symbol for the standard deviation of a distribution. In upper-case form (Σ) it indicates the arithmetic operation of addition or summation. (When a distinction between the standard deviation of a sample and that of a population is important, the Roman letter "s" is used to indicate the standard deviation of the sample.)

119. A *significant difference*, statistically speaking, is a large enough difference between two comparable statistics computed from separate samples so that the probability that the difference may be attributed to chance is less than some defined limit. If the difference as large as the observed difference could not be expected to occur by chance more than five times in one hundred, the difference is sometimes said to be significant at the 5 per cent level of confidence. The significance of a difference depends not only on the magnitude of the difference, but also upon the precision of the two measures used to obtain the difference. Hence, a difference too small to be of any significance can often be made statistically significant by the use of sufficiently large samples. Conversely, the use of very small samples can make measures so imprecise that a difference may be statistically insignificant even when it is large enough to be of considerable practical significance.

120. A *skewed distribution* is an asymmetrical distribution in which most of the scores are closer to one end of the distribution than they are to the other. Skewed distributions ordinarily have only one mode, but the tails or extremities are unequal in length. If the longer tail of the distribution extends toward the lower end of the score scale, the distribution is said to be negatively skewed. If the longer tail extends to the higher end of the score scale, the distribution is said to be positively skewed.

121. *Sociometry* is a technique for revealing group structure. It is based on data obtained by asking each member of the group

which other members, usually two to five, he would prefer to have as a friend, a teammate, a group leader, or some other associate. These choices are often displayed graphically on a chart known as a "sociogram."

122. The *Spearman-Brown formula* is used to predict the reliability of a lengthened test, assuming that the material added to the test is highly similar to that already present in it. The Spearman-Brown formula may be written

$$r_n = \frac{nr_s}{1 + (n - 1)r_s}$$

when r_n is the reliabilty coefficient of the lengthened test, r_s the reliability coefficient of the original short test, and n the number of times that the original length has been increased. The Spearman-Brown formula has wide uses, but perhaps the most common use is in stepping up the correlation between scores on halves of a test to obtain an estimate of the reliability of the total test.

123. A *specific determiner* is some characteristic in the statement of a true-false test item which supplies an unintended clue to the correct answer. For example, statements including the words "every," "always," "entirely," "absolutely," and "never" are more likely to be false than true. Similarly the statements containing the words "sometimes," "usually," "often," and "ordinarily" are more likely to be true than false.

124. In a *speed test* the rapidity with which a task is completed is an important factor determining the score on the test. Some speed tests consist of tasks of uniform and relatively low difficulty so the student's score is determined almost entirely by how fast he works, not by the difficulty of the tasks he accomplishes. Any test with a time limit short enough to prevent many examinees from finishing is at least partially a speed test.

125. A *split-halves reliability coefficient* is obtained by using one-half of the items on the test, sometimes the odd-numbered items, to yield one score for an examinee and the other half of the items to yield another, independent score. The correlation between the scores on these two half-tests, corrected with the aid of the Spearman-Brown formula, provides an estimate of the reliability of the total test.

126. The *standard deviation* is a measure of variability, dispersion, or spread of a set of scores around their mean value. Mathematically, the standard deviation is the square root of the mean of the squared deviations of the scores from the mean of

the distribution of scores. The more closely the scores in a distribution cluster about the mean, the smaller the standard deviation. In a normal distribution, 68.26 per cent of all of the scores lie within one standard deviation of the mean.

127. The *standard error of measurement* is an estimate of the standard deviation of the errors of measurement associated with the test scores in a given set. The standard error of measurement is estimated by multiplying the standard deviation of the scores by the square root of one minus the reliability coefficient. Approximately two-thirds of the errors of measurement in a given set of test scores will be less than the standard error of measurement. The largest error of measurement in a set of one hundred scores is likely to be less than three times the standard error of measurement.

128. A *standard score* is one derived from a raw score so that it can be expressed on a uniform standard scale without seriously altering its relationship to other scores in the distribution. A simple type of standard score is the z-score, which expresses each raw score as a positive or negative deviation from the mean of all raw scores on a scale in which the unit is one standard deviation. In another type of standard-score scale, the transformation is arranged to yield a normal distribution of standard scores. The use of standard scores simplifies comparisons and interpretations of scores.

129. A *standardized test* is one which has been constructed in accord with detailed specifications, one for which the items have been selected after tryout for appropriateness in difficulty and discriminating power, one which is accompanied by a manual giving definite directions for uniform administration and scoring, and one which is provided with relevant and dependable norms for score interpretation. Standardized tests are ordinarily constructed by test specialists, with the advice of competent teachers, and are offered for sale by test publishers. Unfortunately not all tests offered as standardized tests have been prepared as carefully as the foregoing description suggests.

130. A *stanine score* (from standard nine) is a single-digit standard score on a nine-unit scale. The distribution of stanine scores in the population from which they were derived has a mean of 5 and standard deviation of 2. Stanine scores are normalized standard scores so that, in the population from which they were derived, the proportions of each stanine score are approximately these:

Stanine Score	1	2	3	4	5	6	7	8	9
Per cent of Scores	4	7	12	17	20	17	12	7	4

131. A *statistic* is a number used to describe or characterize some

aspect of a sample. For example, the number of cases in the sample, the mean value of the measures in the sample, the standard deviation of those measures, and the correlation between two sets of measures for the members of the sample are statistics. Corresponding to every statistic in the sample there is a parameter in the population.

132. The *statistical validity* of scores from a test, or any other measures, is ordinarily indicated by the coefficient of correlation between those scores and appropriate criterion measures. For example, the statistical validity (predictive validity) of an aptitude test is expressed by the coefficient of correlation between the scores of students on the aptitude test and their subsequent scores on some good measure of achievement.

133. In the *subjective evaluation* of a student's answers to essay test questions, or of his performance in other situations, the score assigned is determined by the personal opinion and judgment of the scorer. It is not determined by a prescribed scoring key or by the specifications in detail of the requirements for answers which will receive various scores.

134. A *subtest* is a part of a test, composed of similar items having a distinct purpose, for which a separate score may be provided. The reliability of scores on short subtests is generally low.

135. A *table of specifications* includes a test outline which specifies what proportion of the item shall deal with each content area and with each type of ability. It may also include other specifications, such as the number of items in the test, the time to be allowed for its administration, and descriptions of kinds of items, which will or will not be included in the test. The content outline for a test is often presented in the form of a two-dimensional grid with content areas represented along one dimension and pupil abilities or educational outcomes along the other. The number or proportion of items to be devoted to each content area and to each educational outcome is specified in the table.

136. A *test* is a general term used to designate any kind of device or procedure for measuring ability, achievement, interest, and other traits. A test is also defined as any systematic procedure for comparing the behavior of two or more persons. In ordinary speech, the terms "examination," "quiz," and "test" are often used interchangeably. However, the term "quiz" ordinarily refers to something short and informal, the term "test" to a longer more carefully prepared series of questions, and the term "examination" to a very comprehensive process.

137. A *test exercise* is a structural unit of a test for which a single set of directions is provided. A test exercise, unlike a test item, ordinarily requires more than one response.

138. A *test item* is the smallest independent unit of a test. Each statement to be judged true or false, each question to which an answer is to be selected, each incomplete statement to which a completion is to be selected, each blank in a sentence or paragraph to be filled in, is a separate test item.

139. *Test-retest reliability* is calculated by correlating scores for the same students on two administrations of the same test. The size of a test-retest reliability coefficient indicates not only the precision of measurement of the test, but also the stability of the trait being measured. Test-retest reliability coefficients do not indicate how adequately or representatively the items in the test sample the whole field to be covered by the test. Hence, retest reliability coefficients are usually higher than equivalent forms reliability coefficients. In general, the greater the interval of time between test and retest, the lower the retest reliability coefficient will be. Because of practice effects and the difficulty in maintaining motivation when examinees are asked to take the same test the second time, retest reliability coefficients are calculated less frequently than other types.

140. In a *time-limit test* pupils are allowed an exact amount of time on which to work on a test, usually short enough to prevent most of them from completing the test. A student's score on a time-limit test is influenced considerably by the speed with which he works on it. When time-limit tests are used as standardized tests, it is highly important for the examiner to see that the timing corresponds exactly with that specified in the directions for test administration.

141. A *trait* is any attribute of persons which is possessed in differing amounts by different members of a group or class. It is a physical characteristic or a relatively stable mode of behavior. Such things as height, intelligence, quality of handwriting, or understanding of chemical principles are traits.

142. A *true-false item* consists of a statement which the examinee is asked to judge to be true or false. A true-false item might be regarded as a form of the multiple-choice item in which only two answer options are provided and in which the answer options are the same for all items.

143. A *true score* is an idealized error-free score for a particular person on a particular test. It may also be defined as the mean of

an infinite number of independent measurements of the same trait, using equivalent forms of the test. The second definition assumes that as the number of independent measurements of the same trait in the same person is increased, the average value of the errors associated with those measurements approaches zero. The actual score a person does receive on a particular test can hence be regarded as the sum of his true score and a positive or negative error of measurement associated with that particular measurement.

144. A *T-score* is a normalized standard score on a scale such that the distribution of T-scores in the population from which they are derived has a mean of 50 and a standard deviation of 10. The original T-scores, devised by McCall and named in honor of Thorndike and Terman, were limited to scores which would be made on a standard test by an unselected group of twelve-year-old children.

145. The *validity* of a test is often defined as the degree to which it measures what it purports to measure, or as the extent to which a test does the job for which it is intended. Reliability is a necessary but not a sufficient condition for validity. The validity of an achievement test depends not only on the reliability of the scores it yields, but also on the extent to which the content of the test represents a balanced and appropriate set of tasks sampling the outcomes of the course or instructional program. For some types of tests for which good independent criterion measures are available, statistical coefficients of validity can be obtained. These are coefficients of correlation between scores on the test and the criterion measures.

146. The *variance* is a measure of the dispersion of scores about their mean. The variance is the mean of the squared deviations of the scores from their mean. Hence, it is equal to the square of the standard deviation.

147. In *weighted scoring* the number of points awarded for a correct response is not the same for all items in the test. In some cases, weighted scoring involves the award of different numbers of points for the choice of different responses to the same item.

148. In a *work-limit test* the test is short enough, or the time allowed long enough, to permit all or nearly all of the examinees to finish. The objective of the work-limit test is to determine how much the examinee can do, regardless of how fast or slowly he works.

149. A *work-sample test* is a performance test which provides a controlled tryout of the examinee's behavior under conditions as similar as possible to those he will encounter in a work situation. In a work-sample test the relevance of the tasks is high.

150. A *z-score* is a standard score. In a complete distribution of z-scores, the mean is zero and the standard deviation 1. Raw scores are converted into z-scores by subtracting the mean from the raw score and dividing the difference by the standard deviation. Thus, z-scores are equally likely to be positive or negative. They ordinarily range from about -3 to about $+3$. To avoid the loss of too much precision in converting raw scores to z-scores, the z-scores are ordinarily expressed to tenths or hundredths of the standard deviation unit. If a z-score is multiplied by 10 and added to 50, the result is another kind of standard score, sometimes designated as a "Z-score."

Index